David Johnston

**Random Number Generators—Principles and Practices**

David Johnston

# Random Number Generators—Principles and Practices

—

A Guide for Engineers and Programmers

DE
—
G
PRESS

ISBN 978-1-5015-1513-2
e-ISBN (PDF) 978-1-5015-0606-2
e-ISBN (EPUB) 978-1-5015-0626-0

**Library of Congress Control Number: 2018949266**

**Bibliographic information published by the Deutsche Nationalbibliothek**
The Deutsche Nationalbibliothek lists this publication in the Deutsche Nationalbibliografie;
detailed bibliographic data are available on the Internet at http://dnb.dnb.de.

Typesetting: VTeX UAB, Lithuania
Printing and binding: CPI books GmbH, Leck

www.degruyter.com

This book is dedicated to the memory of George Cox, without whom my work in random number generators would never have started and who was a tenacious engineering partner.

Thank you to my wife, Tina, for putting up with me disappearing every weekend for two years to write this book. To Charles Dike, Rachael Parker, James Shen, Ammon Christiansen and Jesse Walker, Jian Zhong Wang, Kok Ching Eng, Beng Koi Lim, Ping Juin Tan and all the other engineers who worked with me to achieve higher performance random number generators a reality in Intel products; to Nichole Schimanski for answering many of my dumb mathematics questions; to the many academics who inspired me and provided important insights and findings, including Yvgenny Dodis, Ingrid Verbauwhede, Vladimir Rožić, Bart Massey, Hugo Krawczyk, Boaz Barak, Russell Impagliazzo, and Avi Wigderson, thanks.

# About De|G PRESS

## Five Stars as a Rule

De|G PRESS, the startup born out of one of the world's most venerable publishers, De Gruyter, promises to bring you an unbiased, valuable, and meticulously edited work on important topics in the fields of business, information technology, computing, engineering, and mathematics. By selecting the finest authors to present, without bias, information necessary for their chosen topic *for professionals*, in the depth you would hope for, we wish to satisfy your needs and earn our five-star ranking.

In keeping with these principles, the books you read from De|G PRESS will be practical, efficient and, if we have done our job right, yield many returns on their price.

We invite businesses to order our books in bulk in print or electronic form as a best solution to meeting the learning needs of your organization, or parts of your organization, in a most cost-effective manner.

There is no better way to learn about a subject in depth than from a book that is efficient, clear, well organized, and information rich. A great book can provide life-changing knowledge. We hope that with De|G PRESS books you will find that to be the case.

https://doi.org/10.1515/9781501506062-201

# Contents

# Preface

Many books and most academic papers on random numbers turn out to be either highly mathematical and difficult to follow, or the opposite, offering little useful engineering insight. In contrast, this book is aimed at the practicing programmer or hardware engineer. The use of mathematics is kept to a level appropriate for the topic, with an emphasis on working examples and codes that run and can be used and experimented with. The reader would benefit from being able to program a computer, possessing the sort of mathematics common in undergraduate engineering courses and preferably having an interest in random numbers.

Random Number Generators have many uses. From modeling stochastic systems to randomizing games, to picking lottery winners, to playing board games (using dice), to randomizing cryptographic protocols for security.

The most critical application is in cryptographic security, where random numbers are an essential component of every cryptographic application. There can be no cryptographic security without secure, unpredictable random numbers.

While random numbers may appear to be a trivial and simple topic, it turns out that there are many counterintuitive concepts and many subdisciplines, including random number testing, random number generation, entropy extraction, public key generation, and simulation.

Unfortunately, in cryptography, random number generation has proven difficult to get right and there are many examples of cryptographic systems undermined by poor quality random number generators.

A number of programs have been written to accompany this book. They are mostly written in Python 2 and C. Electronic copies of this code are available through Github (https://github.com/dj-on-github/RNGBook_code). In addition a number of externally available software tools are used. Appendix D provides pointers to all the other software used in this book and a reference to relate listings to their location in the book.

https://doi.org/10.1515/9781501506062-202

# 1 Introduction

My first professional encounter with random numbers happened while implementing the 802.11 WEP (Wired Equivalent Privacy) protocol in a WiFi chip. This required that random numbers be used in the protocol and the approach I took was to take noisy data from the wireless receive hardware and pass it through an iterated SHA-1 hash algorithm. Once a sufficient amount of noisy data had been fed in, the output of the hash was taken to be a random number.

Given that at the time I was largely ignorant of the theory behind random number generation in general and entropy extraction in particular, the solution was not terrible, but with hindsight of a decade of working on random number generators there are some things I would have done differently.

Subsequent to attending the IEEE 802.11i working group to work on the replacement protocol to WEP (one of the security protocol standards famously back-doored by the NSA and thereby introducing bad cryptography into standards) and later on the 802.16 PKMv2 security protocol, the need for random numbers in security protocols and the problems specifying and implementing them, led to my career being diverted into a multiyear program to address how to build practical random number generators for security protocols that can be built in chips, tested, mass manufactured, and remain reliable and secure while being available to software in many contexts. Ultimately this emerged as the RdRand instruction and later the RdSeed instruction in Intel CPUs. A decade later, the requirements are still evolving as new needs for random number generators that can operate in new contexts emerge.

My initial model for this book was for it to be the book I needed back when first implementing a hardware random number generator for the 802.11 WEP protocol. I would have benefited greatly from a book with clear information on the right kinds of design choices, the right algorithms, the tradeoffs, the testing methods, and enough of the theory to understand what makes those things the correct engineering choices. The scope of the book grew during its writing, to cover nonuniform RNGs, a much expanded look at various types of random number testing, nonuniform RNGs, software interfaces for RNGs, and a mix of software tools and methods that have been developed along the way.

Since the early 2000s, the requirements for random number generators have evolved greatly. For example, the need for security against side channel and fault injection attacks, security from quantum computer attacks, the need for smaller, lower power random number generators in resource-constrained electronics, and the need for highly efficient RNGs and floating point hardware RNGs for massively parallel chips.

Random numbers are used in many other fields outside of cryptography and the requirements and tradeoffs tend to be different. This book explores various noncryptographic random number applications and related algorithms. We find examples of

https://doi.org/10.1515/9781501506062-001

random number uses occurring in simulations, lotteries, games, statistics, graphics, and many other fields.

To give a taste of what will be covered in this book, the following are three examples of random bits represented in hex format. They all look similarly random, but the first is statistically uniform and is generated using a very secure, nonpredictable random number generator suitable for cryptography, while the second is statistically uniform but completely insecure and predictable and the third is neither statistically uniform nor cryptographically secure.

**Listing 1.1:** Output of a Cryptographically Secure RNG

```
E8E03922F6759144BDF8FD850A9F459D15709084A058C2447AB4AC22B9787B35
E43F8ED014DB8F7BC2877E79E722C5C950BAF7C1ECBD3F4B91116B8D6BB97A6F
D7DEB1BFE3370A92AAC1BB47A07617DD0C6F2061AA149F378D3461EFB70BC5F3
9D6C75E43949102E91915E9DC074AB1CC9E4D89EDEBE84EC7B47A528EA040859
2B4419CBE814C481BF9D277ABEC0D52BF87FBD5C477BCBD8AE40D8E74E904D85
FD56D0321FC55E20FB973616C8CA641B20BDE07B7428DE4565D6728A82589F2F
6D0AD798F0BD2CCD7A222C2B54BD309925E824CA66793681C05743DEF3EF0868
CE121A2265BE29FA4A0D80086859CAD7E6AB1A0D550295B88478E9A7DC1AABFD
441727708B22AEB9D5C58C5D6F4356AD2979062BFE4C25534F8497862DD104F2
6CBD49AF08C52B55E23251598A3E713D7A068BDA374DE51F66F1502030CF28B6
956C2F681EAAACB7EC7F9F33D7CBBD2527F8A623C0344D3CEDA65C6312BB8B79
BA02B15C2A536CE3BDD4A63E2947A2C79C1CFC835077917913881451CD655E50
```

**Listing 1.2:** Output of a Uniform, Insecure RNG

```
B7F4E5C40A7C151D654898AA7E12508D56446BCED37864F5F12B712D8EF87FCB
6C6FFA364601091ED0DEF6895156848BB95F16EA805CB4D8B96BB97C19AD97E0
30898D7F6BAF8B7B11E6CB331C908E6F1958828835471648BDC14A20C4FB7921
8C0A9DFA6B189F45B159E9ACA36941483A2082D154B0DC701BE6778026992ADE
30A296E239D2239EF823159623D5A26F2585B77F491BA7439775B8A72FAC6365
877039B56D96277500CD6C7DBE084B06F61886EDF2C959E6448B88619A68FB12
062FCC04A6C56D7264F4D06FA2CC24D9F4B51A47E7D000C61C16AB8375F90725
ED216F647269F0A25AB4C8F9B36ED9242B77B74DD4362B97B787F65DCB52C159
8FA1BB5002127DD5F2988DC432A2A3EAA774526B866FEBC06635C7F1C244ACEE
565FD626B28245F8730A8C3400E0C9F55741DDC1BC3DFE98A5D7F2A39870CEF1
779CF3F0E9D554CCE630C732AD8CD9959B212EE9B542B8B3B060F15229AEA3B2
6BB346EDD19ED238D8BD83588536AC62D39B87A43F0C370703A301FBE86CADE5
```

**Listing 1.3:** Output of a Nonuniform, Insecure RNG

```
3D231558968E6514D6584DF4559E4C833E770226B83D23676CDDB2D8857C8E80
AC839B5EBE231102126DF551D3986C288065C2772C6614137B380194D51F6E3D
27C8ABBB2E0538285244D4EB2930BA0EB90A034F0F85BC1BED6BE37F52A9D3FD
B0D3F55F40BA9BDA2DD17EB66F54DF0CB35BADDC5EDF1BB638F037ACCC9231E4
FE26C963DC8647F7ECB21C851A184D8EA970F9E4770220DF2EC2C7A8CCD11E5D
3974D7355A55F5031C7CF123F5DB0EB81D3DDE8D359C6455334A1C62B1F964E6
BB583BA383AE86B84240D383A681A0867B4AC49286DC8848D91DCCC4BAC59C18
853C9D150CBEF54152C3C960B3FB0E60DF0A6AA10078843B213C453C90D5E1FC
```

C53D397A527761411C86BA48B7C1524B0C60AD859B172DB0BAE46B712936F08A
DA7E75F686516070C7AD725ABCE2746E3ADF41C36D7A76CB8DB8DA7ECDD2371F
D6CA8866C5F9632B3EDBCC38E9A40D4AE94437750F2E1151762C4793107F5327
D206D66D8DF11D0E660CB42FE61EC3C90387E57D11568B9834F569046F6CEDD0

The first is generated from a random number generator in an Intel CPU that has a metastable entropy source, followed by an AES-CBC-MAC entropy extractor and an SP800-90A and 90C XOR construction NRBG, with an AES-CTR-DRBG. This RNG uses algorithms that are mathematically proven to be secure in that it is algorithmically hard to infer the internal state from the output and impossible to predict past and future values in the output when that state is known.

The second is generated with a PCG (Permuted Congruential Generator) RNG. PCGs are deterministic RNGs that have excellent statistical properties, but there is no proof that it is hard to infer the internal state of the algorithm from the output, so it is not considered secure.

The third is generated with an LCG (Linear Congruential Generator) RNG. LCGs are simple deterministic RNG algorithms for which there are a number of statistical flaws. It is trivial to infer the internal state of the algorithm and so to predict future outputs. So, it is proven to be insecure.

Later chapters on NRBGs, DRBGs, entropy extractors, uniform noncryptographic random number generators and test methods will explore the differences between these different types of random number generator and how to test for their properties.

## 1.1 Classes of Random Number Generators

Things that make random numbers are generically called Random Number Generators (RNGs). These fall into two major types: Pseudo-Random Number Generators (PRNGs) and True Random Number Generators (TRNGs). Unfortunately, TRNG is a term that is not well defined. It is interpreted in different ways by different people in industry and academia.

PRNGs are deterministic algorithms that generate a "random looking" sequence of numbers. However, given the same starting conditions, a PRNG will always give the same sequence. Hence, the name "Pseudo-Random" Number Generator.

Typically, a PRNG will be implemented as software or digital hardware. As we will see later, there is a special class of PRNG, the "Cryptographically Secure" PRNG or CS-PRNG, which while producing a deterministic sequence, provides guarantees on how hard it is to predict numbers in the sequence, such that the PRNG is usable for cryptographic purposes.

TRNGs are nondeterministic systems. They inevitably require a hardware component to sense "noise" or "entropy" in the environment that can be turned into nondeterministic numbers. Since a computer algorithm follows a fixed set of instructions, it is impossible to write a nondeterministic random number generator algorithm that works in isolation. You must have a physical hardware component to pass a nondeterministic source of data into the system to form what is often called a TRNG.

For example, the command line program "djenrandom" is a program to generate random numbers of various types. The "pure" model only produces random numbers that should be indistinguishable from random. However, by default, it internally uses a deterministic PRNG without any source of physical randomness. In the example below, we can see that we invoke the pure mode "-m pure" and pass the output to the "head" command to see only the first two lines, that is, "djenrandom -m pure| head -2." The result is the same every time, as we would expect from a deterministic PRNG algorithm, which always has the same initial state:

```
> djenrandom -m pure | head -2
BAA0D0E8CB60A3917EA080E11B5E089333C16DAC72DD57AAE470712D5C7D5621
FE06BA76C496828F45BD469E01F50CD45E36C7869D60AAF26EB1E0DED9A02CAA
> djenrandom -m pure | head -2
BAA0D0E8CB60A3917EA080E11B5E089333C16DAC72DD57AAE470712D5C7D5621
FE06BA76C496828F45BD469E01F50CD45E36C7869D60AAF26EB1E0DED9A02CAA
> djenrandom -m pure | head -2
BAA0D0E8CB60A3917EA080E11B5E089333C16DAC72DD57AAE470712D5C7D5621
FE06BA76C496828F45BD469E01F50CD45E36C7869D60AAF26EB1E0DED9A02CAA
>
```

We can persuade djenrandom to use a nondeterministic random seed (which it pulls from the Linux /dev/random service) using the "-s" argument (s stands for "seed"), to make it act as a TRNG. Here, we see that when acting as TRNG, the result is different every time:

```
>  djenrandom -s -m pure | head -2
B6DC13426156F65791F4AA5358D631AC805ECAE78DDDDD7D9A38A60E87CF64BA
40386087CA176AE0C4AE95F16E163F78FACB0BFAD56669CF4F9EE471241C7F46
> djenrandom -s -m pure | head -2
7616B7E1CB28F268BAB2083659A69D8577DA86538BEDFD9CA9FB21200EF70204
A078441938A921B7E01F09092BCDB392CF4BCC8400F120C12472703BA91FFC25
> djenrandom -s -m pure | head -2
C4284E7C8C042E59D44AD591C978C86DEFECBF32DF426AA7CA1B77FD02F46607
07BD9E153A38C0A733FC9C0F262987E0FA5C3DDFF4204850537B3FF55562627E
>
```

Physical noise sources are never perfectly random. The common term for perfectly random is "IID", meaning Independent and Identically Distributed. IID data is allowed to be biased, but there must be no correlation between values in an IID sequence and the data should also be statistically stationary, meaning the bias or any other statistic cannot change with time.

There is always some bias, correlation, and nonstationarity even if it is too small to be detected; so it is common and often necessary for a TRNG to have some form of post processing to improve the random qualities of the data. We look at this in Chapter 3, Entropy Extraction.

It is common but not always true, that sources of physical noise into a computer tend to be slow and PRNGs tend to be fast. So it is common in real systems to feed the output of a slow TRNG into a fast CS-PRNG to form a hybrid system that is cryptographically useful, nondeterministic, and fast. It is also appropriate to first pass the entropy gathered from the noise source into an extractor before the CS-PRNG. The data from the noise source is partially random and nondeterministic. The data from the entropy extractor will be slower than from the noise source, but should, if in a correctly designed RNG, be close to perfectly uniform, unpredictable, and nondeterministic. Once the data from the entropy extractor has seeded a CS-PRNG, the output of the CS-PRNG should be statistically uniform, cryptographically hard to predict, and faster.

So, as we pass through the chain, the properties of the random numbers can be labelled as "Bad", "Close to perfect and ideal for cryptography" and then "Good enough for cryptography", whereas the performance can go from "Slow" to "Slower" to "Fast". See Figure 1.1.

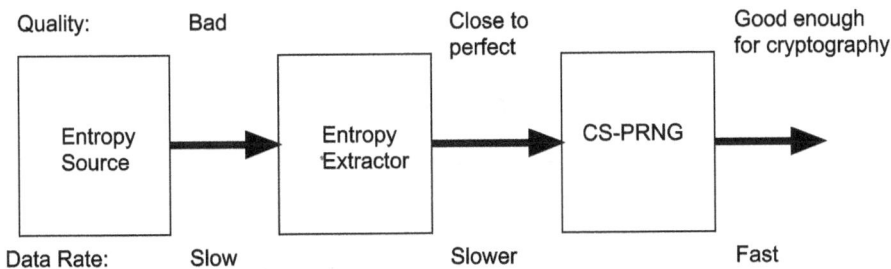

**Figure 1.1:** Properties, as numbers, pass through an RNG.

Subsequent Chapters 2, Entropy Sources, 3, Entropy Extraction, and 4, Cryptographically Secure Pseudorandom Number Generators will explain why.

## 1.2 Naming RNGs

There are commonly used names for different types of random number generators and there are standardized names, which are completely different. See Table 1.1. For example, the NIST SP800-90A, B, and C standards define a set of names that are different from the commonly used ones above. See Table 1.2.

**Table 1.1:** Table of RNG Names.

| Type of RNG | Common Name or Acronym |
|---|---|
| Any RNG | RNG |
| Any Deterministic RNG | PRNG |
| Any Nondeterministic RNG | TRNG |
| A Noise Sampling Circuit | Noise Source |
| A noise sample circuit with post processing | TRNG or Entropy Source |
| A cascade of TRNG or full entropy source followed by a CS-PRNG | TRNG |

NIST Use a different set of names for the same concepts:

**Table 1.2:** Table of NIST Names for RNGs.

| SP800-90 Term | Meaning |
|---|---|
| RBG | Random Bit Generator |
| DRBG | Deterministic Random Bit Generator |
| SEI | Source of Entropy Input |
| ES | Entropy Source |
| FES | Full Entropy Source |

## 1.3 Disambiguating RNG Types

Given the types and names above we can draw up a taxonomy of RNGs. All RNGs are RNGs, but can be split into two top level groups of deterministic and non-deterministic RNGs.

The deterministic RNGs may or may not be cryptographically secure. An example of an insecure property is lacking prediction resistance, whereby an observer can look at the output values and infer the internal state and so predict the future outputs. Another example is lacking backtracking resistance, where an observer can compute previous values from a sequence by looking at a set of later values. Secure random number generators will have the prediction resistance and backtracking resistance properties.

Nondeterministic RNGs may be only a noise source, or a system with a noise source and algorithmic post processing to produce high quality random numbers. Depending on the application, the quality of the output may or may not matter.

No naming system, whether just in common use or standardized, addresses all these cases, and this has led to a lot of confusion about what a random number generator really is. A common question, "Is that a TRNG (True Random Number Generator)" might elicit the response from me: "Do you mean a nondeterministically seeded PRNG with well-defined computational prediction bounds or do you mean a full entropy source comprising noise source with an extractor?" Put more clearly, this is asking (a) Is there an entropy source producing unpredictable bits? (b) Is there an entropy extractor turning those unpredictable bits into fully unpredictable bits, each with a 50% probability of being 1 and each bit being independent of the others? (c) Is there a secure PRNG algorithm that prevents an observer of the output bits being able to predict future value from the PRNG or infer past values from the PRNG?

These are the common features of a secure PRNG and so form one possible definition of a TRNG (True Random Number Generator), while the TRNG term is used very loosely in practice.

The different RNG types are identified based on the properties of the construction of the RNG. The essential major components of secure RNGs are the entropy source (or noise source), the entropy extractor (or conditioner or entropy distiller), and optionally a PRNG (or deterministic random bit generator).

Insecure random number generators are common outside the field of cryptography for many purposes, including simulation, system modeling, computer graphics, and many other things. These can be uniform or be designed to follow some nonuniform distribution such as a Gaussian distribution. The figures of merit for these types of generator tend be based on speed performance or closeness to some statistical model. Figure 1.2 gives a sequence of questions that divides the various common RNG types.

The NIST SP800-90A, B, and C specifications do not concern themselves with insecure RNGs, and so do not specify names for insecure RNGs, although the names they do specify tend to be different from common use. For example, SP800-90A calls a PRNG (Pseudo-Random Number Generator) a DRBG (Deterministic Random Bit Generator), a TRNG (True Random Number Generator), an NRBG (Nondeterministic Random Bit Generator), and an entropy source an SEI (Source of Entropy Input).

Generally, PRNGs do not have specific terms to separate secure PRNGs from insecure PRNGs. Similarly, there is no commonly used term to distinguish a simple noise source from a noise source with post processing to increase the per-bit entropy. In common terminology, both might be called a TRNG, whereas NIST SP800-90B and C do distinguish between an NRBG (Nondeterministic Random Bit Generator) and an SEI (Source of Entropy Input). In the NIST arrangement, an SEI is a component of an NRBG.

## 1.4 Nonuniform RNGs

There is a class of RNG that is designed to generate random numbers that follow a distribution other than a uniform distribution, for example, a Gaussian distribution,

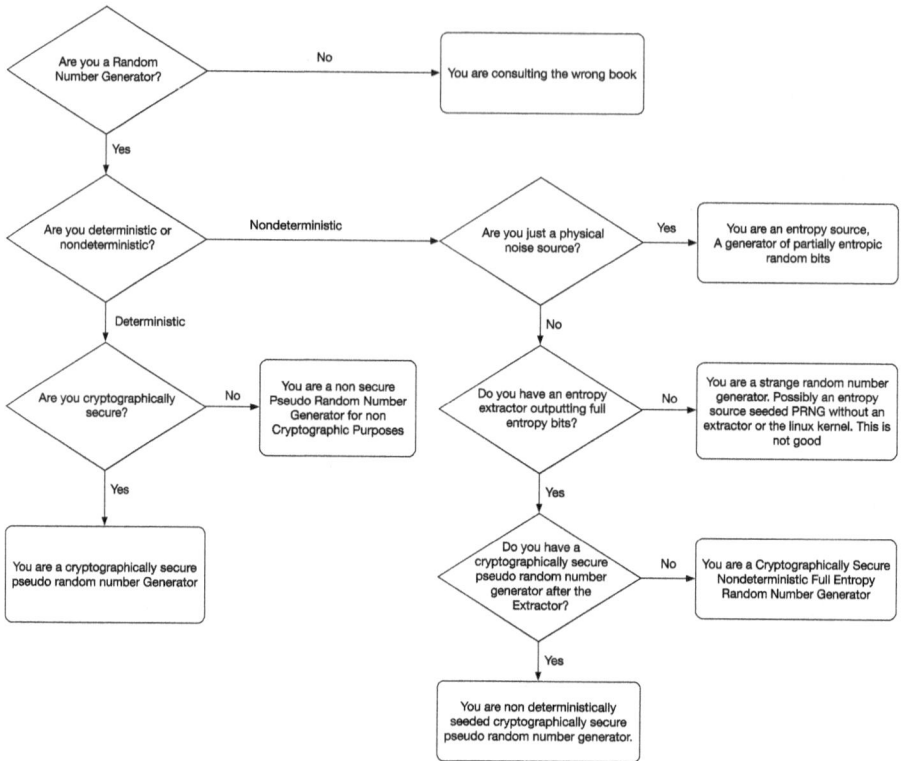

**Figure 1.2:** RNG Type Flowchart.

binomial distribution, gamma distribution, or one of the many other distributions defined in mathematics.

These typically operate by starting with a uniform distribution and then applying a transform to generate the required distribution from the uniform distribution.

We look at some nonuniform RNGs in Chapter 7 on Gaussian RNGs.

## 1.5 Noncryptographically Secure PRNG Algorithms

This class of RNG generates uniformly distributed random numbers. However, they are not designed to be unpredictable. It is possible for future and past values to be predicted from a sequence of values from such an RNG. This makes them unsuitable for cryptographic uses.

There are many noncryptographic uses of noncryptographically secure PRNGs. For example, database hashing algorithms are used to create a randomized distribution that minimize collisions in the database, where different bits of data land in the same place. Simulation programs often need random stimulus to drive their model.

But they require repeatability, so each run has a seed number and the seed number can be used to cause the PRNG to produce the same output and so the same simulation run. Nonsecure PRNG algorithms tend to be simpler and faster than cryptographically secure PRNGs, since they do not make use of the extensive cycles of linear and non-linear transformations needed in a cryptographically secure algorithm. Efficiency is often a goal of the design of such algorithms.

Some examples of commonly used insecure PRNG algorithms are:

1. Linear Congruential Generators (LGCs): A simple family of generators that computes $X_{n+1} = (aX_n + c) \mod m$.
2. XORShift: A simple generator with good statistical properties based on XORs and shifts of its state variables.
3. Permuted Congruential Generators (PCGs): A family of generator with excellent statistical properties, based on introducing a XorShift based permutation output stage to the LCG loop.

A number of such algorithms are looked at in Chapter 6 on noncryptographic PRNGs.

## 1.6 Cryptographically Secure PRNG Algorithms

Cryptographically secure PRNGs, while behaving deterministically, are designed so that an observer seeing a subset of the output values cannot predict any other past, present, or future values from the output of the PRNG.

Examples of commonly used secure PRNGs are:

1. SP800-90A DRBGs: This includes the CTR-DRBG, the Hash-DRBG, and the HMAC-DRBG. The Dual-EC-DRBG is a famous example of a back-doored RNG that was removed from the SP800-90A specification after the back door properties were made widely known.
2. ChaChaCha and its predecessor Salsa20, using shifts, additions, and xors on its state variables; used in OpenSSL and in the OpenBSD and NetBSD Random Number service.
3. BlumBlumShub: A number-theoretic RNG with well-proven security properties, but very inefficient compared to the other PRNGs in this list.

Generally, we think of a PRNG having an internal "state", that is, a number of bits. The state of those bits determines the next output value, and each time a value is output, the internal state is changed so that the next number appears random with respect to all previous and future values.

The mechanism for determining the output from the state and the mechanism for updating the state can be distilled into a next-state function $f_{ns}(s_i)$ and a state output function $f_{out}(s_i)$. These are arranged as shown in Figure 1.3.

$$f_{ns}(s_i) \rightarrow s_{i+1}$$
$$f_{out}(s_i) \rightarrow x_i$$

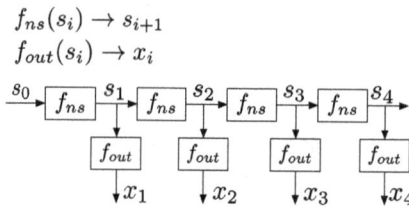

**Figure 1.3:** CSPRNG State Diagram.

The primary security property for a CSPRNG is that an adversary with visibility of the outputs $x_i$ cannot infer the internal state. The adversary infers the state by inverting $f_{out}$, thus computing $s_i$ from $x_i$ and earlier outputs $x_{i-n}$. So, it is necessary for the output function $f_{out}$ to be hard to invert.

Another property desirable for a CSPRNG is backtracking resistance. If the state $s_i$ is revealed, we know the adversary can predict future outputs by repeatedly applying $f_{ns}$ to $s_i$. We want it to be hard for the adversary to compute earlier outputs from the state. Therefore, the state update function $f_{ns}$ should be hard to invert, so that $s_{i-1}$ cannot be computed from the inverse of $f_{ns}$. That is, computing

$$s_{i-1} = f_{ns}^{-1}(s_i)$$

is computationally hard.

Another property for a CSPRNG is forward prediction resistance, whereby even with knowledge of some internal state $s_i$, future states cannot be computed. This is not a property of all CSPRNGs and, for example, is an optional property in SP800-90A. The means to achieve forward prediction resistance is to inject fresh entropic data into each state update. So the next state function now has two parameters, the previous state $s_i$ and fresh entropy $E_i$:

$$s_{i+1} = f_{nspr}(s_i, E_i)$$

Thus, future state values are both a function of the previous state and future entropy data that has not been generated yet. In real-world RNGs, this is typically achieved by running the entropy source continuously, taking the new bits that are available from the entropy source at the time of the update and stirring them into the current or next state of the update function, using xor, or a cryptographic mixing function.

Note that while it is easy to create PRNGs that have these desirable properties, by simply using known good cryptographic functions with the noninvertibility properties required, there are many examples where they do not have such properties, either through poor design, or through deliberately hidden methods to invert the update and output functions or leak the state. The now classic example of a deliberately flawed RNG is the SP800-90 Dual-EC-DRBG, which we look at in Section 4.1.

CSPRNGs have an additional function to reseed the state of the PRNG with fresh entropy. Typically this is always performed at the start of the PRNG being run and may be performed periodically, or on request at later points in time.

### 1.6.1 Example of CSPRNG: The SP800-90A CTR DRBG

This is a quick look at the SP800-90A CTR DRBG. We look at this and other CSPRNG algorithms in more detail in Chapter 4. Details of the SP800-90A CTR DRNG are in Section 4.1.3.

**State:** The state of the algorithm consists of three variables, $V$ (vector) a 128 bit number, $K$ (Key) a key, one of 128, 192, or 256 bits (depending on the key size of the AES function used), and finally $C$ (count), the count of the number of generated outputs since the last reseed.

**Generate Function:** The output function is called generate(). The function increments $V$ and $C$ and the output using the AES algorithm invoked with the key input $K$ and vector input $V$.

```
generate():
    V = V+1
    C = C+1
    x = AES(K,V)
    output x
```

**Update Function:** The next state function is called update(). This computes a new value for $K$ and $V$ so that backtracking resistance is achieved. The key $K$ that was used in updating to the new $K$ is lost, so inverting the procedure would require searching all the possible values for $K$.

```
update():
    K' = K xor AES(K,V+1)
    V' = V xor AES(K,V+2)

    V = V+2
    K = K'
    V = V'
```

The above example assumes that the key size is the same as the block size of the AES. If the key size was 256 bits, then the CTR algorithm would be extended in order to get enough bits to update the key. In the listing below, the CTR algorithm is run for three invocations of AES to get 256 bits of CTR output for a 256 bit key update and a further 128 bits for the vector update.

```
update(K,V):
    K_lower' = K_lower xor AES(K,V+1)
    K_upper' = K_upper xor AES(K,V+2)
    V' = V xor AES(K,V+3)

    V = V+3
    K = K_upper' | K_lower'
    V = V'
```

There are other details in the full specification that have been omitted here, such as the personalization strings, initialization, additional entropy input, and handling of multiple key sizes.

It is from these two algorithms that the term CTR DRBG is derived. Given $K$ and $V$, the output value and the values to XOR into $K$ and $V$ in the update are drawn from the output of AES in CTR (CounTeR) mode. CTR mode involves taking an IV (initialization vector) and incrementing it with a counter. For each increment, the value $IV + n$ is encrypted with the key $K$. This yields a series of output values that are indistinguishable from random. This is shown in Figure 1.4.

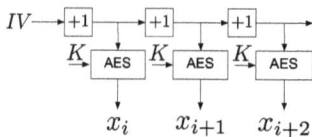

**Figure 1.4:** CTR Mode.

In the CTR DRBG, $V$ is used as the IV (Initialization Vector) and the outputs from the CTR mode operation are used to provide the data output and the update values for $K$ and $V$. This is shown for the 128 bit key case in Figure 1.5, which requires three invocations of AES in the CTR algorithm, one each for output data value, the key update, and the vector update.

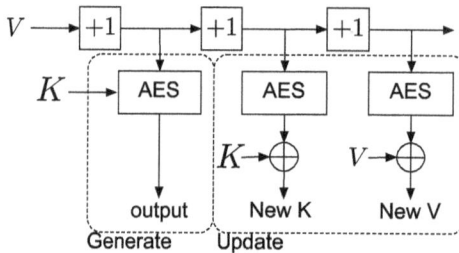

**Figure 1.5:** CTR DRBG Relationship to CTR Mode.

Chapter 4 goes into detail on the design of a number of cryptographically secure RNGs.

### 1.6.2 Attacking CSPRNGs

Assuming there is no low effort algorithm to compute the internal state from the output values, the way to predict the past or future outputs of a secure PRNG is to try guessing all the possible internal states and compare the output from those states against the observed output. When you find a match, you have the internal state.

If you had a PRNG with 16 bits of internal state and you had three output values $A$, $B$, and $C$, all you need to do to determine future values $D$, $E$, and $F$ is to try running the algorithm for three steps starting from each of the $2^{16}$ (that is 65536) possible internal states. If the output matches $A$, $B$, and $C$, then you have the internal state and you can keep going to predict future outputs. Obviously this is a trivial task for a modern computer.

The following program implements a weak PRNG using AES-CTR mode. It is weak because the key is only 16 bits in length. It generates 6 output values. Then the attack algorithm executes a small loop which searches through all the $2^{16}$ possible keys to find a key that decrypts the first three random values to three values that increment by 1. Those decrypted three values are the sequence of vector values $V$, $V+1$ and $V+2$. Once it has found the key, it goes on to generate the next three outputs, which match the final three values from the weak RNG, showing that it has managed to predict future values, by inverting the output function to get $K$ and $V$ from the output data.

**Listing 1.4:** Weak PRNG Example

```python
#!/usr/bin/env python

# A weak RNG with only 16 bit keys
from Crypto.Cipher import AES
key = 0x2984 # 16 bit key.
V = 0x0123456789abcdef0123456789abcdef # 128 bit vector

def byteify(n):
    bytelist = list()
    for j in xrange(16):
        bytelist.append((n >> (8*j)) & 0xff)
    return(bytes(bytearray(bytelist)))

def debyteify(bytelist):
    bi = 0
    for i in xrange(16):
        bi = (bi << 8) + ord(bytelist[15-i])
        #print "debyteify  %x" % ord(bytelist[15-i])
    return (bi)

def printbytes(h,b):
    st = h
    for i in xrange(16):
        st = st + "%02x" % ord(b[15-i])
    print st

cipher = AES.new(byteify(key), AES.MODE_ECB)
outputs = list()
for i in xrange(6):
    outputs.append(cipher.encrypt(byteify(V)))
    V += 1

# Now outputs[] contains 6 randomish values
```

```
for i in xrange(len(outputs)):
    print "Output_%d_:_%032x" % (i,debyteify(outputs[i]))

# Now search for the key using first three numbers.
for i in xrange(65536):
    trialkey = byteify(i)
    cipher = AES.new(trialkey,AES.MODE_ECB)
    try1 = debyteify(cipher.decrypt(outputs[0]))
    try2 = debyteify(cipher.decrypt(outputs[1]))
    try3 = debyteify(cipher.decrypt(outputs[2]))

    if (try3 == (try2+1)) and (try2 == (try1+1)):
        print "Key_%04x_works" % i
        break
# Now predict the next 3 values
predict1 = cipher.encrypt(byteify(try3+1))
predict2 = cipher.encrypt(byteify(try3+2))
predict3 = cipher.encrypt(byteify(try3+3))

print "Prediction_for_outputs_3-5:"
print "%032x" % debyteify(predict1)
print "%032x" % debyteify(predict2)
print "%032x" % debyteify(predict3)
```

So, a necessary feature of a secure PRNG is that it has enough internal state bits that it is not computationally feasible to try every possible value. Typically a secure PRNG would have 256 bits or more internal state. In the CTR-DRBG, the key size determines the security level. With a key size of 128 bits, it would take 10 782 897 524 556 318 080 696 079 years for a computer to search the key space at a rate of 1 million keys per second. With a 256 bit key it would take 366 922 989 192 195 209 469 576 219 385 149 402 531 466 222 607 677 909 725 256 622 years.

## 1.7 Controlled Defect RNGs

In order to test extractor algorithms or calibrate entropy estimation algorithms, it is necessary to create random numbers with known deviations from a uniform distribution such as bias or serial correlation.

The tool, djenrandom, made available with this book is an example of a program that implements a set of controlled defect RNGs. The four defect models supported are
1. Bias, where the probability of a bit being 1 can be controlled.
2. Correlation, where the serial correlation of the bitstream can be controlled.
3. SUMS (Step Update Metastable Source), a model which closely models a metastable entropy source with feedback and can produce data with bias, serial correlation, and nonstationarity all at the same time.

4. SINBIAS (Sinusoidal Bias), a model which varies the bias of generated data sinusoidally.

Links to the software tools, including djenrandom are given in Appendix D.

Chapter 11, Software Tools looks at using djenrandom for defective data generating in greater detail, along with looking at a number of other software tools.

## 1.8 Noise Source Circuits

In order that an RNG is nondeterministic, it needs some source of nondeterministic data. This requires hardware that is capable of taking nondeterministic events from the environment and turning them into bits. This type of circuit is commonly called a *noise source* or *entropy source*. Noise sources are circuits rather than algorithms. However, noise sources should be combined with a deterministic post processing algorithm to improve the entropy quality. These algorithms are called *entropy extractors* or *conditioners*. This book treats noise sources as only the noise sampling circuit and the extractor/conditioner algorithms separately.

Examples of noise source circuits include:

1. RO (Ring Oscillator)/Phase error accumulation sources. This is a widely used but often easily attacked class of noise source. A ring oscillator is a loop of inverters which self oscillates. When sampled periodically, the accumulated phase noise of the loop results in random bits being sampled. It is common for RO circuits to be implemented with multiple ROs, each with mutually prime loop lengths as a mechanism to prevent them from running in phase with each other, although this is rarely successful.
2. Metastable Phase Collapse Ring Oscillators. This is a class of entropy source that entails running a number of independent ROs. These are then joined together in one big loop. The multiple independent phases of the circuit at the point of circuit switch will collapse to a single large loop oscillation. The collapse is metastable, driven by noise and the resulting phase error is random with an exponential distribution resulting from the metastable resolution time. This circuit was documented in a paper from Samsung [24].
3. Feedback Stablized Metastable Latch. This is a practical form of entropy source in silicon chips that repeatedly forces a latch into metastability and lets it resolve to a 1 or 0. Noise is supposed to drive the resolution to 1 or 0 and so the resulting bits have entropy. Typical latches have bias that would lead to the same value each time, so a stabilization loop is needed to load one side or the other of the latch to keep it operating in a balanced metastable mode. This kind of entropy source is seen in Intel CPUs. A conference paper by Rachael Parker describes the circuit and derives a closed form equation for the min entropy of metastable latch based noise sources [16].

4. Analog Modular Multiplier Loop/Infinite Noise Multiplier. This involves iteratively amplifying a noisy source (such as from a diode or resistor) until it exceeds a particular voltage, whereupon the voltage is divided in half. Each time the circuit is iterated, a single bit is output, based on whether the voltage is above or below 50% of the module threshold. This circuit is seen in some plug-in USB RNG devices.

5. Reverse Biased Zener. This involves amplifying and sampling the noise from a reverse biased diode. This kind of circuit is often used in board level RNG circuits. It is notoriously hard to ensure that these circuits work well when manufactured in volume, but single circuits are easy to tweak to make them work.

6. Demod Error Vector. This method is used in some chips with radio demodulators. These typically supply an error vector register that measures the distance of each received symbol from the ideal symbol and is a function of the noise in the sender, the receiver, and the intervening radio path. While the radio is receiving data, the error vector from the demodulator tends to have high entropy. This kind of noise source has been implemented in Bluetooth and 802.11 chips, where no alternate entropy source was provided.

Chapter 2 examines entropy sources in greater detail.

## 1.9 TRNG Extractor/Conditioning Algorithms

An entropy extractor is an algorithm that takes in data that is typically partially entropic and outputs data that is either more entropic than the input, or is close to fully entropic. It is impossible to create a deterministic algorithm that outputs more entropy than is input into the algorithm. Since we want the entropy per bit at the output to be more entropic than the entropy per bit at the input, the number of bits at the output of an extractor has to be smaller than the number of bits consumed at the input. So, $\text{entropy}_{in} \geq \text{entropy}_{out}$ and $\text{len}(\text{entropy}_{in}) > \text{len}(\text{entropy}_{out})$.

The theory of entropy extractors tends to be a very mathematical area of computer science and that is a fine topic for a different book. In this book we look primarily at the practical implementation aspects of extractors.

Examples of entropy extractors include:

1. AES-CBC-MAC. An extractor algorithm in the current draft of SP800-90B. It is used in Intel CPUs as the entropy extractor that conditions the seeds for the CS-PRNG from which the RdRand instruction gets its random numbers.

2. Von Neumann and Yuval Perez whiteners. These are debiaser algorithms that, when fed independent random input values, guarantee unbiased outputs. Unfortunately, this algorithm is widely misused in various chips, by being fed from a serially correlated source, so the input bits are not independent.

3.  BIW (Barack Impagliazzo Wigdersen) Extractor. An example of a multiple input extractor. These extractors tolerate inputs with nonindependent inputs. However, the separate inputs must be independent from each other. The BIW extractor takes 3 independent inputs. It is noted for its efficient implementation and is suitable for use in resource-constrained environments.
4.  2-EXT Extractor. This is another multiple input extractor taking two independent inputs. It is notable since it has been shown to be secure from quantum computer attacks.
5.  Many XOR Extractor. This is an ad-hoc extractor that entails simply XORing together the output of multiple separate entropy sources. This structure has been seen in a number of mobile phone chips. As an extractor, it has poor properties and therefore needs the noise sources to be of high quality and highly independent from each other.

## 1.10 The Structure of Secure RNG Implementations

The components of a general secure RNG include the functional parts (entropy source, extractor, CS-PRNG) typically along with self test features such as BIST (Built In Self Test) and OHT (Online Health Test). See Figure 1.6.

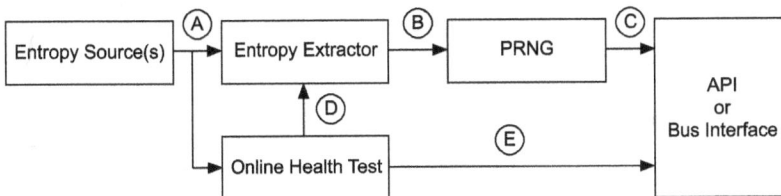

**Figure 1.6:** RNG Structure.

### 1.10.1 Point A, the Raw Data

In this structure, the entropy source outputs unprocessed entropic data to point A, which is sent into the entropy extractor from point A.

The data at point A is sometimes named *raw data*, because it has not yet been post processed by the extractor or PRNG. Thus, the data at the output C is sometimes referred to as *cooked* data.

It is important that the input requirements of the extractor are met by the output properties of the entropy source at point A. For example, an AES-CBC-MAC extractor will typically require the input data to have a min entropy of > 0.5 bits per bit. A multiple input extractor would require each of the inputs to be independent of each other and also have some level of min-entropy. The quality of the data at point A generally is described in terms of min-entropy and basic statistics such as mean, serial correlation, and stationarity.

This raw data is also fed to the online health test, which is typically a statistical test to ensure the entropy source is correctly functioning. This may run full time or on demand.

### 1.10.2 Points D and E, the Health Status Feedback

The results of the online testing would typically be made available at the RNG's main interface via point E, but also it can (and should) be used to inform the extractor when the quality of the data is meeting its input requirements via point D.

### 1.10.3 Point B, the Seed Quality Data

The output of the extractor will generally be close to full entropy, if the input requirements of the extractor are met, or in the case of single input extractors, it is possible to show only computational predication bounds rather than min-entropy when the input is only guaranteed to have a certain level of min-entropy [7]. It has been shown mathematically that getting to 100% full entropy is impossible, but is it possible to get arbitrarily close to full entropy. The gap between the actual min-entropy and full entropy in extractor theory is referred to as $\varepsilon$ (epsilon).

The data at point B might constitute the output of the RNG, or it might provide the seed input to the PRNG to initialize or update the PRNG's state to be nondeterministic.

### 1.10.4 Point C, the PRNG Output

The PRNG typically takes in a seed from point B either initially or periodically to inject nondeterminism into its state. It will then proceed to generate outputs Each step employs an output function to generate an output from the current state and also generate a next state from the current state.

The data at the PRNG output stage generally cannot be treated as having an amount of min-entropy. Instead, it has a certain computational prediction bound. This is because by observing past values from the output, there is always a brute force algorithm that can search through all the possible values of the internal state to find the state that would have generated the previous values. A secure PRNG algorithm ensures that the amount of computation required is too high to be practically implemented.

The current progress towards quantum computers makes it relevant to also consider the computations prediction bounds for a quantum computer. Some RNGs, such as number-theoretic RNGs like BlumBlumShub, are completely insecure against a quantum computer. Conventional cryptographic RNGs based on block ciphers or hashes or HMACs, tend to have their security strength reduced to the square root of the security against a classical computer. So, the industry is in a process of doubling the key sizes of RNGs to prepare for future quantum computer threats.

## 1.11 Pool Extractor Structures

The most basic way of viewing an entropy extractor is that it takes in $n$ bits and outputs $m$ bits of data which are passed onto the next stage.

A more useful structure is to have the extractor include its earlier result in the next result. For example, if you were using AES-CBC-MAC with a 128 bit block size, with a 4:1 extractor ratio the algorithm would be: Given Inputs:

$$\text{in}_a \quad \text{where } \text{len}(\text{in}_a) = 128$$
$$\text{in}_b \quad \text{where } \text{len}(\text{in}_b) = 128$$
$$\text{in}_c \quad \text{where } \text{len}(\text{in}_c) = 128$$
$$\text{in}_d \quad \text{where } \text{len}(\text{in}_d) = 128$$

and output

$$\text{out}_x = \text{AES\_CBC\_MAC}(\text{key}, \text{in}_a|\text{in}_b|\text{in}_c|\text{in}_d) \tag{1.1}$$

So 512 bits of input data are compressed down to 128 bits of extract data.

If the extractor maintained a pool of 128 bits, it could use AES-CBC-MAC to mix in the input raw entropy into the pool by including the pool in the AES-CBC-MAC calculation. This is simply achieved by including the previous output in the input to the CBC MAC algorithm:

$$\text{out}_x = \text{AES\_CBC\_MAC}(\text{key}, \text{out}_{x-1}|\text{in}_a|\text{in}_b|\text{in}_c|\text{in}_d)$$

So, if there were periods of low entropy from the entropy source, the pool would maintain the complexity of the output of the extractor. Also, the extractor could keep running while the raw entropy data is flowing in, until the PRNG needed a seed, so the extractor ratio would be as large as possible for each reseeding.

A third enhancement available with a pool structure is that when the OHT tags a set of input bits as not meeting the test requirement, they can still be mixed into the pool so that any residual entropy is not lost. The AES-CBC-MAC algorithm can be continued until a required number of healthy input samples are mixed into the pool. This forms an active response to attacks on the entropy source that try to reduce the entropy of the source. As the number of unhealthy samples increases, the amount of samples mixed into the pool increases.

The AES-CBC-MAC can be broken down into multiple single AES operations. The pseudocode in Listing 1.5 shows this pool method in terms of an individual AES operation executed once per loop.

**Listing 1.5:** Pool Extractor Pseudocode

```
extractor_ratio = 4
pool = 0
healthy_samples = -1
    while healthy_samples < extractor_ratio:
        if healthy_samples = -1:
            pool = AES(key,pool)
            healthy_samples++
        else:
            pool = AES(key, pool xor input)
            if sample_was_healthy:
                healthy_samples++
```

This will continue to extend the CBC-MAC until enough healthy samples are received and will also mix in the previous pool value. The extensibility of CBC-MAC is considered a weakness when used as a MAC, but in this context as an extractor, it is a strength.

The Intel DRNG exhibits this behavior. The reseed of the AES-CTR-DRBG requires 256 bits, so it performs two parallel CBC-MACs, each generating 128 bits of seed data to make 256 bits.

Similar mechanisms could be implemented with hashes or HMAC, both of which are suitable extractor algorithms.

## 1.12 What Key to Use?

In Chapter 3 on entropy extraction, there is a discussion of seeded extractors and how getting a uniform seed is a chicken-and-egg problem. How can you get a uniform seed from an extractor when the extractor needs a uniform seed at its input and uniform data is not available from the physical world?

So what is the right key to use for CBC-MAC extractors? The key needs to be independent of the raw entropy coming in, but it may also be static and public.

A value like all zeroes or all ones would not be independent from failure modes of an entropy source or entropy sources exhibiting high bias.

The approach taken in Intel CPUs was to encrypt the value 1 with the key 0 using AES. This value should have no algorithmic or statistical connection to raw data coming in from the entropy source. This approach was discussed and shown to be safe in [21].

The approach taken in the TLS protocol, with the HKDF extractor, is to use a key of 0 when a random key is not available.

This same rationale could be used with other seeded constructs. But first, the mathematical proof of the properties of the extractor should be consulted to check that such a seed will suffice.

## 1.13 Multiple Input Extractors

Multiple input extractors, as the name suggests, take multiple independent inputs. It is necessary that the inputs be independent. Consider if two inputs did not need to be independent, then instead, a single input of dependent bits could be split into two sets of data and meet the input requirements. This task could be done inside the extractor. So, the only reason to ask for multiple inputs is that those inputs are independent.

Figure 1.7 shows the way a multiple input extractor takes input from multiple independent entropy sources and outputs a single stream of random numbers that are very close to perfectly uniform, provided that the quality of the input entropy is high enough. Each multiple input extractor is designed for a specific number of inputs. Two and three input extractors are shown in Figure 1.7, because Section 3.10 goes into detail on two multiple input extractors, the BIW three input extractor and the 2-EXT two input extractor.

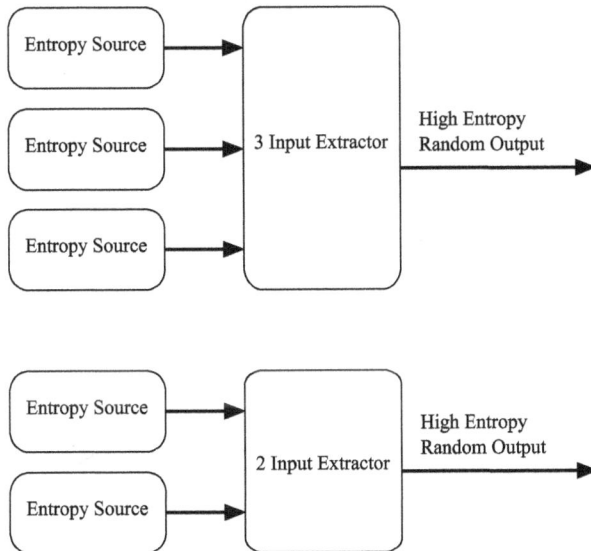

**Figure 1.7:** Three Input Extractor and Two Input Extractor.

Multiple input extractors tend to use basic arithmetic or algebraic methods rather than rely on cryptographic primitives such as block ciphers or hashes. This leads to such extractors being small and efficient to implement compared to cryptographic extractors. However, the cost is that multiple independent entropy sources are needed. So, the savings in implementation costs of the extractor need to be factored against the additional implementation costs of the entropy sources.

# 2 Entropy Sources

Entropy sources are physical systems that take noise from the environment and turns it into random bits. Usually these are electrical circuits. There are some examples of partly mechanical entropy sources, but these are not generally useful, except as a curiosity, because they tend to be very slow and unreliable. Therefore, we will focus on electronic entropy sources in this chapter.

Ideal binary random numbers are IID (independent and identically distributed) and have a bias of 0.5; so, 1 is as likely as 0.

However, entropy sources can never achieve this property directly. The physical world from which noise is sampled only yields data that has some level of correlation, bias, and nonstationarity. Entropy extractor algorithms are, therefore, used to convert the partially entropic output of an entropy source into data that closely approximates full entropy IID data.

In this chapter, we look at *entropy sources*. In the next chapter, we look at *entropy extractors,* which take partially entropic data from an entropy source and convert it to almost fully entropic data.

## 2.1 Ring Oscillator Entropy Sources

A common type of entropy source is the ring oscillator. This is a circuit that has an odd number of inverters in a ring, so that when powered, it oscillates. The period of the oscillation varies over time as a result of noise in the circuit, and so, periodically, sampling the phase of the circuit at some point on the ring should yield partially entropic data. The longer the time between the samples, the greater the amount of phase noise contributing to the values that are read, so the statistical properties of the data improve with longer sampling intervals. A simplified circuit for a ring oscillator is shown in Figure 2.1.

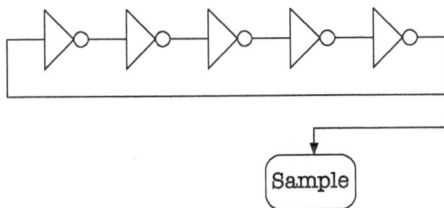

**Figure 2.1:** Ring Oscillator Circuit.

The inverter, represented by a triangle with a circle on the output, takes a binary value, 0 or 1, and outputs the opposite value. With 0 on the input, it will output 1. With 1 on the input, it will output 0.

https://doi.org/10.1515/9781501506062-002

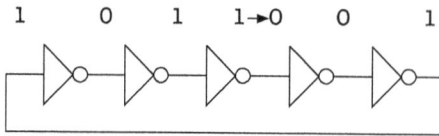

**Figure 2.2:** Ring Oscillator Circuit Values.

In Figure 2.2, the binary value alternates from 0 to 1 to 0 as it crosses the inverters. However, since there is an odd number of inverters, there must be a discontinuity point where there is an input value that equals the output value. The output of that inverter gate, therefore, changes to the opposite value. The discontinuity, as a result, moves on to the next inverter. This discontinuity carries on cycling around the circuit. If you look at the waveform at any particular point, then you will see that the value oscillates up and down, changing once for each time the discontinuity makes a trip around the circuit.

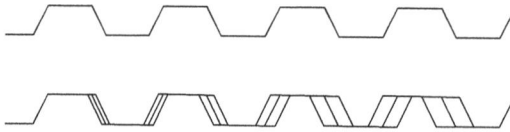

**Figure 2.3:** Ring Oscillator Waveform.

The upper trace in Figure 2.3 shows what you would see if you observed the voltage of a point in the ring oscillator circuit changing over time, using an oscilloscope.

The lower trace shows what you would get if you were to take multiple traces and overlap them. Aligning the left-hand edge, you would see the uncertainty in the loop time, since the timing of the traces will vary as a result of noise randomly affecting the time it takes for a signal to pass through a gate. The second edge shows a small amount of variation. The size of this variation usually follows a normal distribution. We will call that time $\sigma_t$, which is the normal random variate with the standard deviation of the loop time uncertainty. The diagram is an exaggerated view; it typically takes thousands of clock periods for a full cycle of timing uncertainty to accumulate.

The uncertainty in the next edge is the sum of the previous uncertainty and the same uncertainty in the current cycle. As time progresses, the uncertainty of the edge timing increases until the uncertainty is larger than a single loop period.

The variance of two normal random variates added together is the sum of the two variances of the two variates. So, if sampling at a period $t_{sample}$ is equal to $N$ average cycles, then

$$\sigma^2_{t_{sample}} = \sum_1^N \sigma_t^2,$$

$$\sigma_{t_{sample}} = \sqrt{\sum_1^N \sigma_t^2}.$$

So, with a ring oscillator circuit, measure the timing uncertainty. Then find which value of $N$ will lead to $\sigma_{t_{sample}}$ being several times greater than the loop time $t$. You can set the sample period $t_{sample} = Nt$, and you can expect the value of a point in the circuit sampled every $t_{sample}$ seconds will appear random.

## 2.1.1 Ring Oscillator Entropy Source Problems

Ring oscillator entropy sources have been popular mostly because the circuit appears very easy to implement. However, they have been found to have some issues. The output of a ring oscillator is serially correlated. As the sample period $t_{sample}$ increases, the serial correlation reduces, but it never goes away completely. This has been a problem when the von Neumann debiaser or the Yuval Perez debiaser is used as the entropy extractor. It is a requirement of those two debiaser algorithms that the input data samples be independent of each other. However, samples from serially correlated data are not independent and so may lead to a lower output entropy than is expected from a Von Neumann or Yuval Perez debiaser. The Von Neumann and Yuval Perez debiaser algorithms are described in Sections 3.4 and 3.5.

A second problem is that ring oscillators have been shown to be vulnerable to injection attack, where a periodic signal is injected via the power supply or via an electromagnetic coupling device. This can lead to the ring oscillator locking to the frequency of the injected signal, and so, the loop time becomes predictable and the entropy is lost.

For example, at the CHES 2009 Conference, the paper [12] was presented showing a frequency injection attack on a chip and pin payment card, where they rendered the random data predictable and were therefore able to cryptographically attack the authentication protocol. The paper is available at http://www.iacr.org/archive/ches2009/57470316/57470316.pdf.

There are some common design mistakes with ring oscillator entropy sources. A number of ring oscillator implementations implement multiple ring oscillators and combine the outputs by XORing them together on the assumption that the sample outputs from the rings are independent. See Figure 2.4.

The problem with this is that it makes it more susceptible to injection attacks, because with multiple oscillators there tends to be multiple modes in which the oscillators will lock with each other. When sequences that are locked to each other in phase or frequency are XORed together, they cancel and make a low entropy repeating sequence. The more oscillators, the more the number of opportunities for an injection attack to work. Thus, if you are implementing a ring oscillator entropy source, then the best number of loops to implement is 1. However, if you need higher performance, using multiple loops is a way to achieve higher performance. An appropriate way to combine the output of multiple loops is to independently feed them into an entropy extractor that is tolerant of correlation between the input bits, as shown in Figure 2.5.

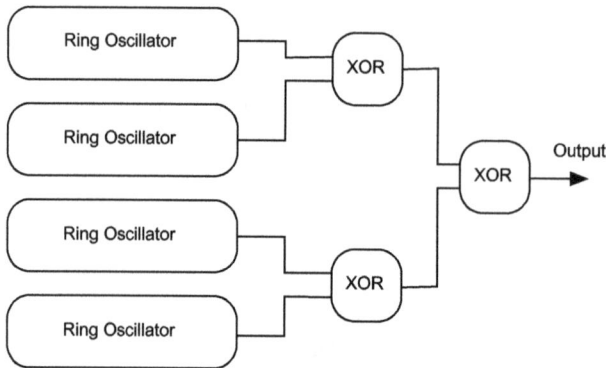

**Figure 2.4:** Multiple Ring Oscillators Poorly Combined.

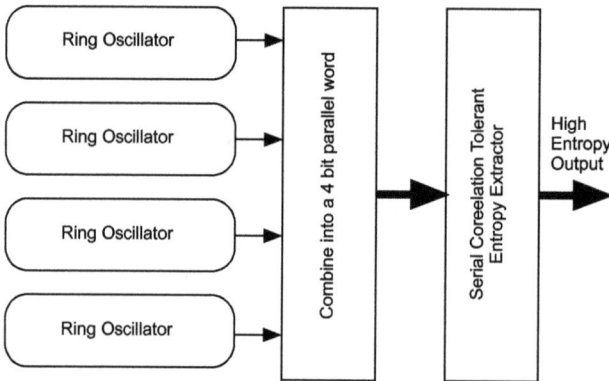

**Figure 2.5:** Multiple Ring Oscillators Well-Combined.

In a secure RNG, you would also need an online health test per loop. It would make sense to have tests that both check the loops have not failed and test that the loops are not correlated with each other, so they can detect an injection attack or loop locking failure. Chapter 9 goes into greater detail on online health testing algorithms in general and correlation detection algorithms in particular.

## 2.2 Metastable Phase Collapse Ring Oscillator Entropy Sources

There is no commonly used name for this sort of entropy source; I call it the Metastable Phase Collapse Ring Oscillator Entropy Source. I am not aware of a published version of this type of entropy source. It represents an attractive alternative to ring oscillator sources, using similar technology in a different configuration.

A paper was published with a related, but different, idea by Samsung engineers. We will take a look a that design in Section 2.3.

The Metastable Phase Collapse Ring Oscillator Entropy Source involves a ring of ring oscillators. Each ring oscillator is of a different length, so that they oscillate at different frequencies.

Two properties of the ring sizes will help prevent locking between the rings.

First, make the size of the rings different enough that one loop cannot simply shift its frequency a little bit to match the other.

Second, ensure the LCM (lowest common multiple) of the two loop frequencies is large compared to the loop periods, so they will not easily find a common multiple of their base frequencies at which they will both oscillate. Choosing frequencies that are relatively prime might hypothetically have this property, since the LCM of two different primes $p$ and $q$ is $p \times q$. However, the frequencies are not bound to integer relationships, so some extensive testing should be employed to ensure that the circuit cannot be coaxed to lock its loops together using injection attacks.

A control signal causes the rings to switch between being several independent rings into one large ring.

Here, we will take a look at the what happens with multiple discontinuities in a ring oscillator in order to understand how this entropy source behaves. To simplify the diagrams, we will shrink the inverter gates to arrows as shown in Figure 2.6. A filled arrow represents a nongate that is outputting logic zero, and a hollow arrow represents an inverter gate that is outputting logic one. The oscillator loop is shown as a chain of these inverter gates, and the number of inverter gates is indicated in the middle. With an odd number of inverter gates, there will be a travelling discontinuity as discussed in Section 2.1. This is shown as the dot on the loop where two gates with the same output value meet.

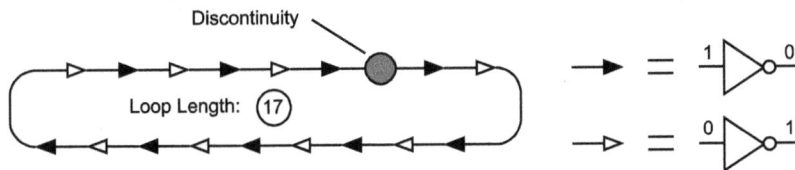

**Figure 2.6:** Single Ring Oscillator.

It is not possible to have two discontinuities in a ring with an odd number of gates. Try stringing an odd number of gates together in alternating sequence with two discontinuities; you will see that one of the discontinuities will cancel out.

However, you can have an odd number of discontinuities. Figure 2.7 shows a ring of 17 gates with three discontinuities and a ring of 19 gates with five.

When two discontinuities meet they will cancel each other out. So, the odd number of discontinuities will be maintained. Over time, the discontinuities in a ring oscillator with multiple discontinuities will collide and cancel out until there is only a single discontinuity left. You can consider the motion of the discontinuities as following a random walk relative to a discontinuity travelling at exactly the average loop

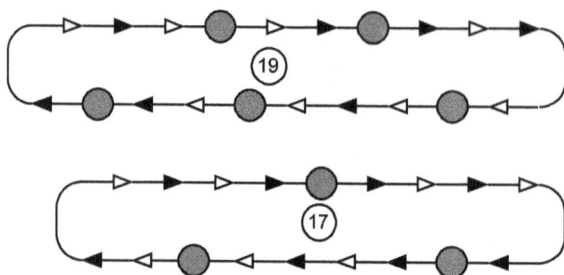

Figure 2.7: Multiple Discontinuities in a Ring Oscillator.

frequency. Each passage through a gate will be a little slower or a little faster, depending on the noise in the system. Adding these together over time amounts to a random walk. Since they are performing a one dimensional random walk on a loop instead of an infinitely long line, then, as the distance of the two random walks of two discontinuities gets larger and both add up to the loop size, they will collide. Thus, multiple discontinuities on the same loop will very quickly walk into each other and cancel.

The design of the entropy source uses an odd number of ring oscillators so that when connected in a large loop there are still an odd number of gates in the large loop. Multiplexors configure the loops either as individual loops or as one large loop.

In Figure 2.8, a configuration of three ring oscillators connected via multiplexors is shown.

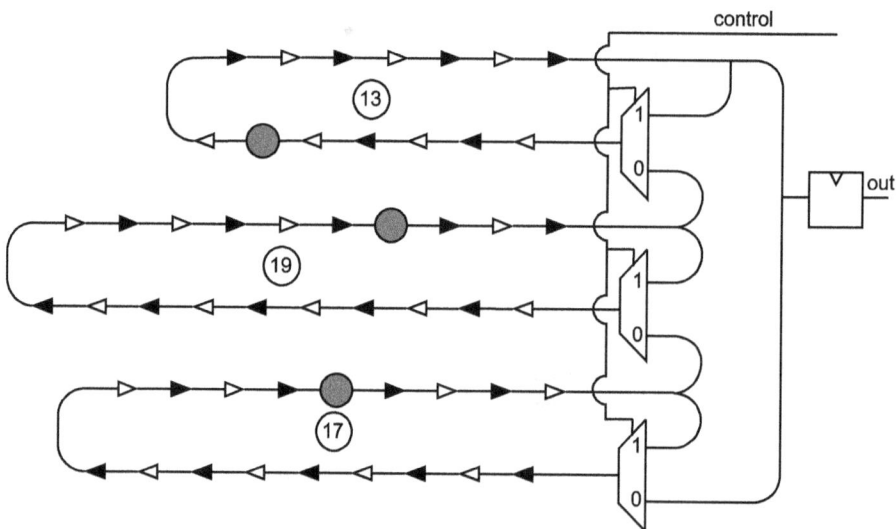

Figure 2.8: Metastable Ring Oscillator Circuit.

With the control signal high, the loops operate independently, with the output of the loop fed back into the input. With the control signal low, the loops are joined into

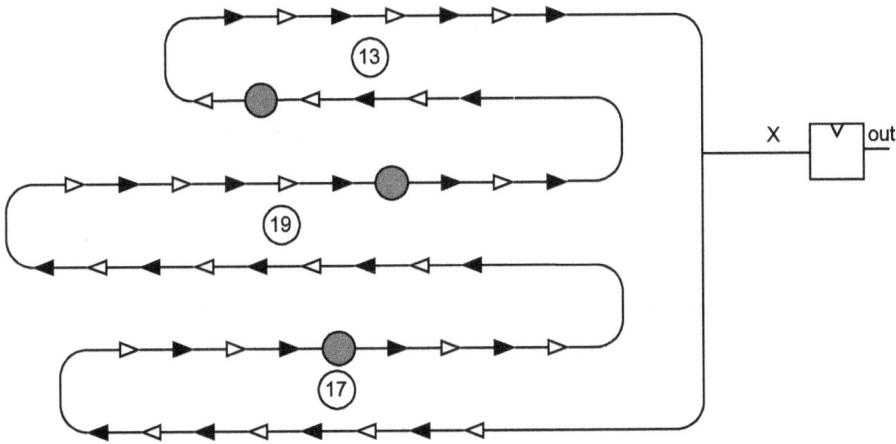

**Figure 2.9:** Large Oscillator Configuration of Metastable Ring Oscillator.

one big loop with 49 elements, as in Figure 2.9. The three discontinuities that were present in the three oscillators are now on the main ring and these will quickly cancel to a single discontinuity. It is possible at the point in the ring where the multiplexors are, to be in phase when the two rings attach. So, this can also introduce two extra discontinuities in the large ring when the multiplexors are switched from the three ring mode to the large ring mode.

While oscillating as independent rings, the phase of the rings should be to some extent independent of each other. On the switch to the single large ring, those multiple discontinuities are all present on the ring. This state of having multiple discontinuities in the loop is a metastable state. There is a vanishingly small probability that the discontinuities travel around the loop at exactly the same speed and never collide. In reality, over a short period of time, noise will vary the timing of the travel of the discontinuities and the multiple phases will collapse together into one phase. The transition from multiple phases to a single phase is metastable, and noise drives the collapse to a stable state with a single discontinuity, making the timing of the collapse and the resulting phase of the slow oscillation nondeterministic.

In Figure 2.10, we see the fast oscillation measured at the output of the 13 gate loop when the control signal is high, and we see it switch to a low frequency oscillation of the large loop when the control signal is low. The state of $X$ is sampled by the output flip-flop on the rising edge of the control signal, which comes at the end of the slow

**Figure 2.10:** Signal Trace of Metastable Ring Oscillator.

oscillation period, by which time the metastable state of the loop that started with at least three discontinuities has had time to resolve to a state with one discontinuity.

So, the circuit operates with a low frequency square wave on the control signal, switching the circuit between the two modes. The phase of the circuit at a chosen point is captured a short time after the switch to the large ring mode. This is the random bit and so the circuit generates 1 bit for each cycle of the control signal.

An attraction of ring oscillator RNGs is that they can be built from basic logic components and are, therefore, easily portable between different silicon processes. The attractions of metastable entropy sources include their robustness from attack, that they are easily mathematically modeled and exhibit a high measured min entropy and high rate of entropy generation.

The Metastable Phase Collapse Ring Oscillator Entropy Source combines the benefits of the ring oscillator with some of the benefits of a metastable source, albeit without the high speed of single latch metastable sources.

## 2.3 Fast Digital TRNG Based on Metastable Ring Oscillator

The title "Fast Digital TRNG Based on Metastable Ring Oscillator" is the title of the paper [24] available at https://www.iacr.org/archive/ches2008/51540162/51540162.pdf.

This paper describes a similar structure to the multiple ring oscillator structure in Section 2.2. However, in place of the ring oscillator loops, there is a single inverter gate that is switched between being in self feedback mode, or being in a loop of all the inverters. This is directly equivalent to the phase collapse source in Section 2.2 with all loops having only 1 inverter, as shown in Figure 2.11.

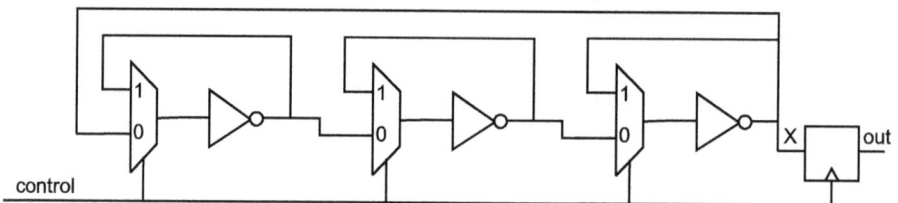

**Figure 2.11:** Fast Digital TRNG Based on Metastable Ring Oscillator.

In a silicon implementation of an inverter gate, connecting it back on itself will not behave as a ring oscillator, since the loop time is too short for the signals to make full transitions between low and high logic states. Instead, the voltage rests somewhere in the middle between the high voltage and low voltage as shown in Figure 2.12.

This is a stable state while the feedback loop is connected, but when the loop is broken and the inverters are all connected in a big loop, the state with the voltage in the middle of the range is metastable, so the voltages at each node move to a logic 1

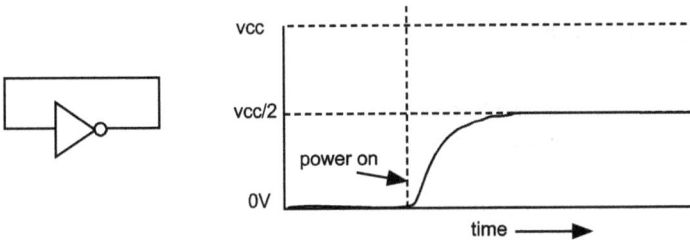

**Figure 2.12:** Single Inverter Feedback.

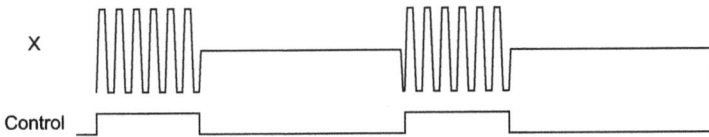

**Figure 2.13:** Signal Trace of Metastable Ring Oscillator With Single Inverter Feedback.

or 0, driven by noise; this ultimately resolves to a single loop with a single travelling discontinuity. The resulting timing diagram is as shown in Figure 2.13.

There is a problem with connecting an inverter directly back on itself in a fast silicon CMOS process, as in Figure 2.12. When the output voltage is in the middle of the range, there is what is called a *crowbar current* passing from the power supply input to the 0 V connection. The $P$ transistors connected to the power supply and the N transistors connected to the 0 V line will both be partially switched on. In a normal configuration, either one or the other transistor is switched of, so current does not flow from the power supply to the 0 V line. This crowbar current will consume excess power and will limit the device lifetime. Therefore, it is commonly forbidden in silicon design rules to connect an inverter in that manner. However, there are more complex circuit topologies, where additional transistors limit the crowbar current. Therefore, such a circuit would need some custom circuit design, rather than using standard logic inverter gates.

## 2.4 Feedback Stabilized Metastable Latch Entropy Source

The Feedback Stabilized Metastable Latch Entropy Source is possibly the most robust and reliable form of entropy source for implementation on a silicon chip. Its favorable properties include:
- High performance.
- Low power consumption.
- Easily modeled min-entropy.

–   Very reliable (e. g., zero known failures in over 400 million instances in Intel chips
     delivered).
–   Robust against a number of attack strategies.
–   Relatively easy to port between silicon processes.

These are the reasons that we chose to use this sort of entropy source in mass production after it was first developed.

The basic idea is that if you build two inverters into a stable back to back configuration, as in Figure 2.14, the two nodes, A and B, will resolve either to a 0.1 stable
state or a 1.0 stable state when powered on. The choice of 0.1 or 1.0 is driven by noise,
because the two gates are identical. Once the noise kicks the node voltages a little
bit in one direction, the logic gates will operate as open loop amplifiers and drive the
voltages to the state toward which the noise pushed it.

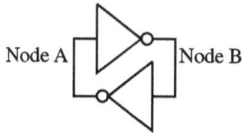

Node A        Node B

**Figure 2.14:** Back-to-Back Inverters.

In order to cycle the generator quickly, switches, implemented with transistors, can
be put on nodes A and B or in the power supplies of the gates, to force the gates to one
of the two unstable states, 0,0 or 1,1.

If you build such a circuit, you will find that it tends to always output the same
binary value. This is because when you build a pair of gates like this in silicon, one
usually turns out to be stronger than the other. So, when resolving from a 1,1 or 0,0
state to a 0,1 or 1,0 state, one gate always wins and, therefore, overcomes the ability of
noise to drive the resolution.

This can be modeled by dropping a ball on a hill. See Figures 2.15 and 2.16.

The ball will either fall to the left or the right and the resulting output, 0 or 1, will
depend on which way it rolls.

The hill represents the transfer function of the metastable circuit. The ball can
land on it at the top (equivalent to the 1,1 state) and stay there indefinitely. But the
probability of it remaining on the top reduces exponentially with increasing time, and
very quickly noise will drive the ball to fall one way or the other.

The position of the hill is fixed and it represents the relative strengths of the logic
inverters. If one gate is stronger the hill will be further to the left. If the other is stronger,
the hill will be further to the right. Over a large population of devices, the position of
the hill will take on a Gaussian distribution, but in any single device the position will
remain in the same spot.

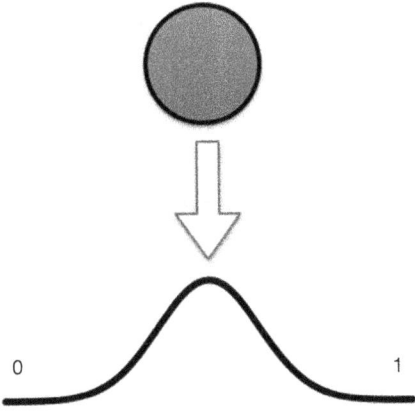

Figure 2.15: Ball Being Dropped on a Hill.

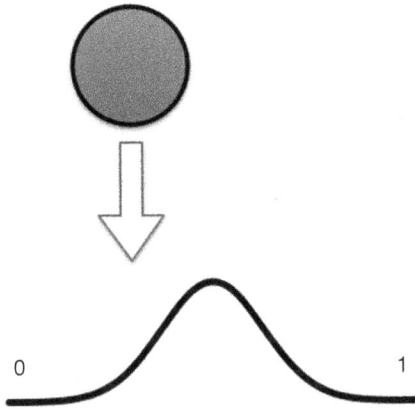

Figure 2.16: Ball Being Dropped on a Hill With Bias.

It is easy to visualize that, if the hill is to one side of the ball, then the ball will always roll to the same side.

The ball represents the state of the circuit and this has noise, which is a time-varying position of the ball. The static variation of the hill can be dubbed "the manufacturing variation," modeled as $\sigma_m$. The dynamic variation of the ball can be dubbed "the noise variation" $\sigma_n$.

As indicated in Figure 2.17, the ball's position is jiggling left and right with a Gaussian distribution having standard deviation $\sigma_n$. The hill is at some position chosen from a Gaussian distribution having standard deviation $\sigma_m$.

We can see that if the noise of the ball's position takes it to either side of the hill's peak, then the output will be able to take on either value.

However, if the noise of the ball's position is small compared to the noise of the hill's position, then the ball will likely only land on one side. So, for a good entropy

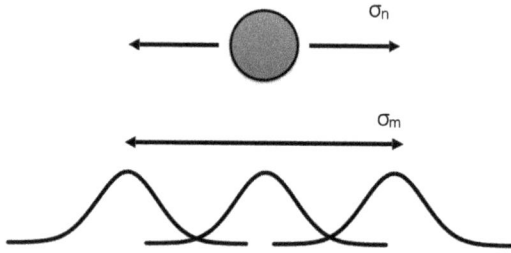

**Figure 2.17:** Ball Being Dropped on a Hill With Variation.

source, we want

$$\sigma_n \gg \sigma_m.$$

The question of how much bigger $\sigma_n$ needs to be than $\sigma_m$ is answered in a paper [16] by Rachael Parker. The answer is a factor of at least 10. However, when we build such a circuit in modern-day silicon processes, we find the difference is only about a factor of 5.

The solution is to put in some compensatory circuits to pull the hill into the middle. In effect, reducing $\sigma_m$, so that it is sufficiently small compared to $\sigma_n$.

The approach taken in an early Intel entropy source design was to load one of the nodes with a feedback circuit. When a 1 came out, the load would be increased, driving the hill in the direction that leads to a greater probability of a 0 result. When a 0 came out, the load would be decreased, driving the hill in the direction that leads to a greater probability of a 1 result.

Unfortunately, this did not work well, because it proved to be too sensitive to environmental noise. An improved design incorporated a dual differential feedback, which loaded both sides of the circuit, and when a 1 was generated, the loads were increased on one side and decreased on the other. When a 0 came out, the loads were moved the opposite way on both sides. With this balanced operation, the circuit turned out to be highly robust and this is what has been used in Intel product since the first production version in the Ivy Bridge CPU.

A simplified schematic of this circuit is shown in Figure 2.18. It shows two capacitors that load the two sides of a latch through a transistor. Charge is pulled and pushed on and off the capacitors in opposite directions, with each data bit output.

This has the effect of driving the bias to 50%, since an excess of 1s will lead to more 0s, and an excess of 0s will lead to more 1s. However, the secondary effect is that following a 1, the probability of a 0 is increased and vice versa. So, serial correlation has been introduced to the output data.

One way to think of this is that the feedback circuit is converting bias into serial correlation and the mathematics of this is exactly the same as the mathematics of the ball-on-hill example, except with a feedback process moving the hill towards the center more often than not, once for each time the ball drops on a hill.

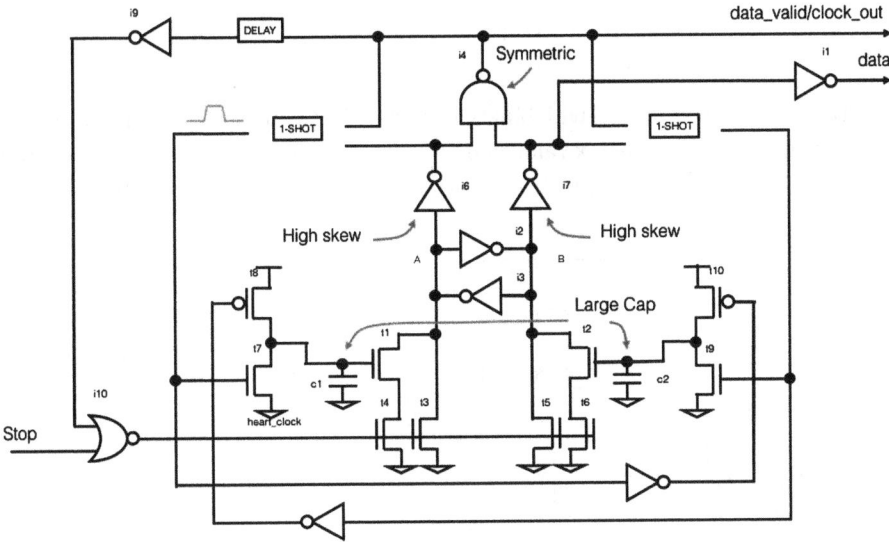

**Figure 2.18:** Metastable Latch Entropy Source Circuit.

## 2.5 Infinite Noise Multiplier Entropy Source

The infinite noise multiplier is a circuit suitable for board level implementation. It makes use of linear amplifiers and so is not ideal for implementing in CMOS digital integrated circuits. Another name for the circuit is "Modular Noise Multiplier".

The starting point for understanding the infinite noise multiplier is to consider the operation of a successive approximation ADC (Analog to Digital Converter). This device measures an analog voltage and returns a digital number representing that voltage. It does this in a series of steps. On the first step, it places a reference voltage in the middle of the voltage range. If the measured voltage is above the reference, then it returns a 1, otherwise it returns a 0. This is the most significant bit of the resulting digital number. The reference voltage is then moved to the middle of the remaining range, depending on the value of the bit. The process repeats, returning bits with decreasing significance and moving the reference voltage to the middle of the remaining range, successively closer to the actual voltage being measured. Figure 2.19 shows an example structure of a 7-bit successive approximation ADC.

The first bit generated goes to the bit 6 (the 7th bit) of the register, so if the bit sequence turns out to be 1100011, the register values will evolve as follows:

|       |   | Value | Register | Register Output |
|-------|---|-------|----------|-----------------|
| MSB   | 7 | 1     | 1xxxxxx  | 1000000         |
|       | 6 | 1     | 11xxxxx  | 1100000         |
|       | 5 | 0     | 110xxxx  | 1100000         |
|       | 4 | 0     | 1100xxx  | 1100000         |
|       | 3 | 0     | 11000xx  | 1100000         |

|       |   |           |         |
|-------|---|-----------|---------|
| 2     | 1 | 110001x   | 1100010 |
| LSB 1 | 1 | 1100011   | 1100011 |

The register is preloaded with binary 1000000. So, the initial Vref is in the middle of the range. Therefore, each x value will be output as a 0 on its respective wire to the DAC (Digital to Analog Converter), as shown in the register output column.

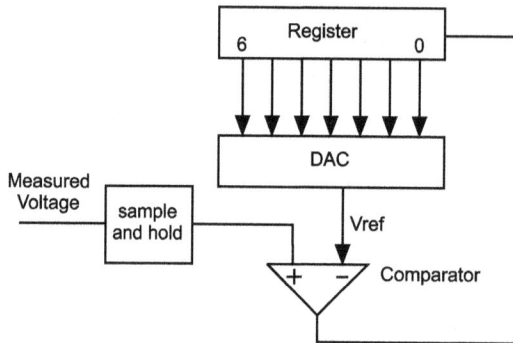

Figure 2.19: Successive Approximation ADC.

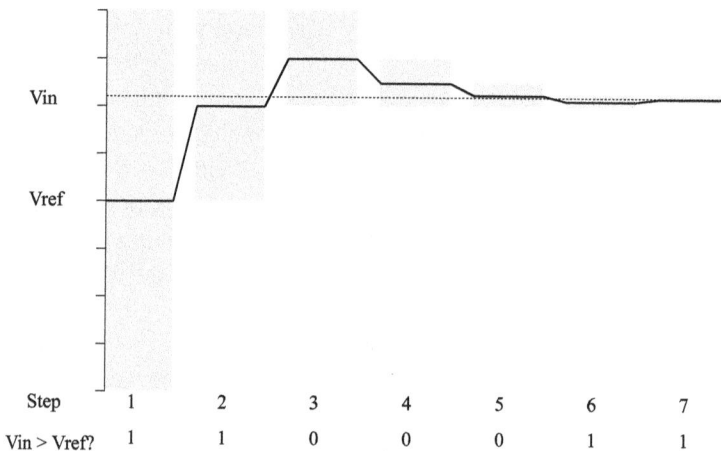

Figure 2.20: Successive Approximation ADC Operation.

Figure 2.20 shows how the reference voltage changes with each step of the ADC, narrowing the comparison range to the half of the previous range that the input voltage is within. In the example in the picture, the output sequence is 110011.

The limit on the resolution of a successive approximation ADC is the noise in the circuit. As the lower significant bits of the measurement are reached, the noise becomes larger, relative to the size of the step in the reference voltage, until the noise dominates and the circuit is only measuring that noise. The ADC uses a DAC to generate the reference voltage.

The idea behind the infinite noise multiplier is to simply carry on continuously measuring the noise, rather than the signal. This does not work with a normal successive approximation DAC structure, since repeating a reference DAC that can continue with infinite precision is not possible. So, instead of moving the reference point with a DAC, the measured signal is moved by amplifying it by a factor of 2, and the reference voltage remains in the middle. If a 1 is returned, then the signal is reduced by subtracting the reference voltage. If a 0 is returned, then the signal is left alone and multiplied again.

The basic loop in the circuit is equivalent to the following Python code:

**Listing 2.1:** Infinite noise multiplier algorithm.

```
def update(v):
    v = 2*v
    if v > vref:
        output(1)
        v = v - vref
    else:
        output(0)

    return v
```

This process ends up continuously amplifying the noise in the circuit such that it varies around the reference voltage. With a perfectly accurate multiply and subtraction circuit and a perfectly stable reference voltage, the circuit would output full entropy. However, inevitable inaccuracies with these parts of the circuit lead to bias and correlation in the output, which leads to reduced min-entropy. The actual entropy out tends to be a function of the accuracy of the multiply and substract steps.

Figure 2.21 shows how the infinite noise multiplier is different from the successive approximation ADC. The $V_{ref}$ signal remains constant and the input voltage is manipulated, multiplying it by 2 and then, if the resulting voltage is greater than $V_{ref}$, the input voltage is reduced by $V_{ref}$. The output bit on each cycle is the result of the $V_{ref}$ comparison. We see that, given the same input level as with the successive approximation ADC, it gives the same binary output value of 1100011.

While we can see that the initial voltage at $V_{in}$ gets turned into a binary number, the circuit can keep cycling, and so moving further to the right of the diagram in Figure 2.21. Each time it cycles, the noise is multiplied by 2 and the magnitude of the remaining signal reduces relative to the noise. Thus, the noise quickly dominates the resulting output bits.

A reference design, including circuit diagrams for various implementations and supporting software for a USB device, is available at https://github.com/waywardgeek/infnoise.

Vin

Vref

| Step | 1 | 2 | 3 | 4 | 5 | 6 | 7 |
|---|---|---|---|---|---|---|---|
| Vin > Vref? | 1 | 1 | 0 | 0 | 0 | 1 | 1 |

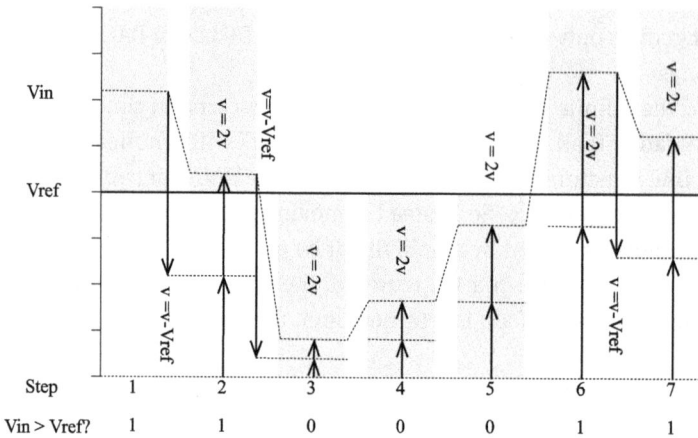

**Figure 2.21:** Infinite Noise Multipler ADC.

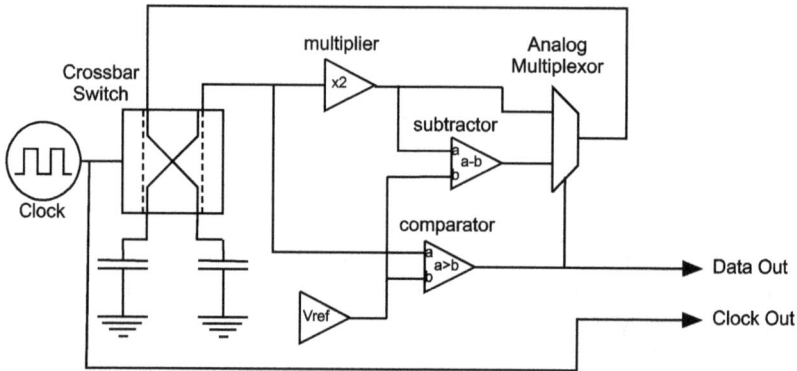

Crossbar Switch

multiplier
x2

Analog Multiplexor

subtractor
a-b

Clock

comparator
a>b

Vref

Data Out

Clock Out

**Figure 2.22:** Infinite Noise Multiplier Schematic.

These circuit designs are switched capacitor-type circuits. The charge on one capacitor is the current state that the circuit then amplifies by 2, and if necessary, subtracts $V_{ref}$. It puts the resulting voltage onto a second capacitor. A switching circuit then swaps the two capacitors, so the output capacitor becomes the input capacitor.

There are a number of different ways to implement this and the above URL gives a few different detailed designs. Figure 2.22 is a simplified schematic of one of the types of design. It skips over many of the details of analog design so that it can be understood by people not familiar with analog circuit design. Two capacitors are connected via a crossbar switch that swaps the connections to the capacitors, controlled by a clock signal. The voltage $V_{cap}$ on the current state capacitor goes into the circuit and two voltages are computed, $V_{cap} \times 2$ and $(V_{cap} \times 2) - V_{ref}$. A comparator checks if the current voltage is greater than $V_{ref}$, and if so, $(V_{cap} \times 2) - V_{ref}$ volts are driven onto the output capacitor; otherwise, $V_{cap} \times 2$ volts are driven onto the output capacitor. The clock switches, the output capacitor becomes the current state, the current state capacitor becomes the output, and the process starts again with the next clock cycle.

Like ring oscillator circuits, the infinite noise multiplier is fairly slow, but is less susceptible to injection attack than ring oscillators. It also lends itself to board level implementations much better than metastable latch and ring oscillator circuits, so is ideal for plug in USB type entropy sources. I am unaware of any attempts to build one on a chip with a digital semiconductor process.

Some implementations are available as plug in USB devices, one called the OneKey https:/onekey.com and another available at https://github.com/waywardgeek/infnoise.

Therefore, if you have a computer in which there is not an entropy source but there is type-A USB interface, this sort of device can be used to provide nondeterministic random data.

## 2.6 Diode Breakdown Noise Entropy Source

There are a variety of types of noise that occur in electronics, such as shot noise, flicker (or 1/f) noise, and thermal noise. There is a specific form of noise that occurs in semiconductor diodes when reverse biased at the avalanche breakdown voltage, where current starts running backward through the diode.

A very old technique for generating electrical noise in random number generators is to reverse bias a diode at the avalanche breakdown point and then amplify that noise and sample it. There are many examples of circuit topologies available on the Internet for avalanche noise based entropy sources. They typically fall into one of two types: a zener diode based noise source and a transistor diode based noise source. The example below is a general model for a circuit topology that puts a transistor diode into breakdown, amplifies the resulting noise, buffers it and then converts it to digital voltage levels.

The breakdown voltage of the reverse biased diode in common general purpose transistors varies between about 7 and 11 volts. In Figure 2.23, the reverse biased diode is in the leftmost transistor Q1. The voltage Vcc and resistor R1 should be set to limit the current through Q1 to a small number from 10 to 100 nA.

The current through Q1 is noisy with avalanche breakdown noise and it passes on through the base of Q2, which amplifies that current. So, the current into the collector of Q2 is an amplified version of the noise current through Q1. As it is passing through R1, the voltage at the input to C1 is $Vcc - R1(Iq1 + Iq2)$, where Iq1 is the current through Q1 and Iq2 is the current through Q2. Vcc is the supply voltage.

I have not given specific values for components, voltages or currents, because the appropriate breakdown current for generating the most noise varies quite a lot between different transistors and even between transistors of the same type and manu-

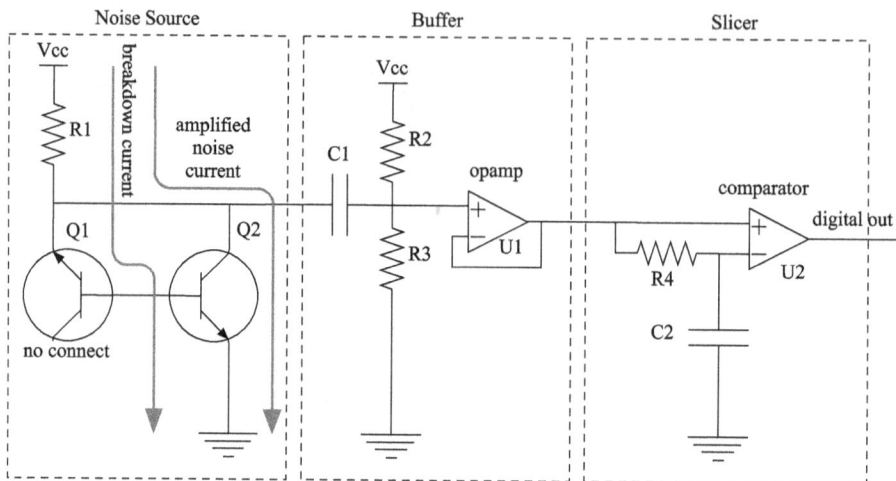

**Figure 2.23:** Diode Avalanche Breakdown Noise Source.

facturer. So, some experimentation will be needed to find the right current and resulting right component values.

The noise voltage is, hopefully, at least 50 mV peak to peak. The signal source is fairly high impedance. So, the next stage is a simple unity gain buffer to create a low impedance output capable of driving the next stage. Capacitor C1 removes the DC component of the signal. The two resistors R2 and R3 are of equal value and center the voltage in the middle of the rail. Alternatively, you could generate a virtual ground with another opamp and hook it up via a resistor, or you might have both positive and negative rails and the signal can be centered around 0 V. The resistors need to be of high value, such as 1 or 2 MegaOhms.

The final stage is a slicer. The RC network R4 and C2 create a smoothed voltage, approximately in the middle of the signals peak-to-peak range. So, the comparator outputs a 1 when the input signal is higher than its average and a 0 when the input is lower. This digital output signal can be captured on a GPIO pin of a microprocessor, or fed into a digital sampling circuit.

The challenge with breakdown noise entropy sources is that of manufacturability. It is always possible to get a transistor or diode to produce noise by passing reverse current through the diode. However, the precise conditions under which a large amount of noise is generated vary from device to device, and from circuit board to circuit board. For an individual board, tweaking it to work is relatively easy, but tweaking millions of boards is not generally acceptable in electronics manufacturing, which is why we can find many good examples of people's breakdown noise source designs, but we do not tend to find them used in mass manufactured products, where phase error accumulation or metastable resolution sources are preferred.

# 3 Entropy Extraction

An imperfect source of entropy will have some property that makes the nature of its output different from the output from a fully random, full entropy source. The output of a circuit designed to sense electrical noise and turn it into random bits is always subject to bias, correlation, and nonstationarity.

Systematic relationships between the data values, which otherwise look random, can be the basis of reduced entropy of the data. The output of a seeded deterministic PRNG might appear to output a perfectly random megabyte of data, but be seeded with a full entropy 256 bit number. Thus, an observer with sufficient computational power could predict future outputs of the PRNG by examining the $2^{256}$ possible output sequences that the PRNG can make and seeing which one the observed output matches. Once found, the PRNG becomes completely predictable. The entropy was 256 bits, not 1 megabyte.

The process for taking nonfull entropy data and transforming it so it has higher entropy rate is called entropy extraction or entropy distillation. The analogy with distillation is strong. In distillation of alcohol, a quantity of dilute alcohol is put into the distillery and a smaller quantity of more concentrated alcohol comes out the other side. In entropy distillation, a number of bits of data that contains a smaller number of bits of entropy is passed through the extraction process and a smaller quantity of less dilute data comes out with a smaller number of bits of entropy than went into the input, but the ratio of the number of bits of entropy per bit of data from the output is improved, relative to the number of bits of entropy per bit of data at the input.

Though the term entropy distillation is a more appropriate term for a process that inputs more data and outputs less data, but with higher entropy rate, and the distillation of alcohol is a good analogy, the term entropy extraction is more commonly used.

It is impossible to get more entropy out of a deterministic algorithm than is put in, but it is possible to get more entropy per bit, provided that there is the same or less total entropy out than entropy in. The NIST SP800-90A specification defines the term "entropy rate" as the number of bits of entropy per bit of data in a collection of bits.

Figure 3.1 shows the close similarity between entropy distillation and alcohol distillation.

An important distinction, therefore, is between the entropy of the data and the entropy rate of the data. The entropy is the total entropy in the data. The entropy rate is the total entropy in the data divided by the number of bits in the data. An extractor increases the entropy rate, but does not increase the entropy.

Consistent with this is that if an extractor is working, outputting data with a higher entropy rate than the input, it is also outputting less data than the input and usually less entropy also, because some of the entropy gets lost in the processing. Sometimes a goal of entropy extractor design is to minimize this entropy loss.

https://doi.org/10.1515/9781501506062-003

Input:
L units of liquid =
M units of alcohol +
N units of other liquid

Alcohol Distillation Apparatus

$L = N + M$
$L = Y + Z + A + B$
$Y <= M$
$N <= Z$

Output:
X units of liquid =
Y units of alcohol +
Z units of other liquid

Input:
Heat Energy

Waste Output:
Heat Energy +
A units of alcohol +
B units of other liquid

Input:
L bits of data =
M bits of entropy +
N bits of predictability

Entropy Extraction Apparatus

$L = N + M$
$L = Y + Z + A + B$
$Y <= M$
$N <= Z$

Output:
X bits of data =
Y bits of entropy +
Z bits of predictability

Input:
Electrical Energy

Waste Output:
Heat Energy +
A units of entropy as heat +
B units of predictable bits of
information as heat

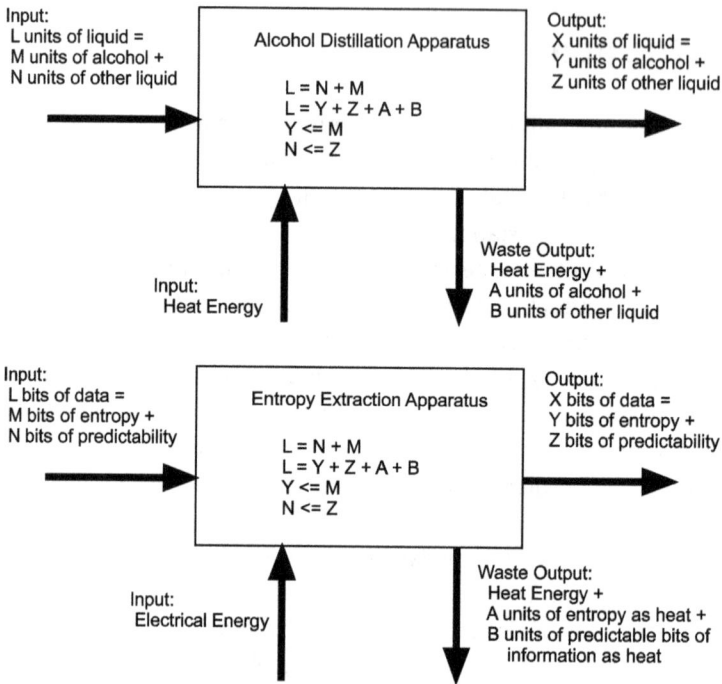

**Figure 3.1:** Similarity Between Alcohol Distillation and Entropy Distillation.

## 3.1 The Simplest Extractor, the XOR Gate

The XOR gate takes in two binary values and outputs 1. If the inputs are different, $(0, 1)$ or $(1, 0)$, then output is 1. If the inputs are the same, $(0, 0)$ or $(1, 1)$, then the output is 0. An alternative name is the inequality gate, since it outputs the value 1 if the inputs $A$ and $B$, $A \neq B$, are given. See Table 3.1.

In electronics this is denoted with the XOR symbol (Figure 3.2):

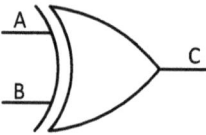

A

C

B

**Figure 3.2:** XOR Gate Symbol.

In mathematics, it is sometimes denoted as addition, since addition modulo two gives the same result. Sometimes it is denoted as a plus sign in a circle, for example:

$$A \oplus B.$$

If we assume we have a constantly biased input, then for each unpredictable bit the probability of getting a 1 may or may not be the same as the probability of getting

**Table 3.1:** XOR Truth Table.

| Input 1 | Input 2 | Output |
|---------|---------|--------|
| 0 | 0 | 0 |
| 0 | 1 | 1 |
| 1 | 0 | 1 |
| 1 | 1 | 0 |

a 0, but the sum of the two probabilities is always 1.

$$P(0) + P(1) = 1$$
$$P(0) = 1 - P(1)$$

We can look at the XOR in terms of the probability of the output value given the probability of the input values. The probability that the output is 0 is equal to the probability that

(input1 = 0  and  input2 = 0)  or  (input1 = 1  and  input2 = 1).

The probability that the output is 1 is equal to the probability that

(input1 = 0  and  input2 = 1)  or  (input1 = 0  and  input2 = 1).

So,

$$P(\text{output} = 0) = P(0)P(0) + P(1)P(1)$$
$$P(\text{output} = 1) = P(0)P(1) + P(1)P(0) = 2P(0)P(1)$$
$$P(\text{output} = 1) = 2(1 - P(1))P(1) = 2(P(1) - (P(1)^2)).$$

Figure 3.3 shows the bias for the output of the XOR gate is always closer to the horizontal 0.5 bias line than the input bias, because the curve bulges out towards the 0.5 line relative to the diagonal input bias line. The dotted line is a reflection of the input bias line, so it can easily be seen that the XOR output is always closer to the 0.5 bias line.

Thus, the XOR gate is taking two equally biased inputs and yielding a single output, which is either equally or less biased, depending on the inputs. With perfect input bias of 0.5 on either input, the output is equally biased at 0.5. With both inputs with the worst case bias of either 1.0 or 0.0, the output will also have the worst case bias of 1.0 or 0.0.

If we allow the bias on the inputs to be different, we can create a table of the probabilities $P(A = 1)$ and $P(B = 1)$, varying between 0.0 and 1.0 as shown in Table 3.2.

We see that where one input bias is 0.5, the output bias is 0.5 regardless of the other input. At all other points the bias is not 0.5.

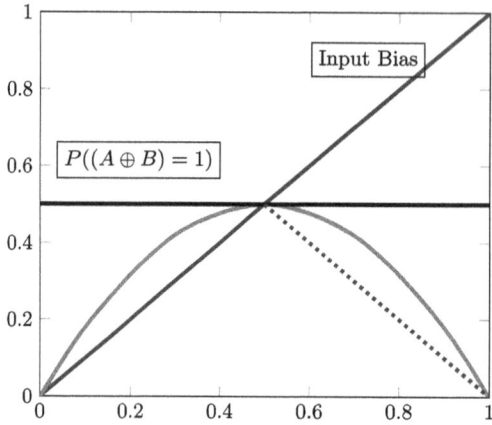

Figure 3.3: Bias of Output of XOR Gate.

**Table 3.2:** Bias of Output of XOR Gate Given Input Bias A and B.

| | | \multicolumn{11}{c}{$P(A = 1)$} | | | | | | | | | |
| | | 0.0 | 0.1 | 0.2 | 0.3 | 0.4 | 0.5 | 0.6 | 0.7 | 0.8 | 0.9 | 1.0 |
|---|---|---|---|---|---|---|---|---|---|---|---|---|
| | 0.0 | 0.00 | 0.10 | 0.20 | 0.30 | 0.40 | 0.50 | 0.60 | 0.70 | 0.80 | 0.90 | 1.00 |
| | 0.1 | 0.10 | 0.18 | 0.26 | 0.34 | 0.42 | 0.50 | 0.58 | 0.66 | 0.74 | 0.82 | 0.90 |
| | 0.2 | 0.20 | 0.26 | 0.32 | 0.38 | 0.44 | 0.50 | 0.56 | 0.62 | 0.68 | 0.74 | 0.80 |
| | 0.3 | 0.30 | 0.34 | 0.38 | 0.42 | 0.46 | 0.50 | 0.54 | 0.58 | 0.62 | 0.66 | 0.70 |
| | 0.4 | 0.40 | 0.42 | 0.44 | 0.46 | 0.48 | 0.50 | 0.52 | 0.54 | 0.56 | 0.58 | 0.60 |
| $P(B = 1)$ | 0.5 | 0.50 | 0.50 | 0.50 | 0.50 | 0.50 | 0.50 | 0.50 | 0.50 | 0.50 | 0.50 | 0.50 |
| | 0.6 | 0.60 | 0.58 | 0.56 | 0.54 | 0.52 | 0.50 | 0.48 | 0.46 | 0.44 | 0.42 | 0.40 |
| | 0.7 | 0.70 | 0.66 | 0.62 | 0.58 | 0.54 | 0.50 | 0.46 | 0.42 | 0.38 | 0.34 | 0.40 |
| | 0.8 | 0.80 | 0.74 | 0.68 | 0.62 | 0.56 | 0.50 | 0.44 | 0.38 | 0.32 | 0.26 | 0.20 |
| | 0.9 | 0.90 | 0.82 | 0.74 | 0.66 | 0.58 | 0.50 | 0.42 | 0.34 | 0.26 | 0.18 | 0.10 |
| | 1.0 | 1.00 | 0.90 | 0.80 | 0.70 | 0.60 | 0.50 | 0.40 | 0.30 | 0.20 | 0.10 | 0.00 |

We are interested in how far 0.5 the output bias is. The closer the better. So we can plot the same table, but label it with the distance from 0.5 computed as $|0.5 - P(1)|$.

In Table 3.3, we can see that at no point is the output further from 0.5 than either of the inputs.

We can show this mathematically by considering the case where the bias on the two inputs $A$ and $B$ can take any value between 0 and 1.

$$P(A = 1) = 1 - P(A = 0),$$
$$P(B = 1) = 1 - P(B = 0).$$

The output of XOR is 1 when $A, B = 0, 1$ or $A, B = 1, 0$.
So,

$$P((A \oplus B) = 1) = P(A = 1)P(B = 0) + P(A = 0)P(B = 1).$$

**Table 3.3:** Distance From 0.5 of XOR Gate Output Bias Given Bias of Inputs A and B.

|          |     | $P(A = 1)$ | | | | | | | | | | |
|----------|-----|------|------|------|------|------|------|------|------|------|------|------|
|          |     | 0.0  | 0.1  | 0.2  | 0.3  | 0.4  | 0.5  | 0.6  | 0.7  | 0.8  | 0.9  | 1.0  |
|          | 0.0 | 0.50 | 0.40 | 0.30 | 0.20 | 0.10 | 0.00 | 0.10 | 0.20 | 0.30 | 0.40 | 0.50 |
|          | 0.1 | 0.40 | 0.32 | 0.24 | 0.16 | 0.08 | 0.00 | 0.08 | 0.16 | 0.24 | 0.32 | 0.40 |
|          | 0.2 | 0.30 | 0.24 | 0.18 | 0.12 | 0.06 | 0.00 | 0.06 | 0.12 | 0.18 | 0.24 | 0.30 |
|          | 0.3 | 0.20 | 0.16 | 0.12 | 0.08 | 0.04 | 0.00 | 0.04 | 0.08 | 0.12 | 0.16 | 0.20 |
|          | 0.4 | 0.10 | 0.08 | 0.06 | 0.04 | 0.02 | 0.00 | 0.02 | 0.04 | 0.06 | 0.08 | 0.10 |
| $P(B = 1)$ | 0.5 | 0.00 | 0.00 | 0.00 | 0.00 | 0.00 | 0.00 | 0.00 | 0.00 | 0.00 | 0.00 | 0.00 |
|          | 0.6 | 0.10 | 0.08 | 0.06 | 0.04 | 0.02 | 0.00 | 0.02 | 0.04 | 0.06 | 0.08 | 0.10 |
|          | 0.7 | 0.20 | 0.16 | 0.12 | 0.08 | 0.04 | 0.00 | 0.04 | 0.08 | 0.12 | 0.16 | 0.20 |
|          | 0.8 | 0.30 | 0.24 | 0.18 | 0.12 | 0.06 | 0.00 | 0.06 | 0.12 | 0.18 | 0.24 | 0.30 |
|          | 0.9 | 0.40 | 0.32 | 0.24 | 0.16 | 0.08 | 0.00 | 0.08 | 0.16 | 0.24 | 0.32 | 0.40 |
|          | 1.0 | 0.50 | 0.40 | 0.30 | 0.20 | 0.10 | 0.00 | 0.10 | 0.20 | 0.30 | 0.40 | 0.50 |

To simplify the equations we will say

$$x = P(A = 1),$$
$$y = P(B = 1).$$

So,

$$P((A \oplus B) = 1) = x(1 - y) + y(1 - x)$$
$$= x - xy + y - xy$$
$$= x + y - 2xy.$$

Bias is better if it is closer to 0.5. So, we will measure the deficiency of bias to be the distance from 0.5.

$$\text{defc(bias)} = |\text{bias} - 0.5|.$$

We want to show that the output of the XOR gate always has equal or better bias than both of the inputs. To show

$$\text{defc}(A \oplus B) \leq \text{defc}(A),$$

we must show that

$$|x + y - 2xy - 0.5| \leq |x - 0.5|.$$

By symmetry, showing this would also imply

$$|x + y - 2xy - 0.5| \leq |y - 0.5|.$$

By contradiction, if

$$|x + y - 2xy - 0.5| > |x - 0.5|,$$

then

$$|x + y - 2xy - 0.5| - |x - 0.5| > 0.$$

By the triangle inequality

$$|x + y - 2xy - 0.5 - x + 0.5| \geq |x + y - 2xy - 0.5| - |x - 0.5|,$$

so $|y - 2xy| > 0$ for both $x$ and $y$ being between 0 and 1.
However, if $x = \frac{1}{2}$ and $y = \frac{1}{2}$, then

$$|y - 2xy| = |0.5 - 0.5| = 0.$$

This contradicts $|y - 2xy| > 0$.
Therefore, by contradiction

$$|x + y - 2xy - 0.5| \leq |x - 0.5|.$$

So, $P((A \oplus B) = 1)$ is always equally distant from or closer to 0.5 than the biases on both input $A$ and input $B$.

It is important to note that this only holds for statistically independent inputs. If the value of the two inputs $A$ and $B$ were correlated in some way, for example, $A$ is more likely to equal not($B$) than $B$, then the output of XOR would be biased toward 1, since the 10 and 01 patterns are more likely than 00 or 11. If this correlation is large enough, the output can turn out to be more biased than the input bits.

## 3.2 A Simple Way of Improving the Distribution of Random Numbers that Have Known Missing Values Using XOR

With an n bit uniformly distributed random source, there are $2^n$ different possible numbers and each are equally likely; so, $P(x) = \frac{1}{2^n}$ for all $x \in \{0, \ldots, 2^{n-1}\}$. See Figure 3.4.

Now consider an $n$ bit random binary source that is uniformly distributed, except for one value that never occurs. Let us choose 0. There are $2^n$ possibilities, but the one missing value 0 cannot happen, $P(0) = 0$. So, there are $2^n - 1$ remaining possibilities each with equal likelihood and their probabilities add up to one, so instead of

$$\forall x \in \{0..2^{n-1}\} : P(x) = \frac{1}{2^n},$$

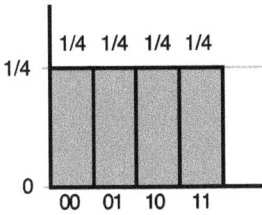

Here $n = 2$ and all four 2-bit values are equally likely; so, their probabilities are

$$\frac{1}{2^n} = \frac{1}{4}.$$

The four binary value probabilities add to 1:

$$P(00 \text{ or } 01 \text{ or } 10 \text{ or } 11) = P(00) + P(01) + P(10) + P(11) = 1.$$

**Figure 3.4:** Uniform 2-Bit Distribution.

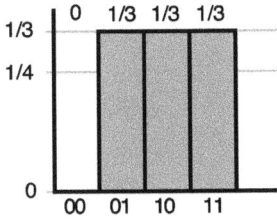

Here, there are three equally likely values

$$P(01) = \frac{1}{3}, \quad P(10) = \frac{1}{3}, \quad P(11) = \frac{1}{3},$$

but

$$P(00) = 0.$$

Again, the sum of all outcomes gives 1.

**Figure 3.5:** Nonuniform 2-Bit Distribution.

we have

$$\forall x \in \{1..2^n - 1\} : P(x) = \frac{1}{2^n - 1}, \quad P(0) = 0.$$

So, three outcomes (01, 10, and 11) in the nonuniform distribution are all a little bit more likely than in the uniform distribution $\frac{1}{2^n-1}$ rather than $\frac{1}{2^n}$, except for 00, which does not ever occur, and so, has probability 0. See Figure 3.5.

If you had such a random source, how could you make it uniform?

You could run it through a cryptographic hash algorithm and truncate the output. Or better, you could concatenate 2 numbers and hash the result, taking out the original sized number. This would be undistinguishable from a uniform random sequence.

However, hashing is an expensive algorithm with multiple steps. We can combine multiple binary numbers with XOR. It typically takes just one computer instruction to XOR two 64-bit numbers together. So, it is a lot cheaper than executing a hash function but the result outputs a distribution that is closer to uniform rather than perfectly uniform. We would like to know how effective this computationally cheaper method actually is so we can know if it is advisable to use it in place of more expensive methods.

In the case of XORing a pair of 2-bit numbers, we can add the probabilities of the results. There are 4 possibilities in the first number and 4 in the second. So, the total number of possible input combinations is $4 \cdot 4 = 16$ (see Table 3.4).

If you add the probabilities of the combinations that yield each output – 00, 01, 10, and 11 – you get the resulting probabilities of each combination $A$ and $B$, as shown in Table 3.5.

**Table 3.4:** Probabilities of XORing 2 Two-Bit Numbers.

| A | B | $P(A)$ | $P(B)$ | $A \oplus B$ | $P(A \wedge B)$ |
|---|---|---|---|---|---|
| 00 | 00 | 0 | 0 | 00 | 0 |
| 00 | 01 | 0 | $\frac{1}{3}$ | 01 | 0 |
| 00 | 10 | 0 | $\frac{1}{3}$ | 10 | 0 |
| 00 | 11 | 0 | $\frac{1}{3}$ | 11 | 0 |
| 01 | 00 | $\frac{1}{3}$ | 0 | 01 | 0 |
| 01 | 01 | $\frac{1}{3}$ | $\frac{1}{3}$ | 00 | $\frac{1}{9}$ |
| 01 | 10 | $\frac{1}{3}$ | $\frac{1}{3}$ | 11 | $\frac{1}{9}$ |
| 01 | 11 | $\frac{1}{3}$ | $\frac{1}{3}$ | 10 | $\frac{1}{9}$ |
| 10 | 00 | $\frac{1}{3}$ | 0 | 10 | 0 |
| 10 | 01 | $\frac{1}{3}$ | $\frac{1}{3}$ | 11 | $\frac{1}{9}$ |
| 10 | 10 | $\frac{1}{3}$ | $\frac{1}{3}$ | 00 | $\frac{1}{9}$ |
| 10 | 11 | $\frac{1}{3}$ | $\frac{1}{3}$ | 01 | $\frac{1}{9}$ |
| 11 | 00 | $\frac{1}{3}$ | 0 | 11 | 0 |
| 11 | 01 | $\frac{1}{3}$ | $\frac{1}{3}$ | 10 | $\frac{1}{9}$ |
| 11 | 10 | $\frac{1}{3}$ | $\frac{1}{3}$ | 01 | $\frac{1}{9}$ |
| 11 | 11 | $\frac{1}{3}$ | $\frac{1}{3}$ | 00 | $\frac{1}{9}$ |

**Table 3.5:** Output probabilities when XORing 2 two-bit numbers.

| $A \oplus B$ | $P(A \oplus B)$ |
|---|---|
| 00 | $\frac{3}{9}$ |
| 01 | $\frac{2}{9}$ |
| 10 | $\frac{2}{9}$ |
| 11 | $\frac{2}{9}$ |

Table 3.5 shows how, compared to the original nonuniform distribution, the probability of each case is closer to the ideal uniform probability of $\frac{1}{4}$ than it was in the original distribution. We have taken two values from two nonuniform random processes and produced one value, which is from a more uniform distribution.

In each case, for the equation $C = A$ XOR $B$, where $A$ and $B$ are two-bit binary numbers, the probabilities can be written out as follows:

$$P(C = 00) = P(A = 00 \,\&\, B = 00) + P(A = 01 \,\&\, B = 01)$$
$$+ P(A = 10 \,\&\, B = 10) + P(A = 11 \,\&\, B = 11)$$
$$P(C = 01) = P(A = 00 \,\&\, B = 01) + P(A = 01 \,\&\, B = 00)$$
$$+ P(A = 10 \,\&\, B = 11) + P(A = 11 \,\&\, B = 10)$$
$$P(C = 10) = P(A = 00 \,\&\, B = 10) + P(A = 01 \,\&\, B = 11)$$
$$+ P(A = 10 \,\&\, B = 00) + P(A = 11 \,\&\, B = 01)$$

$$P(C = 11) = P(A = 00 \; \& \; B = 11) + P(A = 01 \; \& \; B = 10)$$
$$+ \, P(A = 10 \; \& \; B = 01) + P(A = 11 \; \& \; B = 00).$$

We could iterate this, XORing multiple 2-bit nonuniform numbers into one, computing the probabilities using the above equations, feeding back the new probabilities. Since this is like just stirring each new value into a pool, we will call the current state of the probabilities the "pool" and the numbers being XORed-in the "input".

Here is a program in python to iterate these equations, computing the resulting distribution from XORing a new nonuniform value into a pool value. We use python here because it has simple support for rational fractions and so does not lose arithmetic precision in each step, like floating point numbers might.

**Listing 3.1:** xor_iterate.py

```python
def xor_iterate(n):
    next_prob=dict()
    one_third = Fraction('1/3')
    p_input = {0:0, 1:one_third, 2:one_third, 3:one_third}
    p_pool = p_input
    print("Iteration␣P(00)␣␣␣␣P(01)␣␣␣␣P(10)␣␣␣␣P(11)")
    for i in range(n):
        prob00  = p_input[0]*p_pool[0]
        prob00 += p_input[1]*p_pool[1]
        prob00 += p_input[2]*p_pool[2]
        prob00 += p_input[2]*p_pool[3]

        prob01  = p_input[0]*p_pool[1]
        prob01 += p_input[1]*p_pool[0]
        prob01 += p_input[2]*p_pool[3]
        prob01 += p_input[3]*p_pool[2]

        prob10  = p_input[0]*p_pool[2]
        prob10 += p_input[1]*p_pool[3]
        prob10 += p_input[2]*p_pool[0]
        prob10 += p_input[3]*p_pool[1]

        prob11  = p_input[0]*p_pool[3]
        prob11 += p_input[1]*p_pool[2]
        prob11 += p_input[2]*p_pool[1]
        prob11 += p_input[3]*p_pool[0]

        p_pool = {0:prob00, 1:prob01, 2:prob10, 3:prob11}

        iter = "%d" % (i+1)
        print(iter.rjust(4)+("␣␣␣␣␣␣␣%4f␣%4f␣%4f␣%4f"
        % ( p_pool[0], p_pool[1], p_pool[2], p_pool[3])))
```

When executed the output is

```
>>> import xor_iterate
>>> xor_iterate.xor_iterate(13)
Iteration P(00)     P(01)     P(10)     P(11)
    1        0.333333 0.222222 0.222222 0.222222
    2        0.222222 0.259259 0.259259 0.259259
    3        0.259259 0.246914 0.246914 0.246914
    4        0.246914 0.251029 0.251029 0.251029
    5        0.251029 0.249657 0.249657 0.249657
    6        0.249657 0.250114 0.250114 0.250114
    7        0.250114 0.249962 0.249962 0.249962
    8        0.249962 0.250013 0.250013 0.250013
    9        0.250013 0.249996 0.249996 0.249996
   10        0.249996 0.250001 0.250001 0.250001
   11        0.250001 0.250000 0.250000 0.250000
   12        0.250000 0.250000 0.250000 0.250000
   13        0.250000 0.250000 0.250000 0.250000
```

The probabilities quickly converge to a uniform distribution of $P = \frac{1}{4}$ for each value. The three right-hand columns are all the same. So, we need only look at P(00) and one other. Plotting them as lines, shows the convergence of the probabilities toward uniform as the iteration count increases, as shown in Figure 3.6.

So, we have the basis for a very simple algorithm to turn nonuniform distributions into uniform distributions by XORing multiple values together until a uniform distribution is achieved. So long as you know the input distribution, you can calculate the amount of input values needed to compute a single value from a distribution with a chosen amount of uniformity.

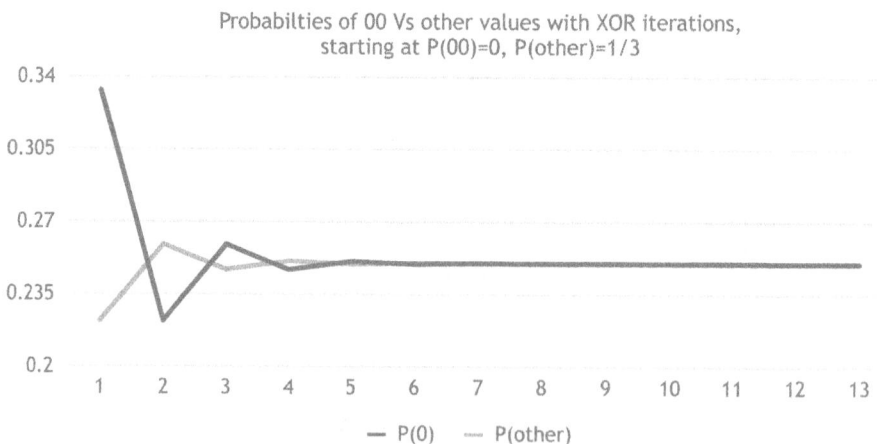

Figure 3.6: Two-Bit XOR Bias Convergence.

### 3.2.1 Is This Efficient?

This simple XOR iteration is cheap computationally, but the process consumes multiple nonuniform random numbers to produce 1 uniform random number.

If the supply of nonuniform random numbers is cheap and plentiful, then this algorithm is more efficient than hashing two values together, using a hash algorithm like SHA256.

However, if the supply of nonuniform random numbers is not so cheap, for example, they come from a slow entropy source hardware, it may take less time and fewer resources to compute the hash over two numbers and truncate.

### 3.2.2 Why This Might Matter: Two Real-World Examples with Very Different Results

#### 3.2.2.1 Example 1: Intel x86 RdRand Instruction

All Intel CPUs, from Ivy Bridge onwards, contain an instruction called RdRand. When executed with a 64-bit-destination register, it returns a 64-bit random number into that register. However, just like the example above, it will never return a zero. All other values are returned with equal probability. So,

$$P(0) = 0 \quad \text{and} \quad P(\text{other}) = \frac{1}{2^{64} - 1}. \tag{3.1}$$

This is a lot more uniform than the 2-bit example. The difference between 0 and $\frac{1}{2^{64}-1}$ is a lot smaller than the difference between 0 and $\frac{1}{3}$. But, if you are generating cryptographic keys for instance, then you would want to have a sufficiently uniform distribution.

We saw in the above 2-bit example that the probabilities for all values other than 0 are identical. So, we can simplify the equations a bit, computing just for $P(0)$ and $P(\text{other})$.

The routine in Listing 3.2 does the same calculation for 64-bit numbers with 0 missing from the distribution. It uses the mpmath library to allow us to do floating point calculations with arbitrary precision. Here, we choose to use 200-bit precision, which is sufficient.

**Listing 3.2:** 64 bit XOR Iteration

```
from mpmath import *

def xor_iterate64(n):
    mp.prec = 200
    oo2sf   = mpf(1)/mpf(2**64)
    oo2sfmo = mpf(1)/mpf((2**64)-1)
    ttt64   = mpf(2**64)
    ttt64m1 = mpf((2**64)-1)
```

```
ttt64m2 = mpf((2**64)-2)

p_input_0 = mpf(0)
p_input_other = oo2sfmo

p_pool_0 = p_input_0
p_pool_other = p_input_other

for i in xrange(n):
    p_0     = p_input_0 * p_pool_0
    p_0     += ttt64m1 * p_input_other * p_pool_other

    p_other = p_input_0 * p_pool_other
    p_other += p_input_other * p_pool_0
    p_other += ttt64m2 * p_input_other * p_pool_other

    p_pool_0 = p_0
    p_pool_other = p_other
    difference = p_pool_0 - p_pool_other

    print "Iteration   %"d % (i+1)
    print "  P(0) "    ,p_pool_0
    print "  P(Other"),p_pool_other
    print "  Difference ",difference
    print
```

When run, we see that on the $4^{th}$ iteration, when 5 values have been XORed together, the probabilities converge to a uniform distribution, with a precision of 200 binary digits. After only one iteration (XORing two values), the difference between the two probabilities is less than $3 \times 10^{-39}$, which is more than sufficient for cryptographic purposes.

```
>>> import xor_iterate as xi
>>> xi.xor_iterate64(6)
Iteration   1
 P(0)      5.42101086242752217033113759205528043413702130341688594422258e-20
 P(Other) 5.42101086242752217003726400434970855711297533088675477228e-20
 Difference  2.93873587705571877024045972528210464997834847714904449876e-39

Iteration   2
 P(0)      5.42101086242752217003726400434970855711297533088675477228e-20
 P(Other) 5.42101086242752217003726400434970855712890625000000000009e-20
 Difference  -1.59309191113245227728796545442054514435269511107663077320e-58

Iteration   3
 P(0)      5.42101086242752217003726400434970855712890625000000000009e-20
 P(Other) 5.42101086242752217003726400434970855712890625e-20
 Difference  8.63616855509444462538635186280039957111600036443628138502e-78

Iteration   4
 P(0)      5.42101086242752217003726400434970855712890625e-20
 P(Other) 5.42101086242752217003726400434970855712890625e-20
 Difference  0.0
```

### 3.2.2.2 Example #2 FIPS 140-2 Random Number Generators

The FIPS (Federal Information Processing Standard) 140-2 includes the following requirement for compliant RNGs in Section 4.9.2:

> *Continuous random number generator test.* If a cryptographic module employs Approved or non-Approved RNGs in an Approved mode of operation, the module shall perform the following continuous random number generator test on each RNG that tests for failure to a constant value.
> 1. If each call to as RNG produces blocks of n bits (where $n > 15$), the first n-bit block generated after power-up, initialization, or reset shall not be used, but shall be saved for comparison with the next n-bit block to be generated. Each subsequent generation of an n-bit block shall be compared with the previously generated block. The test shall fail if any two compared n-bit blocks are equal.

This test is required to be applied continuously to the output of the RNG. So, a FIPS 140-2 compliant RNG that outputs 16-bit values would have every value that matched the previous value fail the test and be eliminated from the output sequence.

This obviously reduces the entropy of the RNG. Whether or not this is a back door in the specification added by the NSA is, at the time of writing, not known.

What we know about every output is that it could be one of any of the $2^{16}$ values, except for the previous value output. So, there are $2^{16} - 1$ possible values out of a number space of $2^{16}$ values. In cryptographic terms, a nonuniformity of $\frac{1}{2^{16}-1}$ is more than sufficient bias to enable cryptographic attacks in algorithms like DSA (Digital Signature Algorithm), which are vulnerable to tiny amounts of bias in the supplied random numbers.

It would be simple to detect this flaw. Search for matching pairs. You should expect to find one in every 65536 pairs. After examining a few megabytes of data, the absence of any matching pairs will be solid evidence that this entropy-destroying procedure is in place in the system you are using.

So, here, we build a simulation, where the missing value is the last value that was output. Therefore, we will need to generate a random sequence, pass it through the FIPS 140-2 4.9.2 continuous test procedure, and use that to tell us which value cannot occur on each step, and so, compute the resulting probabilities.

A problem with this algorithm is that for each iteration it has to evaluate $2^{16} \cdot 2^{16} = 2^{32}$ combinations, thus making it very slow. The code is written to take a "bits" parameter, so we can try it out on fewer bits to see how it behaves. We start with a little function in Listing 3.3 to pull random numbers and limit them to "bits" bits.

**Listing 3.3:** Variable Width Random Bits Function

```
import os
```

```
from struct import *

def rand16(bits):
    a = os.urandom(2)
    therand16 = unpack('H',a)[0]
    if therand16 < 0:
        therand16 += 0x8000
    mask = (2**bits)-1
    therand16 = therand16 & mask
    return therand16
```

Then, we iterate through the XOR process, each time taking an input distribution that is uniform except for the last random value such that $P$(previous value) = 0.

Since we expect a distribution with many different values, we will just output the minimum and maximum probabilities in the distribution, which is sufficient to know how bad or good it is. The is implemented in Listing 3.4.

**Listing 3.4:** XOR Iteration WITH CRNGT

```
from mpmath import mpf
import mpmath as mp


def xor_iterate_fips(bits=16, iterations=16):
    mp.prec = 200
    oo2s    = mpf(1)/mpf(2**bits)
    oo2smo  = mpf(1)/mpf((2**bits)-1)
    ttt16   = mpf(2**bits)
    ttt16m1 = mpf((2**bits)-1)
    ttt16m2 = mpf((2**bits)-2)

    # fetch the first random number to initialize the comparison value
    # as per FIPS 140-2 4.9.2
    rt = random_things(bits)

    therand = rt.rand16()
    mask = (2**bits)-1
    lastrand = therand & mask

    # initial the input probabilities. The lastrand gets 0
    # others get 1/(2^16 -1)
    p_input = list()
    next_p = list()
    p_pool = list()
    for i in xrange(2**bits):
        p_input.append(0)
        p_pool.append(oo2smo)
        next_p.append(0)
```

```
        p_pool[lastrand] = 0

    print "Initial␣rand␣=␣%X" % lastrand

    for i in xrange(iterations):
        therand = rt.rand16() # lastrand will not occur
        mask = (2**bits)-1
        therand = therand & mask

        # fill in the input distribution
        for j in xrange(2**bits):
            p_input[j] = oo2smo
            next_p[j]=0
        p_input[lastrand] = 0

        for a in xrange(2**bits):
            for b in xrange(2**bits):
                axorb = a ^ b
                p_axorb = p_input[a] * p_pool[b]
                next_p[axorb] += p_axorb

        lastrand = therand

        for j in xrange(2**bits):
            p_pool[j] = next_p[j]

        print "Iteration␣␣%d␣-␣random#␣=␣%X" % (i+1, lastrand)
        print "␣␣minP␣␣␣␣",min(p_pool)
        print "␣␣maxP␣␣␣␣",max(p_pool)
        print "␣␣Difference␣",(max(p_pool)-min(p_pool))
        print

xor_iterate_fips()
```

For this first try, we run it with 2 bits, to match the 2-bit example earlier in this
section.

```
>>> a = xi.xor_iteraten_fips(bits=2,iterations=13)
Initial rand = 3
Iteration  1 - random\# = 1
  minP      0.222222222222222222222222222222222222222222222222222222222222
  maxP      0.333333333333333333333333333333333333333333333333333333333333
  Difference  0.111111111111111111111111111111111111111111111111111111111111

Iteration  2 - random\# = 3
  minP      0.222222222222222222222222222222222222222222222222222222222222
  maxP      0.259259259259259259259259259259259259259259259259259259259259
  Difference  0.037037037037037037037037037037037037037037037037037037037037

Iteration  3 - random\# = 0
  minP      0.246913580246913580246913580246913580246913580246913580246913
```

```
maxP        0.2592592592592592592592592592592592592592592592592592592926
Difference  0.0123456790123456790123456790123456790123456790123456790012346

Iteration   4 — random\# = 3
minP        0.2469135802469135802469135802469135802469135802469135802469 1
maxP        0.2510288065843621399176954732510288065843621399176954732510 3
Difference  0.0041152263374485596707818930041152263374485596707818930041151

Iteration   5 — random\# = 1
minP        0.2496570644718792866941015089163237311385459533607681755829 9
maxP        0.2510288065843621399176954732510288065843621399176954732510 3
Difference  0.0013717421124828532235939643347050754458161865569272976680384

Iteration   6 — random\# = 0
minP        0.2496570644718792866941015089163237311385459533607681755829 9
maxP        0.2501143118427069044352994970278920896204846822130772748056 7
Difference  0.0004572473708276177411979881115683584819387288523090992226794

Iteration   7 — random\# = 1
minP        0.2499618960524310318549001676573693034598384392623075750647 8
maxP        0.2501143118427069044352994970278920896204846822130772748056 7
Difference  0.0001524157902758725803993293705227861606462429507696997408 9313

Iteration   8 — random\# = 3
minP        0.2499618960524310318549001676573693034598384392623075750647 8
maxP        0.2500127013158563227150332774475435655133871869125641416450 8
Difference  0.0000508052634252908601331097901742620535487476502565665802 97763

Iteration   9 — random\# = 1
minP        0.2499957662280478924283222408508188114955376043624786194516 4
maxP        0.2500127013158563227150332774475435655133871869125641416450 8
Difference  0.0000169350878084302867110365967247540178495825500855221934 32743

Iteration   10 — random\# = 0
minP        0.2499957662280478924283222408508188114955376043624786194516 4
maxP        0.2500014112573173691905592530497270628348207985458404601827 9
Difference  0.0000056450292694767622370121989082513392831941833618407311440403

Iteration   11 — random\# = 3
minP        0.2499995295808942102698135823167576457217264004847198466057 4
maxP        0.2500014112573173691905592530497270628348207985458404601827 9
Difference  0.0000018816764231589207456707329694171130943980611206135770480134

Iteration   12 — random\# = 0
minP        0.2499995295808942102698135823167576457217264004847198466057 4
maxP        0.2500001568063685965767288058944141180927578665050933844647 5
Difference  0.0000006272254743863069152235776564723710314660203735378590 1595262

Iteration   13 — random\# = 2
minP        0.2499999477312104678077570647018619606357473778316355385117 5
maxP        0.2500001568063685965767288058944141180927578665050933844647 5
Difference  0.0000002090751581287689717411925521574570104886734578459530 0521382
```

We can see that it converges to uniform more slowly than the case with the static missing value. Interestingly, if we run the same program many times using a different random sequence each time, we find it converges to exactly the same min and max distribution, even though the input is changing randomly. Here is the final difference between the highest and lowest probability in the output distribution, after thirteen iterations over four independent runs with different data:

```
Run 1 :  0.00000020907515812876897174119255215745701048867345784595300521382
Run 2 :  0.00000020907515812876897174119255215745701048867345784595300521382
Run 3 :  0.00000020907515812876897174119255215745701048867345784595300521382
Run 4 :  0.00000020907515812876897174119255215745701048867345784595300521382
```

Increasing the bit-size, we find that it converges to uniform faster, but the program runs slower. Here is the $14^{th}$ iteration with 9 bit outputs, which took a minute to run:

```
Iteration  14 - random\# = 158
  minP      0.00195312499999999999999999999999999999999976404051634652182651 9
  maxP      0.00195312500000000000000000000000000000000000461760241983323233
  Difference  2.36421243895461496713961481889375749039520047158660801592 79e-41
```

At 16 bits the program does not complete the first iteration. With more efficient programming or a faster computer, it may be possible to complete this computation. The results on a bit-width of 9 show that XORing 16 values from a FIPS 140-2 RNG is sufficient to render the output distribution uniform enough for cryptography. Therefore 16 iterations will also be sufficient for 16 bit-numbers passing through a CRNGT.

## 3.3 Debiasing Algorithms

There are a number of commonly used algorithms for debiasing data. These algorithms are designed to take in nonuniform random bits and output unbiased random bits, where the ratio of 1s to 0s tends to 1:1, as the number of bits becomes larger. These algorithms should not be treated as general entropy extraction algorithms, although they can be used as such in special cases. For example, when the input data has zero serial correlation, the von Neumann whitener and Yuval Peres whitener can be used as an extractor. Below, we look at three algorithms. The von Neumann whitener, the Yuval Peres whitener, and Blum's method [3].

## 3.4 Von Neumann Debiaser Algorithm

The von Neumann debiaser, often called the von Neumann whitener, is an algorithm to turn a number of biased independent bits into a smaller number of unbiased independent bits. The algorithm is as follows:
–   Take a string of an even number of $m$ bits $z_0 \ldots z_{m-1}$.

$$z_{i\ldots m-1} = 1, 0, 0, 0, 1, 0, 1, 0, 0, 1, 0, 0, 1, 0, 0, 1, 1, 1, 1, 0, 1, 0,$$
$$0, 0, 0, 1, 0, 0, 0, 1, 1, 1, 0, 1, 1, 0, 0, 0, 0, 1, 1, 0, 1, 0$$

- Divide $z$ into $n$ pairs $x_{0...n-1}$, where $n = \frac{m}{2}$

$$x_{i...n-1} = 10, 00, 10, 10, 01, 00, 10, 01, 11, 10, 10, 00, 01, 00, 01, 11, 01, 10, 00, 01, 10, 10$$

- Discard all pairs 00 and 11.

$$10, 10, 10, 01, 10, 01, 10, 10, 01, 01, 01, 10, 01, 10, 10$$

- For each the 10 and 01 pairs, output the second bit of the bit-pair. That is, for each pair 10, output 0, and for each pair 01, output 1.

$$\text{output} = 0, 0, 0, 1, 0, 1, 0, 0, 1, 1, 1, 0, 1, 0, 0$$

The logic of this algorithm is that the only transition that can follow a 0-to-1 transition is a 1-to-0 transition and vice versa. So, the number of 1-to-0 transitions will be equal to the number of 0-to-1 transitions; that will yield the same number of 1s and 0s. Since the bits are split into pairs and the bits are statistically independent, the algorithm will randomly miss about half of the transitions, where it lands between pairs. This gives the output data both an approximately even bias and no serial correlation, provided that the input data has no serial correlation.

Implementing this in hardware is quite simple, since all it requires is mapping the four combinations of 2-bit patterns into output bits or nothing.

A simple bitwise implementation could be as shown in Listing 3.5.

**Listing 3.5:** Von Neumann Debiaser

```
def von_neumann_debiaser(bits):
    result = list()
    l = len(bits)/2
    for i in xrange(l):
        twobits = bits[l*2:(l*2)+2]
        if twobits = [0,1]:
            result.append(1)
        elif twobits = [1,0]:
            result.append(0)
    return result
```

In software, an efficient implementation might use byte tables to map the input bytes to output bits. One table contains the bit patterns and the other contains the number of bits in each pattern.

For example, the hex byte $0 \times 82$ in binary is 10000010, which splits into 10 00 00 10, which gets mapped to two bits 1 an 1. So, the table entry at position $0 \times 82$ would contain $0 \times 03$, which represents the 11 in the two lower bits. The length tables at position $0 \times 82$ would contain 2, which is the count of the number of bits.

The code in Listing 3.6 creates these tables by running each byte through the debiaser algorithm and printing the resulting table.

**Listing 3.6:** Von Neumann Debiaser Table Generator

```python
#!/usr/bin/env python

count_table = [0 for x in xrange(256)]
pattern_table = [0 for x in xrange(256)]

for i in xrange(256):
    abyte = i
    count = 0
    pattern = 0
    for j in xrange(4):
        pair = abyte & 0x03
        abyte = abyte >> 2
        if (pair == 1):    # 01 case
            pattern = (pattern << 1) | 0x01
            count = count + 1
        elif (pair == 2):    # 10 case
            pattern = pattern << 1
            count = count + 1
    count_table[i] = count
    pattern_table[i] = pattern

print "Pattern_Table"
for y in xrange(16):
    line = pattern_table[y*16:(y*16)+16]
    linelist = [("0x%02x" % x) for x in line]
    line = ",".join(linelist)
    print line

print "Count_Table"
for y in xrange(16):
    line = count_table[y*16:(y*16)+16]
    linelist = [("%d" % x) for x in line]
    line = ",".join(linelist)
    print line
```

When we run this program it outputs two tables, the first being the 256-bit patterns, the second being the number of bits to use in each pattern. The pattern table followed by the count table is:

```
0x0,0x0,0x1,0x0,0x0,0x0,0x2,0x0,0x1,0x1,0x3,0x1,0x0,0x0,0x1,0x0
0x0,0x0,0x2,0x0,0x0,0x0,0x4,0x0,0x2,0x2,0x6,0x2,0x0,0x0,0x2,0x0
0x1,0x1,0x3,0x1,0x1,0x1,0x5,0x1,0x3,0x3,0x7,0x3,0x1,0x1,0x3,0x1
0x0,0x0,0x1,0x0,0x0,0x0,0x2,0x0,0x1,0x1,0x3,0x1,0x0,0x0,0x1,0x0
0x0,0x0,0x2,0x0,0x0,0x0,0x4,0x0,0x2,0x2,0x6,0x2,0x0,0x0,0x2,0x0
0x0,0x0,0x4,0x0,0x0,0x0,0x8,0x0,0x4,0x4,0xc,0x4,0x0,0x0,0x4,0x0
0x2,0x2,0x6,0x2,0x2,0x2,0xa,0x2,0x6,0x6,0xe,0x6,0x2,0x2,0x6,0x2
0x0,0x0,0x2,0x0,0x0,0x0,0x4,0x0,0x2,0x2,0x6,0x2,0x0,0x0,0x2,0x0
```

```
0x1,0x1,0x3,0x1,0x1,0x1,0x5,0x1,0x3,0x3,0x7,0x3,0x1,0x1,0x3,0x1
0x1,0x1,0x5,0x1,0x1,0x1,0x9,0x1,0x5,0x5,0xd,0x5,0x1,0x1,0x5,0x1
0x3,0x3,0x7,0x3,0x3,0x3,0xb,0x3,0x7,0x7,0xf,0x7,0x3,0x3,0x7,0x3
0x1,0x1,0x3,0x1,0x1,0x1,0x5,0x1,0x3,0x3,0x7,0x3,0x1,0x1,0x3,0x1
0x0,0x0,0x1,0x0,0x0,0x0,0x2,0x0,0x1,0x1,0x3,0x1,0x0,0x0,0x1,0x0
0x0,0x0,0x2,0x0,0x0,0x0,0x4,0x0,0x2,0x2,0x6,0x2,0x0,0x0,0x2,0x0
0x1,0x1,0x3,0x1,0x1,0x1,0x5,0x1,0x3,0x3,0x7,0x3,0x1,0x1,0x3,0x1
0x0,0x0,0x1,0x0,0x0,0x0,0x2,0x0,0x1,0x1,0x3,0x1,0x0,0x0,0x1,0x0
```

```
0,1,1,0,1,2,2,1,1,2,2,1,0,1,1,0
1,2,2,1,2,3,3,2,2,3,3,2,1,2,2,1
1,2,2,1,2,3,3,2,2,3,3,2,1,2,2,1
0,1,1,0,1,2,2,1,1,2,2,1,0,1,1,0
1,2,2,1,2,3,3,2,2,3,3,2,1,2,2,1
2,3,3,2,3,4,4,3,3,4,4,3,2,3,3,2
2,3,3,2,3,4,4,3,3,4,4,3,2,3,3,2
1,2,2,1,2,3,3,2,2,3,3,2,1,2,2,1
1,2,2,1,2,3,3,2,2,3,3,2,1,2,2,1
2,3,3,2,3,4,4,3,3,4,4,3,2,3,3,2
2,3,3,2,3,4,4,3,3,4,4,3,2,3,3,2
1,2,2,1,2,3,3,2,2,3,3,2,1,2,2,1
0,1,1,0,1,2,2,1,1,2,2,1,0,1,1,0
1,2,2,1,2,3,3,2,2,3,3,2,1,2,2,1
1,2,2,1,2,3,3,2,2,3,3,2,1,2,2,1
0,1,1,0,1,2,2,1,1,2,2,1,0,1,1,0
```

These tables allow us to implement the von Neumann debiaser by inputting a byte, using the value of the byte to index into the tables to get the number of bits and the value of the bits to output.

The code in Listing 3.7 reads a binary file and using the above tables, performs the von Neumann debiasing algorithm and outputs to a second file.

**Listing 3.7:** Table Driven Von Neumann Debiaser

```python
#!/usr/bin/env python

import sys

pattern_table=[ 0x0,0x1,0x0,0x0,0x1,0x3,0x1,0x1,0x0,0x2,0x0,0x0,0x0,0x1,0x0,0x0,
                0x1,0x3,0x1,0x1,0x3,0x7,0x3,0x3,0x1,0x5,0x1,0x1,0x1,0x3,0x1,0x1,
                0x0,0x2,0x0,0x0,0x2,0x6,0x2,0x2,0x0,0x4,0x0,0x0,0x0,0x2,0x0,0x0,
                0x0,0x1,0x0,0x0,0x1,0x3,0x1,0x1,0x0,0x2,0x0,0x0,0x0,0x1,0x0,0x0,
                0x1,0x3,0x1,0x1,0x3,0x7,0x3,0x3,0x1,0x5,0x1,0x1,0x1,0x3,0x1,0x1,
                0x3,0x7,0x3,0x3,0x7,0xf,0x7,0x7,0x3,0xb,0x3,0x3,0x3,0x7,0x3,0x3,
                0x1,0x5,0x1,0x1,0x5,0xd,0x5,0x5,0x1,0x9,0x1,0x1,0x1,0x5,0x1,0x1,
                0x1,0x3,0x1,0x1,0x3,0x7,0x3,0x3,0x1,0x5,0x1,0x1,0x1,0x3,0x1,0x1,
                0x0,0x2,0x0,0x0,0x2,0x6,0x2,0x2,0x0,0x4,0x0,0x0,0x0,0x2,0x0,0x0,
                0x2,0x6,0x2,0x2,0x6,0xe,0x6,0x6,0x2,0xa,0x2,0x2,0x2,0x6,0x2,0x2,
                0x0,0x4,0x0,0x0,0x4,0xc,0x4,0x4,0x0,0x8,0x0,0x0,0x0,0x4,0x0,0x0,
                0x0,0x2,0x0,0x0,0x2,0x6,0x2,0x2,0x0,0x4,0x0,0x0,0x0,0x2,0x0,0x0,
```

```
                   0x0,0x1,0x0,0x0,0x1,0x3,0x1,0x1,0x0,0x2,0x0,0x0,0x0,0x1,0x0,0x0,
                   0x1,0x3,0x1,0x1,0x3,0x7,0x3,0x3,0x1,0x5,0x1,0x1,0x1,0x3,0x1,0x1,
                   0x0,0x2,0x0,0x0,0x2,0x6,0x2,0x2,0x0,0x4,0x0,0x0,0x0,0x2,0x0,0x0,
                   0x0,0x1,0x0,0x0,0x1,0x3,0x1,0x1,0x0,0x2,0x0,0x0,0x0,0x1,0x0,0x0]

count_table = [ 0,1,1,0,1,2,2,1,1,2,2,1,0,1,1,0,
                1,2,2,1,2,3,3,2,2,3,3,2,1,2,2,1,
                1,2,2,1,2,3,3,2,2,3,3,2,1,2,2,1,
                0,1,1,0,1,2,2,1,1,2,2,1,0,1,1,0,
                1,2,2,1,2,3,3,2,2,3,3,2,1,2,2,1,
                2,3,3,2,3,4,4,3,3,4,4,3,2,3,3,2,
                2,3,3,2,3,4,4,3,3,4,4,3,2,3,3,2,
                1,2,2,1,2,3,3,2,2,3,3,2,1,2,2,1,
                1,2,2,1,2,3,3,2,2,3,3,2,1,2,2,1,
                2,3,3,2,3,4,4,3,3,4,4,3,2,3,3,2,
                2,3,3,2,3,4,4,3,3,4,4,3,2,3,3,2,
                1,2,2,1,2,3,3,2,2,3,3,2,1,2,2,1,
                0,1,1,0,1,2,2,1,1,2,2,1,0,1,1,0,
                1,2,2,1,2,3,3,2,2,3,3,2,1,2,2,1,
                1,2,2,1,2,3,3,2,2,3,3,2,1,2,2,1,
                0,1,1,0,1,2,2,1,1,2,2,1,0,1,1,0]

def von_neumann_debiaser(bits):
    global pattern_table
    global count_table

    bitlist = list()
    bytelist = list()

    for byte in bytes: # VN Debiaser table lookup
        pattern = pattern_table[ord(byte)]
        count = count_table[ord(byte)]
        if count > 0:
            for i in range(count):
                bit = ((pattern >> i) & 0x01)
                bitlist.append(bit)

    while len(bitlist) > 7: # Turn 8 bits to a byte
        outbyte = 0
        bits = bitlist[:8]   # Pull 8 bits of the front
        outbitlist = bitlist[8:]
        for bit in bits:           # Turn them into a byte
            outbyte = outbyte << 1
            outbyte = outbyte + bit
        bytelist.append(outbyte) # add it to the output

    while len(bytelist) > 256: # Write out in chunks
        data = bytearray(bytelist)
        outf.write(data)
        outbytelist = list()

# get filename
filename = sys.argv[1]
outfilename = sys.argv[2]

outbitlist = list()
outbytelist = list()

outf = open(outfilename,"wb")
```

```
with open(filename,"rb") as f:
    bytes = f.read(256) # Read a chunk of bytes
    while bytes:
        for byte in bytes: # VN Debiaser table lookup
            pattern = pattern_table[ord(byte)]
            count = count_table[ord(byte)]
            if count > 0:
                for i in range(count):
                    bit = ((pattern >> i) & 0x01)
                    outbitlist.append(bit)

        while len(outbitlist) > 7: # Turn 8 bits to a byte
            outbyte = 0
            bits = outbitlist[:8]   # Pull 8 bits of the front
            outbitlist = outbitlist[8:]
            for bit in bits:         # Turn them into a byte
                outbyte = outbyte << 1
                outbyte = outbyte + bit
            outbytelist.append(outbyte) # add it to the output

        while len(outbytelist) > 256: # Write out in chunks
            data = bytearray(outbytelist)
            outf.write(data)
            outbytelist = list()

        bytes = f.read(256) # Read in the next 32
# The last line
data = bytearray(outbytelist)
outf.write(data)

f.close()
outf.close()
```

A shortcoming of the von Neumann debiaser algorithm is that the amount of data output is nondeterministic when fed by nondeterministic data. The number of instances of 00 and 11 in the bit pairs, which will be dropped, is unpredictable.

A more serious shortcoming is that the properties of the algorithm rely on the input data being independent of each other. So, there must be zero serial correlation. This is not a property that is typical of practical entropy source designs. There are many instances of real-world hardware random number generators, where the serially correlated output from an entropy source was fed into a von Neumann debiaser; this is one of the causes of RNG failure in cryptosystems.

For an extreme example, if we feed in 32 bits of data, with the worst case negative serial correlation of −1.0, then the input is

$$1,0,1,0,1,0,1,0,1,0,1,0,1,0,1,0,1,0,1,0,1,0,1,0,1,0,1,0,1,0,1,0$$

The output would be

$$0,0,0,0,0,0,0,0,0,0,0,0,0,0,0,0$$

which is as biased as possible and is an example of how serially correlated input causes the debiasing properties of the algorithm to fail.

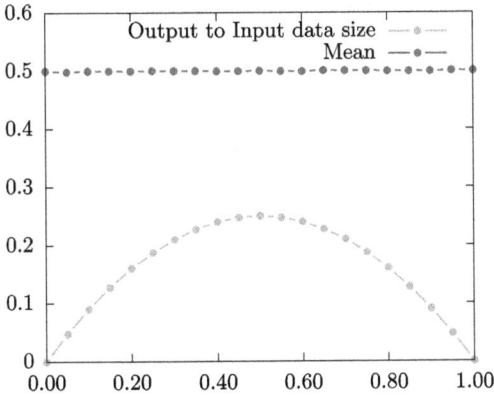

**Figure 3.7:** Von Neumann Debiaser Output Bias and Output Size vs Input Bias.

Therefore, in the following examples we experiment with feeding in biased data, but not serially correlated data. In Figure 3.7, we pass files of 1 mibibyte of biased data through a von Neumann whitener algorithm with bias varying in 0.05 steps from 0.0 to 1.0 and show the output bias and output size ratio.

We can see how the bias remains close to 0.5 across the full range. However, the file size reduces as the bias increases, and when the bias reaches the extremes of 1 and 0, the output size is 0 bytes.

## 3.5 Yuval Peres Debiaser Algorithm

The Yuval Peres Debiaser [17] is an extension of the von Neumann debiaser. The principle is that the data that are discarded are fed back into the debiaser. This can continue iteratively, with the bits discarded by the second pass being fed into the debiaser a third time, and so on, until there is no more data to process or the iteration limit is reached. The Yuval Peres Debiaser paper [17] shows that the amount of extracted entropy rapidly approaches the Shannon limit as the number of iterations increases.

The algorithm is defined recursively. The algorithm description in the paper is written in a mathematical style and may be hard to decode for a nonmathematician. The snippet from the paper where the algorithm is described is shown in Figure 3.8.

What this is saying is that with a number of bits $x_1, \ldots, x_n$ and a chosen depth $v$, we define the depth 1 function $\Psi_1(x_1, \ldots, x_n)$ to be the von Neumann debiaser algorithm over $x_1, \ldots, x_n$.

We define the Yuval Peres debiaser function as $\Psi_v(x_1, \ldots, x_n)$, where $v > 1$. It is the concatenation of three bit strings.

The first is the von Neumann debiaser algorithm run over those bits $x_1, \ldots, x_n$.

The second is $\Psi_{v-1}(u_1, \ldots, u_{\frac{n}{2}})$, where $u_1, \ldots, u_{\frac{n}{2}}$ is the XORing of each pair of bits within $x_1, \ldots, x_n$, and so, is half as long as the $x$ bit string.

**2. The iterated procedures.** The von Neumann extraction procedure
$\Psi_1: \Omega \to \Omega$ is defined by

$$\Psi_1(x_1, x_2, \ldots, x_{2n+1}) = \Psi_1(x_1, \ldots, x_{2n}) = (y_1, \ldots, y_k),$$

where $y_i = x_{2m_i}$ and $m_1 < m_2 < \cdots < m_k$ are all the indices $m \leq n$ for
which $x_{2m} \neq x_{2m-1}$.

(∗) The iterated procedures $\Psi_\nu$, $\nu \geq 2$ are defined inductively. Given
$x_1, \ldots, x_{2n}$, denote $u_j = x_{2j-1} \oplus x_{2j}$ ($\oplus$ is addition modulo 2) and $v_j = x_{2i_j}$,
where $i_1 < i_2 < \cdots < i_{n-k}$ are all the indices $i \leq n$ for which $x_{2i} = x_{2i-1}$
and $k$ is again the number of indices $m \leq n$ such that $x_{2m-1} \neq x_{2m}$. Let

$$\Psi_\nu(x_1, \ldots, x_{2n}) = \Psi_1(x_1, \ldots, x_{2n}) * \Psi_{\nu-1}(u_1, \ldots, u_n) * \Psi_{\nu-1}(v_1, \ldots, v_{n-k}).$$

Finally, define $\Psi_\nu$ for sequences of odd length by $\Psi_\nu(x_1, \ldots, x_{2n+1}) = \Psi_\nu(x_1, \ldots, x_{2n})$. To verify that the $\Psi_\nu$ are extraction procedures, it is convenient to extend the class of processes considered. Recall the notion of *ex-
changeable* random variables ([3], Section VII.4).

**Figure 3.8:** Yuval Peres Debiaser Algorithm Snippet. Snippet from "Iterating von Neumann's Procedure for Extracting Random Bits".

The third is $\Psi_{v-1}(v_1, \ldots, v_{\frac{n}{2}})$, where $v_1, \ldots, v_{\frac{n}{2}}$ is made from a string formed with a 0 for
each 00 pair and a 1 for each 11 pair in the $x_1, \ldots, x_n$ bitstring, essentially, taking 1 bit
for each discarded bit pair from the von Neumann debiaser.

So, for $X = x_1, \ldots, x_n$, $U =$ the XOR of the bit pairs in $X$ and $V = a$, mapping of 00
pairs to 0 and 11 pair to 1 from $X$ and with || being the concatenation operator

$$\Psi_V(X) = \Psi_1(X) || \Psi_{v-1}(U) || \Psi_{v-1}(V).$$

The code in Listing 3.8 is a naive, bitwise implementation of the Yuval Peres debiaser. It implements a recursive function. It operates over lists of bits passed in as a
parameter.

**Listing 3.8:** Yuval Peres bitwise debiaser

```
def yuval_peres_debiaser(bits,depth):
    if len(bits) < 2:
        return list()

    if depth < 2:
        newbits = von_neumann_debiaser(bits)
        return newbits

    l = len(bits)/2

    # The first part
    first = von_neumann_debiaser(bits)

    u = list()   # The second part, xor the bit pairs
    for i in xrange(l):
        u.append(bits[2*i] ^ bits[(2*i)+1])
    second = yuval_peres_debiaser(u,depth-1)

    v = list() # The third part. map 00->0, 11->1
```

```
for i in xrange(l):
    if bits[2*i] == bits[(2*i)+1]:
        v.append(bits[2*i])
third = yuval_peres_debiaser(v,depth-1)

return first+second+third
```

The program code available with this book in the file yp_debiaser.py wraps this code with a program to read in a binary file and write out the result. The first parameter is the depth parameter. The next two parameters are the input and output filenames.

For example, to run a depth 2 Yuval Peres debiaser over biased data with bias of 0.35 using the same file of biased data used with the von Neumann debiaser test, we can do the following:

```
$ python yp_debiaser.py 2 bias_0p35_a.bin yp_0p35.bin
$
```

Then, we can examine the mean and serial correlation of the output with djent.

```
$ djent -b yp_0p35.bin
 opening yp_0p35.bin as binary
 Symbol Size(bits) = 1
   Shannon IID Entropy = 1.000000 bits per symbol
   Optimal compression would compress by 0.000007 percent
   Chi square: symbol count=3347081, distribution=0.32,
   randomly exceeds 57.08 percent of the time
   Mean = 0.500155
   Monte Carlo value for Pi is 3.142992 (error 0.04 percent).
   Serial Correlation = 0.001104
$
```

We can see that the output data has a mean close to 0.5; it passes the Chi-Square test of randomness and the serial correlation is insignificant. So, the algorithm is working as intended.

The file size is 418386 bytes, compared to the source file size of 1 mibibyte.

As we increase the depth, the processing time increases and the amount of output data increases. See Table 3.6.

**Table 3.6:** Yuval Peres Debiaser Input-to-Output File Size.

| Depth | File Size | Output:Input Ratio |
|-------|-----------|--------------------|
| 1 | 238547 | 0.227 |
| 2 | 418386 | 0.399 |
| 3 | 555112 | 0.529 |
| 4 | 658612 | 0.628 |
| 5 | 736805 | 0.703 |
| 6 | 795669 | 0.759 |

This highlights a danger with the Yuval Peres debiaser. The data we are processing here has a bias of 0.35. So, the min-entropy measured in bits is $-\log_2(\max(0.35, 1 - 0.35)) = 0.6215$.

Multiplying this by the number of input bytes 1048576 gives us a maximum of 651677 full entropy bytes that could be extracted from the input data. However, the Yuval Peres debiaser can run right through that limit and output more data bits than there are bits of entropy in the source data.

So, when choosing the depth, it is important to know the worst case input bias and to set the depth of the Yuval Peres debiaser such that it does not output more data than there is entropy. In this example, the maximum depth we would choose is 3 because the input to output file ratio of 0.529 is less than the entropy to data size ratio of 0.6215, whereas, the output-to-input file ratio for depth four is 0.628, which is greater than that limit. So, 3 is the largest depth for which there are fewer output bits than bits of entropy in the input data.

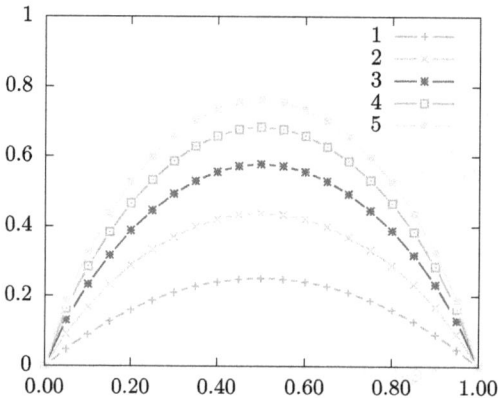

**Figure 3.9:** Yuval Peres Debiaser File Output Size vs Bias and Iteration Count.

In the plot in Figure 3.9, the Yuval Peres debiaser algorithm has been run over biased data with bias going from 0 to 1 in 0.05 steps and five curves are produced for iteration limits from 1 to 5. An iteration limit of 1 is analogous to the von Neumann whitener. We can see the output file size increasing both with the number of iterations and with the closeness of the bias to 0.5.

## 3.6 Blum's Method Debiaser Algorithm

The von Neumann and Yuval Peres debiasers both require the input bits to be independent of each other. A paper by Blum [3] describes an algorithm that can extract unbiased bits from a class of serially correlated data that can be generated using a finite Markov chain.

The limitation to the generators that can be modelled with finite Markov chains is that the algorithm is of mostly academic interest. Real-world entropy source circuits tend to have infinite states and tracking those states well is not possible.

For example, the Markov diagram in Figure 3.10 has four states $S_1, S_2, S_3, S_4$ and each state has two possible exit paths that are chosen at random, but with each path having a specific probability of being chosen. The sum of the probabilities of each exit path is 1, since a path will always be chosen.

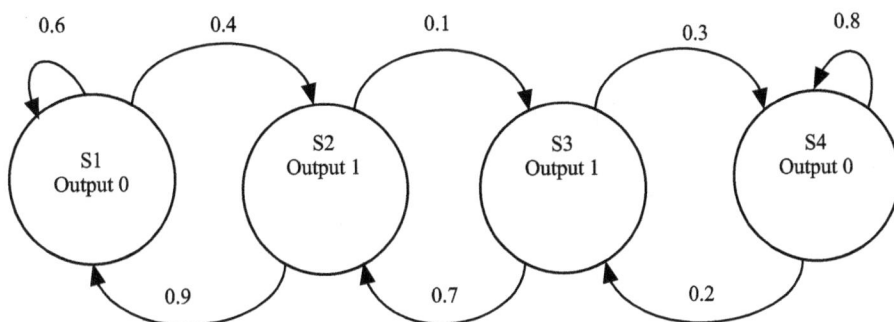

Figure 3.10: Markov Chain Generating Dependent Random Bits.

Each time a state is visited, a 1 or 0 is output. We can see that the probability of a particular value being output is a function of the previous state and so the output bits are serially dependent.

The python code in Listing 3.9 will generate 1024 bits of data, using the above Markov model.

Listing 3.9: blum_whitener_1.py

```python
#!/usr/bin/env python

import random

# Tuple of (state number, output value, destination state,
#           destination probability, other destination state)
states = [0,(1, 0, 2, 0.4, 1),(2, 1, 3, 0.1, 1),(3,1,4,0.3,2),(4,0,3,0.2,4)]

state = 1
out_value = 0
out_string = ""
index = 0

for i in xrange(4096):
    (s,ov,dest1,dest_prob,dest2) = states[state]
    if ov == 1:
        out_value = out_value + (0x01 << index)
    index += 1

    if index == 8:
        out_string += "%02x" % out_value
```

```
        out_value = 0
        index = 0

    if len(out_string) == 64:
        print out_string
        out_string = ""

    if random.SystemRandom().random() < dest_prob:
        state = dest1
    else:
        state = dest2
```

Running this, we get some random looking output.

```
$ python2 blum_whitener_1.py
541421152a252a1029142209aa50081229412988808124025a4884043040030
0a8a040804a47a2611851c03409812a0105a462025540ba34abaab314a118944
48a212421d0d01d8b090013c8a50804008821a04b05045844a355803011e9c10
48912a74a1240540c219049c6252a2540585a8ab329a04540824a2221d215c15
1449a0142284be1229a2088d11109180e28ac2850495bb480e1491a4540550a4
c7116e0529a8e82a44400250e840c40000b08a4e45044105452212510915080 0
01442549458888441120d1950a51492222d20d1026d5558aa8126200ece8544a
54ea22a144295440241211555122145224544aa22a4a429345008928094a1a14
002ba853299d20085c54a08a7297908a421d51856122a44029281417210020a8
847c41226880c186220909a42a083016252281504049aac8185f12217281b812
4421502520bdf1550a114e141020551255a20080200ad530e5722112e9a2008a
0a948802211200d0558a0472ca4580aaaa0842254926b2c1100785a0225d1242
012a52140844552912c58311024a1000000a45d1151551221511702e052a1149
a44f020111705488ca00001a5415a592120a494485542a084140008840101e38
01014640391544144219000c5420122855545254510 2114a5740511049974809
11152807900a091a400c074209044589520 4a8432841baa24804804d293a2950
$
```

We can test this with djent, and we find it to have substantial bias and serial correlation.

```
$ python2 blum_whitener_1.py | djent -l 1
    Shannon IID Entropy = 0.900217 bits per symbol
    Optimal compression would compress by 9.978303 percent
    Chi square: symbol count=4089, distribution=552.46,
    randomly exceeds 0.00 percent of the time
    Mean = 0.316214
    Monte Carlo value for Pi is 3.811765 (error 21.33 percent).
    Serial Correlation = -0.191129
$
```

The 1986 paper by Blum [3] describes four algorithms ($A$, $B$, $C$, and $D$) of increasing complexity. It shows algorithm A to be flawed and goes on to make improved versions of $B$, $C$, and $D$. Here, we will show algorithm B.

The algorithm maintains a state element $S_i$ for each state of the Markov chain. Each state can hold a value from the set $\{\lambda, H, L, 0, 1\}$. As the Markov chain is run, the state elements are updated. Landing in a state with $S_i = H$ or $S_i = L$ will result in a 1 or

0 being output respectively; that state element is then set to λ to indicate it has been used. Otherwise, a state element takes on the 0 or 1 value of the Markov chain element visited. When the history of the previous two states is 1.0, the state is marked with *H*. If it is 0.1 it is marked with an *L*.

The effect is to tag states as outputting a 1 or 0 (identified in the paper as *H* or *L* for "heads" or "tails") following a 01 or 10 transition, but to not output the value until the state is revisited.

**Listing 3.10:** blum_whitener_2

```python
#!/usr/bin/env python

import random
import sys

# Tuple of (state number, output value, destination state,
#           destination probability, other destination state)
states = [0,(1, 0, 2, 0.4, 1),(2, 1, 3, 0.1, 1),(3,1,4,0.3,2),(4,0,3,0.2,4)]

state = 1
out_value = 0
out_string = ""
index = 0
count = 0
ic = 2**16  # input count

# State bits can be L, 0, 1, H or T.
# Initiatize all states to L
state_bits = ['L' for x in states]
i = 1
for j in xrange(ic):
    # Step 1
    s = ""
    for st in state_bits:
        s = s+str(st)
    if (state_bits[i] == 'H') or (state_bits[i] == 'T'):
        if (state_bits[i] == 'H'):
            out_value = out_value + (0x01 << index)
            index += 1
        elif (state_bits[i] == 'T'):
            index += 1
        state_bits[i] = 'L'
        count += 1
        if index == 8:
            out_string += "%02x" % out_value
            out_value = 0
            index = 0

        if len(out_string) == 64:
            print out_string
            out_string = ""

    # Step 2
    # Run the Markov Chain one step to get 1 or 0
    (s,ov,dest1,dest_prob1,dest2) = states[i]

    if random.SystemRandom().random() < dest_prob1:
```

```
            next_state = dest1
    else:
            next_state = dest2
    (s,ov,dest1,dest_prob2,dest2) = states[next_state]

    exit_bit = ov

    # Step 3
    s = str(state_bits[i])

    if state_bits[i] == 'L':
        state_bits[i] = exit_bit
    elif (state_bits[i] == 0) or (state_bits[i] == 1):
        if exit_bit == state_bits[i]:
            state_bits[i] = 'L'
        else:
            if state_bits[i] == 1 and exit_bit == 0:
                state_bits[i] = 'H'
            else:
                state_bits[i] = 'T'
    # Step 4
    i = next_state

print >> sys.stderr,   "Bits_in:",ic,",_Bits_out:",count,"_Ratio:",(float(count)/ic)
```

The number of iterations in this Listing was increased to 65536 because the number of outputs per state is reduced with the Blum whitener. Running this, we get more random looking output as follows:

```
$ python2 blum_whitener_2.py
2c3fc9b75ae0456f550e0df8b1156e2a674115ff1669d8b9c4a1f478b229e762
cee9653817cb4c141ad61b4ee5aa0a71410c4dbd0f6162988380b40331a62639
50b9c103a2ace48c34e576ce1c8a5194879b862f9577da0ed63cefaa783a8de1
ce33acd43946634758806a232fb6277bd542197de2fc3ae9938ae8a1c0a802e2
62afcbbf0219f4529a9e47338f9f7526241d23075110dff424c99b7970f67640
6bc6f6605a0364b4c5d3b1dcc21ae0c3ef1bf247193a0b1a66cb283ddb094075
48c5c8dcd561853b6612c2be3fa2e88dee9871a2168d13e73a30f421509b414d
a99295f141cc59fa073f68515cb978b97e77dab3acd8c2e2e0d7134c563a6ff0
2fa7cfc6ad230a11cc505219b20106531a33bc58ac9ed2d7b19fb9551fd76461
b9e8ab9a44fb0d614aa950da1487ea64200125de056e294b8f529f13a9b0046a
493f3353b168aa8e949b1ebca909bdb1fd6841c877ca8421f3846f172e012a47
8657000c7a63732b63e562da96843dc6b2bccabfb8a0328bb4334b5a2eea1bbe
5a6d4567a38e7898121ac0f29ff4aa42dfb27f559448d50a212877d30ed3afb9
b47e4b80d3452d880485109c6451e198f77525b5e5047db678c613e340bc3505
e93b84154008b86554caefbbfbd6c6a73331db86daf02f9c5a810e873fdd1c29
ee43ecc5dcde8dbf24b4d30833203402ce06324aadf7719203a31a18a8067f5c
cd098e343d6b11f15bb93f8a1ebf26992ec669215f8178f9abee9275142146fb
9cf26208fca71f62324f7bb31f98d55eba25f8bd35903cf1dbb80fd43b649cf7
1a548b4a46f4d289aa298962f6f470a9313eab9ab67a5982cb698b09dd6a168c
07d440538817cc5068dbe4548159dbefbfaec5a4798ad07438a75de96ce1459e
c0e0d1357f6844c9fd557a6f580b9b169a660cafff47013236a502b1780b0f1e
144e8c9d18cb9a42b7d0f1d6fa911244feda91f9dff88f32aafb78d304f481ff
```

```
70835cd31e0a7a3a1c9cf93924b24ef53d0fb11e09839511528fefb278fe9a22
3cb378825af8536fc6d09a24267b82c5b6ef1dc9da33335f92ccf0cb54e6eb2c
72a15bb427888f54cfdb892b508da2e3b432c81a19d23d42a94e55a85dab80c5
eeafe5410d7334f7b14ca573b4af3f3fb4f3d2d8e03b69a24c1929a69f952864
564440c8c8616bb6d67acb4b5819c9c95d6576439e7f34b0c867f5ce9d64c49c
6ac41a2131615df1af099e61335ac7342ed601134428096546a5ac8a0d4b2cbd
631d12f430f7403d2cdc1de544b353256fcbd66f96ba7d9a513b4777f96cf3c3
d2a07d6ea84f261abcd479091157042af5ceeed5cf053796ed8276a3f7bf94a1
03344d96cfd51ad4ac3bb5c74b2d450d5cdefcdb60a0f63903f017abed037a59
f8dc629dfb59377c1ccfb9a5966e97c4186621d09631ecb752737e1d1cc39acc
5ee7b4490787bf991e1dd9e5029bf5531ec5cdba832eb52b0fdd27ed9b8ce5cc
5133c2a4c5dd34db0b7b1296dbc15b426059288af45f9dd788458441cb87aabc
0aa6abf92e3fa0b206e82cd031f37be773abff7bacf83c4895f02cfd1795a639
490787b3cbf09a80576a066a78560058c863b594bf22a30bc067bdb23466996f
ce4b7213c2ed1efc42a039958a77e509d0be44c5c2c64d8674c44ab891b1edfb
6480e25945c90a8fbd9ed6d261570f1d23630e6e22915c6e4c00e67232888977
42d545d3cb5cff8b21915fba3d2552d208884030ae5cb96387dfa82ddf516c7d
5bacfbb41c537bfe2a9c58b543f00939c9732b623e84fa557faf1f4a98b74ff7
da01f84a953719b8ada229139513be167ac68ef359f8cd8b5dab5bb4efe037b3
81d6174b72f2f46c031bb1b10d4fcb0aa5b2778bb6c57175d0eee57a7ec960c9
61e359d0e9c1f3954b3e9a3c6a32cdf90ba46eaea7b5bede123ad1e96c471cae
51d95ac4237f888b6a061a17ecb96694f0e513528441b1f55171ae4c8ba0fcc5
0a38594a2a720c8fe77baedf2319c4278f4f7bea931edcb9bc679295be0611c5
f6a08137d9bf0eae1d0bd4b3993a073b6f4d5e43a5632b5703dba0560fd7c262
a9d8ce58bd623ae17e8ba3bcebe880804dd44196f84df6d349e04de25c1f0bfd
d21b4eed3d3c04f4d9933c9f46cbf07121ca1613721366f365347a7e963da674
Bits in: 65536 , Bits out: 12533  Ratio: 0.19123840332
$
```

We see that the ratio of input bits to output bits is now only 0.191. However, if we test the data with djent, we see that the bias and serial correlation has been corrected.

```
$ python2 blum_whitener_2.py | djent -l 1
Bits in: 65536 , Bits out: 12565  Ratio: 0.19172668457
   Shannon IID Entropy = 0.999869 bits per symbol
   Optimal compression would compress by 0.013108 percent
   Chi square: symbol count=12537, distribution=2.28,
   randomly exceeds 13.12 percent of the time
   Mean = 0.506740
   Monte Carlo value for Pi is 2.957854 (error 5.85 percent).
   Serial Correlation = 0.010667
$
```

This is not a very useful algorithm in the real world, because entropy sources are not strict Markov chains and one cannot track the state of an entropy source the way that this algorithm tracks the state in a Markov chain. However, it shows that correcting for correlation is possible.

## 3.7 Cryptographic Entropy Extractors

Here, we start looking at cryptographic entropy extractors of the sort that are typically used in cryptographically secure random number generators. First, we consider Pinkas Proof, which limits us from achieving a perfect solution. Then, we look at single input, seeded extractors, which get "close enough" to uniform output to be cryptographically useful, despite the Pinkas proof. Finally, we look at multiple-input extractors, which allow extraction from low-entropy sources, where single-input extractors do not.

## 3.8 Pinkas Proof, or Why We Cannot Have Nice Things

In a paper by John McInnes and Benny Pinkas entitled "On the Impossibility of Private Key Cryptography with Weakly Random Keys" [14], it was shown that it is impossible to take a weakly random source of entropy, that is, any source with less than perfect min-entropy and compress it to make a perfect random key with full min-entropy; so, it is impossible to generate such a key to work perfectly with a one-time-pad style encryption.

   Therefore, there is no situation in which you can have a deterministic extraction algorithm that can take the imperfectly random output of a single entropy source and convert it to a full entropy key. See Figure 3.11.

This Doesn't Happen

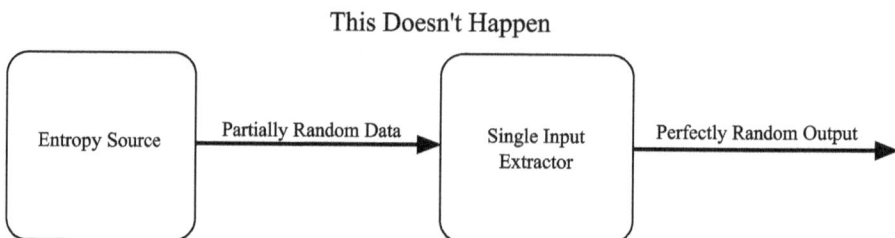

**Figure 3.11:** The Thing That the Pinkas Proof Shows is Impossible.

This might seem like a problem for cryptography, which it is. In order to do entropy extraction with provable security properties, we need to do something else. The two primary solutions to this problem are seeded extractors and multiple-input extractors; a third solution that is common, but misguided, is to use a cryptographic hash function as a single input extractor, despite the existence of the proof in [14]. There are no known good attacks, if the hash function and the entropy source is good. However, that construction is theoretically unsound.

## 3.9 Seeded Entropy Extractors

A seeded entropy extractor is an algorithm that takes in partially random data on one input and a uniformly random seed in a second input. It has been shown that such algorithms, which produce outputs good enough for cryptography, can exist. See Figure 3.12.

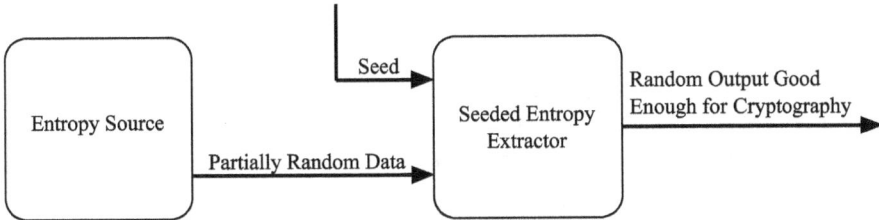

**Figure 3.12:** Seeded Entropy Extractor.

An obvious shortcoming of the seeded extractor approach is that in a universe like ours, with copious sources of partially random data, but no sources of perfectly random data, how could the first seeded extractor work without the uniform seed? This is a real problem and in seeded extractors, inadequate seed sources are usually used.

Examples of algorithms used for seeded entropy extractors include the CBC-MAC algorithm and the HMAC algorithm. Notably, both these algorithms are MACs (Message Authentication Code), which are algorithms that take in an arbitrary amount of data and a fixed length key (which is used as the seed input when used as an extractor) and outputs a fixed size value. In the paper "Randomness extraction and key derivation using the CBC, cascade and HMAC modes" [7], it is proven that HMAC and CBC-MAC are secure entropy extractors.

The draft SP800-90B standard specifies three approved extractors, CBC-MAC, CMAC, and HMAC. While [7] derives very specific bounds for the amount of input entropy needed to achieve the desired computational security at the output, the NIST specification makes an arbitrary requirement that there be twice as much entropy in as data out. See Figure 3.13.

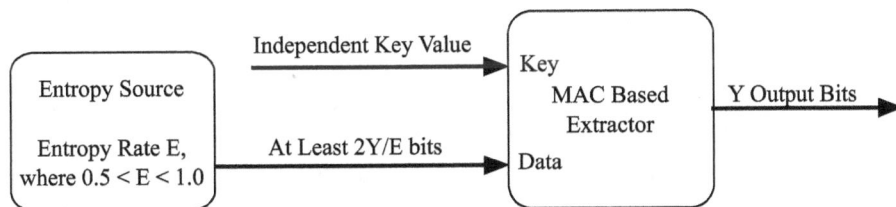

**Figure 3.13:** NIST 2X Entropy Ratio Requirement.

So in an RNG seeking certification against the NIST specs, for example, to use in a FIPS 140-2 certified product, it is simple to compute how much data needs to be fed in for each seed out, but this level is more conservative than is necessary, and for any noncertified implementation, [7] can be referenced to find a more efficient bound for how much input data is needed per seed.

### 3.9.1 CBC-MAC Entropy Extractor

CBC-MAC is an algorithm that generates a MAC, which is typically used in communication protocols to authenticate that a message is from a holder of a key.

There are a number of attacks against CBC-MAC, if used improperly and other algorithms like HMAC or CMAC are preferred for generating MACs. However, as an entropy extractor, CBC-MAC is a good algorithm.

The algorithm takes an input message and splits it into $n$ blocks of data $m_1$ to $m_n$ equal to the block size of the encryption algorithm used; for example, in the case of AES, this would be 128 bits.

The first block, $m_1$, is passed through an encryption block cipher. The next block $m_2$ is XORed with the output of the previous block cipher, and the result passed through the block cipher. This is repeated for each of the $n$ blocks, and the final output of the final stage is the MAC.

As in Figure 3.14, the first stage is often drawn as having $m_1$ XORed with 0, so all the stages are of the same form.

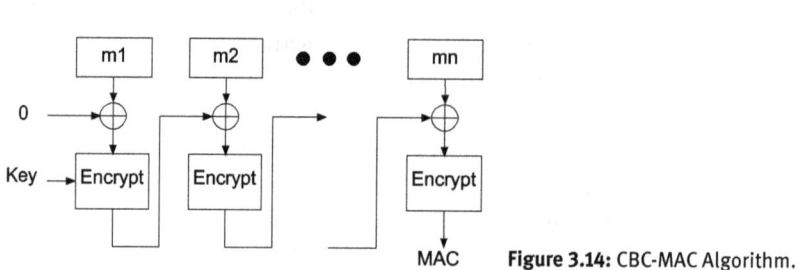

Figure 3.14: CBC-MAC Algorithm.

There are a number of things to take into account when using a MAC algorithm as a MAC. This includes things such as padding and preventing extension attacks. However, when used a MAC, as an extractor it is simpler. Just make the input data length be a multiple of the block size so that it can be evenly divided into $n$ blocks with no remainder or padding. The output is the full entropy random value.

The proof of the properties of CBC-MAC as an extractor relies on the input entropy rate being greater than 50%. That is, for $n$ bits of data, there are at least $\frac{n}{2}$ bits of entropy.

The NIST requirement states that for full entropy output, at least twice as many bits of entropy must be fed in than the number of bits removed. For AES, the output is 128 bits. Thus, at least 256 bits of entropy is needed at the input. Since the source is less than 100% entropic and must be at least 50% entropic for CBC-MAC to work as an extractor, a good choice of the number of blocks is to assume a 50% entropy rate so there are at least 64 bits of entropy in each 128-bit input block. Therefore, at least $\frac{256}{64} = 4$ input blocks are needed for each output block.

The key should either be a uniform random number or some value that is independent of the input data. It need not be a secret; the Intel DRNG uses CBC-MAC for its extractor and the key is a static number formed by encrypting the value 0 with the key of value 1 with AES. This forms a random-looking number that is independent of any entropy source that is not deliberately trying to copy that number.

In python, CBC-MAC is available in the Crypto library, so a python example would not show the inner loop. The example below is written in C, using the aes128k128d function available from the djenrandom codebase for the AES function.

It reads a file as binary and pulls 64 bytes at a time, passing the 64 bytes through AES-CBC-MAC and the 16 bytes (128 bit) output is the extracted random number, which is printed out. It continues reading and extracting until the end of the file is reached.

**Listing 3.11:** cbc_mac.c

```c
#include <stdio.h>
#include <string.h>
#include "aes128k128d.h"

int main(int argc, char** argv) {
    FILE *fp;
    char filename[256];
    unsigned char buffer[64];
    int c,i;
    int finished = 0;
    unsigned char feedforward[16];
    char output[64];
    unsigned char key[16];
    unsigned char initdata[16];

    // Clear start value and compute key
    for (i=0;i<16;i++){
        feedforward[i] = 0;
        key[i] = 0;
        initdata[i] = 0;
    }
    initdata[0] = 1;
    aes128k128d(key,initdata,key);

    // Get the file name
    if (argc == 2) {
        strcpy(filename,argv[1]);
    }
    else {
        printf("Error:_Enter_single_filename_as_argument\n");
        exit(1);
```

```
}

// Loop through the file, running CBC-MAC.
fp = fopen(filename,"rb");
while (finished == 0) {
    c = fread(buffer,1,64,fp);
    if (c==64) {
        for (i=0;i<4;i++) {
            xor_128(buffer+(i*16), feedforward, feedforward);
            aes128k128d(key,feedforward, feedforward);
        }
        for (i=0;i<16;i++) sprintf(&output[i*2],"%02X",feedforward[i]);
        output[32] = 0;
        printf("%s\n",output);
    }
    else finished = 1;
}
fclose(fp);
exit(0);
}
```

This is compiled with the AES code file:

```
$ gcc cbc-mac.c aes128k128d.c -o cbc-mac
$
```

We run it from the command line and point it to a file from which to extract. So, in the following example, djenrandom is used to create 1 kibibyte of negatively serially correlated data. Then, the CBC-MAC program is called to extract from that data.

```
$ djenrandom -s -m correlated --correlation=-0.2 -b -k 1 > sccdata.bin
$ ./cbc-mac sccdata.bin
F863922E0911DF1C304DB2378162686A
3EC3F205CF219DFC28FDF70386657EC4
3DD8761F20D7A0FE0FDD38D76E113AED
2E84E9FE696A56D687287D6E18BF9EE3
BCCA13F6271DC4F340CB5C58F0472DE3
EF206EDF30DA0437E484C329C688EECE
3C67F6FE9FD63C6FA28A91AE8A5FF45F
2E9FAF210F426D30082CD765BDEA152B
4CDF219119C8E3A6BA0A429DDAD0EAF7
867B10181D10C45B024061C1CCD0432E
11353332797F41918577771443FC590C
2318E6D4767D4F594656495155687A44
3EE1F68D38AA64DB5980ADFAA02B318A
587E6F3C53059A9F213C80EB17E0967B
12E64AFA9F6A12AADA4730317A66B3D5
7619EB11DA3196B9D84E3B8C1034950F
```

### 3.9.2 CMAC Entropy Extractor

CMAC was created as a successor to CBC-MAC. It addresses some problems with CBC-MAC, such as extension attacks. Like CBC-MAC it uses an underlying block cipher algorithm, AES being the common choice.

CMAC works equally well as an extractor as CBC-MAC, although it is a little less efficient, since more invocations of AES are required per output.

First two subkeys $K1$ and $K2$ are created from the input key $K$. From the NIST SP800-38B specification:

1. Let $L = \text{Encrypt}_K(0)$.
2. If $\text{MSB}(L) = 0$ then $K1 = L << 1$ else $K1 = (L << 1)$ XOR Rb.
3. If $\text{MSB}(L) = 0$ then $K2 = K1 << 1$ else $K2 = (K1 << 1)$ XOR Rb.

Rb is a constant that depends on the block size of the cipher.

When the block-size is 128 bits, Rb = 0x00000000000000000000000000000017.

When the block-size is 64 bits, Rb = 0x000000000000001B.

As with CBC-MAC, the MAC algorithm needs to deal with padding, but in the case of extraction, we can simply make the input entropy be a multiple of the block length.

The progression of the algorithm is identical to CBC-MAC, until we get to the final stage, when $K1$ is XORed into the final value before the final block cipher.

$K2$ is used when there is padding. However, since we can avoid padding for extraction, the $K2$ computation can be skipped.

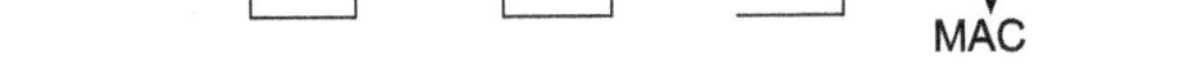

Figure 3.15: CMAC Algorithm.

The C code below is the core CMAC algorithm written in C. The full program with test vectors is available at http://www.deadhat.com/wmancrypto/cmac_0.1.c. The same file reading code from the CBC-MAC example can be used to turn it into a command line program. See Figure 3.15.

**Listing 3.12:** cmac.c

```
/* Take note that in the NIST CMAC specification
    the MSB is byte index 0, so the carries go the
    other way to the way you might expect */
void leftshift128(unsigned char *a, unsigned char *out) {
```

```
        unsigned char x;
        int carry;
        int i;
        carry=0;

        for (i=15; i >= 0 ; i--) {
                x = a[i] << 1;
                if (carry == 1) {
                        x = x | 0x01;
                }
                else {
                        x = x & 0xfe;
                }

                out[i] = x;
                carry = 0;
                if ((a[i] & 0x80)==0x80) carry = 1;
        }
}


/**********************************************************/
/* int cmac()                                             */
/* Computes the 128 bit CMAC of the plaintext             */
/**********************************************************/

int cmac(   unsigned char *key,
            unsigned char *k1,
            unsigned char *k2,
            unsigned char *plaintext,
            unsigned int length,
            unsigned char *t)
{

        unsigned char l[16];
        unsigned char lshl[16];

        unsigned char r[16] = {0x00,0x00,0x00,0x00, 0x00,0x00,0x00,0x00,
                               0x00,0x00,0x00,0x00, 0x00,0x00,0x00,0x87 };
        unsigned char zeroes[16] = {0x00,0x00,0x00,0x00, 0x00,0x00,0x00,0x00,
                                    0x00,0x00,0x00,0x00, 0x00,0x00,0x00,0x00 };

        unsigned char c[16] = {0x00,0x00,0x00,0x00, 0x00,0x00,0x00,0x00,
                               0x00,0x00,0x00,0x00, 0x00,0x00,0x00,0x00 };
        unsigned char temp[16] = {0x00,0x00,0x00,0x00, 0x00,0x00,0x00,0x00,
                                  0x00,0x00,0x00,0x00, 0x00,0x00,0x00,0x00 };
        unsigned char mn[16] = {0x00,0x00,0x00,0x00, 0x00,0x00,0x00,0x00,
                                0x00,0x00,0x00,0x00, 0x00,0x00,0x00,0x00 };
        unsigned char *m;
        unsigned int n;
        unsigned int i;
        unsigned int remainder;

        /* Compute subkeys K1 and K2 */
        aes128k128d(key, zeroes, l);
        if ((l[0] & 0x80) == 0x80) { /* if MSB of L is set */
                leftshift128(l,lshl);
                xor_128(lshl,r,k1);
        }
        else {
                leftshift128(l,k1);
```

```
};

if ((k1[0] & 0x80) == 0x80) {  /* if MSB of K1 is set */
        leftshift128(k1,lsh1);
        xor_128(lsh1,r,k2);
}
else {
        leftshift128(k1,k2);
};

/* Compute the MAC */
n = length/16;
remainder = length % 16;

if (remainder != 0) {n++;};

for (i=0; i<16; i++) {c[i] = 0x00;}; /* Clear C0 */

for (i = 0; i< n-1; i++) {
        m = (unsigned char *)(plaintext+(16*i));
        xor_128(c,m,temp);
        aes128k128d(key, temp, c);
};

                         /* Final block */
if (remainder == 0) {
        m = plaintext+(16*(n-1));
        xor_128(m, k1, mn);
        xor_128(c, mn, temp);
        aes128k128d(key,temp, t);
}
else {
        for (i=0; i<16; i++) temp[i]=0x00; /* clear temp */
                               /* copy last fragment into temp */
        m = plaintext+(16*(n-1));
        for (i=0; i<remainder; i++) {
                temp[i] = m[i];
        }
                           /* set the leftmost bit of the padding */
        temp[remainder] = 0x80;
        xor_128(temp, k2, mn);
        xor_128(mn, c, temp);
        aes128k128d(key, temp, t);
}
};
```

### 3.9.3 HMAC Entropy Extractor

The HMAC algorithm uses an underlying hash algorithm to create a MAC. Like the CMAC, it deals with attempts to append or prepend data to an existing MAC by modifying the initial and final blocks.

There is no requirement on the key size. For a key longer than the block size of the hash, it is hashed down to the block-size. For a shorter key, it is padded up to the block-size with 0s added to the right of the key.

```
if length(key) > blocksize:
    key = hash(key)
else if length(key) < blocksize:
    pad = 0 repeated (blocksize - length(key)) times
    key = key || pad
```

When the key is the same size as the block size of the hash, nothing is done to the key. So, for an entropy extractor, where we are choosing the size of the key, we can choose to set the key size to the block-size and skip the initial key transformation step.

Two pad patterns are used; the input pad and the output pad.

The input pad is the byte 0x36 repeated up to the block-size: $\frac{blocksize}{8}$ bytes of 0x36 XORed with the key.

The output pad is the byte 0x5c repeated up to the block-size: $\frac{blocksize}{8}$ bytes of 0x5c XORed with the key.

For example, when using SHA-256, the block-size is 256 bits or 32 bytes.

```
input_pad = 0x3636363636363636363636363636363636
            363636363636363636363636363636363636  XOR key
output_pad = 0x5c5c5c5c5c5c5c5c5c5c5c5c5c5c5c5c
             5c5c5c5c5c5c5c5c5c5c5c5c5c5c5c5c  XOR key
```

Then the output of the HMAC is computed as

```
X = hash(input_pad || message)
output = hash(output_pad || X)
```

The simple python example below takes a filename and a key on the command line. For each output, 512 bits are pulled from the file and passed through HMAC with the key. The output is printed out as hex.

**Listing 3.13:** hmac_extactor.py

```
#!/usr/bin/env python

import hmac
import hashlib
import base64
import sys

# get filename
filename = sys.argv[1]
key = sys.argv[2]

with open(filename,"rb") as f:
    bytes = f.read(128) # Read 1024 bits
    while len(bytes) == 128:
        digest = hmac.new(key, msg=bytes, digestmod=hashlib.sha256).digest()
        astr = ""
        for byte in digest:
            astr += "%02X" % ord(byte)
        print astr
```

```
        bytes = f.read(128)
f.close()
```

Running the code, we again generate 1 kibibyte of negatively serially correlated data and run it through the program, which takes in 512 bits at a time from the file, extracts a value from it, using HMAC-SHA256, and outputs the value as hex.

```
$ djenrandom -b -m correlated --correlation=-0.2 -k 1 > sccdata.bin
$ python hmac_extractor.py sccdata.bin this_is_a_key
BE2939AF83E0AFF6D93AD4D40F55AF9CE142C3837A8391FC6EE7BFE2C58F7EA7
C9D9901D5C3B658B7832875BA486D8BC397A0FA8B50E08F5455FD355BC24985F
EBFD03F8D934A079104C3660BB3B6FB31CC137ED2CA54E303AE1264603C007CF
274B5B0D612867B296AB3771069842AAF47884EB0C7ADE85D2F1A9CD5D527AEC
AE821C5DF602E275717F13DF4E14FD1C690FF9FE519C90A1B79A92CCA038626A
656CDE12AFE8597D4BCB8765C79BA3845B7CBF7CD3A0F8DBFAC0406D8DEB24D1
39C75D308280D688F948209D13843E665192890B7C277D81380AFE88E6C9C7C7
DD7008491B1D42432503A9244707FC02E3CC913F6FF7C19A3AC3E4378560A904
```

## 3.10 Multiple Input Entropy Extractors

As the name implies, multiple-input entropy extractors take multiple-input data values. These separate inputs must be statistically independent of each other for the properties of the extractor to hold. See Figure 3.16.

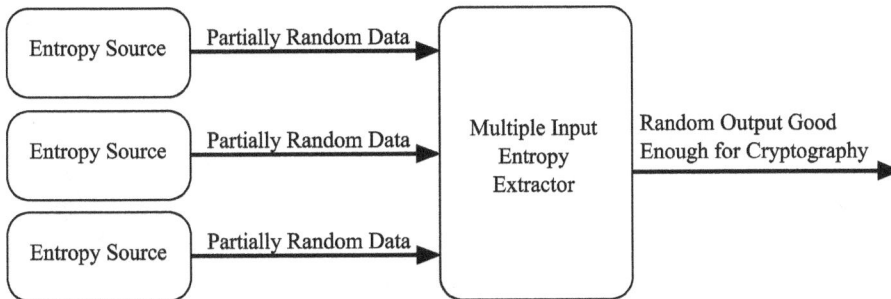

**Figure 3.16:** Multiple Input Entropy Extractor.

This sort of extractor typically is used either to generate full entropy seeds from high-quality, close to uniform entropy, sources, or to sufficiently improve the entropy from multiple low-quality entropy sources, in order to use the output as the input to a seeded entropy extractor. In one construction below (2EXT) is the explicit structure of the 2-input extractor, with the first stage creating a seed for the second stage, which is a seeded extractor.

One way of thinking about why source-independence of a multiple-input extractor is a necessary part of the definition of a multiple-input extractor is that, if correlation was allowed between the two or more inputs, then the extractor could simply take in one source and split the input into blocks, and feed those into the two or more inputs of an algorithm wrapped by the input-splitting algorithm. So, the whole algorithm would be a single input extractor.

Here, we look at two multiple-input extractor algorithms. First, the three input BIW (Barack, Impagliazzo, Wigderson) extractor, which is extraordinarily efficient and second 2-EXT, a 2-input extractor, which is somewhat more complex but has the additional interesting property of having been proven to be a quantum-secure entropy extractor.

### 3.10.1 Barak, Impagliazzo, Wigderson 3 Input Extractor

This extractor is described in [1]. It takes three independent inputs of each of the same bit width and each input must have a min-entropy above some limit. The entropy at the output will be the same bit width and the min-entropy will be improved, relative to the lower limit of the min-entropy on each of the inputs.

A beneficial property is that the input min-entropy does not need to be above any specific value. So, poor quality sources with min-entropy below 0.5 can be used. This is in contrast to many single-input extractors, for example, the CBC-MAC single-input extractor that needs the input min-entropy to be greater than 0.5.

It is a valid approach to use a BIW extractor with weak sources to produce partially entropic data with min-entropy greater than 0.5, which is then fed into a MAC-based extractor to produce a close-to-full entropy output.

#### 3.10.1.1 BIW Extractor Structure

The extractor structure is exceedingly simple. We call the three inputs $A$, $B$, and $C$. Treat the three $n$-bit input values as elements of a $G(s^n)$ Galois field. The output is computed as follows:

$$\text{output} = (A \cdot B + C),$$

where the multiply and add operations are performed within the Galois field. So, "add" is equivalent to an $n$-bit bitwise XOR and "multiply" is performed with a shift-add structure. Both these operations are very low computational complexity and are easy to implement.

#### 3.10.1.2 BIW Extractor Properties

Lemma 3.14 of [1] states:

There exists an absolute constant $c > 0$, such that, for every prime $p$, every $\delta > 0$, and every distributions $\mathcal{A}, \mathcal{B}, \mathcal{C}$ over GF($2^p$), with $H^\infty(\mathcal{A}), H^\infty(\mathcal{B}), H^\infty(\mathcal{C}) > \delta p$, the distribution $A \cdot B + C$ is $2^{-\epsilon m}$-close to having min-entropy at least $\min\{(1+\epsilon)m, 0.9 \log |\mathbb{F}|\}$, where $\epsilon = c\delta$.

To nonmathematicians, that may be hard to understand. So, here is a clearer description of the result.

Take three inputs $A, B, C$, each of bit width $p$.

All three inputs take a number from a source that has min-entropy greater than some fraction of $p$. That fraction is called $\delta$. So, for example, with sources each with min-entropy $> 0.5$, $\delta = 0.5$, $\delta$ is the measure of the quality of the sources.

Take a number computed as $D = A \cdot B + C$.

The resulting number $D$ is from a distribution that has (or is very close to having) some min-entropy.

The amount of min-entropy of the output is the lower order of

$$(1 + (c\delta))m$$

and

$$0.9 \log |\mathbb{F}|,$$

where $m$ is defined in the in section 3.3.1 of [1], where it states that $A$, $B$, and $C$ have min-entropy of at least $m$. Therefore, in our case, $m$ is the number of bits in the input words, times the min-entropy per bit. So, for example, a 13-bit input with 0.7 bits per bit of min-entropy, $m = 0.7 \cdot 13 = 9.1$.

The result tells us that $c > 0$, so for bits widths of $p = 13$, $m = 13$, and entropy sources with min entropy of 0.7, $\delta = 0.7$. So $(1 + (c\delta))m > m$.

The log in the second bound is base 2, since we are working in bits. So, for example, for 13-bit field $0.9 \log |\mathbb{F}| = 0.9 \cdot 13$.

So, the min-entropy of the output $D$ is generally going to be $> 0.9$ bits-per-bit of output.

Most importantly, the min-entropy of the output is better than that of the inputs regardless of what the input min-entropy is.

So, with weak sources, you can combine them to make a source with min-entropy better than 0.5. Thus, making that output suitable to feed into a single input extractor that requires min-entropy $> 0.5$ in order to produce cryptographically secure outputs.

### 3.10.1.3 How the BIW Extractor Works

We start with the idea of two partially random independent inputs being used to index into a two-dimensional table. If the table contains "random-looking" values, then, we might expect the results to look random. If the table looks very regular, then we might not expect the output to look random.

For example, using two inputs $x$ and $y$ that are partially random numbers between 0 and 9, to index into the column and row, respectively, of the addition table, outputs might not end up looking very random.

| + | 00 | 01 | 02 | 03 | 04 | 05 | 06 | 07 | 08 | 09 |
|---|----|----|----|----|----|----|----|----|----|----|
| 00 | 00 | 01 | 02 | 03 | 04 | 05 | 06 | 07 | 08 | 09 |
| 01 | 01 | 02 | 03 | 04 | 05 | 06 | 07 | 08 | 09 | 10 |
| 02 | 02 | 03 | 04 | 05 | 06 | 07 | 08 | 09 | 10 | 11 |
| 03 | 03 | 04 | 05 | 06 | 07 | 08 | 09 | 10 | 11 | 12 |
| 04 | 04 | 05 | 06 | 07 | 08 | 09 | 10 | 11 | 12 | 13 |
| 05 | 05 | 06 | 07 | 08 | 09 | 10 | 11 | 12 | 13 | 14 |
| 06 | 06 | 07 | 08 | 09 | 10 | 11 | 12 | 13 | 14 | 15 |
| 07 | 07 | 08 | 09 | 10 | 11 | 12 | 13 | 14 | 15 | 16 |
| 08 | 08 | 09 | 10 | 11 | 12 | 13 | 14 | 15 | 16 | 17 |
| 09 | 09 | 10 | 11 | 12 | 13 | 14 | 15 | 16 | 17 | 18 |

But, if we instead indexed into a random looking table like the one below, it might end up looking more random.

| | 00 | 01 | 02 | 03 | 04 | 05 | 06 | 07 | 08 | 09 |
|---|----|----|----|----|----|----|----|----|----|----|
| 00 | 81 | 81 | 39 | 32 | 84 | 14 | 12 | 54 | 84 | 97 |
| 01 | 17 | 30 | 66 | 15 | 00 | 77 | 12 | 06 | 25 | 41 |
| 02 | 43 | 83 | 02 | 63 | 71 | 30 | 39 | 68 | 92 | 55 |
| 03 | 11 | 80 | 76 | 36 | 64 | 23 | 09 | 08 | 28 | 65 |
| 04 | 26 | 57 | 10 | 83 | 33 | 11 | 90 | 29 | 80 | 53 |
| 05 | 51 | 78 | 28 | 13 | 23 | 80 | 21 | 65 | 23 | 89 |
| 06 | 07 | 54 | 36 | 86 | 35 | 25 | 03 | 78 | 13 | 77 |
| 07 | 38 | 33 | 42 | 58 | 78 | 26 | 84 | 22 | 62 | 81 |
| 08 | 45 | 02 | 12 | 80 | 95 | 13 | 33 | 24 | 53 | 01 |
| 09 | 05 | 88 | 09 | 65 | 52 | 27 | 78 | 01 | 01 | 44 |

Now, consider what happens when you index into a rectangular window within this table, by constraining the random variables $x$ and $y$ to vary within a smaller range. You can see that some windows are better than others. If we choose the same window in both tables, then we can see that one window has more distinct numbers than the other.

| + | 00 | 01 | 02 | 03 | 04 | 05 | 06 | 07 | 08 | 09 |
|---|----|----|----|----|----|----|----|----|----|----|
| 00 | 00 | 01 | 02 | 03 | 04 | 05 | 06 | 07 | 08 | 09 |
| 01 | 01 | 02 | 03 | 04 | 05 | 06 | 07 | 08 | 09 | 10 |
| 02 | 02 | 03 | 04 | 05 | 06 | 07 | 08 | 09 | 10 | 11 |
| 03 | 03 | 04 | 05 | 06 | 07 | 08 | 09 | 10 | 11 | 12 |
| 04 | 04 | 05 | 06 | 07 | 08 | 09 | 10 | 11 | 12 | 13 |
| 05 | 05 | 06 | 07 | 08 | 09 | 10 | 11 | 12 | 13 | 14 |
| 06 | 06 | 07 | 08 | 09 | 10 | 11 | 12 | 13 | 14 | 15 |
| 07 | 07 | 08 | 09 | 10 | 11 | 12 | 13 | 14 | 15 | 16 |
| 08 | 08 | 09 | 10 | 11 | 12 | 13 | 14 | 15 | 16 | 17 |
| 09 | 09 | 10 | 11 | 12 | 13 | 14 | 15 | 16 | 17 | 18 |

|    | 00 | 01 | 02 | 03 | 04 | 05 | 06 | 07 | 08 | 09 |
|----|----|----|----|----|----|----|----|----|----|----|
| 00 | 81 | 81 | 39 | 32 | 84 | 14 | 12 | 54 | 84 | 97 |
| 01 | 17 | 30 | 66 | 15 | 00 | 77 | 12 | 06 | 25 | 41 |
| 02 | 43 | 83 | 02 | 63 | 71 | 30 | 39 | 68 | 92 | 55 |
| 03 | 11 | 80 | 76 | 36 | 64 | 23 | 09 | 08 | 28 | 65 |
| 04 | 26 | 57 | 10 | 83 | 33 | 11 | 90 | 29 | 80 | 53 |
| 05 | 51 | 78 | 28 | 13 | 23 | 80 | 21 | 65 | 23 | 89 |
| 06 | 07 | 54 | 36 | 86 | 35 | 25 | 03 | 78 | 13 | 77 |
| 07 | 38 | 33 | 42 | 58 | 78 | 26 | 84 | 22 | 62 | 81 |
| 08 | 45 | 02 | 12 | 80 | 95 | 13 | 33 | 24 | 53 | 01 |
| 09 | 05 | 88 | 09 | 65 | 52 | 27 | 78 | 01 | 01 | 44 |

This leads us to the Erdős–Szemerédi theorem from [9]. This result shows that, where $A$ is a set of integers (such as the constrained set of $x$ and $y$ values considered in the previous paragraph), we have

$$\max(|A + A|, |A \cdot A|) \geqslant |A|^{1+c_1},$$

where $|A + A|$ is the number of distinct integers in the window into the addition table, and $|A \cdot A|$ is the number of distinct integers in the window into the multiplication table. Later it was shown that $c_1 \geqslant \frac{1}{3}$.

In less formal terms, this is saying that, if you index into a window in the addition table and also index into the same window into the multiplication table, the number of distinct integers, in at least one of those windows, will be larger than the size of the set $A$ by a certain amount. It does not matter which window you choose. It remains true for all $A$ by $A$ sized windows. Bourgain, Katz, and Tao [4] extended this result to elements in finite fields.

The BIW extractor paper [1] uses these results to show that the min-entropy from the result of the expression $A \cdot B + C$ is greater than the lowest min-entropy in $A$, $B$ or $C$. Either the multiplication part adds enough min-entropy or the addition part does. So, by combining both, they guarantee an increase in min-entropy. They go on to show the bounds for fields of the form $GF(2^p)$, and so, we have a result we can implement, since elements of fields of the form $GF(2^p)$ map nicely to bits in a binary number, and computer arithmetic over those elements in the field is simple and cheap.

### 3.10.1.4 Measured Results for the BIW Extractor

First, we look at what happens when we supply a BIW extractor with biased input data.

Section 19.2 gives the following equation for the min-entropy of biased data:

$$H_\infty(X) = -\log_2(\max(P(1)^n, P(0)^n)),$$

where $n$ is the number of bits in each input word, and $b$ is the bias of the bits.

We can plot a graph of min-entropy against bias and also plot the measured min-entropy of data with that bias passed through the entropy extractor to compare the efficiency of the extractor.

The output entropy is measured using the Markov–Renyé min-entropy estimate algorithm. The calculated min-entropy of the input is plotted and the $X$ axis is the bias of the input data. See Figure 3.17.

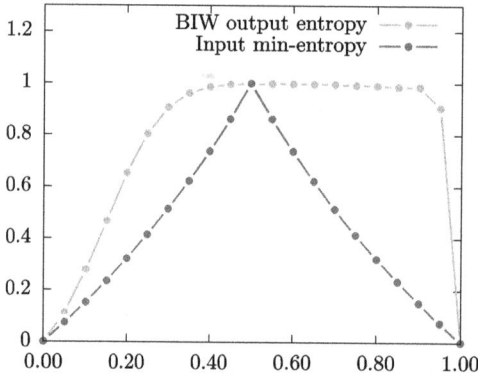

**Figure 3.17:** Measured Min-Entropy of BIW Output Against the Bias of Input Data and the Source Min-Entropy.

We can see that for bias between 0.2 and 0.8, the output measured min-entropy is above 0.5. The entropy drops off more quickly as the bias approaches 0 than when the bias approaches 1. This is because in $A \cdot B + C$, if $A = 0$, then the entropy in $B$ is lost because it is multiplied by 0. The reverse is also true: if $B = 0$, then, the entropy in $A$ is lost because it is multiplied by 0. So, as the probability of all bits being 0 increases, the amount of lost entropy increases.

Now, we will look at what happens when we feed serially correlated data into the BIW extractor. For serially correlated binary data with serial correlation $s$, the min entropy per bit is

$$H_\infty(X) = -\log_2\left( \max\left( \frac{s+1}{2}, \frac{s+1}{2} - 1 \right) \right).$$

Again, the output entropy is measured with the Markov–Renyé min-entropy estimate algorithm. The input entropy is calculated with the above equation, and the $x$ axis is the serial correlation coefficient, from −1 to +1. See Figure 3.18.

We can see how the measured output min-entropy is maintained at close to full entropy across a wide range of serial correlation in the input data streams.

### 3.10.1.5 BIW Extractor Code Example

The python code in Listing 3.14 implements the Galois field multiply gmul(a,b) and the Galois field add gadd(a,b). biw(a,b,c) implements the BIW extractor. The code uses a

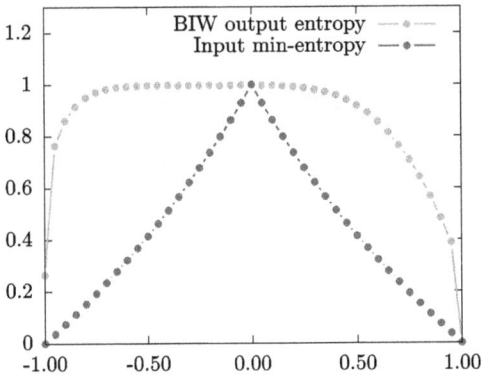

**Figure 3.18:** Measured Min-Entropy of BIW Output Against Serial Correlation and the Source Min-Entropy.

13-bit field, using the irreducible polynomial $m(x) = x^{13} + x^5 + x^3 + x + 1$. For other bit widths, you should choose irreducible polynomials of the degree equal to the bit width.

As you can see, the BIW algorithm itself takes one line of code. The Galois multiplication will typically be available as a library function.

**Listing 3.14:** biw.py

```python
def gmul(a, b):
    poly = 0x001b # 0x201b with the msb lopped off.
    degree = 13

    z = 0
    if a & 1:
        r = b
    else:
        r = 0
    for i in xrange(1, degree+1):
        if (b & (1 << (degree-1))) == 0:
            b = z ^ ((b << 1) & ((1 << degree) - 1))
        else:
            b = poly ^ ((b << 1) & ((1 << degree) - 1))
        if a & (1 << i):
            r = r ^ b
        else:
            r = r ^ z
    return r

def gadd(a, b):
    return a^b

def biw(a,b,c):
    return gadd(gmul(a,b),c)
```

### 3.10.2 2-EXT 2-Input Extractor

This extractor is described in [6]. It takes two independent inputs of each of the same bit width and, like the BIW extractor, each input must have a min-entropy above some limit. The min-entropy at the output will be improved relative to the lower limit of the min-entropy on each of the inputs.

This extractor also has the property of being a quantum-secure extractor, and so, is an important part of a random number generator that is designed to be secure against a quantum computer attack.

#### 3.10.2.1 2-EXT Extractor Structure

The 2-EXT extractor has two major components, a blender and a seeded extractor. The seeded extractor may be any good seeded extractor, such as the HMAC algorithm or a Trevisan extractor. The blender algorithm is specified in the 2-EXT paper [6]. The output of the blender is used as the seed input to the seeded extractor and one of the inputs to the blender is also used as the data input to the seeded extractor.

In the paper [6], 2-EXT is described as

$$TWOEXT(X, Y) = EXT(Y, BLE(X, Y)),$$

which equates to the data path in Figure 3.19.

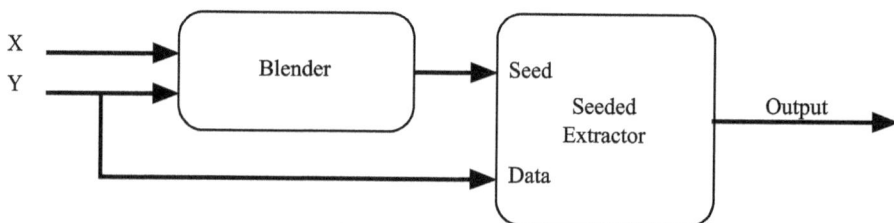

**Figure 3.19:** 2-EXT Structure.

The first stage of the paper shows that the output of a strong blender $BLE(X, Y)$ can be used as the seed input to a strong seeded entropy extractor. The second stage described an existing family of strong blender algorithms based on matrix operations and shows a new efficient way to construct the matrices.

The 2-EXT extractor blender stage uses a series of square matrices, one for each output bit. The sides of the matrices are of the same length as the 2-input bit strings $X$ and $Y$. The matrices contain only binary bits, treated as GF(2) elements. The $X$ input is left multiplied by a matrix and an inner product multiply is performed between the result of the matrix multiplication and the $Y$ input. This is repeated for each output bit, with the same $X$ and $Y$ input, but a different matrix for each output bit.

For a $k$-bit output blender, we have $k$ matrices $\{A_1, \ldots, A_k\}$. The $k$ output bits are computed as

$$\mathrm{BLE}_A(X, Y) = ((A_1 x) \cdot y, \ldots, (A_k x) \cdot y)$$

The dot $\cdot$ denotes an inner product multiply, and $A_n x$ denotes a matrix multiply of $A_n$ by $x$.

The matrices need to be full rank. We can show this with a toy example, where the bit lengths of $X$ and $Y$ are each 4 bits, and we output 4 bits. This gives an extraction ratio of 2:1, with 8 input bits ($X$ and $Y$) and 4 output bits.

The matrices $A_1, \ldots, A_4$ might be as follows (the matrix construction will be explained later):

$$A_1 = \begin{pmatrix} 1 & 0 & 0 & 0 \\ 0 & 1 & 0 & 0 \\ 0 & 0 & 1 & 0 \\ 0 & 0 & 0 & 1 \end{pmatrix}, \quad A_2 = \begin{pmatrix} 0 & 1 & 0 & 0 \\ 0 & 0 & 1 & 0 \\ 1 & 0 & 0 & 1 \\ 1 & 0 & 0 & 0 \end{pmatrix},$$

$$A_3 = \begin{pmatrix} 0 & 0 & 1 & 0 \\ 1 & 0 & 0 & 1 \\ 1 & 1 & 0 & 0 \\ 0 & 1 & 0 & 0 \end{pmatrix}, \quad A_4 = \begin{pmatrix} 1 & 0 & 0 & 1 \\ 1 & 1 & 0 & 0 \\ 0 & 1 & 1 & 0 \\ 0 & 0 & 1 & 0 \end{pmatrix}.$$

The input $X$ consists of 4 bits $X_0, X_1, X_2, X_3$, and, similarly, $Y$ consists of 4 bits $Y_0, Y_1, Y_2, Y_3$.

We construct $X$ and $Y$ into a column matrices and the output bits are computed as $A_i X \cdot Y$. Each calculation yields one bit of the output $\mathrm{Out}_0, \ldots, \mathrm{Out}_3$.

$$\mathrm{Out}_0 = \begin{pmatrix} 1 & 0 & 0 & 0 \\ 0 & 1 & 0 & 0 \\ 0 & 0 & 1 & 0 \\ 0 & 0 & 0 & 1 \end{pmatrix} \begin{pmatrix} X_3 \\ X_2 \\ X_1 \\ X_0 \end{pmatrix} \cdot \begin{pmatrix} Y_3 \\ Y_2 \\ Y_1 \\ Y_0 \end{pmatrix},$$

$$\mathrm{Out}_1 = \begin{pmatrix} 0 & 1 & 0 & 0 \\ 0 & 0 & 1 & 0 \\ 1 & 0 & 0 & 1 \\ 1 & 0 & 0 & 0 \end{pmatrix} \begin{pmatrix} X_3 \\ X_2 \\ X_1 \\ X_0 \end{pmatrix} \cdot \begin{pmatrix} Y_3 \\ Y_2 \\ Y_1 \\ Y_0 \end{pmatrix},$$

$$\mathrm{Out}_2 = \begin{pmatrix} 0 & 0 & 1 & 0 \\ 1 & 0 & 0 & 1 \\ 1 & 1 & 0 & 0 \\ 0 & 1 & 0 & 0 \end{pmatrix} \begin{pmatrix} X_3 \\ X_2 \\ X_1 \\ X_0 \end{pmatrix} \cdot \begin{pmatrix} Y_3 \\ Y_2 \\ Y_1 \\ Y_0 \end{pmatrix},$$

$$\mathrm{Out}_3 = \begin{pmatrix} 1 & 0 & 0 & 1 \\ 1 & 1 & 0 & 0 \\ 0 & 1 & 1 & 0 \\ 0 & 0 & 1 & 0 \end{pmatrix} \begin{pmatrix} X_3 \\ X_2 \\ X_1 \\ X_0 \end{pmatrix} \cdot \begin{pmatrix} Y_3 \\ Y_2 \\ Y_1 \\ Y_0 \end{pmatrix}.$$

Composed into equations, we get:

$$Out_0 = X_3Y_3 + X_2Y_2 + X_1Y_1 + X_0Y_0,$$
$$Out_1 = X_2Y_3 + X_1Y_2 + X_3X_0Y_1 + X_3Y_0,$$
$$Out_2 = X_1Y_3 + X_3X_0Y_2 + X_3X_2X_1 + X_2Y_0,$$
$$Out_3 = X_3X_0Y_3 + X_3X_2Y_2 + X_2X_1X_1 + X_1Y_0.$$

Since the bits are treated as elements in GF(2), a multiplication is equivalent to a boolean AND, and an addition is equivalent to a boolean XOR. So, in python this might be implemented as follows:

**Listing 3.15:** ble.py

```python
def ble(x3,x2,x1,x0,y3,y2,y1,y0):
    out0 = x3*y3 ^ x2*y2 ^ x1*y1 ^ x0*y0
    out1 = X_2 Y_3 + X_1 Y_2 + X_3 X_0 Y_1 + X_3 Y_0
    out2 = X_1 Y_3 + X_3 X_0 Y_2 + X_3 X_2 X_1 + X_2 Y_0
    out3 = X_3 X_0 Y_3 + X_3 X_2 Y_2 + X_2 X_1 X_1 + X_1 Y_0
    return (out3, out2, out1, out0)
```

In digital logic, it could be implemented with the following circuit (Figure 3.20):

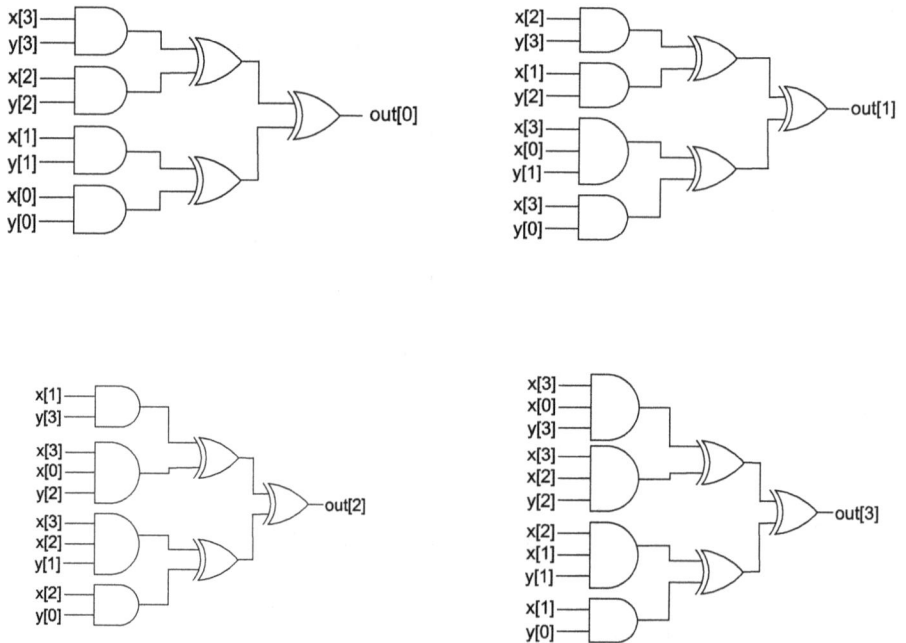

**Figure 3.20:** 2-EXT Blender Logic.

In a real-world implementation, you may want to use larger input strings in order to support a larger blender output, so the seed of the extractor stage is large enough to be useful.

The blender structure can work with random full rank matrices. So, to generate those, simply fill matrices of the appropriate size with random bits, then check if the matrix has full rank. If not, try again until you find a full-rank matrix. Repeat this process until you have one matrix for each bit of the output.

In the paper, Dodis et al. describe a number theoretic way of directly constructing matrices that will work for the blender. This yields sparser matrices than the random method, and so, the resulting computations are fewer. The description in the paper is very terse and made me and even a couple of friends with mathematics PhDs scratch our heads. After some experimentation, the algorithm in the paper was determined. It is as follows:

For bit strings of length $\ell$, choose a Galois field of the form $GF(2^\ell)$ and generate a basis as the string of values $x_1, x_2, \ldots, x_\ell$. This can be computed by taking any primitive element $m$ and computing $1, m, m^2, m^3, \ldots, m^{\ell-1}$.

In our $GF(2^4)$ example, there is only one primitive polynomial $x^4 + x + 1$. The bitfield encoding of powers of $\alpha$, where $\alpha$ is a zero of $x^4 + x + 1$, is

0001, 0010, 0100, 1000, 0011, 0110, 1100, 1011, 0101, 1010, 0111, 1110, 1111, 1101, 1001,

which in human numbers is

$$x_1 \cdots x_{15} = 1, 2, 4, 8, 3, 6, 12, 11, 5, 10, 7, 14, 15, 13, 9.$$

Now, for the tricky bit, each matrix $A_n$ is computed by left multiplication of an element in the field $y$ by $x_i$. As stated in the article,

$$A_i : y \in GF[2^\ell] \mapsto x_i y.$$

This yields the set of matrices. What was not obvious was how. It turned out that $A_i$ refers to a matrix that, when multiplied by $y$ with $y$ expressed as a column vector, results in a row vector that encodes for the element you would get, if you performed the normal Galois field multiplication $x_i y$. So, for each multiplier $x_i$, there is a square matrix that has the same effect as when multiplied as $x_i$.

In order to work out the matrix construction, a program was written to try all possible $4 \times 4$ binary matrices, perform the matrix multiplication, and see which matrix yielded the same answer as the Galois field multiplication. After identifying these matrices, it was simple to inspect them and determine the process to generate them.

Many engineers may not be familiar with Galois field theory. To clarify the process, the mechanics of the process to make the matrices are as follows:

Start with $A_1 = I$, the identity matrix, with the sides being the same length as the number of bits in the $X$ or $Y$

$$A_1 = \begin{pmatrix} 1 & 0 & 0 & 0 \\ 0 & 1 & 0 & 0 \\ 0 & 0 & 1 & 0 \\ 0 & 0 & 0 & 1 \end{pmatrix}.$$

The matrix $A_{n+1}$ is computed by first taking $A_n$ and rotating the contents right by 1:

$$\begin{pmatrix} 0 & 1 & 0 & 0 \\ 0 & 0 & 1 & 0 \\ 0 & 0 & 0 & 1 \\ 1 & 0 & 0 & 0 \end{pmatrix}.$$

Then take element $x_n$ from the basis sequence and form it into a column vector, with the lowest order bits being at the bottom, increasing to the highest order bits at the top. In this case, we have a $x_2 = 2$, which as a binary column vector would be

$$x_2 = \begin{pmatrix} 0 \\ 0 \\ 1 \\ 0 \end{pmatrix}.$$

Then, take this column and XOR it into the leftmost column of the shifted matrix to get the matrix we want

$$A_2 = \begin{pmatrix} 0 & 1 & 0 & 0 \\ 0 & 0 & 1 & 0 \\ 1 & 0 & 0 & 1 \\ 1 & 0 & 0 & 0 \end{pmatrix}.$$

For the next one, $A_3$, take $A_2$ and shift it right:

$$\begin{pmatrix} 0 & 1 & 0 & 0 \\ 0 & 0 & 1 & 0 \\ 1 & 0 & 0 & 1 \\ 1 & 0 & 0 & 0 \end{pmatrix} \longrightarrow \begin{pmatrix} 0 & 0 & 1 & 0 \\ 0 & 0 & 0 & 1 \\ 1 & 1 & 0 & 0 \\ 0 & 1 & 0 & 0 \end{pmatrix}.$$

Make a column vector out of $x_3$,

$$x_3 = 4 = \begin{pmatrix} 0 \\ 1 \\ 0 \\ 0 \end{pmatrix},$$

and XOR it into the shifted matrix

$$A_3 = \begin{pmatrix} 0 & 0 & 1 & 0 \\ 1 & 0 & 0 & 1 \\ 1 & 1 & 0 & 0 \\ 0 & 1 & 0 & 0 \end{pmatrix}.$$

Repeat the process to generate one matrix for each output bit required.

The code, in Listing 3.16, make_ext2_matrices.py to generate these matrices. It uses the gf2.py library that is provided with it to perform the GF(2) matrix manipulations. The basis vector and the $A_i$ matrices are output as text.

The degree of the generator polynomial, the element used to generate the basis vector, and the number of output bits are set on lines 7 to 9 of the program. The largest degree supported by the gf2 library is 512.

**Listing 3.16:** EXT2 Matrix Construction.

```python
#!/usr/bin/env python

import gf2 as gf
import copy

degree = 32 # largest power of the generator polynomial.
element = 2 # Element to raise powers of for the basis
seedlength = 4 # Output bit length of the blender.
                # Also the number of matrices to generate

A = list()
# Create A_1, an identity matrix
A.append(gf.make_identity_matrix(size=degree))

# Compute basis element list x_i
basis = gf.moarrrr_power_to_the_alpha(element, degree=degree, length=seedlength)
print "Basis_x_i_=_", ["0x%x" % x for x in basis[:seedlength]]
for x in range(1,seedlength):
    # compute A_{i+1}
    matrix = copy.deepcopy(A[x-1]) # copy A_{x-1}
    gf.rotate_right_matrix(matrix) # Shift ot right

    #get basis element as a column vector
    element = basis[x]
    columnv = gf.element2column(element, size=degree)

    # XOR the column vector into the left column of the matrix
    for y in xrange(degree):
        matrix[y][0] = matrix[y][0] ^ columnv[y][0]

    # Add the resulting matrix to the list
    A.append(copy.deepcopy(matrix))

for i,x in enumerate(A):
    print "matrix_A_%d" % (i+1)
    print gf.matrix2str_binary_2d(x)
```

In Figure 3.21, we show an example structure for the 2-EXT extractor with bit widths suitable for cryptographic purposes. The seeded extractor is HMAC-SHA256,

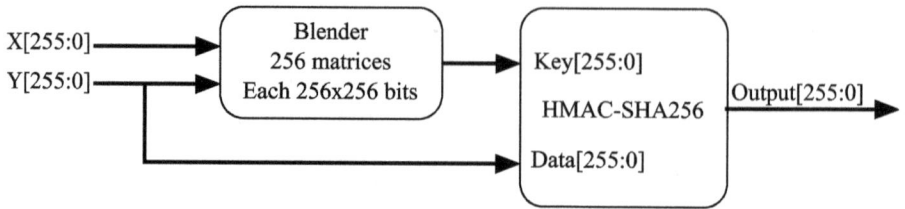

**Figure 3.21:** Example Implementation of 2-EXT.

which is compliant with the draft SP800-90B specification. The output of the blender goes into the key input of the HMAC extractor. The 256 $X$ input bits go both into the blender and the data input of the HMAC function, consistent with the 2-EXT extractor architecture.

For the blender arithmetic, the generator function for the Galois field used to make the matrices can be chosen as the lowest weight 256-bit irreducible polynomial $x^{256} + x^{10} + x^5 + x^2 + 1$.

Figure 3.21 shows the 2-EXT structure annotated with these bit size and algorithm options. The total input size is 512 bits, every 256 bits from two independent entropy sources. The output size is 256 bits. So, the extraction ratio is 2:1.

# 4 Cryptographically Secure Pseudorandom Number Generators

In this chapter we look in detail at some of the PRNG (Pseudo Random Number Generator) algorithms and their specifications. The algorithms in the specifications (with the exception of ANSI and ISO/IEC standards) are freely available and do not need to be restated directly here. Instead, we focus on illustrating how the algorithms fit into the update-output function model.

## 4.1 SP800-90A

The three SP800-90 specifications (SP800-90A, SP800-90B, and SP800-90C) are the NIST (The US National Institute for Standards and Technology) Random Number Generator specifications. It is published by the NIST CSRC (Computer Security Resource Center) http://csrc.nist.gov/ and written by the NIST CSRC, the NSA (US National Security Agency), and also with a small number of contributions from industry and the public.

The SP800-90 standard was initially published as a single document without A, B, and C suffixes. The first standard was published in June 2006. That document was withdrawn and replaced with "SP800-90 Revised" in March 2007.

The standard defined 4 DRBGs, each with many optional features allowed by the specification. Two were based on hash functions, the HASH DRBG, and the HMAC DRBG; one based on block ciphers, the CTR DRBG; one based on number theory, the Dual-EC-DRBG.

There was concern within industry and academia regarding the Dual-EC-DRBG specification. Shortly after publication of the first version of the specification, at the rump session of Crypto 2007 (an academic cryptography conference), Dan Shumow and Niels Ferguson gave a talk entitled "On the possibility of a Back Door in the NIST SP800-90 Dual-EC-DRBG" that described the back door mechanism https://rump2007.cr.yp.to/15-shumow.pdf. In addition, the Dual-EC algorithm was slow and was described in mathematical language that made it inaccessible to many. Thus, while SP800-90 algorithms were widely adopted, the Dual-EC-DRBG was not, yet it remained in the standard.

In January 2012, NIST revised SP800-90 with minor updates and changed the name from SP800-90 to SP800-90A http://nvlpubs.nist.gov/nistpubs/Legacy/SP/nistspecialpublication800-90a.pdf. They started the process of developing SP800-90B and SP800-90C, which were specifications for entropy sources and full RNG constructions, respectively.

Following revelations in 2013 by Edward Snowden that the NSA had put back doors into cryptographic and communication standards, it became widely reported

https://doi.org/10.1515/9781501506062-004

in the media that the Dual-EC-DRBG had been back-doored by the NSA. This led to NIST removing the Dual-EC-DRBG from the standard and this was published as SP800-90Arev1 http://nvlpubs.nist.gov/nistpubs/SpecialPublications/NIST.SP.800-90Ar1.pdf in June 2015. There was a comment period for this, and unlike previous drafts, there were many comments from industry and academia. So, there were a number of other changes in the details of the specification.

It is notable that NIST was not motivated to remove the back-doored algorithm from the standard until there was widespread media attention, even though it was commonly understood to be back-doored by cryptographers and engineers for 6 years prior to the media attention.

The S800-90A Revision 1 remains the standard at the time of writing, whereas SP800-90B and SP800-90C remain in draft form and have not become standards.

The DRBG algorithms in SP800-90A include optional components, the personalization string, Additional Input (for forward prediction resistance), and the derivation function "*df*" (a poor type of entropy extractor), which is optional for the CTR DRBG but mandatory for the Hash DRBG and not an option for the HMAC DRBG. This makes KAT (Known Answer Testing, see Chapter 8) testing for the purposes of certification of implementations a challenge, due to the high number of possible combinations of algorithm choice and key sizes.

### 4.1.1 SP800-90A Hash DRBG

The hash DRBG builds algorithms around an underlying hash function, for example, SHA-256 and SHA-512.

**State:** The size of the state variable depends on the output size of the hash functions used. For example, if SHA256 is used, the state variable size will be 256 bits.

The state variables of the Hash DRBG are the seed $V$, $C$ (a working value), and reseed_counter.

The size of V and C in bits are given in Table 4.1 below in the Seed Length column.

**Instantiate Algorithm:** The Instantiate function is called to initialize the DRBG.

**Table 4.1:** Hash DRBG State and Block Sizes.

| Hash Algorithm | Hash Output Block Size | Seed Length |
|---|---|---|
| SHA-1 | 160 | 440 |
| SHA-224 | 224 | 440 |
| SHA-256 | 256 | 440 |
| SHA384 | 384 | 888 |
| SHA-512 | 512 | 888 |

There are four inputs:

entropy_input: Entropic data from the entropy source or extractor.

nonce: A number that is unique to the instance of the DRBG. It may be randomly generated, or generated from a timestamp or a fixed value created differently for each instance of the DRBG. It does not need to be kept secret.

personalization_string: A string of bits that may be zero length.

pr_flag: A binary flag to request prediction resistance.

The initial value of state variable $V$ is computed as shown in Figure 4.1.

The initial value of state variable $C$ is computed as shown in Figure 4.2.

reseed_counter is set to 1.

**Reseed Function:** The reseed function takes in fresh entropy, along with any additional input updates $V$ and $C$ and resets reseed_counter to 1.

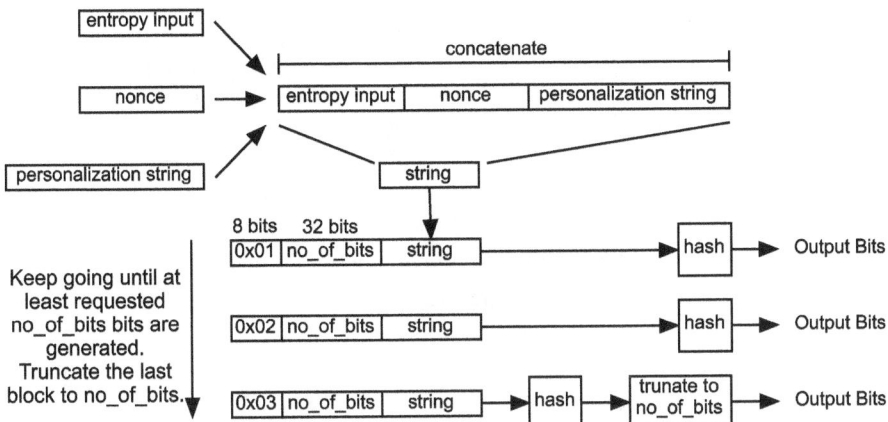

**Figure 4.1:** Computing $V$ in the Hash DRBG Instantiate Function.

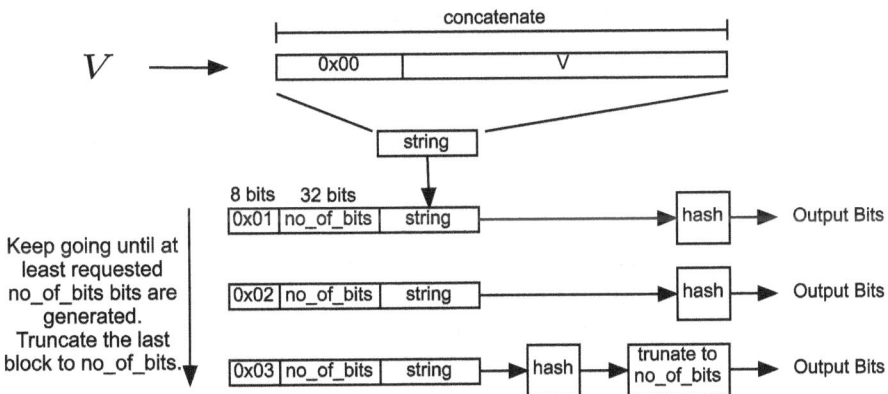

**Figure 4.2:** Computing $C$ in the Hash DRBG Instantiate Function.

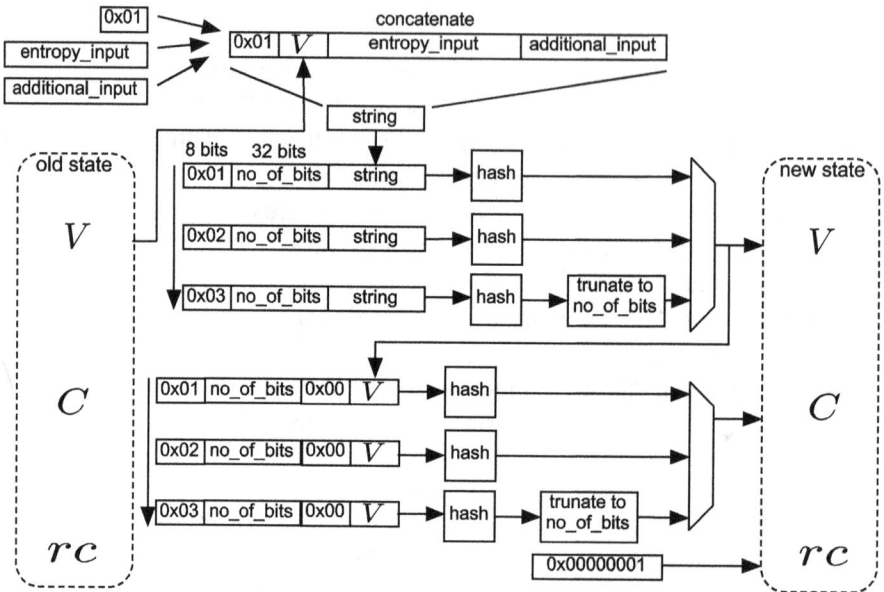

**Figure 4.3:** Hash DRBG Reseed Function.

For $V$, the input entropy, additional input and the previous value of $V$ are formatted into a string which is fed into the hash_df function, which iteratively hashes the string, prefixed with a counter until a sufficient number of bits are generated for the new state of $V$.

The next value of $C$ is generated as a function of this new value of $V$, using the same iterative algorithm as for $V$.

reseed_counter is reset to 1.

The structure of the algorithm is shown in Figure 4.3.

**State Update:** The state update and output function of a generic PRNG are both merged into the generate() function of the hash DRBG, which both generates output data and updates the internal state.

A data flow diagram of the state update is shown in Figure 4.4.

When prediction resistance is requested, additional input entropy data is input, prepended with (0x02 || V) and the resulting string hashed with the underlying hash function to derive the value $w$. Then, update $V$ by adding $w$.

$$V = V + w \bmod \text{ seed length}.$$

If there is no additional input then skip this step.
Compute

$$H = \text{Hash}(0x03||V)$$

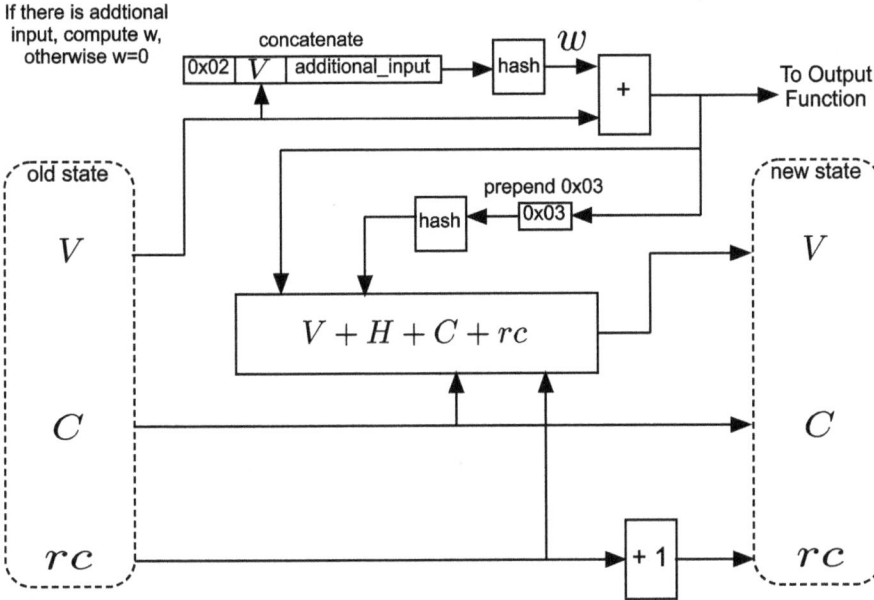

**Figure 4.4:** Hash DRBG State Update.

The new state of V is computed by adding together $V$, $H$, $C$, and reseed_counter.

$$V = V + H + C + \text{ reseed\_counter mod seed length.}$$

$C$ remains unchanged.

reseed_counter is incremented.

**Output Function:** The output function starts with the value of $V$, after it has been updated with $w$ in the update function. A copy of $V$ is taken (called data in the specification) and, in a loop, the value of data is hashed to create some output data and then incremented. Once there is sufficient output data to meet the requested number of bits, the output data is returned, as shown in Figure 4.5.

### 4.1.1.1 Observations on the SP800-90A Hash DRBG

When you compare the generic PRNG structure against output and update functions of the Hash DRBG, the Hash DRBG appears to be more complex than necessary. There are multiple stages of hashing and looping in each stage, when all that is required is a one-way function with the right properties.

The state sizes are not a multiple of the hash output, so truncation of the hash output is required.

The update function uses integer addition on numbers that are 440 or 888 bits for no apparent benefit. In hardware this is slow, in software this requires custom large integer addition code that can be a source of bugs and timing side channels.

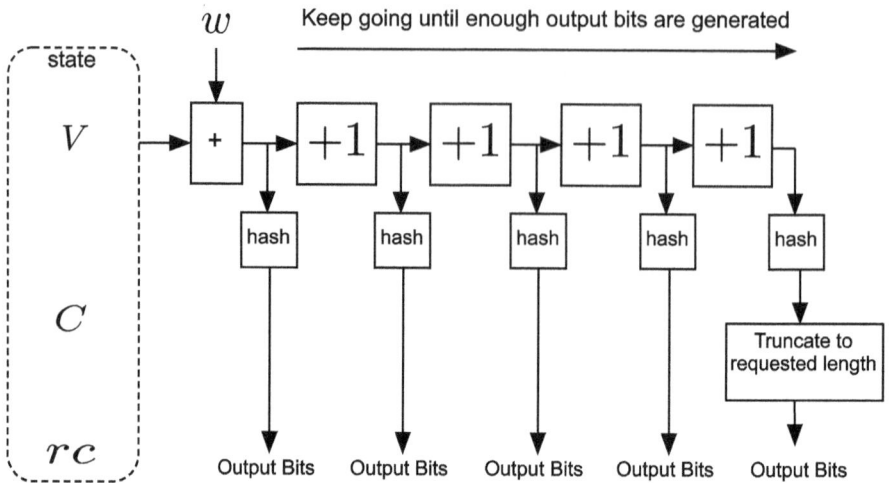

**Figure 4.5:** Hash DRBG Output Function.

The output and update functions are not independent. An intermediate state of the output function $V + w$ is used as input to the output function.

### 4.1.2 SP800-90A HMAC DRBG

The HMAC DRBG builds algorithms around an underlying HMAC-function, such as HMAC-SHA256 or HMAC-SHA512. HMAC is a message authentication algorithm that is built using an underlying hash function. So, the name of an HMAC function is HMAC followed by the hash function it uses. For example, HMAC-SHA256 is HMAC using the SHA256 hash function.

**State:** The size of the state variable depends on the output size of the hash functions used.

The state variable $V$ is the size of the output of the hash function. This follows the sizes given in Table 4.1.

The state variable $K$ is the same size as $V$.

reseed_counter is typically a 32-bit integer, but needs only be large enough to contain the maximum reseed interval for the implementation.

**Update Algorithm:** The HMAC DRBG builds the primary functions (Instantiate, Generate, and Reseed) using the update function. This takes in the current state of $K$ and $V$ and optionally some additional entropy input of arbitrary size and computes new values for $K$ and $V$.

If there is no entropy input to the HMAC_update function, then the function is as follows:

$$\text{string} = V||0x00||\text{input\_entropy}$$

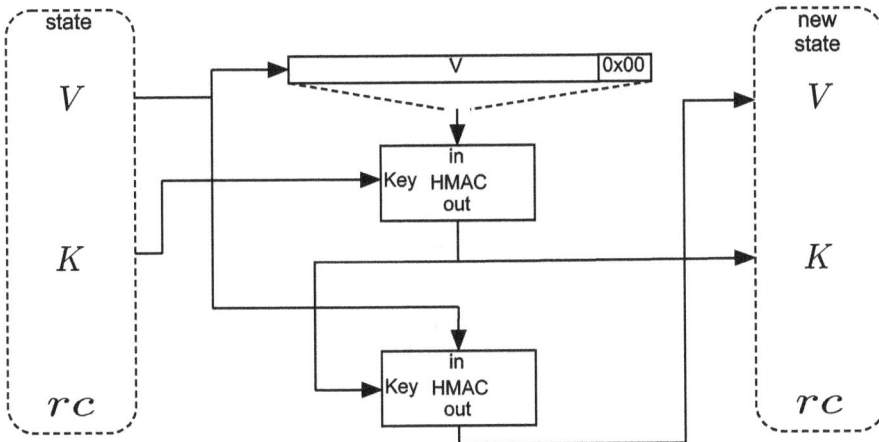

**Figure 4.6:** HMAC DRBG Update Function Without Entropy Input.

$$K = \text{HMAC}(K, \text{string})$$
$$V = \text{HMAC}(K, V)$$

This is shown in Figure 4.6.

If there is entropy input, then, there is a second step to the algorithm and the input is processed twice. Note that the 0x00 inserted into the string in the first HMAC input string is changed to 0x01 in the second invocation.

$$\text{string} = V||0x00||\text{input\_entropy}$$
$$K = \text{HMAC}(K, \text{string})$$
$$V = \text{HMAC}(K, V)$$
$$\text{string} = V||0x01||\text{input\_entropy}$$
$$K = \text{HMAC}(K, \text{string})$$
$$V = \text{HMAC}(K, V)$$

This is shown in Figure 4.7.

**Instantiate Algorithm:** The Instantiate function is called to initialize the HMAC DRBG.

The inputs are the same as for the Hash DRBG:

entropy_input: Entropic data from the entropy source or extractor.

nonce: A number that is unique to the instance of the DRBG. It may be randomly generated, or generated from a timestamp or a fixed value created differently for each instance of the DRBG. It does not need to be kept secret.

personalization_string: A string of bits that may be zero length.

The input material is concatenated into a string seed_material, $K$ is set to 0, and $V$ is set to a string of 0x01 bytes. The update function is called to apply the input entropy

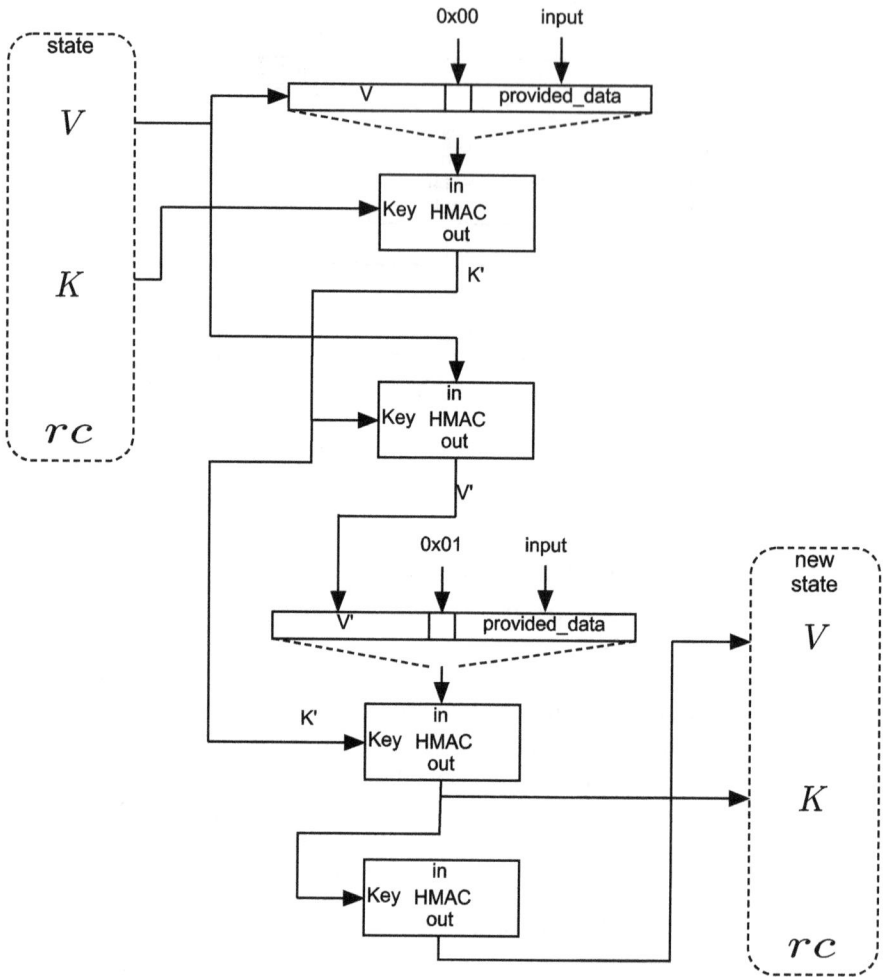

**Figure 4.7:** HMAC DRBG Update Function With Entropy Input.

to the state of the DRBG, and, finally, reseed_counter is set to 1.

$K = 0$

$V = 0x010101\ldots$

seed_material = entropy_input||nonce||personalization_string

$(K, V) = \text{HMAC\_DRBG\_Update}(\text{seed\_material}, K, V)$

reseed_counter = 1

**Reseed Algorithm:** The reseed algorithm is identical to the instantiation algorithm, except that the *nonce* and personalization_string are replaced with the additional_input string and the $K$ and $V$ variables are not cleared.

$$\text{seed\_material} = \text{entropy\_input}||\text{additional\_input}$$
$$(K, V) = \text{HMAC\_DRBG\_Update}(\text{seed\_material}, K, V)$$
$$\text{reseed\_counter} = 1$$

**Generate Function:** As with all the SP800-90 DRBGs, the output function is called Generate() and is tightly linked to the update function.

If there is additional_input provided to the generate function for prediction resistance, then, this is first mixed into the state, otherwise this step is skipped.

$$(K, V) = \text{HMAC\_DRBG\_Update}(\text{additional}_{\text{input}}, K, V)$$

Thereafter, the following steps are run in a loop until the requested number of bits have been generated. If prediction resistance is enabled, the additional_input will contain entropy data, otherwise it will be null.

$$V = \text{HMAC}(K, V)$$
$$\text{Output} = V$$
$$(\text{Key}, V) = \text{HMAC\_DRBG\_Update}(\text{additional\_input}, \text{Key}, V)$$
$$\text{reseed\_counter} = \text{reseed\_counter} + 1$$

### 4.1.2.1 Observations on the SP800-90A HMAC DRBG

Compared to the Hash DRBG, the HMAC DRBG is much better organized. There is a primary function HMAC_DRBG_Update that is used by the instantiation, generation, and reseeding functions. So, there is much less design complexity and it is simpler to ensure the design runs in constant time, thus limiting timing based side channel attacks.

The HMAC function is a known good entropy extractor. Therefore, this DRBG is also effective when there is no entropy extractor feeding full entropy input, and so, the input is partially entropic.

The HMAC DRBG is the most computationally intensive of the three DRBGs. So, it can be thought of as the least efficient, but likely to be the most algorithmically secure structure of the three options.

### 4.1.3 SP800-90A CTR DRBG

The CTR DRBG builds algorithms around the CTR (counter) mode algorithm, using an underlying block cipher function. Presently the only NIST-compliant block cipher options are the AES algorithms, which come with key sizes of 128, 192, and 256 bits.

Triple DES is also a block cipher option in the SP800-90A standard. However, this is an obsolete block cipher with a block size of only 64 bits, which impacts the security of the cipher and is deprecated for new implementations. So, we will ignore the Triple DES option.

**State:** The state variables are $K$, which is equal to the key size of the chosen AES algorithm. $V$ is always 128 bits, since the block size of AES is constant at 128 bits. Although, if larger, block ciphers become an option; the size of $V$ would then be equal to the block size of the block cipher.

The final state variable is reseed_counter.

The reseed_counter is typically a 32-bit integer, but needs only be large enough to contain the maximum reseed interval for the implementation.

Like the HMAC DRBG, there is an update function defined, which is also used by the initialize and reseed functions.

**CTR Algorithm:** The CTR algorithm generates a sequence of pseudorandom blocks from an initialization vector (IV) and a key, by repeatedly incrementing and encrypting the IV value. The IV size is equal to the data block size of the block cipher. The structure of the algorithm is shown in Figure 4.8.

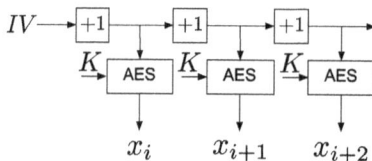

**Figure 4.8:** CTR Algorithm.

This is the underlying algorithm used to generate both the output data and the next state for the CTR DRBG.

For the CTR algorithm to be secure, it is necessary that each value of the incremented IV be unique when used with the same key, otherwise repeated use of the same IV will result in the same output value.

The number of iterations of the increment, encrypt loop in the CTR algorithm is limited to a small integer. So, it is alright if, instead of incrementing the entire 128 bit field of the IV, a subset of the bits of the IV can be incremented. For example, the lower 8 bits might be incremented. Thus, the value of the lower 8 bits might roll over from 0xFF to 0x00. However, as long as the number of iterations is less than $2^8$, all the values of the lower 8 bits visited will be unique.

Older versions of the SP800-90A specification did not permit this behavior, and so, this required a full 128-bit integer addition for the CTR mode. Based on input to NIST from this author, suggesting that the counter operation be permitted to be over a subset of the IV bits, NIST amended the 2012Rev1 specification to allow incrementing a subset of bits. This change was necessary to allow higher-performance hardware implementations of the CTR DRBG. For example, the Intel DRBG that feeds the RdRand instruction in Intel CPUs increments a 16-bit field in the IV in order to achieve the frequency performance necessary for the RdRand instruction.

**Update Algorithm:** The update value takes input provided_data and the state variables Key and $V$ and results in updated values for Key and $V$.

The CTR algorithm is called with the Key as the key and $V$ as the IV. Sufficient blocks of data are generated to supply seedlen bits, where seedlen equals the length of Key + the length of $V$.

If provided_data is input (is not NULL), then, this must be equal in length to seedlen, and this is XORed with the CTR output.

The new value for Key is taken from the left keylength bits of the CTR output. The new value for $V$ is taken from the next 128 bits of the CTR output.

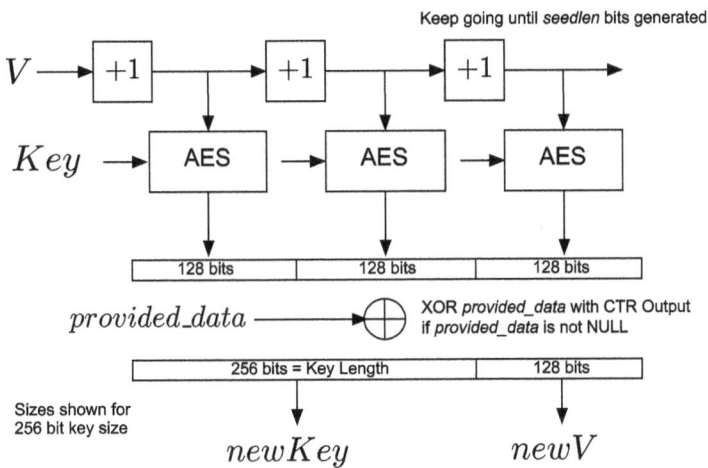

**Figure 4.9:** CTR DRBG Update Algorithm.

Figure 4.9 shows the update procedure for a 256-bit key. If the key size is 128, then, there will be only two invocations of AES to generate 128 bits for the Key update and 128 bits for the $V$ update.

If a key size of 192 bits is used, the length of the block output of CTR algorithm will not equal seedlen, since the output length of CTR mode with AES is a multiple of 128 bits (256, 384, or 512 bits), whereas for 192-bit keys, seedlen = 192 + 128 = 320. Therefore, with 192-bit keys, the leftover output of the CTR operation is discarded. This is a complication that provides a good reason to not use 192-bit keys with the CTR DRBG, particularly in hardware implementations, where data may be shuffled around on 128-bit and 256-bit busses, and nonaligned shifting operations would require additional data shuffling logic.

The update algorithm is used directly as the state update function and also as the reseed function.

**Instantiate Algorithm:** The instantiate function is called to initialize the CTR DRBG.

Inputs are entropy_input and personalization_string. entropy_input must be seedlen bits in length. The specification states "Ensure that the length of the personalization_string is exactly seedlen bits", but, then, goes on to describe a padding procedure, if it is shorter than seedlen. So, it is unclear whether or not personalization_string is required to be seedlen bits long.

personalization_string is an optional input and may be NULL.

The steps are:

Set Key = 0

Set $V$ = 0

If length of personalization_string < seedlen, then append seedlen – len(personalization_string) bits to the right of personalization_string.

Compute seed_material = personalization_string xor entropy_input

Set (Key, $V$) = CTR_DRBG_Update(seed_material, Key, $V$)

Set reseed_counter = 1

Note that aside from zeroing Key and $V$, this procedure is the same as the reseed procedure, and so, a normal implementation would simply clear Key and $V$ and, then, call the reseed function, instead of implementing a separate instantiation algorithm.

To address issues of the startup output of the entropy source having low quality immediately after power on, it is common to call reseed multiple times during initialization to ensure that the state of the DRBG has sufficient entropy. For example, the Intel DRNG calls reseed four times during initialization.

**Reseed Algorithm:** The reseed algorithm takes in new entropy and updates Key and $V$ using that entropy as input to the update algorithm.

The reseed algorithm is identical to the initialization algorithm, except that Key and $V$ are not cleared to zero before being updated.

The steps are:

If length of personalization_string < seedlen, then append seedlen – len(personalization_string) bits to the right of personalization_string.

Compute seed_material = personalization_string $\oplus$ entropy_input

Set (Key, $V$) = CTR_DRBG_Update(seed_material, Key, $V$)

Set reseed_counter = 1

**Generate Algorithm:** The generate algorithm is called to generate random data for output.

If additional_input is supplied with the call to generate, then the generate function begins with a call to update Key and $V$, using the additional_input bits.

$$(Key, V) = CTR\_DRBG\_Update(additional\_input, Key, V).$$

If additional_input is null, then that step is skipped.

The output data is generated using the CTR algorithm, incrementing and encrypting $V$ until the requested amount of data is generated.

The final step is a call to Update to the update function.

$$(Key, V) = CTR\_DRBG\_Update(additional\_input, Key, V),$$

where additional_input may be present or be null.

The specification is not clear, if the additional_input in this call to update is the same as the additional_input in the first call. The algorithm description implies it is, but this makes no sense and the logical inference is that, if used, it would consist of new random data from the entropy source.

Figure 4.10 shows the generate–update algorithm as a single CTR mode expansion from Key and $V$ generating the output data along with the new values for Key and $V$ in the update call.

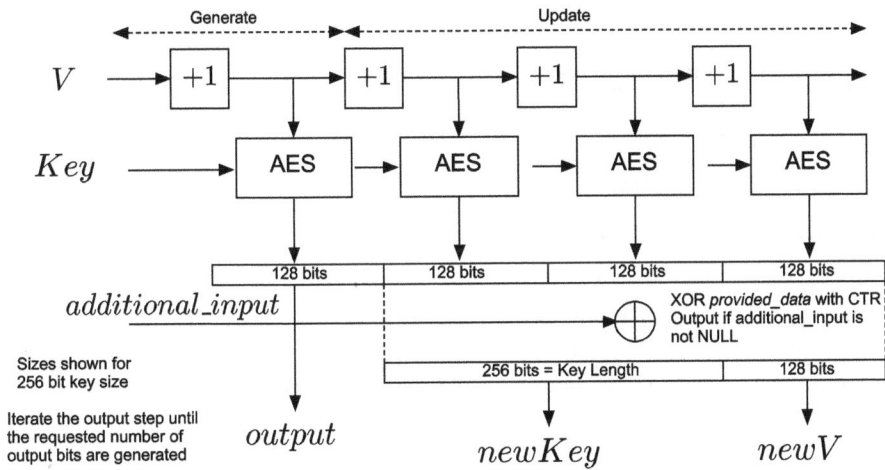

**Figure 4.10:** CTR DRBG Generate Algorithm.

Note that the initial update, when additional_input is given, is not shown.

The generate stage, where the CTR algorithm is run to generate output data may be more than one step. The specification states that the generate part should be iterated until the requested number of bits are generated. In hardware implementations, it is common for the generate step to be a fixed number of iterations (e. g. 1) since the request is typically limited to a fixed size, such as reading from a fixed size register. Software implementations are typically more flexible.

### 4.1.4 Observations On the CTR DRBG

The CTR DRBG is the most computationally efficient of the three DRBGs in the SP800-90A specification. This is because the AES function is significantly computationally cheaper than the SHA or HMAC-SHA algorithms.

The generate function calls update every time it is invoked. In Figure 4.11, the gen blocks indicate the CTR steps to generate output and the Upd blocks indicate the call to update made by the generate function.

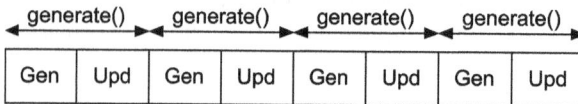

| generate() | | generate() | | generate() | | generate() | |
|---|---|---|---|---|---|---|---|
| Gen | Upd | Gen | Upd | Gen | Upd | Gen | Upd |

**Figure 4.11:** CTR DRBG Generate–Update Sequence.

However, when reseed is called, the final update of the generate sequence is wasted since its state is overwritten with the reseed as shown in Figure 4.12.

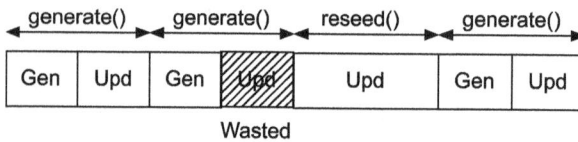

| generate() | | generate() | | reseed() | | generate() | |
|---|---|---|---|---|---|---|---|
| Gen | Upd | Gen | Upd | Upd | | Gen | Upd |

Wasted

**Figure 4.12:** CTR DRBG Wasted Update Before Reseed.

If you are using additional input entropy with each update, there are even more wasted entropy and updates. Every final call to update in the generate call is overwritten by the initial update in the next generate call to stir in the additional entropy. See Figure 4.13.

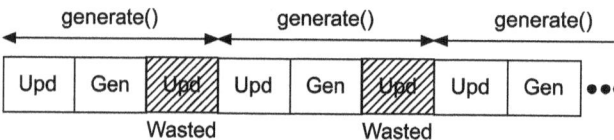

| | generate() | | | generate() | | | generate() | |
|---|---|---|---|---|---|---|---|---|
| Upd | Gen | Upd | Upd | Gen | Upd | Upd | Gen | ••• |

Wasted          Wasted

**Figure 4.13:** CTR DRBG Wasted Additional Entropy With Prediction Resistance Enabled.

The logical thing to do to achieve prediction resistance is just to require a single reseed between each generated output, without any intervening update calls, as shown in Figure 4.14. However, this would be a violation of the SP800-90A CTR DRBG specification, and so, would not be able to be certified as being compliant to SP800-90A.

generate() Reseed() generate() Reseed() generate()

| Gen | Upd | Gen | Upd | Gen |
|------|------|------|------|------|

No Entropy Wasted

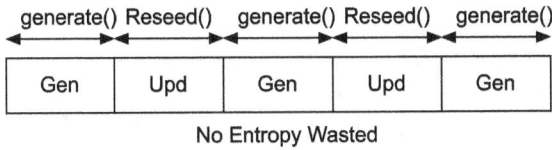

**Figure 4.14:** CTR DRBG More Efficient Prediction Resistance Scheme.

For "non-SP800-90" applications, it would be simpler and faster and have the same security properties as a compliant CTR_DRBG with prediction resistance.

## 4.2 ANSI X9-82

We will not go into detail with the ANSI X9.82 specifications since they are mostly written by the same people that wrote SP800-90 and contain the same algorithms.

The structure of the specifications is different to SP800-90 as shown in Table 4.2.

**Table 4.2:** Relationship Between ANSI X982 and NIST SP800-90.

| ANSI Document | Title | Equivalent NIST Document | Function |
|---|---|---|---|
| X9-82 Part 1 | Overview and Basic Principles | | Introduction to RBGs |
| X9-82 Part 2 | Nondeterministic Random Bit Generators | SP800-90A | HASH, HMAC and CTR DRBGs |
| X9-82 Part 3 | Number Theoretic Random Bit Generators | SP800-90A | Dual-EC (withdrawn) and other number theoretic DRBGs |
| X9-82 Part 4 | Constructions for RBGs | SP800-90 B and C | Entropy Sources, Extractors and how to combine with DRBGs |

The ANSI specifications are not free. At the time of writing, the ANSI specifications each cost (in US Dollars) $60, so $240 for the complete set. Since the NIST documents contain the same information and are freely available, there is not much motivation to pay for the ANSI specifications.

## 4.3 Salsa20

Salsa20 is a secure PRNG, intended for use as a stream cipher. Here, we will look at its design as a PRNG.

A derivative version called "Cha Cha" updated some of the internal algorithms in Salsa20, which we will look at in Section 4.4.

The Salsa20 specification is available from https://cr.yp.to/snuffle/spec.pdf.

In order to get the full specification for the Cha Cha algorithm, you will need to read both the Salsa20 and the Cha Cha specifications. The Cha Cha specification updates some of the inner algorithms in Salsa20 without describing the rest of the algorithm.

The Cha Cha algorithm is a stream cipher, meaning it is a PRNG that produces a stream of pseudorandom bits based on its secret state. To be used as a cipher the stream of bits is XORed with the plaintext to get ciphertext.

The basic structure for the PRNG is a hash function used in counter mode, as shown in Figure 4.15. This is similar to the output function of the SP800-90 Hash DRBG, as shown in Figure 4.5. The hash used here is defined by the specification.

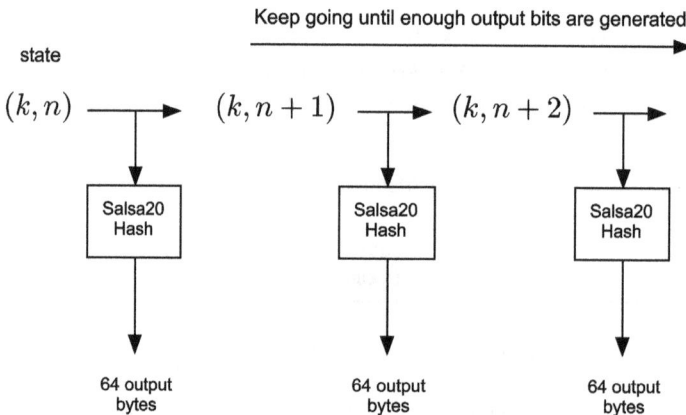

**Figure 4.15:** CTR Mode Output of Salsa20 and Cha Cha.

The counter is the number $n$ and the key is $k$. A notable feature is the large block-size. Each output of the Salsa20 hash is 64 bytes or 512 bits.

You may observe correctly, in Figure 4.15, that we are feeding a key $k$ into each hash. However, a hash function does not take in a key. The key $k$ and $n$ are both placed into specific places in the normal input of the hash. This structure can be viewed as a 64-byte structure arranged as a $4 \times 4$ matrix of 32-bit integers. Each 32-bit integer is built from 4 bytes from the input. Salsa20 operates on this 64-byte structure

$$\begin{pmatrix} x_0 & x_1 & x_2 & x_3 \\ x_4 & x_5 & x_6 & x_7 \\ x_8 & x_9 & x_{10} & x_{11} \\ x_{12} & x_{13} & x_{14} & x_{15} \end{pmatrix}.$$

Each entry $x_n$ is a 32-bit integer with 4 input bytes.

The nonce $n$ is 16 bytes/128 bits. The key $k$ is either 16 bytes/128 bits, or 32 bytes/256 bits. If we split the 128 bit $k$ into 4 32-bit words $k_0$ to $k_3$ and split the 256-bit version of

$k$ into 8 32-bit words $k_0$ to $k_7$, and we split $n$ into 4 32-bit words $n_0$ to $n_4$, we can show how the parts of $k$ and $n$ are positioned in the matrix.

For the 256-bit key, the $k$ and $n$ are placed as follows:

$$\begin{pmatrix} \sigma_0 & k_0 & k_1 & k_2 \\ k_3 & \sigma_1 & n_0 & n_1 \\ n_2 & n_3 & \sigma_2 & k_4 \\ k_5 & k_6 & k_7 & \sigma_3 \end{pmatrix}.$$

The other values $\sigma_0$, $\sigma_1$, $\sigma_2$, and $\sigma_3$ are constants:

$$\sigma_0 = 0x65, 0x78, 0x70, 0x61,$$
$$\sigma_1 = 0x6e, 0x64, 0x20, 0x33,$$
$$\sigma_2 = 0x32, 0x2d, 0x62, 0x79,$$
$$\sigma_3 = 0x74, 0x65, 0x20, 0x6B.$$

For the 128-bit key, the key is placed as follows:

$$\begin{pmatrix} \tau_0 & k_0 & k_1 & k_2 \\ k_3 & \tau_1 & n_0 & n_1 \\ n_2 & n_3 & \tau_2 & k_0 \\ k_1 & k_2 & k_3 & \tau_3 \end{pmatrix}.$$

The other values $\tau_0$, $\tau_1$, $\tau_2$ and $\tau_3$ are constants:

$$\tau_0 = 0x65, 0x78, 0x70, 0x61,$$
$$\tau_1 = 0x63, 0x64, 0x20, 0x31,$$
$$\tau_2 = 0x36, 0x2d, 0x62, 0x79,$$
$$\tau_3 = 0x74, 0x65, 0x20, 0x6b.$$

The example software implementation is written in C in order to take advantage of the implicit modulo 32-bit arithmetic available in C.

The C function in Listing 4.1 implements the placement of $k$ and $v$ in the matrix and then calls the hash function over the matrix.

**Listing 4.1:** Salsa20 Matrix Construction

```
void salsa20kn(uint8_t *k, int klen, uint8_t *n, uint8_t *result) {
    uint8_t key[64];
    int i;
    /* sigma0, tau0 */
    key[0]=101; key[1]=120; key[2]=112; key[3]=97;

    if (klen==16) {
        for(i=0;i<16;i++) key[i+4] = k[i];
```

```
    key[20]=110; key[21]=100; key[22]=32; key[23]=49; /*tau1*/
    for(i=0;i<16;i++) key[i+24] = n[i];
    key[40]=54; key[41]=45; key[42]=98; key[43]=121; /*tau2*/
    for(i=0;i<16;i++) key[i+44] = k[i];
  }
  else if (klen==32) {
    for(i=0;i<16;i++) key[i+4] = k[i];
    key[20]=110; key[21]=100; key[22]=32; key[23]=51; /*sigma1*/
    for(i=0;i<16;i++) key[i+24] = n[i];
    key[40]=50; key[41]=45; key[42]=98; key[43]=121; /*sigma2*/
    for(i=0;i<16;i++) key[i+44] = k[i+16];
  }
  key[60]=116; key[61]=101; key[62]=32; key[63]=107; /*tau & sigma3*/

  salsa20_hash(key,result);
}
```

### 4.3.1 Salsa20 Hash

With the starting state of the matrix, the hash function proceeds by performing an ARX (Add Rotate Xor) operation on groups of 4 32-bit words called quarterround($x$) in the specification.

For 4 words, $x = (a, b, c, d)$, the operation $z = $ quarterround($x$) is

$$z_1 = b \oplus ((a + d) <<< 7),$$
$$z_2 = c \oplus ((z_1 + a) <<< 9),$$
$$z_3 = d \oplus ((z_2 + z_1) <<< 13),$$
$$z_0 = a \oplus ((z_3 + z_2) <<< 18).$$

These operations need to be executed in the order shown. The $+$ is a 32-bit integer addition. The $\oplus$ is 32-bit bitwise xor. The $<<< n$ is the 32-bit left rotate by n operator.

In C, this can be implemented as shown in Listing 4.2:

**Listing 4.2:** Salsa20 quarter round function.

```
uint32_t rol(uint32_t x,uint32_t amount) {
    return ((x << amount ) | (x >> (32 - amount)));
}
uint32_t ror(uint32_t x,uint32_t amount) {
    return ((x >> amount) | (x << (32-amount)));
}

void quarterround(uint32_t y0,uint32_t y1,uint32_t y2,uint32_t y3,
                  uint32_t *z0,uint32_t *z1,uint32_t *z2,uint32_t *z3) {
    *z1 = y1 ^ rol((y0 + y3),7);
```

```
*z2 = y2 ^ rol((*z1 + y0),9);
*z3 = y3 ^ rol((*z2 + *z1),13);
*z0 = y0 ^ rol((*z3 + *z2),18);
}
```

There are two types of round function in the hash. The first is the columnround (see Table 4.3), which performs quarterround on each of the columns in the matrix. This is followed by the rowround (see Table 4.4), which performs quarterround on each of the rows of the matrix.

**Table 4.3:** Column Round.

| $\tau_0$ | $k_0$ | $k_1$ | $k_2$ |
|---|---|---|---|
| $k_3$ | $\tau_1$ | $n_0$ | $n_1$ |
| $n_2$ | $n_3$ | $\tau_2$ | $k_0$ |
| $k_1$ | $k_2$ | $k_3$ | $\tau_3$ |

**Table 4.4:** Row Round.

| $\tau_0$ | $k_0$ | $k_1$ | $k_2$ |
|---|---|---|---|
| $k_3$ | $\tau_1$ | $n_0$ | $n_1$ |
| $n_2$ | $n_3$ | $\tau_2$ | $k_0$ |
| $k_1$ | $k_2$ | $k_3$ | $\tau_3$ |

A C implementation of the doubleround function is shown in Listing 4.3.

**Listing 4.3:** Salsa20 Double Round Function

```
void doubleround(uint32_t *x, uint32_t *z) {
    uint32_t t[16];
    /* ARX Columns */
    quarterround(x[0],x[4],x[8],x[12],    &t[0], &t[4] ,&t[8]  ,&t[12]);
    quarterround(x[5],x[9],x[13],x[1],    &t[5], &t[9] ,&t[13] ,&t[1]);
    quarterround(x[10],x[14],x[2],x[6],   &t[10], &t[14] ,&t[2]  ,&t[6]);
    quarterround(x[15],x[3],x[7],x[11],   &t[15], &t[3] ,&t[7]  ,&t[11]);
    /* ARX  rows */
    quarterround(t[0],t[1],t[2],t[3],     &z[0], &z[1] ,&z[2] ,&z[3]);
    quarterround(t[5],t[6],t[7],t[4],     &z[5], &z[6] ,&z[7] ,&z[4]);
    quarterround(t[10],t[11],t[8],t[9],   &z[10],&z[11] ,&z[8] ,&z[9]);
    quarterround(t[15],t[12],t[13],t[14],&z[15],&z[12] ,&z[13] ,&z[14]);
}
```

The row and column rounds are repeated 10 times for a total of 20 rounds. Two additional functions littleendian and littleendian_inv convert between groups of 4 bytes and words, and back again.

The final step is to add the original words of the input matrix to the final state of the matrix. A C implementation is shown in Listing 4.4.

**Listing 4.4:** Salsa20 Hash Function

```
uint32_t littleendian(uint8_t b0,uint8_t b1,uint8_t b2,uint8_t b3) {
    return (b0 + (b1 << 8) + (b2 << 16) + (b3 << 24)); }

void littleendian_inv(uint32_t b, uint8_t *z) {
    z[0] = (b & 0xff); z[1] = (b >> 8) & 0xff;
    z[2] = (b >> 16) & 0xff; z[3] = (b >> 24) & 0xff; }

void salsa20_hash(unsigned char *xin, unsigned char*zout) {
    uint32_t x[16];
    uint32_t z[16];
    uint32_t temp[16];
    int i;

    for(i=0;i<16;i++)
        x[i] = littleendian(xin[(4*i)],xin[(4*i)+1],
                            xin[(4*i)+2],xin[(4*i)+3]);

    doubleround(x,temp); /* 10 Rounds */
    for(i=0;i<4;i++) {
        doubleround(temp,z);
        doubleround(z,temp);
    }
    doubleround(temp,z);

    /* Add input matrix to final matrix */
    for(i=0;i<16;i++) z[i] = z[i]+x[i];
    for(i=0;i<16;i++) littleendian_inv(z[i],&zout[i*4]);
}
```

The C implementation is written with a main function that calls the Salsa hash function 4 times, with $n$ incrementing each time. The output is 4 64-byte sequences. In the result below, each sequence occupies two lines.

```
$ ./salsa20
bded979a09603c623e662040d898c846a23f7fcbc82c0519a6ec56793a2348ce
c7e59ec50af68e2cef92beb028a7be47b81f76d12abc40f521629e44bee3ab70
53f951ea197070ebefbcc8b787f7bda0c8fff8923f08ea765e4066226993c25e
6742706ee4b0831eb269884b6db02c064d0ec4101491fe196fc19f091e08fb32
f13fab6106a71476c9418f9a6635d43b47b943ff975681aa19bb06a375514c0c
c4a92c5391c5728533bc7463f1ea121f9cc3d284d92d5e9e9a81f32d3ed99249
c7bbc9c3f4d9ad59c6713f3afdaca5d2362a4a979b4b9c3a5885e065a78641d4
bf8aa2b367a970d381230f23642480c23a0f4cdfe204776dfefbfb8a29d76ab9
$
```

The Salsa20 algorithm is designed primarily for software implementation and so the state elements are unsigned 32-bit integers. The 32-bit XOR, modulo $2^{32}$ integer addition, and 32-bit rotate operations are used in the round function, which are operations that map directly to instructions in most CPU instruction sets.

## 4.4 Cha Cha

The Cha Cha specification is available at https://cr.yp.to/chacha/chacha-20080128.pdf.

The changes improve some of the security properties relative to Salsa20 and the structure of the matrix has been improved to better performance in SSE implementations on X86 CPUs.

Reference code is provided at https://cr.yp.to/chacha.html, which includes high-performance assembly implementations using the SSE extensions in Intel and AMD CPUs.

Relative to Salsa20, the quarterround function has been updated to be as follows:

$$z_0 = a + b; \quad z_3 = d \oplus a; \quad z_3 = z_3 <<< 16,$$
$$z_2 = z_2 + z_4; \quad z_1 = b \oplus z_2; \quad z_1 = z_2 <<< 12,$$
$$z_0 = a + z_1; \quad z_3 = z_3 \oplus z_0; \quad z_3 = z_3 <<< 8,$$
$$z_2 = z_2 + z_3; \quad z_1 = z_1 \oplus z_2; \quad z_1 = z_1 <<< 7.$$

The updated C is shown in Listing 4.5.

**Listing 4.5:** Cha Cha quarter round function.

```
void quarterround(uint32_t y0,uint32_t y1,
                  uint32_t y2,uint32_t y3,
                  uint32_t *z0,uint32_t *z1,
                  uint32_t *z2,uint32_t *z3) {
    *z0 =   y0 +  y1;  *z3 = y3 ^ *z0; *z3 = rol(*z3,16);
    *z2 =   y2 + *z3; *z1 =   y1 ^ *z2; *z1 = rol(*z1,12);
    *z0 = *z0 + *z1;  *z3 = *z3 ^ *z0; *z3 = rol(*z3,8);
    *z2 = *z2 + *z3;  *z1 = *z1 ^ *z2; *z1 = rol(*z1,7);
}
```

If you want to do the computation in place on the existing state, then this would be:

$$a = a + b; \quad d = d \oplus a; \quad d = d <<< 16,$$
$$c = c + d; \quad b = b \oplus c; \quad b = b <<< 12,$$
$$a = a + b; \quad d = d \oplus a; \quad d = d <<< 8,$$
$$c = c + d; \quad b = b \oplus c; \quad b = b <<< 7.$$

Keep in mind that, if you implement using the in-place method, the final step involves adding the original matrix. So, you will need to keep a copy of the starting matrix.

The placement of $k$ and $n$ has been rearranged in order to achieve higher performance in SSE implementations.

For the 256-bit key, the $k$ and $n$ is placed as follows:

$$\begin{pmatrix} \sigma_0 & \sigma_1 & \sigma_2 & \sigma_3 \\ k_0 & k_1 & k_2 & k_3 \\ k_4 & k_5 & k_6 & k_7 \\ n_0 & n_1 & n_2 & n_3 \end{pmatrix}.$$

For the 128 bit key, the key is placed as follows:

$$\begin{pmatrix} \tau_0 & \tau_1 & \tau_2 & \tau_3 \\ k_0 & k_1 & k_2 & k_3 \\ k_0 & k_1 & k_2 & k_3 \\ n_0 & n_1 & n_2 & n_3 \end{pmatrix}.$$

These both use the same value for $\sigma_{0,1,2,3}$ and $\tau_{0,1,2,3}$ used in Salsa20. The C implementation of this placement code is shown in Listing 4.6.

**Listing 4.6:** Cha Cha matrix retup code.

```
void chachakn(uint8_t *k, int klen, uint8_t *n, uint8_t *result) {
    uint8_t key[64];
    int i;

    if (klen==16) {
        key[0]=101; key[1]=120; key[2]=112; key[3]=97;         /*tau0*/
        key[4]=110; key[5]=100; key[6]=32; key[7]=49;          /*tau1*/
        key[8]=54; key[9]=45; key[10]=98; key[11]=121;         /*tau2*/
        key[12]=116; key[13]=101; key[14]=32; key[15]=107;  /*tau3*/

        for(i=0;i<16;i++) key[i+16] = k[i];
        for(i=0;i<16;i++) key[i+32] = k[i];
        for(i=0;i<16;i++) key[i+48] = n[i];
    }
    else if (klen==32) {
        key[0]=101;   key[1]=120; key[2]=112; key[3]=97;        /*sigma0*/
        key[4]=110;   key[5]=100; key[6]=32; key[7]=51;         /*sigma1*/
        key[8]=50;    key[9]=45; key[10]=98; key[11]=121;       /*sigms2*/
        key[12]=116; key[13]=101; key[14]=32; key[15]=107;  /*sigma3*/

        for(i=0;i<32;i++) key[i+16] = k[i];
        for(i=0;i<16;i++) key[i+48] = n[i];
    }

    chacha_hash(key,result);
}
```

## 4.5 Blum Blum Shub

BBS (Blum Blum Shub) is by far the simplest and by far the least efficient of the PRNGs discussed in this chapter. It has a security proof that relies on the unproven conjecture that $P \neq NP$ is true.

The algorithm description was published in the IACR proceedings [2].

The algorithm for BBS is generated as follows:

Compute $M = PQ$, where $P$ and $Q$ are large primes. For any kind of security, the primes should be of the order of 2048 bits or greater. See Chapter 16 for details of how to generate large and secure prime numbers.

Select an initial state $x_0$, which must be coprime with $P$ and $Q$. Both primes must be congruent to 3 mod 4.

For each output bit needed, compute $x_{n+1} = x_n^2$ mod $M$, then, output the parity of $x_{n+1}$.

The inefficiency of the algorithm arises from computing $x_n^2$ mod $M$ over large 2048-bit integers, once for each single bit of output.

We use python for this example implementation due to the native support for large integer arithmetic and the standard crypto library that has support for finding RSA key pairs, which provides the correct sort of primes. The code is shown in Listing 4.7.

**Listing 4.7:** Blum Blum Shub Python Code

```python
#!/usr/bin/env python

from Crypto.PublicKey import RSA
key_pair = RSA.generate(2048)
p = key_pair.p
q = key_pair.q

M = p*q;

key_pair2 = RSA.generate(2048)
x = key_pair2.p

result = list()

for i in xrange(256): # Generate 256 bytes
    byte = 0
    for j in xrange(8):
        x = (x*x) % M    # The BBS algorithm
        byte = (byte << 1) | (x % 2)
    result.append(byte)

str = ""   # Print out the output
for i,byte in enumerate(result):
    str += "%02x" % byte
    if (i>1) and ((i+1) % 16 == 0):
```

```
print str
str=""
```

Running this produces appropriate output. However, it is not very fast, taking over five seconds to generate 256 bytes.

```
$time python blumblumshub.py
ea014dbf47e0178a198e966982c0d2b1
7e14c674fed7d9e0c120c1360ff63a7c
d19b11451b509435fa5187013bcaa82c
b20251b85cfbd42999e55483d7353663
16deb98c3287e0f9bf5a1dae2519f39d
755e4c229cb97948bb16bf7588d56721
4442580476b66fd03987bab8ee4343d3
29898d5d96e96a596abf3e49f864398b
949ca44c789af259a7892c206668d886
4918b463d7b8b9de42dad402eb4a98ba
bf5e1d69d1a8d05b8cd729edbf581716
8d2b210328fa3d6c9b326ee166bf5535
ef7a0352912e434c4730ee26d90161dc
a701d93ad4de5a38c91c675abcc1737c
790a9dab25446774b98cb912627aaab7
f601c1f7d4e5899145d5b851ccae3c18

real    0m5.495s
user    0m5.482s
sys     0m0.018s
$
```

# 5 Nondeterministic Random Number Generators

The output of an entropy source is nondeterministic and the output of an entropy extractor fed by a nondeterministic input from an entropy source is also nondeterministic and of higher entropy per bit than the input data and, possibly, very close to full entropy, where each bit is independent of every other bit and has an equal 50% probability of being a 1 or 0.

The difference between a fully nondeterministic random number sequence and a DRBG output that has been nondeterministically seeded is that, with the fully nondeterministic data, there is no amount of work you can do, after seeing prior outputs, that will help you predict future outputs as a function of the prior outputs. With a DRBG output, there is a well-defined amount of work needed to compute the internal state of the DRBG as a function of prior outputs in order to predict future outputs. This is generally described in big-O notation. For example, a DRBG might claim its security bound is $O(2^{256})$, meaning that the best known prediction algorithm takes at least $2^{256}$ steps to compute the internal state from prior data. For security purposes, this computational complexity needs to be large enough that prediction of the outputs is not possible. But, with an NRBG, this is not a concern. There is no prediction algorithm that can do better than chance guessing.

Data that is sufficiently close to full entropy should be good enough for cryptographic purposes, but if you are trying to comply with RNG standards, such as SP800-90C or ANSI X9-82, you will find that there are further requirements that force you to add a PRNG and use one of two different structures, the XOR construction or the oversampling construction. This chapter looks at these two constructions.

The XOR construction is described in Section 9.3, page 33 of the second draft of SP800-90C http://csrc.nist.gov/publications/drafts/800-90/sp800_90c_second_draft.pdf. This specification is still a draft and has not been finalized.

The oversampling construction is described in Section 9.4, page 36 of the second draft of SP800-90C.

Before SP800-90C, these two structures were specified in ANSI X9-82, part 4-2011, and they were written largely by the same group of people that wrote SP800-90C. At the time of writing, ANSI were asking for $60 for a copy of this standard, which is only one of four parts of X9-82. So, we will continue with the SP800-90C version which is available without charge.

In both constructions, the justification for these structures is that, should the entropy source fail to have sufficient entropy during use, the security properties of the RNG would fall back to the security of the DRBG algorithm instead of becoming entirely predictable.

https://doi.org/10.1515/9781501506062-005

## 5.1 The XOR Construction NRBG

The XOR construction specifies that each output of the entropy extractor be XORed with the output of a DRBG. The resulting number forms the output of the NRBG.

In the specification it gives a structure as follows (see Figure 5.1):

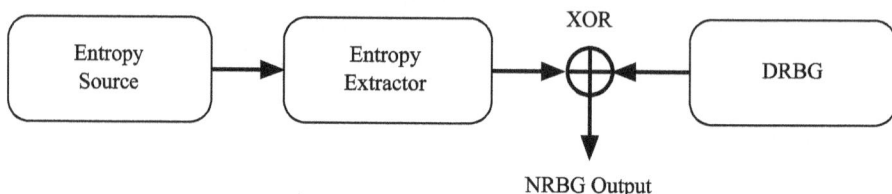

**Figure 5.1:** XOR Construction.

A reasonable criticism of this requirement is that the SP800-90 and ANSI X9-82 specifications already demand online health tests for the output of the entropy source, and so, if both those tests and the entropy source failed, then, the DRBG would mask the failure and the output would look fully random, even though there is no entropy. So, the output is fully deterministic.

A second criticism is that this construction assumes that the online tests are less reliable than the DRBG implementation. In hardware implementations this is often untrue. For example, the logic in the DRBG in Intel CPUs is ten times larger than the online health test logic and the entropy source put together. The failure rate is a simple function of surface area of the circuit, since there is a constant probability of a silicon defect per unit area of silicon. Therefore, it is ten times more likely for there to be an error in the DRBG logic than in the entropy source or online health test logic.

It would be much more efficient to put greater resources into making the online health tests more reliable, for example, by implementing triple modular redundancy (where the circuit is built three times, the outputs compared, and the majority result chosen as the correct one). This would increase the reliability of the circuit and be much less expensive in terms of silicon area than the approach mandated in the XOR construction.

## 5.2 The Oversampling Construction NRBG

The oversampling construction mandates a normal RNG structure with an entropy source, online health test, entropy extractor, and DRBG, but also requires that between each output, the DRBG is reseeded. So, each output of the DRBG has full entropy because the number of bits of full entropy data input to the DRBG, before the output value is emitted, is at least as big as the number of bits in the output value.

Section 4.1.4 describes how this approach is very wasteful of entropy in the CTR DRBG case.

A second criticism is that this NRBG construction interferes with the performance of a high-performance DRBG output, when the DRBG is used both for a DRBG and for an NRBG. This is the case with the Intel RdRand and RdSeed instructions. If it were implemented with the oversampling construction, then whenever the RdSeed (NRBG) instruction were executed, it would force the NRBG to reseed before another output was available from the DRBG. So, the RdRand (DRBG) instruction would then be blocked from returning a number until the reseed had completed.

For this reason, the Intel DRBG circuit that generates random numbers for the RdRand and RdSeed instructions uses the XOR construction, where the RdSeed NRBG maximum output rate is the rate that seeds are available from the extractor. Each output takes an output from the DRBG for the XOR, without requiring the DRBG to be reseeded.

## 5.3 Standards-Based NRBG Summary

In summary, the NRBG structures mandated in SP800-90 and ANSI X9-82 are poor designs that are inefficient, create performance problems, make RNGs unnecessarily large, and prevent other much more reliable approaches to creating reliable RNGs. This has been extensively communicated to NIST in comments on the SP800-90 drafts, but there is no sign that they are taking any notice. It seems that we are stuck with these architectures for standards-based NRBGs.

# 6 Statistically Uniform Noncryptographic PRNGs

In this chapter we look at some examples of statistically uniform, non cryptographic PRNGs. These are PRNG algorithms that aim to output random data that is statistically uniform, but are not intended to have cryptographically secure properties such as prediction resistance or backtracking resistance.

Not requiring cryptographic security enables these PRNG algorithms to be much more efficient than cryptographic PRNG algorithms, often consisting of a sequence of shifts and Xors, or simple arithmetic operations such as multiplying, adding, and modulo operations.

The algorithms shown here are:
- Linear Congruential Generators
- MWC (Multiply With Carry)
- XORSHIFT
- PCGs (Permuted Congruential Generators)

## 6.1 Linear Congruential Generator

LCGs (Linear Congruential Generators) are simple and fast PRNGs that produce approximately uniform output. They were commonly implemented for the random number algorithm in libraries and operating systems. They are not in anyway secure and should not be used as a secure RNG. They also suffer from having significantly nonuniform statistical properties.

An LCG has three parameters:
- A modulus $m$, which determines the size of the group. It is appropriate for $m$ to be prime, so Mersenne primes of the form $m = 2^n - 1$ are particularly useful, since the state will exactly fit into an $n$-bit number.
- A multiplier $a$.
- An addition value $c$.

The algorithm generates a sequence $x_i$.
The algorithm is

$$x_{n+1} = (x_n a + c) \mod m.$$

Repeatedly execute the multiply and addition and output a subset of the bits of $x$.

In an implementation, the state variable $x$ needs to be large enough to hold any number modulo $m$.

For example, Listing 6.1 is a Python implementation using the POSIX rand48 parameters.

https://doi.org/10.1515/9781501506062-006

**Listing 6.1:** LCG Python Program

```python
#!/usr/bin/env python

def lcg(a,c,m,seed):
    x = seed
    while True:
        x = (x*a + c) % m
        yield (x >> 16) & 0xffffffff

lcginst = lcg(a=0x5deece66d,c=11,m=2**48,seed=0x3a6f9eb64)
for i in xrange(10):
    print "0x%08x" % lcginst.next()
```

The output appears random:

```
$ ./lcg.py
0x8b0c5a15
0xf6006961
0x7500c122
0x049939e7
0x803d3108
0x70ae7e90
0x437cfdbc
0x055a2579
0xcffa443e
0x821970f9
$
```

The full state of the LCG is hardly random, and this is why only the upper bits are returned. If we output the state every round of the algorithm, instead of the upper bits, then we can see a clear pattern. The code to do this is in Listing 6.2.

**Listing 6.2:** Full LCG State Output Program

```python
#!/usr/bin/env python

def lcg(a,c,m,seed):
    x = seed
    while True:
        x = (x*a + c) % m
        #yield (x >> 16) & 0xffffffff
        yield x

lcginst = lcg(a=0x5deece66d,c=11,m=2**48,seed=0x3a6f9eb64)

for i in xrange(10):
    x = lcginst.next()
    if (x & 0x01) == 1:
        print "0x%016x_ODD" % x
```

```
        else:
            print "0x%016x_EVEN" % x.
```

This code is the same as the previous LCG code, except that the value yielded from the LCG function returns the full state and the printout code tags ODD onto odd numbers and EVEN onto even numbers.

The output is as follows:

```
0x8b0c5a15119f  ODD
0xf60069615abe  EVEN
0x7500c12256f1  ODD
0x049939e78aa8  EVEN
0x803d3108f993  ODD
0x70ae7e9055a2  EVEN
0x437cfdbc0205  ODD
0x055a25795a2c  EVEN
0xcffa443eecc7  ODD
0x821970f99ac6  EVEN
```

Clearly, the least significant bit of the numbers alternated between 1 and 0, instead of appearing random. This was a feature of the random function in early versions of the Microsoft BASIC language.

Typically, distinguishability tests can distinguish LCGs from random because, as the name suggests, there is a linear relationship between subsequent states of the generator.

Further, 123 kibibytes (1007616 bits, slightly more than the $10^6$ bits required by the SP800-22 tests) of data are generated. The LCG model is used, and the data is analyzed using the SP800-22. We see that the overlapping template matching test returns a FAIL result.

```
$ djenrandom -m lcg -k 123 -b -o lcg.bin
$ python sp800_22_tests.py lcg.bin
... [lots of output skipped]
SUMMARY
-------
monobit_test                                 0.898532530659    PASS
frequency_within_block_test                  0.603460876122    PASS
runs_test                                    0.441857262837    PASS
longest_run_ones_in_a_block_test             0.150963726696    PASS
binary_matrix_rank_test                      0.111458164757    PASS
dft_test                                     0.684402461384    PASS
non_overlapping_template_matching_test       0.999999998408    PASS
overlapping_template_matching_test           0.0               FAIL
maurers_universal_test                       0.999426079498    PASS
linear_complexity_test                       0.516264051158    PASS
serial_test                                  0.876701097409    PASS
approximate_entropy_test                     0.980577297453    PASS
cumulative_sums_test                         0.918827789902    PASS
```

```
random_excursion_test                 0.144610516222      PASS
random_excursion_variant_test         0.0105892759523     PASS
```

## 6.2 Multiply with Carry Uniform PRNG

The Multiply With Carry (MWC) algorithm is a PRNG invented by George Marsargalia. It uses more state than LCGs and so achieves long cycle periods. An implementation benefit of this algorithm is that it does not require safe prime numbers for the modulus and, for example, can use a modulus of $2^n$ or better, $2^n - 1$, which is efficient to implement in software or hardware.

George Marsargalia's Original mother.c code, complete with a clear explanation of the algorithm, was removed from Berkeley University's website, but is available at the Internet archive at https://web.archive.org/web/20100718181751 and http://www.stat.berkeley.edu/classes/s243/mother.c.

The general form of the algorithm has a lag value $r$. There will be a history of $r$ previous values $x_{n-1} \ldots x_{n-r}$, and the current output $x_n$ is a function of the $x[n - r]$ value and the running carry $c_{n-1}$ from the previous round. This is shown in Figure 6.1. Each round computes the next value $x_n$ and the next carry $c_n$. $n$ increments, and the computation shifts to the right one step each round.

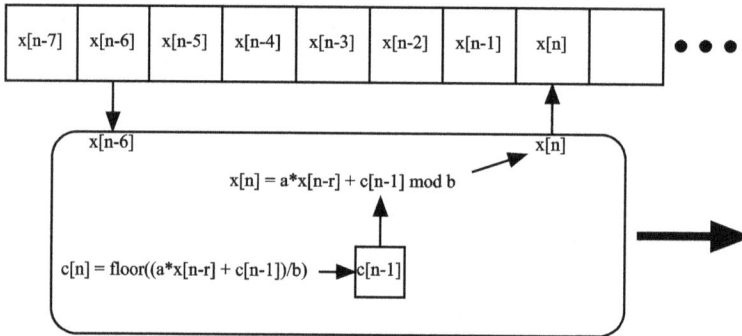

**Figure 6.1:** Multiply with Carry PRNG.

The next state algorithm computes

$$x_n = A \times x_{n-r} + c_{n-1} \quad \bmod b$$

and

$$c_n = \left\lfloor \frac{A \times x_{n-r} + c_{n-1}}{b} \right\rfloor.$$

So, the $r$ most recent state values $x_{n-r} \ldots x_{n-1}$ and the most recent carry value $c_{n-1}$ need to be stored.

In a software or hardware implementation, the state value can be taken as the upper half of bits of the computed value and the carry value as the lower half bits. This is seen in the C implementation below.

Clearly, on the first round, there is no history of values. So, $x_1$ to $x_r$ and $c_{n-1}$ need to be initialized with a random seed and the initial state of $n$ will be $r+1$. Alternatively, seed the first $x_1$ and set $c_1 = 0$ and run it for $2r$ cycles to fill the history buffer.

If we are using a modulus of $2^{32} - 1$, then the values of $x$ will be in the range from 0 to $2^{32} - 2$. So, the initialization needs to ensure that the initialization elements are within this range.

Example code published by George Marsargalia includes versions with $r = 4096$.

The C code in Listing 6.3 uses the same coefficients as the examples, but also properly initializes the state and sets $r = 4096$, $a = 18782$, and $b = 4095$.

**Listing 6.3:** C Implementation of the MWC Algorithm

```c
#include <stdio.h>
#include <stdint.h>
#include "rdrand_stdint.h"

#define R 4096
#define A 17872
#define B 0xffffffff

#define ITERATIONS 100

void init_mwc (uint32_t *state, uint32_t *c, uint32_t *n) {
    uint32_t x;
    int i;

    for (i=0; i<R; i++) {
        do {
            rdrand_get_uint32_retry(10,&x);
        } while (x > (B-1));

        state[i] = x;
    }

    do {
        *c = rdrand_get_uint32_retry(10,&x);
    } while (x > (B-1));
    *n = 0;
}

uint32_t update_mwc (uint32_t *state, uint32_t *c, uint32_t *n) {
    uint64_t t;
```

```
    int ptr;
    *n = (*n + 1) % R;
    ptr = (*n + 1) % R;
    t = ((uint64_t)state[ptr] * (uint64_t)A) + (uint64_t)*c;
    *c = t >> 32;
    state[*n] = t & 0xffffffff;
    return state[*n];
}

int main() {
    uint32_t state[R];
    uint32_t c;
    uint32_t n;
    uint32_t result;
    int i;

    init_mwc(state, &c, &n);
    for (i=0;i<ITERATIONS;i++) {
        result = update_mwc(state, &c, &n);
        printf("%08x\n",result);
    }
}
```

An improvement to the MWC algorithm is the Complementary MWC algorithm. This allows the period of the output sequence to be more easily established, regardless of the size of $r$. This addresses a problem with MWC, where the upper bits can be biased.

With CMWC, the next state algorithm is as follows:

$$x_n = (B - 1) - (A \times x_{n-r} + c_{n-1}) \mod b,$$

where the $c_n$ equation is unchanged, except that $b$ is of the form $2^n$ rather than $2^n - 1$:

$$c_n = \left\lfloor \frac{A \times x_{n-r} + c_{n-1}}{b} \right\rfloor.$$

Since $b$ can now be of the form $2^n$, such as $2^{32}$, the initialization does not need to check for values outside the range from 0 to $2^{32} - 2$.

The CMWC C code is shown in Listing 6.4.

**Listing 6.4:** C Implementation of the CMWC Algorithm

```
#include <stdio.h>
#include <stdint.h>
#include "rdrand_stdint.h"

#define R 4096
#define A 17872
```

```
#define BMINUS1   0xffffffff

#define ITERATIONS 100

void init_mwc(uint32_t *state,uint32_t *c,uint32_t *n) {
    uint32_t x;
    int i;

    for (i=0; i<R; i++) {
        rdrand_get_uint32_retry(10,&(state[i]));
    }

    *c = rdrand_get_uint32_retry(10,&x);
    *n = 0;
}

uint32_t update_mwc(uint32_t *state,uint32_t *c,uint32_t *n) {
    uint64_t t;
    int ptr;
    *n = (*n + 1) % R;
    ptr = (*n + 1) % R;
    t = BMINUS1 - (((uint64_t)state[*n] * (uint64_t)A) + (uint64_t)*c);
    *c = (((uint64_t)state[*n] * (uint64_t)A) + (uint64_t)*c) >> 32;
    state[*n] = t & 0xffffffff;
    return state[*n];
}

int main() {
    uint32_t state[R];
    uint32_t c;
    uint32_t n;
    uint32_t result;
    int i;

    init_mwc(state, &c, &n);
    for (i=0;i<ITERATIONS;i++) {
        result = update_mwc(state, &c, &n);
        printf("%08x\n",result);
    }
}
```

## 6.3 Xorshift Uniform PRNG

The Xorshift algorithm is another algorithm by George Marsargalia. Until PCGs (Permuted Congruential Generators) came along, this algorithm presented the best uniformity of noncryptographic PRNGs. It is exceedingly well-suited for implementation in hardware.

Two algorithms are described, a 32-bit version and a 128-bit version.

A C version of the Xorshift32 algorithm is shown in Listing 6.5. This code is adapted from the implementation in the djenrandom program.

**Listing 6.5:** C Implementation of the XORSHIFT32 Algorithm.

```c
#include <stdio.h>
#include <stdint.h>

void init_xorshift32(uint32_t* state) {
    *state = 0xA634716A;
}

uint32_t xorshift32(uint32_t* state) {
    uint32_t x;

    x = *state;
    x = x ^ (x << 13);
    x = x ^ (x >> 17);
    x = x ^ (x << 5);
    *state = x;
    return x;
}

int main() {
    int i;
    uint32_t x;
    uint32_t state;
    init_xorshift32(&state);
    for (i=0;i<10;i++) {
        x = xorshift32(&state);
        printf("%08x\n",x);
    }
}
```

It can be seen in the xorshift32 function that the operations involve three steps of XORing the state with a shifted version of itself. In hardware, this involves three stages of XOR gates. The bit shifting is achieved by connecting the wires appropriately. So, in hardware, this is a very efficient PRNG.

The output of this program is

```
2b3d89a6
db2990e2
cf812b78
b7259fef
9fd7cde3
ab184416
d0c06ebb
```

```
7ffb6630
74909a6e
9c705980
```

The Xorshift128 variant keeps a longer state, with four 32-bit state variables, but the shifting operation only happens on a 32-bit subset of the state bits, and the state values are rotated through the remaining state. A C implementation of this is shown in Listing 6.6.

**Listing 6.6:** C Implementation of the XORSHIFT128 Algorithm

```
#include <stdio.h>
#include <stdint.h>

void init_xorshift128(uint32_t* state) {
    state[0] = 0xA634716A;
    state[1] = 0x998FCD1F;
    state[2] = 0x6A9B90FE;
    state[3] = 0x7344E998;
}

uint32_t xorshift128(uint32_t* state) {
    uint32_t x;

    x = state[3];

    x = x ^ (x << 11);
    x = x ^ (x >> 8);

    state[3] = state[2];
    state[2] = state[1];
    state[1] = state[0];

    x = x ^ state[0];
    x = x ^ (state[0] >> 19);
    state[0] = x;
    return x;
}

int main() {
    int i;
    uint32_t x;
    uint32_t state[4];
    init_xorshift128(state);
    for (i=0;i<10;i++) {
        x = xorshift128(state);
        printf("%08x\n",x);
    }
}
```

The resulting output appears random. The 128 version appears more uniform to statistical distinguishability tests.

```
f268441d
44c226ce
a3c2fc7c
a678764f
16808631
43212679
f7b4137d
921bc9ca
80b864b6
cae08836
```

## 6.4 Permuted Congruential Generator

At the time of writing, PCGs[1] are the state of the art in uniform noncryptographic random number generators. Cryptographic PRNGs create uniform random numbers with mathematical proof of the difficulty of predicting future values from past values, whereas noncryptographic PRNGs produce uniform random numbers without those guarantees, but at a much lower computational cost.

PCGs are a family of PRNGs with a common structure; an internal RNG, such as an LCG or MGC generator. An MGC is a special case of an LCG, where the additive part is 0. The generator is called the State Transition Function. It contains all the states in the algorithm. The remainder of the algorithm is purely combinatorial.

The output of the state transition function is passed through an output function that permutes the values. This is the transformation that brings much greater statistical uniformity to the output of the state transition function compared to LCG and MCG algorithms.

Then, a part of the resulting value is output. Typically, it is half the bits of the resulting value that are output.

So, the name of a PCG includes the name of the generator, the output function, and the sizes of the state and output. See Figure 6.2.

The paper [15] describes a two-line implementation of a PCG in c:

```
state = state * multiplier + increment;
uint32_t output = state >> (29 - (state >> 61));
```

---

**1** The paper [15] "PCG: A Family of Simple Fast Space-Efficient Statistically Good Algorithms for Random Number Generation" by Melissa E. O'Neill defines the PCG family of algorithms. A web site, http://www.pcg-random.org, provides code examples and technical information.

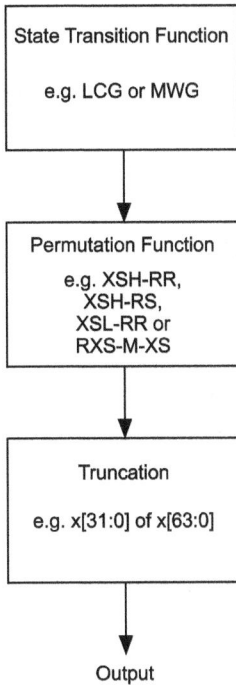

Output          **Figure 6.2:** Permuted Congruential Generator.

The state transition function is the 64-bit LCG:

```
state = state * multiplier + increment;
```

The permutation function is

```
state >> (29 - (state >> 61));
```

The truncation stage is caused by assigning the permutation to a `uint32_t` 32-bit output variable. So, the upper 32 bits of the 64-bit value are dropped.

### 6.4.1 PCG Naming

Examples of PCG permutation algorithm names are:

- PCG-XSH-RR XorShift, Random Rotation;
- PCG-XSH-RS XorShift, Random Shift;
- PCG-XSL-RR XORShift Low Bits, Random Rotation;
- PCG-RXS-M-XS Random XorShift, Multiply, XorShift.

In O'Neill's paper, the state and output size are prepended and the generator is appended in brackets. So, PCG-XSH-RR with 64 bits of state, 32 bits of output, and an LCG generator might be named 64-32-PCG-XSH-RR(LCG).

O'Niell [15] does not go into details of the specifics of the bit level details of each of the operations in the names. Those details are in the provided C++ library and have to be reverse engineered. So, the O'Neill paper, [15], mostly explains the principles and performance of the algorithm family, rather than a complete algorithm suite specification.

For a subset of the algorithm names with specific sizes, the bit level details are given.

### 6.4.2  64-32-PCG-XSH-RR

For 64-32-PCG-XSH-RR it gives:

```
output = rotate32((state ^ (state >> 18)) >> 27, state >> 59);
```

In straight C, this can be implemented as:

```
current64 = (state >> 18) ^ state) >> 27;
rotate_amount =   state >> 59u;
current64 = current64 & 0xffffffff;
current64 = rotate_uint32(current64, rotate_amount);
return current64;
```

The code for djenrandom includes 16-, 32-, and 64-bit variants of XSH_RR, as shown in Listing 6.7.

**Listing 6.7:** PCG_XSH_RR C Implementation

```
/* XSH_RR : Xor Shift, random rotation. Stage in output function.
            Doesn't change state
            Outputs half the state.
    pcg_rotr_8(((state >> 5u) ^ state) >> 5u, state >> 13u)
    pcg_rotr_16(((state >> 10u) ^ state) >> 12u, state >> 28u);
    pcg_rotr_32(((state >> 18u) ^ state) >> 27u, state >> 59u);
    pcg_rotr_64(((state >> 29u) ^ state) >> 58u, state >> 122u);

*/
uint64_t pcg_xsh_rr(t_modelstate* modelstate, t_rngstate* rngstate) {
   uint16_t current16;
   uint32_t current32;
   uint64_t current64;
   int rotate_amount;
   switch (modelstate->pcg_state_size) {
   case 16:
     current16 = ((modelstate->pcg16_state >> 5) ^ modelstate->pcg16_state) >> 5;
     rotate_amount =   modelstate->pcg16_state >> 13u;
     current16 = rotate_uint8(current16, rotate_amount);
     return current16 % 256;
   case 32:
     current32 = ((modelstate->pcg32_state >> 10) ^ modelstate->pcg32_state) >> 12;
     rotate_amount =   modelstate->pcg32_state >> 28u;
     current32 = rotate_uint16(current32, rotate_amount);
     return current32 & 0xffffffff;
   case 64:
```

```
        current64 = ((modelstate->pcg64_state >> 18) ^ modelstate->pcg64_state) >> 27;
        rotate_amount =  modelstate->pcg64_state >> 59u;
        current64 = current64 & 0xffffffff;
        current64 = rotate_uint32(current64,rotate_amount);
        return current64;
    }
    return 0;
}
```

### 6.4.3 64-32-PCG-XSH-RS

For 64-32-PCG-XSH-RS, it gives:

```
output = (state ^ (state >> 22)) >> (22 + (state >> 61));
```

In straight C, this can be implemented as:

```
current = ((state >> 22u) ^ state);
current = (current >> ((state >> 61u) + 22u)) % 4294967296u;
return current;
```

The code for PCG-XSH-RS in djenrandom includes 16-, 32-, and 64-bit variants, shown in Listing 6.8.

**Listing 6.8:** PCG_XSH_RS C Implementation

```
/* XSH_RS : Xor Shift, random xor shift. Stage in output function.
            Doesn't change state
            Outputs half the state.
*/
int pcg_xsh_rs(t_modelstate* modelstate, t_rngstate* rngstate) {
    uint64_t current;
    switch (modelstate->pcg_state_size) {
    case 16:
        current = ((modelstate->pcg16_state >> 7) ^ modelstate->pcg16_state);
        current = ((current >> ((modelstate->pcg16_state >> 14) + 3))) % 256;
        return current % 256;
    case 32:
        current = ((modelstate->pcg32_state >> 11u) ^ modelstate->pcg32_state);
        current = (current >> ((modelstate->pcg32_state >> 30u) + 11u)) % 65536;
        return current % 65536;
    case 64:
        current = ((modelstate->pcg64_state >> 22u) ^ modelstate->pcg64_state);
        current = (current >> ((modelstate->pcg64_state >> 61u) + 22u))
            % 4294967296u;
        return current;
    }
    return 0;
}
```

### 6.4.4 128-64-PCG-XSL-RR

For 128-64-PCG-XSL-RR, it gives:

```
output = rotate64(uint64_t(state ^ (state >> 64)), state >> 122);
```

The same basic C structures used above can be used to implement this and the many other PCG variants.

### 6.4.5 The LCG Generator for PCGs

The LCG generator functions for 16-, 32-, 64-, and 128-bit state sizes are given as follows:

- 16: state = (state × 12829) + 47989;
- 32: state = (state × 747796405) + 2891336453;
- 64: state = (state × 6364136223846793005) + 1442695040888963407;
- 128: state = (state × 47026247687942121848144207491837523525)
                  +117397592171526113268558934119004209487.

### 6.4.6 The MCG Generator for PCGs

The MCG generator functions for 16-, 32-, 64-, and 128-bit state sizes use the same multipliers as the LCG functions but drop the addition step:

- 16: state = state × 12829;
- 32: state = state × 747796405;
- 64: state = state × 6364136223846793005;
- 128: state = state × 47026247687942121848144207491837523525.

# 7 Gaussian or Normally Distributed PRNGs

In this chapter we look at algorithms for generating pseudorandom Gaussian data or for converting uniformly distributed random numbers into Gaussian distributed random numbers. This latter type of algorithm can be either deterministic or nondeterministic, depending on whether or not the input data is deterministic.

The algorithms shown here are:

-  The Box–Muller Algorithm;
-  The Ziggurat Algorithm;
-  The ZIGNOR Algortihm.

## 7.1 Box–Muller Transform Normal Random Variate Algorithm

The Box–Muller transform[1] is a simple algorithm to generate normally distributed random numbers.

The algorithm takes in two uniform random numbers $U_1$ and $U_2$. It then outputs two random numbers $X_1$ and $X_2$ drawn from the standard normal distribution. The algorithm computes $X_1$ and $X_2$ with the following two equations:

$$X_1 = \sqrt{(-2\log_e U_1)}\cos(2\pi U_2)$$

and

$$X_2 = \sqrt{(-2\log_e U_1)}\sin(2\pi U_2).$$

An example Python code is in Listing 7.1.

**Listing 7.1:** Box–Muller Algorithm Python Code

```python
#!/usr/bin/env python

import sys
import random
import math
randsource = random.SystemRandom() # nondeterministic random source

n = int(sys.argv[1])   # Number of random numbers

even_n=n        # Compute the number of pairs necessary to
if (n % 2)==1:  # provide at least n numbers.
    even_n = n+1
```

---

**1** The Box–Muller algorithm was first described in [5].

https://doi.org/10.1515/9781501506062-007

```
for i in xrange(even_n/2):    # Generate n/2 pairs
    u1 = randsource.random()
    u2 = randsource.random()
    x1 = math.sqrt(-2.0*math.log(u1))*math.cos(2.0*math.pi*u2)
    x2 = math.sqrt(-2.0*math.log(u1))*math.sin(2.0*math.pi*u2)

    print x1   # Output the result
    if ((i+1)*2) <= n: # Don't output the last number if n was odd
        print x2
```

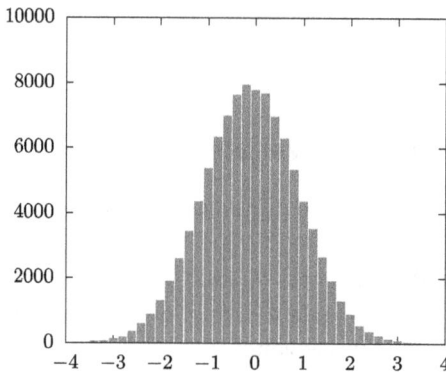

**Figure 7.1:** Histogram of 100 000 Numbers from the Box–Muller Algorithm.

Figure 7.1 shows a histogram of 100 000 numbers output from the Box–Muller algorithm.

## 7.2 The Ziggurat Normal Random Variate Algorithm

In most cases the Ziggurat[2] algorithm is faster than the Box–Muller algorithm. Its running time is nondeterministic. In most cases, it outputs a number in one step, but in about 1% of cases it will call a fallback algorithm, which better models the tails of the normal distribution.

The algorithm models one side of the normal PDF, and the sign of the uniform random number input determines the sign of the resulting variate.

A scaled normal PDF $y = e^{-\frac{1}{2}x^2}$ (to avoid the $\sqrt{2\pi}$ term) is divided into a number of equal area rectangles. In the analysis in the paper, 256 rectangles are used, and in the C source code, 128 are implemented. The diagram in Figure 7.2 shows fewer, exaggerated size rectangles for clarity. The rectangle covers all the curve except for the bottom base strip. If the vertical location lands in this strip, then the fallback algorithm is called.

The improved speed is gained through the use of three lookup tables $w_n$, $k_n$, and $f_n$. So, there is a speed/storage tradeoff with the Box–Muller algorithm. The tables must

---

2 The Ziggurat algorithm was published in [13] in 2000 by George Marsaglia and Wai Wan Tsang.

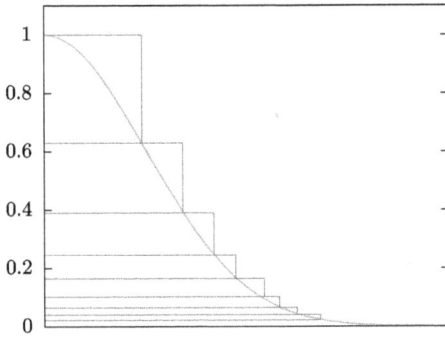

**Figure 7.2:** Ziggurat Algorithm Division of Normal PDF into Rectangles.

be generated before numbers can output. So, there is a startup cost, unless the tables are hard coded in the algorithm.

The primary part of the algorithm takes a signed 32-bit uniform random number, which ranges from −21747483648 to +21747483647. It takes the lower 7 bits $iz$ of this uniform number and indexes into the $k_n$ table to establish whether or not the variate is landing in the tail of the curve or the main body. If it lands in the main body, then it indexes into the $w_n$ table to make the random variate with the appropriate distribution. On average, it lands in the tail once every 127 numbers. If it lands in the tail, then it goes through the fallback algorithm, which takes a number of operations.

```
hz = rand.randrange(-2**31,(2**31)-1)
iz = hz & 127

if (abs(hz)<kn[iz]): # Initial attempt
    return hz*wn[iz]
else:
    < Do Fallback>
```

The $w_n$ table is plotted in Figure 7.3.

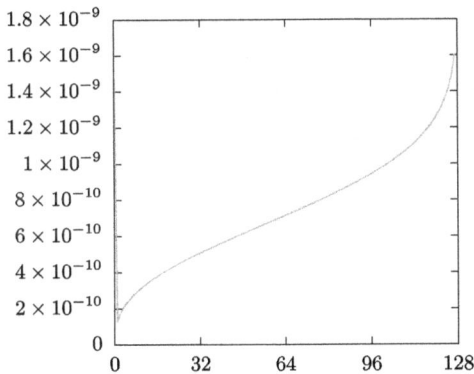

**Figure 7.3:** Ziggurat $w_n$ Table.

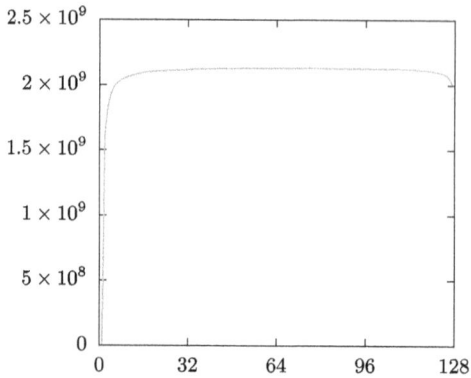

**Figure 7.4:** Ziggurat $k_n$ Table.

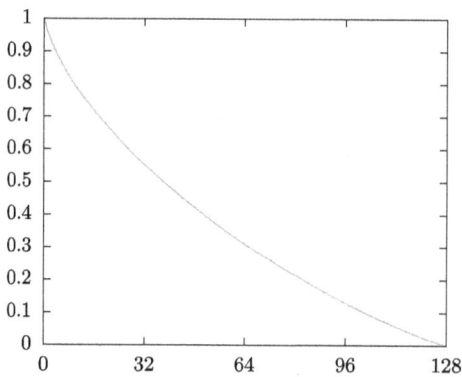

**Figure 7.5:** Ziggurat $f_n$ Table.

The $k_n$ table is plotted in Figure 7.4.

The $f_n$ table is plotted in Figure 7.5.

The C code in [13] is dense and sensitive to the word size of the machine it is compiled on. It will not compile on a modern 64-bit machine without directing the compiler to compile 32-bit code. Also, it uses a built-in PRNG called SHR3, which is statistically not as uniform as we can get from the random service of modern operating systems or improved PRNGs, such as the Permuted Congruential Generators.

The example Python code in Listing 7.2 uses the system random number service instead of the SHR3 PRNG used in the C code in [13].

**Listing 7.2:** Ziggurat Algorithm Python Code

```
#!/usr/bin/env python

import sys
import random
import math

rand = random.SystemRandom() # nondeterministic random source
```

```python
num = int(sys.argv[1])   # Number of random numbers

kn=[0 for x in xrange(128)] # The three lookup tables
wn=[0 for x in xrange(128)]
fn=[0 for x in xrange(128)]

def ziggurat_normal():
    global kn
    global wn
    global fn

    hz = rand.randrange(-2**31,(2**31)-1)
    iz = hz & 127

    if (abs(hz)<kn[iz]): # Initial attempt
        return hz*wn[iz]
    else: # Fallback Algorithm called about 1% of times
        r = 3.442620;
        x=0.0
        y=0.0

        while True:
            x=float(hz)*wn[iz]

            if (iz==0):
                while True:
                    x=-math.log(rand.uniform(0,1.0))*0.2904764
                    y=-math.log(rand.uniform(0,1.0))
                    if ((y+y)<(x*x)):
                        break
                return (r+x)*((int(hz>0)*2)-1)

            if (fn[iz]+(rand.uniform(0,1.0))*(fn[iz-1]-fn[iz])
                                   < math.exp(-.5*x*x)):
                return x

            hz=random.getrandbits(32)
            iz=hz&127
            if(abs(hz)<kn[iz]):
                return (hz*wn[iz])


# Create tables
def build_tables():
    global kn
    global wn
    global fn
    m1 = 2147483648.0
    m2 = 4294967296.0
```

```
dn=3.442619855899
tn=dn
vn=9.91256303526217e-3

# Build the tables kn, wn, fn
q=vn/math.exp(-.5*dn*dn)
kn[0]=(dn/q)*m1
kn[1]=0
wn[0]=q/m1
wn[127]=dn/m1
fn[0]=1.0
fn[127]=math.exp(-.5*dn*dn)

for i in xrange(126,0,-1):
    dn=math.sqrt(-2.*math.log(vn/dn+math.exp(-.5*dn*dn)));
    kn[i+1]=int((dn/tn)*m1);
    tn=dn;
    fn[i]=math.exp(-.5*dn*dn);
    wn[i]=dn/m1;

build_tables()
for i in xrange(num):
    print ziggurat_normal()
```

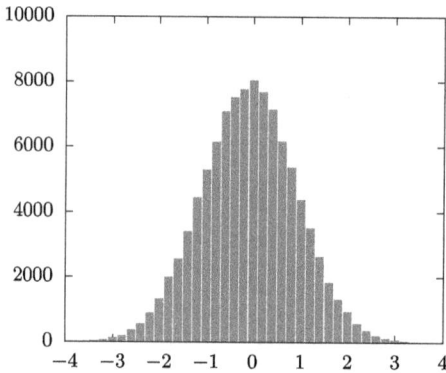

**Figure 7.6:** Histogram of 100 000 Numbers from the Ziggurat Algorithm.

Figure 7.6 shows a histogram of 100 000 numbers output from the ziggurat algorithm.

## 7.3 The ZIGNOR Normal Random Variate Algorithm

The ZIGNOR[3] paper claims improved accuracy with slightly reduced performance relative to the Ziggurat algorithm.

---

3 Jurgen A. Doornik published an improvement to the Ziggurat algorithm in [8] in 2005.

The paper observes that in the Ziggurat algorithm, the 7 bits to choose which box we are in are also the lower 7 bits of the number used to scale the table entry from $w_n$. So, the two numbers are not completely independent. The paper also points out the statistical deficiencies of the SHR3 PRNG and proposes its replacement with the MWC8222 PRNG algorithm (see Section 6.2). Two uniform random numbers are used to ensure the box selection and table scaling are independent.

As with the Ziggurat python code example 7.3, we use the system random number service instead, from which the code fetches both integer and floating point random numbers.

**Listing 7.3:** ZIGNOR Algorithm Python Code

```python
#!/usr/bin/env python

import sys
import random
import math

rand = random.SystemRandom() # nondeterministic random source
num = int(sys.argv[1])   # Number of random numbers

zignor_c = 128
zignor_r = 3.442619855899
zignor_v = 9.91256303526217e-3

adzig_x = [0.0 for x in range(zignor_c+1)]
adzig_r = [0.0 for x in range(zignor_c)]

def tail_computation(dmin,isnegative):
    while True:
        x = math.log(rand.random())/dmin
        y = math.log(rand.random())
        if ((-2*y) < x**2):
            break
    if isnegative:
        return x-dmin
    else:
        return dmin-x

def zignorinit(ic, dr, dv):
    f = math.exp(-0.5 * dr*dr)
    adzig_x[0] = dv/f
    adzig_x[1] = dr
    adzig_x[ic] = 0

    for i in xrange(2,ic):
        adzig_x[i] = math.sqrt(-2.0 * math.log(dv/adzig_x[i-1] +f))
        f = math.exp(-0.5 * (adzig_x[i]**2))
```

```
    for i in xrange(ic):
        adzig_r[i] = adzig_x[i+1]/adzig_x[i]

def zignor():
    while True:
        u = 2.0 * rand.random() -1
        i=rand.getrandbits(32) & 0x7f

        # Top boxes
        if abs(u) < adzig_r[i]:
            return u *adzig_x[i]
        # Lowest box
        isnegative =  (u < 0)
        if i==0:
            return tail_computation(zignor_r,isnegative)

        x = u * adzig_x[i]

        f0 = math.exp(-0.5 * (adzig_x[i] * adzig_x[i] - (x**2)))
        f1 = math.exp(-0.5 * (adzig_x[i+1] * adzig_x[i+1] - (x**2)))

        if (f1 + rand.random() * (f0 - f1)) < 1.0 :
            return x

zignorinit(zignor_c,zignor_r,zignor_v)

for i in xrange(num):
    print zignor()
```

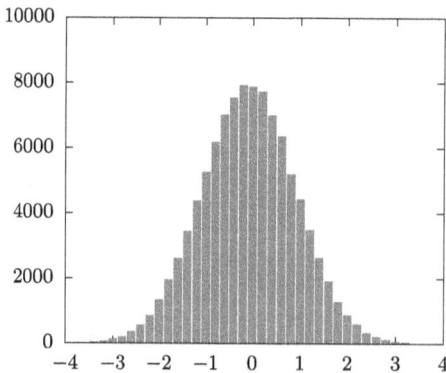

**Figure 7.7:** Histogram of 100 000 Numbers from the ZIGNOR Algorithm.

Running this program to generate 100 000 random floating point numbers yields the normal distribution in Figure 7.7.

# 8 Testing Random Numbers

Effective cryptographic security is dependent on unpredictable random numbers in several ways. Developers of security systems that use random number generators have a need to test the random numbers they use to establish their fitness for use in cryptographic systems and the functionality of the random number generation hardware.

This requires an understanding of the nature of randomness and knowledge of what is being tested for.

Here, we examine seven types of test.

1. Known Answer Test (KAT): A test that checks that deterministic algorithms, such as PRNGs, entropy extractors, and online health tests, are operating correctly.
2. Distinguishability Test: A tests that checks if data are statistically distinguishable from uniform random data.
3. Shannon Entropy Estimation: Measuring the information capacity of the measured data.
4. Min-Entropy Estimation: Measuring the ease of guessing keys made from the measured data.
5. Statistical Prerequisite Measurement: Measuring base statistics such as mean, serial correlation, and stationarity.
6. Online Health Test: A test that continuously checks that the generation of random data is working as the data is generated.

## 8.1 Known Answer Tests

Known Answer Testing is a methodology to show that a random number generator algorithm as implemented conforms to a specification.

Typically there will be a reference implementation written in a high-level language that is used to generate a set of random reference random numbers from an initial seed state. The implementation being tested is put into the same state and run to generate random numbers. The reference numbers and numbers from the implementation are compared and, if the implementation conforms to the algorithm, the numbers will match. See Figure 8.1.

NIST provides known answer vectors for SP800-90A-compliant DRBG algorithms. The NIST SP 800-90A Deterministic Random Bit Generator Validation System (DRBGVS) document http://csrc.nist.gov/groups/STM/cavp/documents/drbg/DRBGVS.pdf describes formats for communicating initial states and a test procedure for each type of DRBG described in SP800-90A.

A descriptor indicates the type of the algorithm being tested, in this case the Hash DRBG using SHA-1:

https://doi.org/10.1515/9781501506062-008

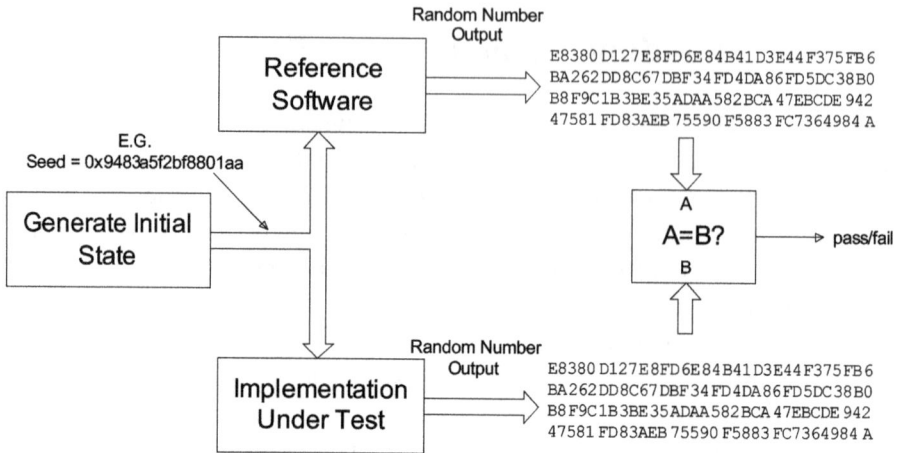

**Figure 8.1:** Known Answer Testing.

```
[SHA-1]
[PredictionResistance = True]
[EntropyInputLen = 128]
[NonceLen = 64]
[PersonalizationStringLen = 0]
[AdditionalInputLen = 0]
[ReturnedBitsLen = 640]
```

It then describes a test procedure:

1. Instantiate DRBG;
2. Generate ReturnedBitsLen random bits, do not print;
3. Generate ReturnedBitsLen random bits, print out;
4. Uninstantiate.

It then lists a series of 15 "challenges" that describe the setup state for each test:

```
COUNT = 0
EntropyInput = 7a0f5bc462fd0d65156d8b1a6ba7387d
Nonce = 1ad732f0b703c3f5
PersonalizationString =
AdditionalInput =
EntropyInputPR = a1b85ba779582722098e7a6c002f5ebb
AdditionalInput =
EntropyInputPR = c335a123499584ec3188a52655294af4
ReturnedBits = ?
```

Known Answer Testing is suitable only for testing deterministic algorithms. In random number testing, it is used to test PRNGs, Entropy Extraction algorithms, and on-line Health Tests.

## 8.2 Distinguishability Tests

This is a statistical hypothesis testing methodology that examines a stream of random bits and computes statistical confidence whether or not the random data under test can be distinguished from a 100% entropic stream of bits.

The result is a pass/fail along with a confidence level (e. g. $P = 0.999$). The pass/-fail indicates whether or not the test algorithm found the data being tested to "look" random. The confidence give the probability (or the inverse) of the hypothesis that the failing result could happen by chance.

Compared to normal statistical tests, this is a bit odd. Normally, you would be looking for a specific hypothesis (e. g., are these two data sets correlated?), and the null hypothesis would be that the two are not correlated. The confidence level would be that of the null hypothesis and you would want its $P$ value (its probability) to be very small. That is, the chance of the null hypothesis being true is very small given the data being tested. Therefore, the opposite of the null hypothesis is very likely.

However, for random number testing, with good data, everything that happens by chance. Every output is equally likely. So, a random number statistical test is not looking to disprove the null hypothesis that the data could have happened by chance. It is looking to prove the hypothesis that the data has some defect, in the form of a detectable deviation from perfect randomness.

Consequently, there is no single perfect randomness test. What you use for testing whether or not data cannot be distinguished from random is a suite of multiple tests that look for a range of specific defects in the data.

Another thing to note about tests that check distingishability from random is that they are really tests of PRNG algorithms, not tests of specific RNGs instances. If you were developing a PRNG algorithm, you would test it against a suite of such tests. A known answer test would be used to test whether an individual instance of a PRNG is correct.

## 8.3 PRNG Test Suites

### 8.3.1 Dieharder

A common open-source PRNG test suite is called dieharder, developed by Robert G. Brown at Duke University. The range of tests in dieharder increases over time. It can be downloaded from http://www.phy.duke.edu/~rgb/General/dieharder.php.

### 8.3.2 NIST SP800-22

Another common test suite is specified in SP800-22 [19] by NIST. NIST provide a software implementation of the SP800-22 test suite at http://csrc.nist.gov/groups/ST/toolkit/rng/documentation_software.html.

The algorithms in SP800-22 are described in detail in Chapter 10.

The dieharder test suite implements a number of the NIST SP800-22 tests.

### 8.3.3 SEMB GM/T 0005-2012

China's SEMB security standards body has published a statistical test suit GM/T 0005-2012 derived from the first version NIST SP800-22, but it excludes some of the controversial tests (such as the Lempel Ziv test) and includes some improved tests such as Maurer's Universal Test Statistic. The later version of SP800-22 caught up with these changes, so the two test suites are very similar.

## 8.4 Entropy Measurements

There are two primary entropy measurements that are useful in measuring random data, Shannon entropy measurements and min-entropy measurement.

These tests are typically run on non post-processed data from an entropy source.

Measuring the Shannon entropy gives a measure of the uniformity of the distribution of symbol frequencies from the source and this gives a measure of the information capacity of the data. A derivation of the equation for Shannon entropy is given in Section 19.1.1, and the procedure is given in Section 8.5.

Measuring min-entropy gives a measure of the difficulty of guessing a value generated from the source. For example, if generated symbols are single bits and the most likely symbols are alternating bits 0101010101..., because the source has negative serial correlation then the optimum guess for the data from the source is 01010101.... A derivation of the equation for min-entropy is given in Section 19.1.2, and the procedure is given in Section 8.6.

The different definitions of entropy, such as Shannon entropy, min-entropy, and max-entropy, are covered in more detail in Chapter 19. In this section, we cover how to test for two variations, Shannon entropy and min entropy.

## 8.5 Shannon Entropy Estimation

Shannon entropy can be considered as the average amount of information in data, resulting from the frequency distribution of the symbols that comprise the data. In communication theory, it describes the information carrying capacity of a channel. The lower the probability of a symbol, the more information it carries when it is sent. Another common way of describing Shannon entropy is as the average entropy, since it takes into account the frequency of all of the symbols in the distribution.

This is described by the standard equation for Shannon entropy.

For a source $X$ producing $n$ different symbols $x_1, x_2, \ldots, x_n$, each of probability $P(x_i)$, the Shannon entropy $H(X)$ is

$$H(X) = -\sum_{i=1}^{n} P(x_i) \log(P(x_i)).$$

The base of the logarithm determines the unit of entropy. With a base of 2, the entropy is measured in bits and one bit of information maps neatly to the concept of a single binary value being able to represent one of 2 states, 1 or 0.

If the base is $e$, the units are called nats. If the base is 10, the units are called Hartlys. In the base 2 case, the term Shannon is also used for the unit, but bit is the more common case.

In this book, base 2 is used and the unit "bit" for representing the quantity of Shannon entropy.

For example, if we have 4 two-bit symbols from a source: 00, 01, 10, and 11 and the frequencies of the symbols are $\frac{1}{8}, \frac{1}{8}, \frac{1}{2}$, and $\frac{1}{4}$, respectively, then, the Shannon entropy of the source is

$$
\begin{aligned}
H(X) &= -\frac{1}{8}\log_2\left(\frac{1}{8}\right) - \frac{1}{8}\log_2\left(\frac{1}{8}\right)\frac{1}{2}\log_2\left(\frac{1}{2}\right) - \frac{1}{4}\log_2\left(\frac{1}{4}\right) \\
&= -\frac{1}{8}(-3) - \frac{1}{8}(-3) - \frac{1}{2}(-1) - \frac{1}{4}(-2) \\
&= \frac{3}{8} + \frac{3}{8} + \frac{1}{2} + \frac{1}{2} \\
&= 1\frac{3}{4}
\end{aligned}
$$

So the average information per symbol is $1\frac{3}{4}$ bits of entropy per symbol. Since there are two bits of data per symbol we can also say there are $\frac{7}{8}$ Shannons per bit of data or slightly more confusingly, there are $\frac{7}{8}$ bits of entropy per bit of data.

## 8.6 Min Entropy Estimation

Min-entropy estimate algorithms come in two forms. The first type of test tries to establish a number that is close to the actual min-entropy of the data. The second type tries to give a lower bound for the entropy in a body of data, under a well-defined model of entropy, such as Rényi entropy. Although it does not tell us what the entropy is, it gives us a bound below which the entropy will not be.

The min-entropy function is denoted as $H_\infty(X)$, where $X$ is a random distribution. The equation for this is

$$H_\infty(X) = H_\infty(p_1, \ldots, p_n) \doteq -\log_2(\max(p_i))$$

So, for any distribution of symbol probabilities $p_1, \ldots, p_n$ from a random variable, the min-entropy, find the highest probability symbol, take $\log_2()$ of that symbol and that will be the min-entropy.

Given the distribution of 2-bit symbols 00, 01, 10, 11 used previously, $\frac{1}{8}, \frac{1}{8}, \frac{1}{2}$, and $\frac{1}{4}$, respectively, we have

$$\max_{p_i} = \max\left(\frac{1}{8}, \frac{1}{8}, \frac{1}{2}, \frac{1}{4}\right) = \frac{1}{2},$$

$$-\log_2\left(\frac{1}{2}\right) = 1.$$

So, we have 1 bit of entropy for every 2 bits of data. The entropy rate is $\frac{1}{2}$.

In order to establish the distribution of symbols from data, you need enough data to build a representative distribution. So, the number of symbols available to test should be much larger than the number of different symbols in the distribution. Fortunately, when testing random numbers, it is easy to simply run the RNG for long enough to produce enough data.

One of the min-entropy tests in SP800-90B is the "Frequency Test", which performs this test, counting the most frequent symbol in the data and deriving the min-entropy from that. However, it reduces the entropy as a function of the amount of the data tested and the confidence level required. Compared to the above approach of computing $-\log_2(\max(p_i))$ from the measured symbol frequencies, the Frequency Test gives a lower bound for the min-entropy instead of an entropy estimate.

The Frequency Test procedure is to compute pmax:

$$\text{pmax} = \max_{i=1..n}\left(\frac{\text{count}_i}{N}\right),$$

where $N$ is the amount of symbols in the data being counted.

With $N$, and a confidence level $\alpha$, compute a fiddle factor $\varepsilon$:

$$\varepsilon = \sqrt{\frac{\log(\frac{1}{1-\alpha})}{2N}}$$

The min-entropy is then computed as

$$\text{min-entropy} = -\log_2(\text{pmax} + \varepsilon).$$

So, having smaller amounts of test data will make the lower bound worse and demanding a higher confidence level will make the lower bound worse. As the quantity of test data increases, the result of the Frequency Test will approach the result of the simple min-entropy test computed using $-\log_2(\max(p_i))$.

## 8.7 Model Equivalence Testing

It is possible to formally analyze a model of a system and to show that the output is random. The model can be simulated and the resulting random data characterized. The random data to be tested is tested for equivalence to the data from the model. This is effective when you have a physical random number generator and you want to show that its design, when built correctly, will behave like a model that is known to make random numbers and that the data it generates looks like the data the model generates.

A simple example is a Gaussian source, where electrical noise with Gaussian distribution is sampled by a quantizing digital system. The modeling of the source may indicate that the distribution of the values has some mean $\mu$, standard deviation $\sigma$, and closely follows a Gaussian distribution.

To perform a model equivalence test, sample a large amount of data from the random source and measure the mean and standard deviation and perform a test to show that the data has a Gaussian distribution. If the measured mean and standard deviation match the values from the model, and the data is shown to have a Gaussian distribution, then, the equivalence of the model and the physical entropy source has been shown.

This allows the model to be used to theorize about the min-entropy of the source. As such, model equivalence testing is often used to show that the model is a true model of the source, rather than to test the source.

## 8.8 Statistical Prerequisite Testing

Certain properties of random numbers, such as bias or statistical independence or correlation are necessary prerequisites for some algorithms. For example, the Yuval Peres whitener (YP) algorithm requires statistically independent numbers at the input for the properties of the YP whitener to hold. Metrics such as the serial correlation coefficient or mean or $\chi^2$ can be used to test for these prerequisites.

These tests tend to be simple mathematical measurements of the data. They can be suitable for analyzing defects in the data (like bias or correlation) or testing that input data meets the requirements of the consuming algorithm.

### 8.8.1 Mean

The mean of data is the sum of all the data divided by the number of values. Given $n$ values $x_0, \ldots, x_{n-1}$,

$$\text{Mean} = \sum_{i=0}^{n-1} \frac{x_i}{n}.$$

If we have uniform random numbers, then as we increase the number of values, the mean tends to approach the mid point $\max(x_i)/2$.

If we know data has some bias, the mean would be a suitable test to show how biased it is. It is not suitable to determine if something is or is not biased, since it does not yield a $P$ value to tell you how likely it is to be biased for any given mean. For that problem, the $\chi^2$ test of randomness is appropriate.

### 8.8.2 Standard Deviation

The formula for the standard deviation of sampled data from normally distributed data is

$$SD = \sqrt{\frac{1}{n-1} \sum (x_i - \bar{x})}.$$

We can see that this formula uses the mean of the data sample $\bar{x}$, and so, to compute the value we first have to run through the data computing the mean $\bar{x}$. Then, we run through the data a second time computing the sum $\sum (x_i - \bar{x})$.

If the data is too big for fit in memory, then, this would be an inefficient algorithm because the file must be read twice.

A number of algorithms have been developed that can compute variance and standard deviation in a single pass. One example is Welford's algorithm.

The python program in Listing 8.1 reads each line of a file once, converting the line to a floating point value and feeding it to Welford's algorithm. Welford's algorithm computes the population variance. Therefore, at the end the program converts it to the population standard deviation and the sample standard deviation.

The program expects the file to contain one floating point or integer value per line.

**Listing 8.1:** Welford's Algorithm

```python
#!/usr/bin/env python
import math
import sys

class welford():
    def __init__(self):
        self.n = 0
        self.mean = 0.0
        self.m2 = 0.0

    def update(self,c):
        if type(c) == list:
            for x in c:
                self.n += 1
                delta = x - self.mean
```

```python
            self.mean += delta/self.n
            delta2 = x - self.mean
            self.m2 += delta*delta2
        else:
            x = c
            self.n += 1
            delta = x - self.mean
            self.mean += delta/self.n
            delta2 = x - self.mean
            self.m2 += delta*delta2

    def results(self):
        pop_variance = self.m2/self.n
        pop_stddev = math.sqrt(self.m2/self.n)
        sample_variance = self.m2/(self.n-1)
        sample_stddev = math.sqrt(self.m2/(self.n-1))
        return (pop_variance,
                pop_stddev,
                sample_variance,
                sample_stddev,
                self.mean,
                self.n)

w = welford()

if sys.argv > 0:   # Get the filename
    filename = sys.argv[1]
    file = open(filename,"r")
else:
    file = sys.stdin

for line in file.readlines(): # process the file
    try:
        value = float(line)
        w.update(value)
    except:
        pass

# Get the results
(p_v, p_sd , s_v, s_sd, mean, n) = w.results()
if n < 2:
    print "Too few samples (%d) to compute standard deviation" % n
else:
    print "n                              : ", n
    print "Mean                           : ",mean
    print "Population Variance            : ",p_v
    print "Population Standard Deviation  : ",p_sd
    print "Sample Variance                : ",s_v
    print "Sample Standard Deviation      : ",s_sd
```

To try this out, djenrandom is invoked to generate 50 000 samples of floating point data with mean of 50 and variance of 9.

```
$ djenrandom -m normal --mean=50 --variance=9 -k 50 > normal_data.dat
```

Then the program is run over the file.

```
$ python welford.py normal_data.dat
n                             :   51200
Mean                          :   49.9953040936
Population Variance           :   9.01365729051
Population Standard Deviation :   3.00227535221
Sample Variance               :   9.01383334194
Sample Standard Deviation     :   3.00230467174
```

We can see that the measured mean is close to 50, the measured variance is close to 9, and the measured standard deviation is close to $\sqrt{9}$.

### 8.8.3 The $\chi^2$ Test of Randomness

The $\chi^2$ (pronouced "kai-squared") test of randomness is specified in Knuth's "Art of Computer Programming" [10]. It uses a $\chi^2$ goodness-of-fit test to measure the probability that the observed bias would have occurred by chance for an unbiased source. Thus, it is only a bias test and cannot distinguish correlation or grouping or other defects in the data.

It is most useful where you know your data to be random, and want to ensure that it is unbiased.

If you consider a set of say 10 000 unbiased perfectly random bits, you would not expect the bias to be exactly 50/50. We expect that there will be some accumulated bias. This is the same thing as the random walk distance considered in Section 18.5. For random data, if you make a bucket for each possible value and place the values from the random data set in their matching bucket, you expect each value to drop into the available buckets evenly, in the case of binary data, 50% 0s and 50% 1s. In the case of $k$ possible values, you can expect each bucket to get $\frac{n}{k}$ values, give or take a little variation due to the randomization. So, in Figure 8.2, you can expect each bucket to get 500 values $\pm$ some variation. The $\chi^2$ distribution gives the probability of that variation.

You can compute an error function (the $\chi^2$ statistic) of how far away from the ideal distribution the data is by summing the squares of the difference between an even distribution and the actual distribution in each bucket.

Given n random numbers, between 0 and $k-1$ separated into buckets, the $\chi^2$ statistic can be computed as the sum are the squares of the difference between the number in each bucket and the expected average number in each bucket.

$$\chi^2 = \sum_{i=1}^{n} \left( \text{bucket}_i - \frac{k}{n} \right)^2$$

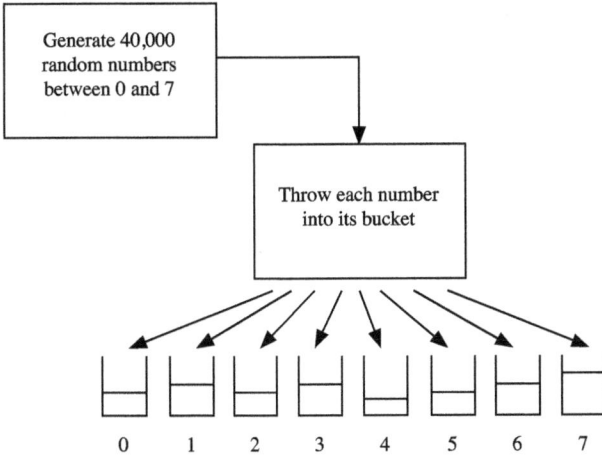

**Figure 8.2:** $\chi^2$ Testing.

This $\chi^2$ statistic follows a $\chi^2(n-1)$ distribution, where $n$ (the number of trials) is also the degrees of freedom of the $\chi^2$ curve. One consequence of this is that a completely even distribution is not the most expected result. In a number of samples the most likely total number of biased buckets is not zero.

In Figure 8.3, you can see how as the number of tested numbers increased, shown as the increasing degrees of freedom, the most expected bias also increases, seen as the rightwards movement of the peak of the curve as *df* increases.

The following R code will generate the $\chi^2$ curves for degrees of freedom between 0 and 7:

**Listing 8.2:** R Chi Square Plot

```
pdf("chisqplot.pdf")
x <- seq(0,19, length = 300)
degf <- c(1,2,3,4,5,6,7)
labels <- c("df=1", "df=2", "df=3", "df=4", "df=5", "df=6", "df=7")
hx = dchisq(x, df=1)
plot(x, hx, type="l", lty=2, ylim=c(0.0,0.6),
  xlab="Chi-Square_Error_Value", ylab="Probability",
  main="Chi_Square_Distributions")
for (i in 1:7) {
        lines(x, dchisq(x,degf[i]), lwd=2, col="black")
}
```

Once you know an error sum, computed over truly random data will follow the $\chi^2$ distributions, you can compute the error sum over the measured data and compare against a $\chi^2$ distribution to determine the proportion of times the error sum of truly random data would exceed the error sum of the measured data. For truly random data, we can expect the Chi square statistic to be greater than the reference $\chi^2$ statistic 50%

**Chi Square Distributions**

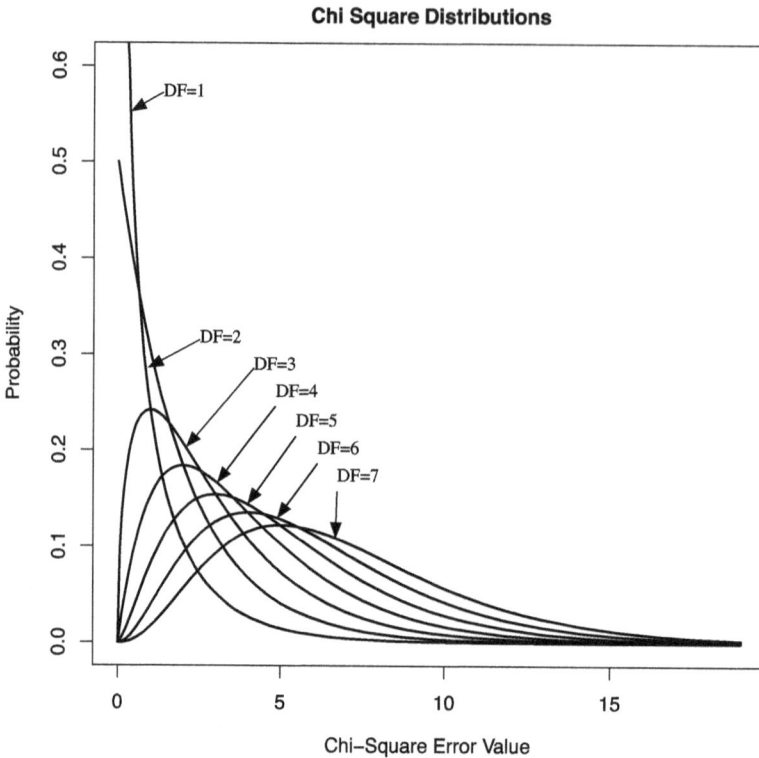

**Figure 8.3:** $\chi^2$ Curves.

of the time and less for 50% of the time. So, the output of a $\chi^2$ test of randomness is the percentage of time the $\chi^2$ result would exceed the expected $\chi^2$ for uniform random data. From that result, a $P$ value is calculated, giving the probability that the source data is random.

The tools "ent" from Fourmilab and the improved version "djent" both implement the $\chi^2$ test. An example of djent being run over 128 kibibytes of uniform binary data is shown in Listing 8.3, giving a $P$ value of 82%.

**Listing 8.3:** Example of djent $\chi^2$ Test Over Uniform Data

```
$ djenrandom -b -k 128 | djent -b
  Shannon IID Entropy = 1.000000 bits per symbol
  Optimal compression would compress by 0.000004 percent
  Chi square: symbol count=1048569, distribution=0.05,
              randomly exceeds 82.00 percent of the time
  Mean = 0.499889
  Monte Carlo value for Pi is 3.143603 (error 0.06 percent).
  Serial Correlation = -0.001133
$
```

The second example in Listing 8.4 uses biased data, and the result is a failing $P$ value of 0.0%.

**Listing 8.4:** Example of djent $\chi^2$ Test Over Biased Data

```
$ djenrandom -b -k 128 -m biased --bias=0.4 | djent -b
  Shannon IID Entropy = 0.971055 bits per symbol
  Optimal compression would compress by 2.894496 percent
  Chi square: symbol count=1048569, distribution=41792.97,
              randomly exceeds 0.00 percent of the time
  Mean = 0.400179
  Monte Carlo value for Pi is 3.614557 (error 15.05 percent).
  Serial Correlation = -0.001721
$
```

The result of the test is a $P$ value between 0 and 1. Biased data tends to send the $P$ value close to the 0 or 1 end. So, if you get a result of 0.999 or 0.001, then it is a strong indication that the data is biased.

However, this result is often misconstrued, with 0.5 being perceived as the "goal" and 0.01 to be a failure. In fact, for truly unbiased random data, the $P$ value is uniform between 0 and 1. So, all values are equally likely. It will land between 0 and 0.1 10% of the time. It will land between 0.9 and 1 10% of the time. Thus, if you run 10000 $\chi^2$ tests of randomness, then you can expect to get an average of 10 results between 0 and 0.001 and 1 result between 0 and 0.0001.

Often the result is given as a percentage. "ent" does this.

So, the right way to use the $\chi^2$ test of randomness is to run several tests and check that the distribution of the output $P$ values looks uniform.

For example, here is the result of running 10 kibibyte of data through the $\chi^2$ test of randomness 20 times, shown to 4 significant digits, using the following command:

```
djenrandom -s -b -k 10 | ent -b | grep exceed | awk '\{print \$5\}'
```

The -s makes djenrandom act as a nondeterministic generator by pulling seed data from the Linux /dev/random service. The -b causes it to output binary data rather than hexadecimal text. The -k 10 causes it to output 10 kibibyte of data. This is piped into ent, and we filter the line with the $\chi^2$ result in it with grep exceed. The final awk plucks out the percentage.

The resulting $P$ values for twenty runs were as follows:

74.26, 68.01, 71.63, 8.19, 94.99, 10.50, 77.99, 86.13, 14.42, 55.25, 89.99, 93.87, 58.09, 56.66, 46.31, 36.74, 28.50, 30.76, 77.99, 74.26

We can capture 10 000 $P$ values by running a little loop, shown here as a bash script.

```
#!/bin/bash

for i in {1..10000}
```

```
do
    djenrandom -s -b -k 10 | ent -b | grep exceed | awk '{print $5}'
done
```

If we plot a histogram of the 10 000 values, then we get the distribution shown in Figure 8.4.

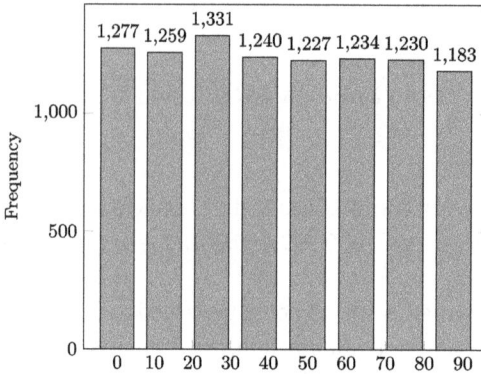

**Figure 8.4:** Distribution of P Values From $\chi^2$ Test Over Uniform Data.

As you can see, even though the data that was tested was a perfect 50/50 biased random source, the normal variation in the bias for any given sample yields a uniformly varying P value. We can try the same thing, but this time we feed in 45/55 biased data using the biased model of the djenrandom command

```
djenrandom -s -m biased --bias=0.45 -b -k 10 | ent -b | grep exceed | awk '\{print \$7\}'
```

The results over 20 runs of the P values are:

0.01, 0.01, 0.01, 0.01, 0.01, 0.01, 0.01, 0.01, 0.01, 0.01, 0.01, 0.01, 0.01, 0.01, 0.01, 0.01, 0.01, 0.01, 0.01, 0.01

So, whereas a single 0.01 might occur by chance 1 in 100 times, with truly random data, a string of them over multiple tests gives a highly confident result that the data is biased. In this case, the joint probability of 20 P values 0.01 or less from unbiased random data is

$$P(20 \text{ P-values each} \leq 0.01) = \frac{1}{100}^{20} = 10^{-40}.$$

So, the probability we are testing unbiased data is very close to zero and we can conclude we have biased data.

From this, we can conclude that the $\chi^2$ test of randomness is a bias test, but one that takes into account that over a number of samples, we expect a certain amount of bias, and a perfect 0.5 bias is less likely than a bias that includes some bias you would expect in perfectly random data. This is what makes it more effective than simply computing the mean. It knows how big to expect the random bias to be as a function of the number of samples. Like many tests in this book, it is appropriate to perform the test a number of times to ensure the individual result was not an outlier.

### 8.8.4 Serial Correlation Coefficient

The serial correlation coefficient (SCC) gives a measure of how much a value in a list of random values is linked to its neighboring bits. Lag-$N$ correlation computes the correlation between each value, and the value that is $N$ positions away in the list. For example, in Lag-3 serial correlation, $x_4$ would be compared with $x_7$. Lag-1 correlation is the same as SCC. So, the SCC is a special case of Lag-$N$ serial correlation, where $N = 1$.

If you have data that are shown to be correlated with time shifted versions of itself, the SCC and Lag-$N$ tests are appropriate to tell you how correlated with itself the data is. In some disciplines, this is called "autocorrelation".

There are two ranges used to report serial correlation. In cryptography, SCC is usually reported in the range $-1$ to $+1$, where 0 is uncorrelated. Positive values indicate that a bit is more likely to equal the previous bit than not. Negative values of SCC indicate a bit is more likely to be the opposite of its previous bit than not.

In signal processing, a range from 0 to 1 is sometimes used, with 0.5 being uncorrelated. Values greater than 0.5 indicate that a bit is more likely to equal the previous bit than not. Values lower than 0.5 indicate a bit is more likely to be the opposite of its previous bit than not.

The ent tool and the SCC[1] algorithm, included in this book, report the $-1$ to $+1$ range.

The correlation coefficient $c$ between two sequences of discrete numbers $x_0, \ldots, x_{n-1}$ and $y_0, \ldots, y_{n-1}$ is

$$c = \frac{n(\sum_{i=0}^{n-1} x_i y_i) - (\sum_{i=0}^{n-1} x_i)(\sum_{i=0}^{n-1} y_i)}{\sqrt{(n \sum_{i=0}^{n-1} x_i^2 - (\sum_{i=0}^{n-1} x_i)^2)(n \sum_{i=0}^{n-1} y_i^2 - (\sum_{i=0}^{n-1} y_i)^2)}}.$$

To compute the serial correlation coefficient of a series of numbers, we compute the correlation coefficient of the series with itself, shifted by one position so it measures how much $x_i$ depends on $x_{i-1}$.

By putting $x_{i-1}$ in place of $y_i$ in the above equation we get the base equation for the serial correlation coefficient scc:

$$\text{scc} = \frac{n(\sum_{i=0}^{n-1} x_i x_{(i+1 \mod n)}) - (\sum_{i=0}^{n-1} x_i)^2}{n(\sum_{i=0}^{n-1} x_i^2) - (\sum_{i=0}^{n-1} x_i)^2}.$$

---

[1] The algorithm for SCC is described in Knuth's *The Art of Computer Programming*, volume 2 [10], Section 3.3.2, Subsection K.

The index of the shifted term in the numerator $(i + 1 \mod n)$ causes the data to be treated as if it were cyclic. The successor to the final value $x_{n-1}$ is treated as if it wrapped around to the start, so it is multiplied by $x_0$. This is not representative of time series data where the final value of the series certainly is not followed by the first. Therefore, a common change is to reduce $n$ by one and do the computation from $x_0$ to $x_{n-2}$, so the final value is only used as the successor to the penultimate value and is not treated as having a successor.

This leads us to examine the implementation of the SCC calculation in the ent tool. ent is written in C, and the code includes a lot of bit twiddling that is not relevant to this analysis. So, the code in Listing 8.5 is a version of the ent SCC code written in python, with only the essential details remaining.

We assume the input is a list of floating point values.

We can see the code implements the wrap around, where it stores the first value as u0 and uses it in the final calculation. The code has three counters (t1, t2, and t3) that are updated as the data is passed into each iteration of the algorithm. The t1 accumulator accumulates the values multiplied by their successor:

$$t_1 = \left( \sum_{i=0}^{n-1} x_i x_{(i+1 \mod n)} \right).$$

In data where the final value is not adjacent to the first value such as time series data, the correct thing to do is to skip the comparison of the first value with the last value, and reduce the total count by 1. The scc algorithm in djent defaults to this behavior but allows wrap-around behavior to be selected.

The counter t2 adds up the values:

$$t_2 = \left( \sum_{i=0}^{n-1} x_i \right).$$

The counter t3 accumulates the square of the values:

$$t_3 = \left( \sum_{i=0}^{n-1} x_i^2 \right).$$

n is the count of the values, equal to $n$ in the equation.

**Listing 8.5:** ent Algorithm for SCC

```python
def ent_scc(values):
    # Initialize
    first = True
    t1 = 0.0
    t2 = 0.0
    t3 = 0.0
    n = 0
```

```
for value in values:
    n += 1

    if first:   # Store first value as u0
        first = False
        last = 0
        u0 = value
    else:
        t1 = t1 + last * value

    t2 = t2 + value
    t3 = t3 + value**2
    last = value

# last cycle wrap around
t1 = t1 + last*u0

# Now compute the SCC from the counters
scc = (n * t1 - (t3*t3))/(n * t2 - (t3*t3))

return scc
```

We can see how the final expression is simply the equation for the SCC, where the summations are contained in the counters.

In computer RNGs, the output is usually a series of bits. The SCC algorithm can be greatly simplified if the data is a binary bit stream. Consider the four possible 2-bit sequences 00, 01, 10, and 11, where the leftmost bit is the earlier bit, and the rightmost bit is the successor.

The t1 counter accumulates t1 = t1 + bit0 * bit1.

So, for the 4-bit pairs, the change in t1 is

```
00 : t1 unchanged
01 : t1 unchanged
10 : t1 unchanged
11 : t1 increments by 1.
```

For t2, if the current bit is 1, increment t2, else t2 remains the same.

For t3, the square of 0 is 0, and the square of 1 is 1. So, t3 is exactly the same as t2.

Therefore, the binary SCC algorithm, without wrap around is as follows:

**Listing 8.6:** Algorithm to Compute SCC Over Binary Time Series

```
def binary_scc(bits):
    # Initialize
    t1 = 0
    t2 = 0
    n = 0
    first = True
```

```
for bit in bits:
    n = n+1
    if first:  # Skip first bit, we need 2 bits
        first = False
    else:
        if (last==1) and (bit==1) t1 += 1
        if (last==1) t2 = t2+1
    last = value

# Now compute the SCC from the counters
n = n-1 # Reduce n because we are not wrapping
scc = (n*t1 - t2*t2)/(n*t2 - t2*t2)

return scc
```

This leads to an efficient hardware implementation of an SCC measurement.

Simply count the frequency of each of the four 2-bit patterns in the data. We will call them count00, count01, count10, and count11. $n$ is the number of patterns counted, that is, $n$ = count00 + count01 + count10 + count11.

Given the behavior of the pattern counters, we know that

```
t1 = count11
t2 = count01 + count11.
```

The SCC computation at the end is then

$$n = count00 + count01 + count10 + count11$$

$$scc = \frac{n(count11) - (count01 + count11)(count01 + count11)}{n(count01 + count11) - (count01 + count11)(count01 + count11)}$$

So, a simple hardware implementation in an RNG is to count the frequency of the four patterns. Then offline, the counts can be read out and the computation done in software.

### 8.8.5 Lag-*N* Correlation

The SCC algorithm computes the correlation between each bit and the next bit. We can extend the SCC algorithm to compute the correlation between each bit and the bit that is $n$ steps away. This is called Lag-*N* correlation, where the correlation is computed between each bit $x_i$ and $x_{i+n}$.

**Listing 8.7:** Algorithm to Compute Lag-N Correlation Over Binary Sequence

```
def binary_lagn(bits,n):
    # Initialize
    t1 = 0
```

```
t2 = 0
count = len(bits)
for i in xrange(count):
    if first:  # Skip first bit, we need 2 bits
        first = False
    else:
        if (bits[i+n % count]==1) and (bits[i]==1) t1 += 1
        if (bits[i]==1) t2 = t2+1

# Now compute the SCC from the counters
lagnc = (count*t1 - t2*t2)/(count*t2 - t2*t2)

return lagnc
```

If we compute the Lag-$N$ correlation coefficient for all values of $N$ and plotted the result, we will get a correlogram. The Lag-0 point is always one, since each value always equals itself. In physical data, the Lag-$N$ correlation usually reduces with increasing $N$.

Figure 8.5 shows a correlogram of binary data generated with a positive SCC of 0.7.

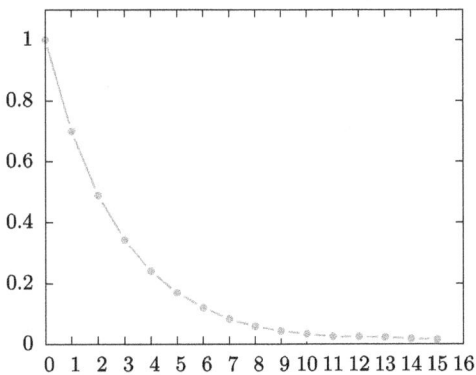

**Figure 8.5:** Correlogram of 81920 Random Bits Generated With SCC = 0.7.

The SCC ranges from –1 to +1. So, to map to probabilities, we need to divide by 2 and add 0.5 to get to range from 0 to 1. Therefore, the probability of 1, given the previous bit, was 1, and if the SCC is 0.7, then it is $0.5 + \frac{0.7}{2} = 0.85$.

As you might expect, if the probability of 1, given the previous bit, was 1 is 0.85, then the probability that the next bit will be one is reduced further. The first bit is 1, so the second bit is 1 85% of the time and 0 15% of the time. The third bit is 1 85% of the time that the second bit is 1, and 30% of the time that the second bit is 0.

To look at correlograms with straightforward probabilistic mathematics, we start by fixing $x_i$ to be 1 and see where it takes us; $b$ is a bit, either 0 or 1, and $\bar{b}$ is the inverse of $b$.

$$P(x_i = b) = 1$$

$$\text{adjbias} = 0.5 + \frac{\text{SCC}}{2}$$

$$P(x_{i+1} = b | x_i = b) = \text{adjbias}$$

$$P(x_{i+1} = \bar{b} | x_i = b) = 1 - \text{adjbias}$$

$$P(x_{i+2} = b | x_i = b) = P(x_{i+1} = b | x_i = b)\text{adjbias} + P(x_{i+1} = \bar{b} | x_i = b)(1 - \text{adjbias})$$

So, for SCC = 0.7, the probability of bits spaced 2 spaces away from each other being the same is $0.85^2 + 0.15^2 = 0.7225 + 0.0225 = 0.745$, and the Lag-2 correlation coefficient is $2(0.745 - 0.5) = 0.49$.

Extending to the $n$th bit, we multiply the previous pair of probabilities by the adjacent probabilities. Then, we convert back from bias to correlation with corr = $2(\text{bias} - 0.5)$.

$$P(x_{i+n} = b | x_i = b) = P(x_{i+n-1} = b | x_i = b)\text{adjbias} + P(x_{i+n-1} = \bar{b} | x_i = b)(1 - \text{adjbias})$$

$$\text{lag}_n = 2(P(x_{i+n} = b | x_i = b) - 0.5)$$

We can compute this iteratively as follows:

**Listing 8.8:** Algorithm to Compute Lag-N Correlation From SCC

```python
#!/usr/bin/env python

def lagn_scc(scc,n):
    # Initialize
    lagns=list()
    probs = list()
    probs.append(1.0) # Lag-0 Correlation == 1
    lagns.append(1.0)

    lag1prob = (scc/2.0)+0.5

    for i in xrange(1,n):
        prob = (lag1prob * probs[i-1]) + ((1-lag1prob)*(1-probs[i-1]))
        probs.append(prob)
        # convert from probability to correlation coef
        lagns.append((prob-0.5)*2.0)

    return lagns, probs

print "#n__lagn_cc_____bias"
lagns,probs = lagn_scc(scc=0.7,n=16)
for i in xrange(len(lagns)):
    print "%02d__%1.8f__%1.8f" % (i,lagns[i],probs[i])
```

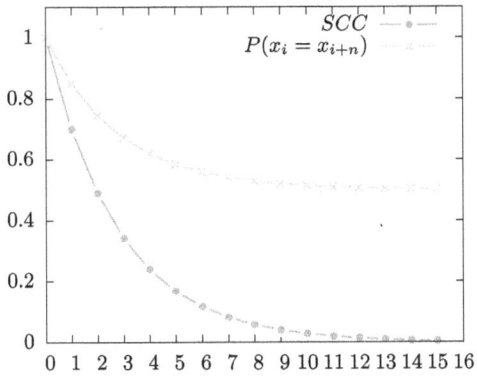

**Figure 8.6:** Lag-*N* Computed From SCC = −0.7.

If we plot the output, we see that as the separation between the bits increases, the bias tends to 0.5, and the SCC tends to 0. See Figure 8.6.

So, the bias of the bit that is 2 steps away from the initial bit that has been fixed to 1 is closer to 50% than the bit that is 1 step away, and this continues to get closer to unbiased as *n* increases.

If the SCC is negative, we get a different result. Each successive bit is more likely to be the opposite of the previous bit. So, a bit two steps away is more likely to be the same. Thus, we get an oscillating curve that converges to unbiased, as shown in Figure 8.7.

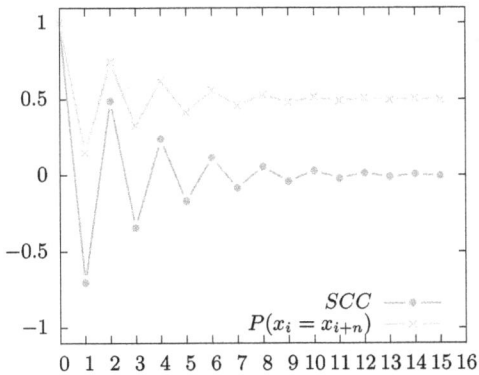

**Figure 8.7:** Lag-*N* Computed From SCC = −0.7.

### 8.8.6 A Note on Bit Ordering

When analyzing random numbers it is important to get the bit ordering correct. In creating Figure 8.5, the initial version had a bug that treated the bits in the bytes of the random file in reverse order, assuming that the last bit came first, and vice versa. The resulting graph, Figure 8.8 showed an interesting shape.

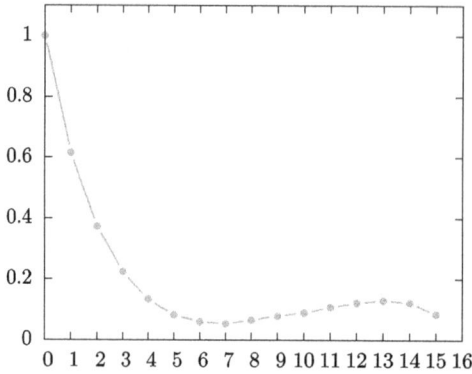

**Figure 8.8:** Correlogram of Bit Reversed Random Data Generated With SCC = 0.7.

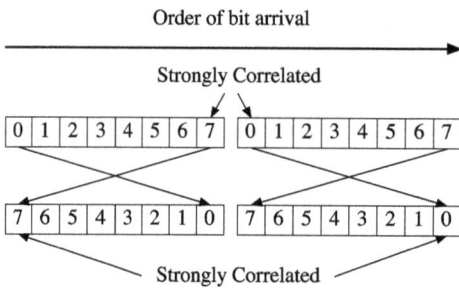

**Figure 8.9:** Effect of Bit Reversal on Serial Correlation.

The secondary peak is consistent with two bits: the last bit of one byte and the first bit of the next byte, which are most strongly correlated with each other, being moved to the opposite ends of their respective bytes. So, it leads to the Lag-$N$ serial correlation coefficient rising to a local peak, where $N$ is close to the distance in bits between these two bits, as shown in Figure 8.9.

If you have data that has a correlogram with unexplained peaks such as this, try bit reversing the data, and see if it makes the peak go away.

### 8.8.7 Efficient Computation of a Correlogram using FFTs

The computation of a correlogram takes $O(n^2)$ multiplications. So, for large amounts of data, this is computationally unfeasible. The Wiener–Khinchin algorithm achieves $O(n \log_2(n))$ multiplications using Fast Fourier Transforms.

Given an array of time series data value $X(t)$,

1. Compute frequency series fs($f$) = FFT($x(t)$).
2. Compute a new series $S(f)$ = fs($f$)fs$^*$($f$) where fs$^*$($f$) is the complex conjugate of fs($f$).
3. Compute the correlogram $R$(lag) = IFFT($S(f)$).

The code below implements the Wiener–Khinchin algorithm. It uses the python numpy library that provides FFT and IFFT functions. Some negatively serially correlated data are created in the main body and fed into the algorithm and the first 32 coefficients are printed out.

**Listing 8.9:** Wiener–Khinchin Algorithm

```python
#!/usr/bin/env python

import math
import numpy
import cmath
import random

def wiener_khninchin(bits):
    n = len(bits)
    if (n % 2) == 1:          # Make it an even number
        raise ValueError("The_number_of_data_samples_must_be_even")

    ts = list()               # Convert to +1,-1
    for bit in bits:
        if bit == 0:
            ts.append(-1.0)
        else:
            ts.append(1.0)

    ts_np = numpy.array(ts)
    fs = numpy.fft.fft(ts_np)   # Compute DFT

    # Multiply each element by its complex conjugate
    fs_out = list()
    for x in xrange(len(fs)):
        theconjugate = fs[x].conjugate()
        newvalue = fs[x]*theconjugate
        fs_out.append(newvalue)
    np_fs_out = numpy.array(fs_out)

    # Take the inverse FFT
    crg = numpy.fft.ifft(np_fs_out)

    # Turn it into a list of reals
    correlogram = list()
    for x in  crg:
        correlogram.append(x.real/n)

    return correlogram

# Make some serially correlated bits
r = random.SystemRandom()
```

```
bits = list()
previous = 0
for i in xrange(256):
    if previous == 0:
        level = 0.2
    else:
        level = 0.8
    ref = r.random()
    if (ref > level):
        newbit = 1
    else:
        newbit = 0
    previous = newbit
    bits.append(newbit)

c = wiener_khninchin(bits) # Compute the correlogram

print "bits:",bits
print
for i in xrange(32):
    print "%02d__%06f" % (i,c[i])
```

In the output we can see the expected results, with the 0 lag position being 1 (since the data are equal to themselves), and the correlation with later bits alternating negative and positive and reducing with distance.

```
00   1.000000
01   -0.593750
02   0.359375
03   -0.187500
04   0.093750
05   -0.109375
06   0.078125
07   -0.140625
08   0.140625
09   -0.093750
10   0.062500
11   -0.046875
12   0.093750
13   -0.187500
14   0.265625
15   -0.250000
16   0.171875
17   -0.125000
18   0.140625
19   -0.171875
20   0.140625
21   -0.109375
22   0.093750
23   -0.000000
```

```
24   -0.046875
25    0.093750
26   -0.093750
27    0.125000
28   -0.093750
29    0.078125
30   -0.093750
31    0.078125
```

When plotted, Figure 8.10 shows the alternating pattern for the correlogram of negatively serially correlated data.

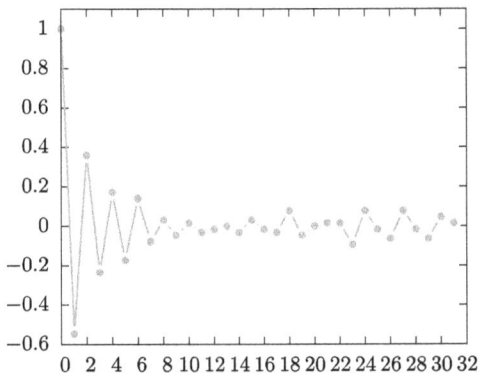

Figure 8.10: Correlogram Using the Wiener–Khinchin Algorithm.

## 8.9 The Problem Distinguishing Entropy and Pseudorandomness

A basic problem faces anyone who is trying to test for entropy, that is, nondeterministic, uniform randomness. To the observer who does not possess the right key, it can be shown that it is computationally infeasible to distinguish true randomness from cryptographically secure pseudorandom data. Yet, to an observer who possesses the key to the PRNG, it is trivial to distinguish a true random stream from a pseudorandom stream generated under that key.

In this way, unpredictability can be a property of what the observer knows. To one observer a random stream may be predictable. To another, the same stream may not be predictable.

So, in the general case, it is impossible to analyze a random number stream and declare it to be entropic. It may be pseudorandom, and you have no way of telling when you are only analyzing the data and not the source.

If you know enough about the source of entropy, then you may be able to compute how entropic the output data is. This tends to involve building a mathematical model of the source and showing mathematically that, if the model is an accurate representation of the source, then the source has some level of min-entropy at its output. Some sources are easy to model, some are not readily analyzable.

If we have a good source of entropy, we can make seeds for a PRNG and run the PRNG. Now, you can show, from the amount of entropy in the internal state of the PRNG, how hard it is to guess that state, and therefore how hard it is to guess the output stream, by showing the PRNG is cryptographically secure.

Another less ideal way of showing a PRNG is "good" in some way is to show that it cannot be distinguished from random data. This does not mean it has any entropy, but if it does, it would meet some security threshold.

## 8.10 Statistical Tests of Uniformity

In Section 10, we look at tests that seek to discover if the data can be distinguished from uniform data, and return a pass/fail result.

One source of these tests is NIST SP800-22Rev1a [19]. This is covered in Chapter 10. Another source is the Dieharder test suite, which is covered in Chapter 11.

## 8.11 Results That are "Too Good"

The Internet is full of examples of random data from various random sources being tested by the statistical analysis program ent. Here is an example of ent being used to test 1 Mibyte of random data from the RdRand instruction in an Intel CPU:

```
$ quickrdrand -b -k 1024 | ent -b
Entropy = 1.000000 bits per bit.

Optimum compression would reduce the size
of this 8388608 bit file by 0 percent.

Chi square distribution for 8388608 samples is 2.68, and randomly
would exceed this value 10.14 percent of the times.

Arithmetic mean value of data bits is 0.4997 (0.5 = random).
Monte Carlo value for Pi is 3.145512182 (error 0.12 percent).
Serial correlation coefficient is 0.000213 (totally uncorrelated = 0.0).
$
```

The result of the $\chi^2$ test is a statement

```
and randomly would exceed this value 10.14 percent of the times.
```

The number 10.14 will become very close to 0 or very close to 100 for data that is biased. If the data is uniformly random, the number will vary uniformly between 0 and 100. Here are the numbers for a sequence of 10 runs of the same procedure, with uniform random data from the RdRand instruction run on a late 2013 model Apple MacBook Pro:

58.49, 64.21, 1.26, 72.63, 40.34, 55.45, 78.88, 52.52, 52.12, 32.92.

One common misunderstanding is that a perfect result would be 50.00, when in reality perfect random data would yield numbers distributed uniformly, like those above, and the probability of getting a specific number like 50.00% to 4 significant digits is $\frac{1}{10000}$.

Try searching the Internet for the string

```
and randomly would exceed this value 50.00 percent of the times.
```

and you will find many examples of people claiming they put the output of an RNG through ent and got that result. Of course, it is a highly suspect result. Ways to get a result of 50.00% include:

- Run the test repeatedly until you get the right answer. This takes on average 10 000 attempts.
- Flip bits in the random data to nudge the value to the desired outcome.
- Edit the text of the output.
- Get very, very, very lucky.

I am not in a position to judge which it might be, but exercise caution in interpreting such results.

## 8.12 Summary

Testing random numbers by looking at the output data, in the absence of the generation process, is of limited use. It can show that data are not random, but it cannot show that data are random.

Proper testing for entropy and subsequent processed random numbers requires a chain of reasoning that shows why the source is random, shows that the source is functioning, and shows that the subsequent extraction and PRNG stages have the desired properties when fed from the source.

# 9 Online Random Number Testing

Entropy sources and deterministic parts of RNGs, including extractors, PRNGs, and supporting hardware and software are subject to failure for a variety of reasons. Where it is important for the random properties of the data to be maintained, such as for security or for the correctness of statistical tests, it is appropriate to perform online testing.

Online testing of random numbers is testing the output of an RNG as the data is generated in order to detect a failure of the source. This is fundamentally different from offline tests covered in Chapter 8, which are intended to test the numbers themselves for random properties. Online tests are intended to test the source, establish that it is functional, and producing random numbers.

The NIST SP800-90 standard describes two online tests: The adaptive proportion test and repetition count test, which are both intended to test the data output from an entropy source. Neither test is a very effective test. In addition, the FIPS 140-2 standard adds the continuous random number generator test (CRNGT), which is intended to test the output of the whole RNG at the DRBG output. However, at best it just reduces the entropy of the data and, at worst, is a cryptographic back door. We will examine these tests and other tests which work.

## 9.1 Tagging or Blocking?

Online tests generally need to happen between the time the data are generated and the time the data are used, so that in the event of a failure the data can be discarded or treated in some way differently from a source that is passing the test.

An online test can either be blocking or tagging. In a blocking test, the data are blocked from being passed from the entropy source to the extractor until the test is complete. If, for example, we have a blocking test that needs to examine 1024 bits of data in order to make a pass or fail decision before the data can be passed on, then, the data has to be stored in some memory.

Figure 9.1 shows an outline of a typical implementation of a blocking online health test. On the left, data is received and tested and placed in memory until the test is complete. Once the result of the test is computed, the data can be passed to an output buffer and made available to the next stage, provided the test passed. If the test failed, the data in memory is deleted and not moved to the output buffer.

In a hardware implementation, storing the data being tested may be an inconvenience and it leads to a tradeoff between the amount of data that the test can examine, and the storage hardware needed to store it.

In a software implementation, it may be a security hazard to leave random data to be used as keys laying around in memory. This makes the architecture of online

https://doi.org/10.1515/9781501506062-009

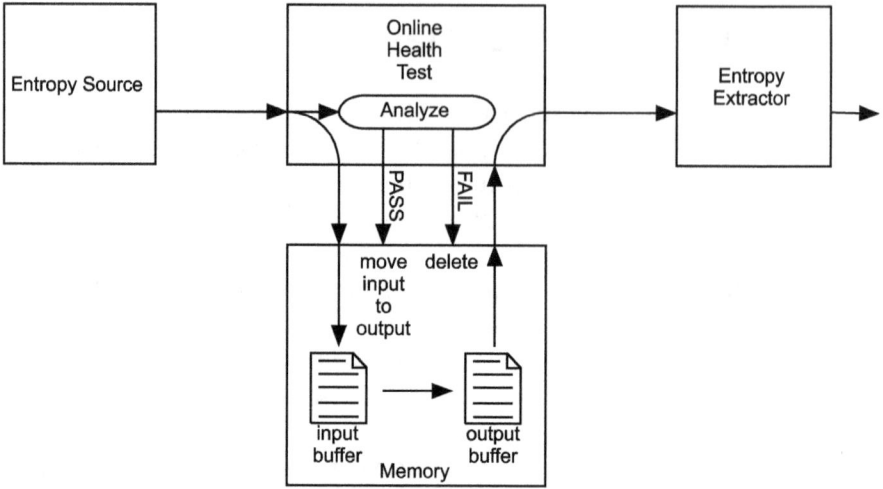

**Figure 9.1:** Blocking Online Health Test Flow.

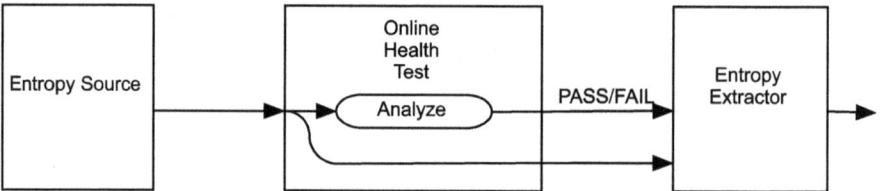

**Figure 9.2:** Tagging Online Health Test Flow.

testing, and how it works with entropy extraction, one of the more important design features of a random number generator.

An alternative test method is tagging, where the data are tested as they fly by onto the next stage, and the test tags the result to the end of a tested block of data as it passes.

Figure 9.2 shows an outline of a typical tagging online health test implementation. The data flows directly through the online health test and onto the extractor. While the data are flowing through, the online health test is examining the data and computing a result. At the end of a data block, the result of the test is also sent to the extractor.

The next stage that receives the tested data, along with the result of the test, typically the entropy extractor, will need to do something appropriate based on the health tag, such as discarding the extracted data, or stirring some more data in before releasing the extracted data to the next stage. For example, a CBC-MAC extractor stirs a number of 128-bit blocks of data into a single 128-bit output value. A typical strategy would be to stir in, say 4 healthy blocks for each 128 bit output, while any blocks tagged as unhealthy are also stirred in, but they are not counted. The extractor will keep going, stirring in all data received until it has received 4 blocks tagged as healthy. The reason for this approach is to allow a high false positive rate online test to be used. Then, a number of healthy data samples will be marked as unhealthy, but it will not break the flow of data; it will just slow it down a bit.

## 9.2 How Much Data to Test?

In the previous section the tradeoff between the test and the storage space hardware size was pointed out. The larger the amount of data tested, the more confidence we can have in the test result, and the more silicon area, power, cost, and attack surface are spent on the memory. Thus, we want to choose a test data size that is large enough to achieve reliable test results and small enough to work with the size and power constraints of the system. Fortunately, for online testing, it turns out the data size does not need to be very large for the tests to be effective.

A common lower limit for the size of the test data is set by the input size of the data to the entropy extractor. For example, an SP800-90B CBC-MAC entropy extractor necessarily works on units of 128 bits of data at a time, since the AES data size is 128. It processes enough of these 128-bit blocks to generate 128 bits of full entropy output.

It turns out that 128 bits is a too small block-size for effective online testing. The random variation of a small number of bits like that yields a high false positive error rate. However, with the right test, 256 bits is a lot more suitable.

So, with an RNG with an AES-based CBC-MAC extractor, online testing of 256 bits at a time is a reasonable design choice. If there is the option to test larger units, then it is better to test those larger units of data. A HMAC-based extractor, for instance, allows an arbitrary input size. Therefore, the system can be designed with an input size that is convenient for testing.

Three of the tests discussed below (APT Section 9.6, RCT Section 9.5, and CRNGT Section 9.4) are "continuous" in that they do not operate on blocks. They continuously update their state as data pass through, until the test meets an error state. This leads to problems with how to deal with such errors during runtime, which is examined in the sections below.

## 9.3 What Should an Online Test Test for?

In the case of offline tests, the three major classes of test are metric tests, which measure some metric-like bias or correlation; entropy estimations tests; and distinguishability tests, which try to establish if the data is uniformly random or not. With the distinguishability and entropy estimation tests, there are usually a battery of tests that look for a variety of different defects. In all cases, the judgment of the test is on the nature of the data, and the amount of data examined by the tests is large, measured in megabytes or gigabytes.

An online test is different in that the data from an entropy source is not expected to be uniformly random, and the type of defect the entropy source might produce is a function of the design of the source. It is not possible in small blocks of data to perform entropy testing or distinguishability testing, but if the failure modes of the entropy source circuit are known, it is entirely possible to test directly for those defects.

So, online tests are characterized as being tests for specific entropy source failure modes over small blocks of data.

Commonly, the failure modes of entropy sources can be characterized as leading to large bias or large serial correlation. Simple cases are flatline outputs, where the data is all ones, or all zeroes. This equated to both high bias and high serial correlation. In cases where there is excess feedback or asymmetry in the feedback in an entropy source circuit, we might expect high negative serial correlation, that is, 010101010... or high bias, for example, 11111111... or 0000000..., and these types of defect are simple to detect.

The basic engineering approach to identifying failure modes is to analyze all SPOF (Single Point of Failure) and DPOF (Double Point of Failure) errors, and see what the output would look like in each of the cases, in simulation. Typically, it will be found that most or all outcomes fall into a small set of output defects.

A common feature of online health tests for entropy source outputs is that the design of the tests is coupled to the failure modes of the source. Stand-alone health tests that do not consider the failure modes of the source are not useful, and this is one of the reasons the standards-based tests are not useful.

In the following sections, we will look at three standards-based online tests, and then look at other tests that have been used in mass production RNGs. The tests are typically simple and easy to implement.

## 9.4 The FIPS 140-2 Continuous RNG Test

The FIPS 140-2 section 4.9.2 CRNGT (Continuous Random Number Generator Test) is a test that is run at the output of a random number generator within a FIPS 140-2 module. The text of the requirements is as follows:

---

*Continuous random number generator test.* If a cryptographic module employs Approved or non-Approved RNGs in an Approved mode of operation, the module shall perform the following continuous random number generator test on each RNG that tests for failure to a constant value.

- If each call to an RNG produces blocks of $n$ bits (where $n > 15$), the first $n$-bit block generated after power-up, initialization, or reset shall not be used, but

> shall be saved for comparison with the next n-bit block to be generated. Each subsequent generation of an *n*-bit block shall be compared with the previously generated block. The test shall fail if any two compared *n*-bit blocks are equal.
> - If each call to an RNG produces fewer than 16 bits, the first *n* bits generated after power-up, initialization, or reset (for some $n > 15$) shall not be used, but shall be saved for comparison with the next *n* generated bits. Each subsequent generation of *n* bits shall be compared with the previously generated *n* bits. The test fails if any two compared *n*-bit sequences are equal.

So, put more simply, if there are two back-to-back values that match, then an error is raised. For a 16-bit output, the rate of a match is 1 match in 65536 numbers. For *n* bits, it is

$$P(\text{match}) = \frac{1}{2^n}.$$

We can test this empirically with a short program.

**Listing 9.1:** crngt.py

```python
#!/usr/bin/env python
import random

bitsize = 16
iterations = 10000000
failcount = 0

maximum = (2**bitsize) -1

prev = random.randint(0, maximum)
for i in xrange(iterations):
    current = random.randint(0, maximum)
    if current == prev:
        failcount += 1
    prev = current

print "From␣0␣to",maximum
print "Errors␣", failcount
print "1␣error␣in␣%d␣numbers" % int(float(iterations)/float(failcount))
```

Running this a few times, we see the match rate is close to 1 in 65536: 68493, 63694, 67114, 67114, etc.

So, for example, the RNG in the Intel Ivy Bridge CPU generates 800 Mbytes of data per second, that is, 400 Million 16 bit words per second. So, the CRNGT would raise $\frac{400000000}{65536} \approx 6013.52$ errors per second on average with a functioning circuit.

The quandary is that FIPS 140-2 gives no guidance as to what to do with these errors. It may or may not be sufficient to just log and ignore the errors. Nobody knows. It is at the whim of the certification lab.

One reasonable approach is to make the output 256 bits wide, so that collisions never happen, because they are too unlikely. However, many computer architectures are limited to passing data in 32- or 64-bit chucks.

At the time of writing this book, the fastest RNGs in the newest server CPUs ran at about 2 Gb/s. A data center with 10 000 CPUs running their RNGs at full speed (common, for example, in SSL network concentrators) would collide at a rate of $\frac{(1\,000\,000\,000)\cdot(10\,000)}{2^n}$ errors per second. For 32-bit values, the data center would raise 2382 errors per second. For 64-bit data, it would be one error every 1 844 674 seconds or once every 21.35 days. For 128-bit data, the error rate is about one every $10^{18}$ years.

As of the corrigendum in 2016 (http://csrc.nist.gov/publications/fips/fips140-2/fips1402annexc.pdf), which added Annex C, FIPS 140-2 stipulates that a random number generator within a FIPS 140-2-compliant module must be SP800-90A-compliant, and so this test is required to be run against the output of an SP800-90A DRBG.

In practice, the test was first defined at a time when SP800-90 did not exist, and the expectation was that the RNG might be simply some ring oscillator with none of the entropy extraction, or DRBG postprocessing that was later mandated by SP800-90.

So this test has undergone an unintended change, in that as FIPS 140-2 evolved, the place in the RNG pipeline in which the test is applied has changed because the specification for RNGs has changed. So, it has moved from being a test on the output of an entropy source to being a test on the output of a DRBG. Meanwhile, the test itself has not been changed, and the SP800-90 specification that was later mandated by FIPS 140-2 defined more appropriate tests to be implemented within the RNG, the Adaptive Proportion Test, and the Repetition Count Test, which (while being poor tests) are at least situated at the right place in the pipeline.

There is another version of FIPS 140-2, ISO/IEC 19790:2012 and a corrigendum ISO/IEC 19790:2012/Cor 1:2015. There is a plan that the next version of FIPS 140-2 (FIPS 140-3) be defined as being the current version of ISO 19790. Instead of updating FIPS 140-2, the US government employees, whose job it is to maintain FIPS 140, chose to put the updates into ISO/IEC 19790 first, and then just adopt that text as FIPS 140-3 by reference.

This change has been awaiting the signature of the Secretary of the US Department of Commerce for a number of years, but his or her signature has not been forthcoming. Why this is relevant is that the CRNGT algorithm has been removed from ISO/IEC 19790, but remains in FIPS 140-2. So, FIPS-compliant cryptographic modules are stuck with the CRNGT algorithm until the switch to ISO/IEC 19790 is made.

The rationale for removing the test in the ISO version is that the ISO specification does tell you specifically what to do with the errors, whereas FIPS 140-2 does not. So, a test like the CRNGT, if it were mandated in the ISO spec, would lead to RNGs that always fail immediately.

## 9.5 The SP800-90B Repetition Count Test

The Repetition Count Test (RCT) is designed to look for a "stuck-at" condition, where the entropy source outputs the same value constantly. When a sequence of the same values is longer than a limited length determined by the test, the test raises a failure condition.

The algorithm is simple, here stated a little differently than the standard for clarity. The value $C$ is the count limit that needs to be set before you run the algorithm.

```
1) Set B=1
2) Set A = The first value from the entropy source
3) Get the next value X
4) If X = A then
        Increment B
        If B = C then
             Raise_an_Error()
        Goto 3
   else
        Set A = X
        Set B = 1
        Goto 3.
```

To find $C$, start with the desired false positive error rate $W$ and compute

$$C = \left\lceil 1 + \frac{(-\log_2(W))}{H} \right\rceil,$$

where $H$ is the min-entropy per sample of data.

In Table 9.1, we compute the value $C$ for various values of $H$ and $W$. The horizontal axis is the exponent $x$ in $2^{-x}$. So, for example, the 32nd column corresponds to the false positive error rate of $W = 2^{-32}$.

**Table 9.1:** Table to Compute $C$ in the Repetition Count Test.

| | | W | | | | | | | | | | | | |
|---|---|---|---|---|---|---|---|---|---|---|---|---|---|---|
| | | **30** | **32** | **34** | **36** | **38** | **40** | **42** | **44** | **46** | **48** | **50** | **58** | **64** |
| H | **0.5** | 61 | 65 | 69 | 73 | 77 | 81 | 85 | 89 | 93 | 97 | 101 | 117 | 129 |
| | **0.6** | 51 | 55 | 58 | 61 | 65 | 68 | 71 | 75 | 78 | 81 | 85 | 98 | 108 |
| | **0.7** | 44 | 47 | 50 | 53 | 56 | 59 | 62 | 64 | 67 | 70 | 73 | 84 | 93 |
| | **0.8** | 39 | 41 | 44 | 47 | 49 | 52 | 54 | 57 | 59 | 62 | 64 | 74 | 81 |
| | **0.9** | 35 | 37 | 39 | 42 | 44 | 46 | 48 | 50 | 53 | 55 | 57 | 66 | 73 |
| | **1** | 31 | 33 | 35 | 37 | 39 | 41 | 43 | 45 | 47 | 49 | 51 | 59 | 65 |
| | **2** | 16 | 17 | 18 | 19 | 20 | 21 | 22 | 23 | 24 | 25 | 26 | 30 | 33 |
| | **3** | 11 | 12 | 13 | 13 | 14 | 15 | 15 | 16 | 17 | 17 | 18 | 21 | 23 |
| | **4** | 9 | 9 | 10 | 10 | 11 | 11 | 12 | 12 | 13 | 13 | 14 | 16 | 17 |
| | **8** | 5 | 5 | 6 | 6 | 6 | 6 | 7 | 7 | 7 | 7 | 8 | 9 | 9 |
| | **16** | 3 | 3 | 4 | 4 | 4 | 4 | 4 | 4 | 4 | 4 | 5 | 5 | 5 |
| | **32** | 2 | 2 | 3 | 3 | 3 | 3 | 3 | 3 | 3 | 3 | 3 | 3 | 3 |

The text of the standard claims the probability of a sequence of length $C$ is connected to the min-entropy $H$, of the source, by the provided equation. This obviously does not hold for negatively serially correlated binary data, where a lower entropy results in a greater probability of subsequent values being different.

## 9.6 The SP800-90B Adaptive Proportion Test

The Adaptive Proportion Test (APT) is similar to the RCT, except that it counts the frequency of a value within a number of output values from the RNG and checks that the frequency is not too high; it does not check that the value is repeated continuously, as in the RCT. The value to be searched for is taken from the data at the start of a block. After a number of values have been examined, the test starts again, picking the next output value as the new value to count.

The algorithm is as follows:

```
Set A = The next output value from the RNG
Set S = 0
Set B = 0
Set C = The cutoff value
Set N = The window size

Repeat forever
    If S = N then
        Set A = The next output value from the RNG
        Set S = 0
        Set B = 0
    Else
        Increment S
        If A = The next output value from the RNG
            Set B = B + 1
            If B > C then raise and error condition
```

There are problems with this test. Curiously, the standard describes some of the problems, whereas the authors did not consider these problems to be sufficient reason to omit the tests from the standard. The text from the standard is as follows:

> – Some noise sources simply do not generate very many samples. If an entropy source never processes as many noise source samples as appear in a window for this test, the test will never complete, and there will be little or no benefit in running the test at all.
> – A larger window size allows for the detection of more subtle failures in the noise source. On one extreme, a window size of 65536 samples can detect relatively small losses in entropy; on the other, a very small window size of

16 samples can reliably detect only the most catastrophic losses in entropy (and is therefore not included in this Recommendation).
- A larger window size means that each test takes longer to complete. Due to the way the Adaptive Proportion Test works, its result is dependent on what value it samples at the beginning of a test run. Thus, the combination of a large window size and a relatively low-rate noise source can ensure that failures take a very long time to detect, even when the test is capable of detecting them.

We will further see that a more serious problem is that the test cannot handle an acceptable false positive error rate for high-speed and high-volume manufactured RNGS.

The standard provides tables for selecting the window size $N$ from four options 64, 256, 4096, and 65536 as a function of the expected entropy per sample $H$. The table ranges from $H = 1$ to $H = 16$. So, for single-bit sources, which inevitably produces less than one bit of entropy per bit of data, there are no suitable entries in the table. Also, for entropy sources with symbol sizes greater than 16, there are no entries in the table. In the case of $H < 1$, the standard mandates that multiple symbols are joined together into a multibit sequence and the per-symbol entropy of the symbols is added together to establish the entropy of each multisymbol symbol. No solution is given for larger output sizes.

Interestingly, the highest entropy per bit (16) in the table for a full entropy source with a 16-bit output is also the lowest bit size allowed with the FIPS 140-2 CRNGT test (FIPS 140-2, Section 9.4). This is one of the many ways in which the testing mechanisms in the SP800-90 and FIPS 140-2 specifications do not work together well. The only symbol size compatible with both tests is 16 bits, whereas the common output sizes of RNGs in computers are 1, 32, or 64 bits per symbol.

The table for selecting $N$, shown in Table 9.2, is given in terms of the entropy loss that the test will detect. Logically, the choice you make would be the largest entropy

**Table 9.2:** Adaptive Proportion Test Entropy Loss Detection Thresholds.

|   | | Window Size $N$ | | |
|---|---|---|---|---|
|   | **64** | **256** | **4096** | **65536** |
| **1** | 67% | 39% | 13% | 3% |
| **2** | 56% | 32% | 11% | 3% |
| **3** | 50% | 31% | 12% | 3% |
| **8** | 54% | 40% | 19% | 6% |
| **16** | 69% | 56% | 40% | 22% |

loss that leaves sufficient entropy to meet the input entropy requirements of the entropy extractor that follows.

So, for example, if you have a 2-bit source and you assume at least 1 bit of entropy per two-bit sample, the maximum acceptable entropy loss is 50%, and so we would look in the $H$ = 2-bit row, and see the largest detectable loss less than 50% is 32% in the 256-bit column. So, you would set $N$ to 256.

The cut-off value $C$ is selected as a function of the min-entropy per sample $H$, the window size $N$, and the acceptable false positive error rate. The standard gives a table computed for the false positive error of $W = 2^{-30}$. However, as we saw in the CRNGT test (Section 9.4), a false positive error rate of $W = 2^{-30}$ is extremely high, and will lead to very frequent errors being raised against a healthy entropy source.

There are two drafts of the SP800-90B specification at the time of writing. The first draft included the following table, computed using a false positive error rate of $W = 2^{-30}$. This is interesting because it is an example of how errors in numerical functions and floating-point precision issues can undermine the design of a test. The left hand column of Table 9.3 is what was in the draft. The right hand column is the corrected version, computed with a correct binomial quantile implementation.

**Table 9.3:** Correction of Cutoff Table.

| Erroneous Cutoff Table, $W = 2^{-30}$ | | | | Correct Cutoff Table, $W = 2^{-30}$ | | | |
|---|---|---|---|---|---|---|---|
| **H** | **64** | **256** | **4096** | **65536** | **H** | **64** | **256** | **4096** | **65536** |
| 1 | 51 | 168 | 2240 | 33537 | 1 | 55 | 176 | 2240 | 33537 |
| 2 | 35 | 100 | 1193 | 17053 | 2 | 39 | 108 | 1193 | 17053 |
| 3 | 24 | 61 | 643 | 8705 | 3 | 27 | 68 | 643 | 8705 |
| 4 | 16 | 38 | 354 | 4473 | 4 | 10 | 44 | 354 | 4473 |
| 5 | 12 | 25 | 200 | 2321 | 5 | 15 | 29 | 200 | 2321 |
| 6 | 9 | 17 | 117 | 1220 | 6 | 11 | 21 | 117 | 1220 |
| 7 | 6 | 15 | 71 | 653 | 7 | 9 | 15 | 71 | 653 |
| 8 | 5 | 9 | 45 | 358 | 8 | 7 | 11 | 45 | 358 |
| 9 | 4 | 7 | 30 | 202 | 9 | 6 | 9 | 30 | 202 |
| 10 | 4 | 5 | 21 | 118 | 10 | 5 | 7 | 21 | 118 |
| 11 | 3 | 4 | 15 | 71 | 11 | 4 | 6 | 15 | 71 |
| 12 | 3 | 4 | 11 | 45 | 12 | 4 | 5 | 11 | 45 |
| 13 | 2 | 3 | 9 | 30 | 13 | 3 | 4 | 9 | 30 |
| 14 | 2 | 3 | 7 | 21 | 14 | 3 | 4 | 7 | 21 |
| 15 | 2 | 2 | 6 | 15 | 15 | 3 | 3 | 6 | 15 |
| 16 | 2 | 2 | 5 | 11 | 16 | 2 | 3 | 5 | 11 |
| 17 | 1 | 2 | 4 | 9 | 17 | 2 | 3 | 4 | 9 |
| 18 | 1 | 2 | 4 | 7 | 18 | 2 | 2 | 4 | 7 |
| 19 | 1 | 1 | 3 | 6 | 19 | 2 | 2 | 3 | 6 |
| 20 | 1 | 1 | 3 | 5 | 20 | 2 | 2 | 3 | 5 |

The entries in the table can be computed by finding the point at $1 - W$ on the binomial distribution of $N$ trials, with $P = 2^{-H}$. In a spreadsheet, the standard suggests the following formula:

```
=CRITBINOM(window_size,2^(-H),1-W)
```

However, when computing this in a spreadsheet for the same false positive error rate, we get different values in the spreadsheet to those found in the standard. In this case, the spreadsheet values are the correct ones, and the values in the standard should be ignored. However, as will be described, the spreadsheet arithmetic is subject to floating point resolution limits, and so cannot be relied upon.

The earlier incorrect table can be computed by creating a binomial quantile function that searches for the point on the binomial CDF curve that returns a value closest to $1 - W$. However, the quantile function is supposed to return that smallest point of the curve that returns a value greater than $1 - W$. This explains the error in the table in the specification. In the python code below, there is a check at the end of the search algorithm to see if the closest index is above or below the threshold, and increase it by one if it is below.

There is a problem with the suggestion to use the Excel CRITBINOM function when trying to compute using lower false positive error rates. For example, it will not work with $W = 2^{-64}$.

When computing this table in Excel for negative integer powers of 2 greater than 53, the table saturates, and each number in the table is equal to the window size. Thus, the error rate will always be 0 and the maximum usable false positive error rate achievable is $W = 2^{-53}$ but at this level there are quantization errors in the result and so the table values are misleading. The errors arise because the floating point format used in Excel, and most programs, has a fractional part of 53 bits. So, at a fractional part of $2^{-53}$, there is only a single binary digit of precision. A reasonable false positive error rate you might want for a high-volume production product might be $2^{-64}$ or lower.

Table 9.4 shows the output of a Python program that generates the above table using 53-bit precision on the left and 200-bit precision on the right.

The program, given in Listing 9.2, computes the binomial quantile function with a library that performs a binary chop search over the binomial CDF function, using the GMPY2 MPFR library, which allows higher precision floating point values. In the case of the code below, 200-bit precision is used.

Tables for the cutoff value for false positive error rates of $W = 2^{-32}$, $W = 2^{-48}$, $W = 2^{-53}$, $W = 2^{-64}$, $W = 2^{-96}$, and $W = 2^{-128}$, with a wider set of block sizes are given in Appendix A.

The difficulty in preparing these tables arose from two issues. First, the limited precision of standard floating point numbers, and, secondly, the problem of computing the binomial CDF for large block-sizes, and small $W$. The binomial CDF is given

**Table 9.4:** Cutoff Tables Computed With Low and High Precision.

| $W = 2^{-64}$, 53 Bit Precision | | | | $W = 2^{-64}$, 200 Bit Precision | | | |
|---|---|---|---|---|---|---|---|
| H | 512 | 1024 | 4096 | 65536 | H | 512 | 1024 | 4096 | 65536 |
| 1 | 384 | 768 | 3072 | 49152 | 1 | 357 | 768 | 2338 | 33930 |
| 2 | 256 | 512 | 2048 | 32768 | 2 | 222 | 512 | 1282 | 17397 |
| 3 | 256 | 512 | 2048 | 32768 | 3 | 141 | 512 | 714 | 8971 |
| 4 | 256 | 512 | 2048 | 32768 | 4 | 92 | 512 | 408 | 4670 |
| 5 | 256 | 512 | 2048 | 32768 | 5 | 63 | 512 | 241 | 2465 |
| 6 | 256 | 512 | 2048 | 32768 | 6 | 44 | 512 | 148 | 1325 |
| 7 | 256 | 512 | 2048 | 32768 | 7 | 33 | 512 | 95 | 730 |
| 8 | 256 | 512 | 2048 | 32768 | 8 | 25 | 512 | 64 | 414 |
| 9 | 256 | 512 | 2048 | 32768 | 9 | 20 | 512 | 45 | 243 |
| 10 | 256 | 512 | 2048 | 32768 | 10 | 16 | 512 | 33 | 149 |
| 11 | 256 | 512 | 2048 | 32768 | 11 | 13 | 512 | 25 | 96 |
| 12 | 256 | 512 | 2048 | 32768 | 12 | 11 | 512 | 20 | 64 |
| 13 | 256 | 512 | 2048 | 32768 | 13 | 10 | 512 | 16 | 45 |
| 14 | 256 | 512 | 2048 | 32768 | 14 | 9 | 512 | 13 | 33 |
| 15 | 256 | 512 | 2048 | 32768 | 15 | 8 | 512 | 11 | 25 |
| 16 | 256 | 512 | 2048 | 32768 | 16 | 7 | 512 | 10 | 20 |
| 17 | 256 | 512 | 2048 | 32768 | 17 | 6 | 512 | 9 | 16 |
| 18 | 256 | 512 | 2048 | 32768 | 18 | 6 | 512 | 8 | 13 |
| 19 | 256 | 512 | 2048 | 32768 | 19 | 5 | 512 | 7 | 11 |
| 20 | 256 | 512 | 2048 | 32768 | 20 | 5 | 512 | 6 | 10 |

as

$$\alpha = \sum_{k=0}^{x} \binom{N}{k} p^k (1-p)^{n-k}.$$

The $\binom{N}{k}$ part becomes very large, for large n, and leads to very slow execution of a program attempting to compute the binomial CDF this way.

The solution involves developing an implementation of the incomplete beta function, using high-precision floating point numbers. This is described in Appendix B.

The binomial CDF can be computed from the incomplete beta function $I_x(a, b)$ with

$$B(n, k, p) = 1 - I_p(k + 1, n - k).$$

Using the above binary search algorithm, the cutoff value for the adaptive proportion test can be computed with the binomial quantile function:

$$C = \text{BQuantile}(\text{windowsize}, 2^{-H}, 1 - W)$$

In Python, first setting the precision and then calling the quantile function (also called the critical value function) would be

```
ctx = gmpy2.context()
ctx.precision = 300
gmpy2.set_context(ctx)

c = binomial_quantile(ws,mpfr('2.0')**(-h),mpfr('1.0')-W)
```

The algorithm and code for the binomial quantile function is in Appendix B.

The cutoff value is computed using the binomial quantile function that computes the smallest $p$ such that

$$\alpha \le B(n, p, x)$$

or, more completely, the smallest $p$ such that

$$\alpha \le \sum_{k=0}^{x} \binom{N}{k} p^k (1-p)^{n-k}.$$

Listing 9.2 generates the cutoff tables, using a high-precision floating point library, and the correct binomial quantile function that is given in Appendix B. The generated tables are given in Appendix A.

**Listing 9.2:** APT Cutoff Table Generating Code

```
#!/usr/bin/env python2

import math
from mpmath import *
from beta_functions import *

PRECISION = 300
mp.dps = PRECISION

wss = [64,256,512,1024,2048,4096,65536]      # Window Sizes
                                  # H Values
hs = [0.1,0.2,0.3,0.4,0.5,0.6,0.7,0.8,0.9]+range(1,21)
for i in xrange(len(hs)): # convert to high precision floats
    hs[i] = mpf(hs[i])

Ws = [32,48,53,64,96,128] # False positive error rate exponents

for wx in Ws:
    W = mpf('2.0')**-wx
    match = True
    print("__W_=_2^-{}".format(wx))
    print("__H{0:5}__{1:5}_{2:5}__{3:5}_{4:5}_{5:5}__{6:5}".\
format(wss[0],wss[1],wss[2],wss[3],wss[4],wss[5],wss[6]))
    print
    for h in hs:
        cs = list()

        for ws in wss:
            cs.append(str(binomial_quantile(ws,mpf('2.0')**(-h),mpf('1.0')-W)))
            print("{0:5.1f}_{1:5}_{2:5}_{3:5}_{4:5}_{5:5}_{6:5}_{7:5}".\
format(float(h),cs[0],cs[1],cs[2],cs[3],cs[4],cs[5], cs[6]))
        print
```

## 9.7 Pattern Counting Health Test

The pattern counting health test is implemented in the RNG in Intel CPUs, and it serves to replace the Adaptive Proportion Test and the Repetition Count Test. This test has been accepted by a certification lab as an acceptable substitute for the standard tests.

The algorithm is a tagging test that tests groups of 256 bits as they come from the entropy source, and tags each block with a single bit healthy flag.

The frequency of 6 different bit patterns within the data is counted over a sliding window. The six patterns are 1, 01, 101, 1001, 010, and 0110. Since the patterns are counted using a sliding window technique, the number of bits looked at for the 2-bit patterns is 257 to account for the single bit that falls off the end, 258 for the 3-bit patterns, and 259 for the 4-bit patterns. The counts just count the pattern arrival and reset on a 256-bit boundary.

In Figure 9.3, we see the structure with the pattern-matchers observing the data as it slides by, producing a pulse whenever they see a match. The pulses are counted and a bounds-matcher checks that the frequency of the patterns were within the expected bounds. An AND gate asserts a 1 if all the pattern frequencies are within the bounds.

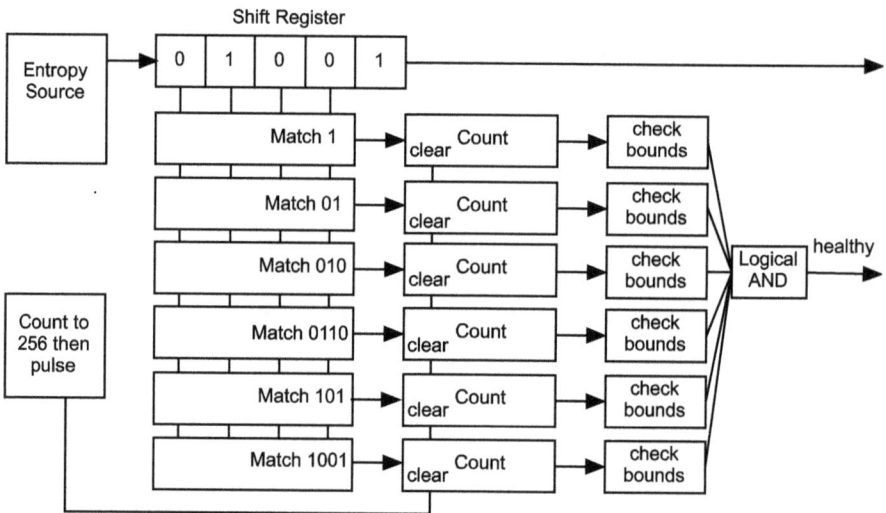

**Figure 9.3:** Pattern Count Online Health Test.

Every 256 arrival clocks a pulse and clears the counters to start again. In the actual design, this pulse goes to many other bits of logic to signal that a new tested block of data is available.

The choice of patterns is selected to cover both the bias (with the 1 pattern) and the reducing frequency with longer patterns. Patterns of 5 bits or longer would be too infrequent within a 256-bit pattern to be useful. However, with a longer data block, you might choose to include longer patterns.

The pattern bounds used in Intel 10 nm and 14 nm products were based on empirical measurement of data from healthy entropy sources, and were set to equalize the false positive error probability of each pattern. The values were also tuned to achieve an overall false positive error probability of 1%:

The bounds are shown in Table 9.5.

**Table 9.5:** Frequency Bounds for Pattern Count Online Health Test.

| Pattern | Min | Max |
|---------|-----|-----|
| 1 | 96 | 159 |
| 01 | 44 | 87 |
| 101 | 9 | 58 |
| 0110 | 4 | 35 |
| 101 | 9 | 58 |
| 1001 | 4 | 35 |

The Python program in Listing 9.3 implements this test. It reads a binary file, splits it into blocks of 256 bits and runs the pattern count online health test over each block, overlapping at the ends for the multibit patterns.

Usually this test would be implemented in hardware, right next to the entropy source, since the algorithm is specifically designed to be efficient in hardware.

**Listing 9.3:** Pattern Count Online Health Test

```python
#!/usr/bin/env python

import math
import sys

previous = [0,0,0]

def oht(bitlist):
    global previous
    bitlist259 = previous + bitlist
    previous = bitlist[253:]
    counts = [0,0,0,0,0,0]
    for i in xrange(256):
        if bitlist259[i+3] == 1:
            counts[0] += 1
        if bitlist259[i+2:i+4] == [0,1]:
            counts[1] += 1
        if bitlist259[i+1:i+4] == [0,1,0]:
            counts[2] += 1
        if bitlist259[i:i+4] == [0,1,1,0]:
            counts[3] += 1
        if bitlist259[i+1:i+4] == [1,0,1]:
            counts[4] += 1
        if bitlist259[i:i+4] == [1,0,0,1]:
```

```
            counts [5] += 1
      return counts

def check_bounds (counts):
      if (counts [0] <= 96) or (counts [0] >= 159): return False
      if (counts [1] <= 44) or (counts [1] >= 87): return False
      if (counts [2] <= 9)  or (counts [2] >= 58): return False
      if (counts [3] <= 4)  or (counts [3] >= 35): return False
      if (counts [4] <= 9)  or (counts [4] >= 58): return False
      if (counts [5] <= 4)  or (counts [5] >= 35): return False
      return True

# get filename
filename = sys.argv [1]

passfail =[0.0,0.0]
with open(filename,"rb") as f:
      bytes = f.read(32) # Read 256 bits
      while len(bytes) == 32:
            bitlist = list ()
            for byte in bytes:
                  for i in range(7,-1,-1):
                        bit = ((ord(byte) >> i) & 0x01)
                        bitlist.append(bit)
            counts = oht(bitlist)
            if check_bounds(counts):
                  passfail[0] += 1.0
            else:
                  passfail [1] += 1.0
            bytes = f.read(32)
f.close ()

print "Passing_Blocks:_",passfail[0]
print "Failing_Blocks:_",passfail[1]
print "Fail_Percentage_=_",(passfail[1])/(passfail[0]+passfail[1])*100.0,"%"
```

Running this over data with an SCC of −0.3, we see a 43% error rate.

```
$ djenrandom -m correlated --correlation=-0.3 -k 10 -b > b.bin
$ ./pattern_count_oht.py b.bin
Passing Blocks:    181.0
Failing Blocks:    139.0
Fail Percentage =    43.4375 %
```

## 9.8 Online Mean and Serial Correlation Test

If you use an entropy source circuit that uses electrical feedback to keep the bias centered at 50% ones and 50% zeroes, then you will generally find that the serial correlation coefficient (SCC) of the data is the property that is directly related to the min entropy of the data.

So, in a random number generator with a feedback stabilized entropy source, when you need the min-entropy of the data to be above some threshold to meet the input requirements of the entropy extractor, it is a reasonable approach to measure the SCC, and set bounds, on the maximum acceptable SCC.

Unfortunately, the equation to compute the SCC is somewhat complicated (see Section 8.8.4), particularly if you plan to implement it in hardware. Fortunately, when the data consists of only binary ones and zeroes, the equation can be greatly simplified, and the algorithm to test that the SCC is within a minimum and maximum SCC range can be greatly simplified.

It is entirely possible to have data that have significant bias, and yet have no serial correlation. This result might be expected if the feedback mechanism of the entropy source has failed in some way. So, the feedback centering disappears and is replaced by significant bias. So for such an online health test, both the mean and SCC need to be measured.

Section 8.8.4 goes into the details of the formulas and code for measuring SCC. In this section, we are concerned with the results of the SCC measurement, when measuring small blocks of data in an online health test.

A short Python program to compute the SCC of 256-bit blocks over data from a binary file is shown in Listing 9.4.

**Listing 9.4:** Serial Correlation Coefficient Online Health Test

```python
#!/usr/bin/env python

import math
import sys

previous = [0,]

def scc256(bitlist):
    global previous
    bitlist257 = previous + bitlist
    previous = bitlist[255:]
    count1 = 0
    counts = [0,0,0,0]
    for i in xrange(256):
        if bitlist[i] == 1:
            count1 += 1
        if bitlist257[i:i+2] == [0,0]:
            counts[0] += 1
        if bitlist257[i:i+2] == [1,0]:
            counts[1] += 1
        if bitlist257[i:i+2] == [0,1]:
            counts[2] += 1
        if bitlist257[i:i+2] == [1,1]:
            counts[3] += 1
    return (count1, counts)

def compute_mean_scc(count1, counts):
```

```
n = 256
top = (n*counts[3]) - ((counts[2] + counts[3])*(counts[2]
        + counts[3]))
bottom = (n*(counts[2] + counts[3]))
            - ((counts[2] + counts[3])*(counts[2] + counts[3]))
scc = float(top)/float(bottom)
mean = float(count1)/256.0
return (mean,scc)


filename = sys.argv[1] # get filename

print "mean,␣scc"
with open(filename,"rb") as f:
    bytes = f.read(32) # Read 256 bits
    while len(bytes) == 32:
        bitlist = list()
        for byte in bytes:
            for i in range(7,-1,-1):
                bit = ((ord(byte) >> i) & 0x01)
                bitlist.append(bit)
        (count1,counts) = scc256(bitlist)
        (mean,scc) = compute_mean_scc(count1,counts)

        print mean,"␣",scc
        bytes = f.read(32)
f.close()
```

The output is a list of the mean and SCC values, computed from the 256-bit blocks in a format compatible with Gnuplot. Running over 64-kibits of data, which is 256 blocks of 256 bits, we get 256 results showing the mean and SCC of each block. We generate 64 kibits of uniform data in a binary file using the djenrandom program as follows:

```
$ djenrandom -b -k 8 > pure_8k.bin
$
```

Then we run it through the program in Listing 9.4:

```
$ ./scc_mean_oht.py pure_8k.bin > scc_mean_oht.dat
$
```

When we plot the distribution of the SCC values, we get Figure 9.4.

So, due to the relatively small size of the block, there is some variation in the measured SCC, even though the actual SCC of the generated data tends to 0, as the size of the data gets large. With a large enough number of data blocks, this distribution of the SCC measurements would become a normal distribution.

The measured values of SCC vary by about 0.2 above and below the actual SCC. With larger block sizes, the variation would reduce. With smaller block sizes, the variation would increase.

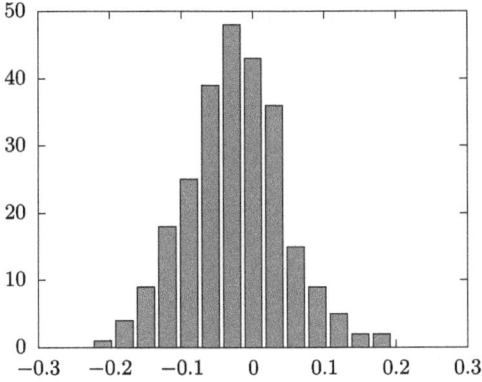

**Figure 9.4:** Distribution of SCC Measurements of Uniform 256 Bit Blocks.

We saw in Section 3.9.1 that a common requirement for the min-entropy of data being input to a seeded extractor is that there be at least 0.5 bits of entropy per 1 bit of random data. So, to ensure that all the data is above 0.5 bits of entropy per bit of data, it is normal to require an engineering margin. For example, test for the SCC being greater than the SCC value. If so, that implies min-entropy of the data is 0.75 bits of entropy per bit of data. Then the test is unlikely to pass data below 0.5 bits of entropy per bit of data.

The min-entropy $h$ of data with some SCC is

$$h = -\log_2\left(\max\left(\frac{scc+1}{2}, 1 - \frac{scc+1}{2}\right)\right).$$

Let us assume the min-entropy $h$ of some data that is serially correlated, but is unbiased, is 0.5 and $\max(\frac{scc+1}{2}, 1 - \frac{scc+1}{2}) = \frac{scc+1}{2}$. It follows that

$$2^{-0.5} = \frac{scc+1}{2},$$

$$\frac{1}{\sqrt{2}} = \frac{scc+1}{2},$$

$$\frac{2}{\sqrt{2}} = scc+1,$$

$$\sqrt{2} = scc+1,$$

$$scc = \sqrt{2} - 1,$$

$$scc \approx 0.41421.$$

By symmetry, in the case where $\max(\frac{scc+1}{2}, 1 - \frac{scc+1}{2}) = 1 - \frac{scc+1}{2}$, the other point where $h = 0.5$ is $-scc$.

So, the serial correlation levels at which $h = 0.5$ are approximately $+0.41421$ and $-0.41421$.

Using the code in Listing 9.4 to measure the SCC of a 256-bit block of data, we can create a loop to find the range of measured values for many different actual values of

SCC, and output the data as CSV, for plotting in a spreadsheet as a scatterplot. This code is shown in Listing 9.5.

**Listing 9.5:** Serially Correlated Data, Actual Against Measured

```python
def gen_scc_data(scc):
    prev = 0
    for i in range(256):
        bits = list()
        for j in range(256):
            paeqb = (scc+1.0)/2.0
            if prev == 1:
                p1 = paeqb
            else:
                p1 = 1-paeqb
            uniformrand = random.random()
            if uniformrand < p1:
                bit = 1
            else:
                bit = 0
            bits.append(bit)
            prev = bit
        yield bits


print "scc,_measured_scc"

for sccint in range(41):
    scc = -1.0 + (sccint * 0.05)
    for bitlist in gen_scc_data(scc):
        (count1,counts) = scc256(bitlist)
        (mean,measured_scc) = compute_mean_scc(count1,counts)
        print scc,",",measured_scc
```

The resulting plot shows the range of the measured SCC for data generated with actual SCC varying from −1 to +1, in increments of 0.05. See Figure 9.5.

If we want to test for a min-entropy of at least 0.5, then we can see that testing for −0.41421 < SCC < 0.41421 will not work, since the variation of values worse than 0.41421 cause them to appear to be within the good range at times.

In Figure 9.6, we have highlighted the SCC range, equating to-min entropy better than 0.5 on both axis. The SCC points in the middle box, where the two ranges overlap show that we can select a narrower range of measured SCC, which will always be within the box. We can see that measuring and testing for −0.2 < SCC < 0.2 will always give a positive result, when the actual min-entropy is better than 0.5 bits per bit of data.

The block-size of 256 bits was chosen to make the diagrams clear. In a commercial design that I was involved in designing, in order to tighten the spread of the measured SCC, the block-size was set to 1024. The higher the block-size, the less conservative the bounds need to be.

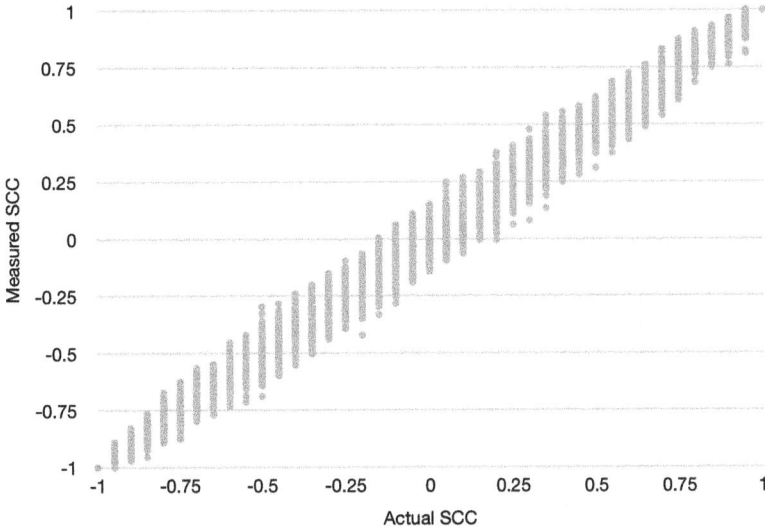

**Figure 9.5:** Actual SCC Against Measured SCC for 256 Bit Blocks.

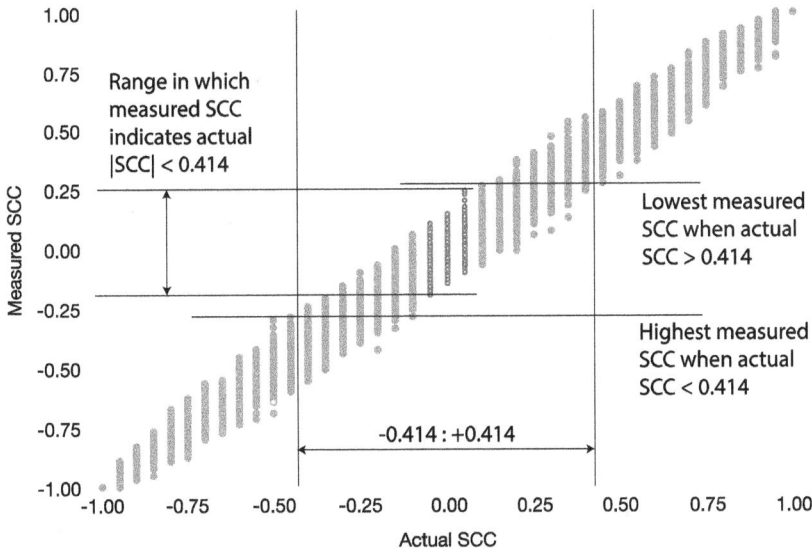

**Figure 9.6:** Constrained Range for SCC Against Measured SCC for 256-Bit Blocks.

If we increase the block-size to 1024 bits, we get the spread in Figure 9.7.

If we increase the block-size to 16384 bits, then we get the spread in Figure 9.8.

So, using larger block-sizes allows us to have to use less extra margin to identify that blocks are within the required SCC bounds.

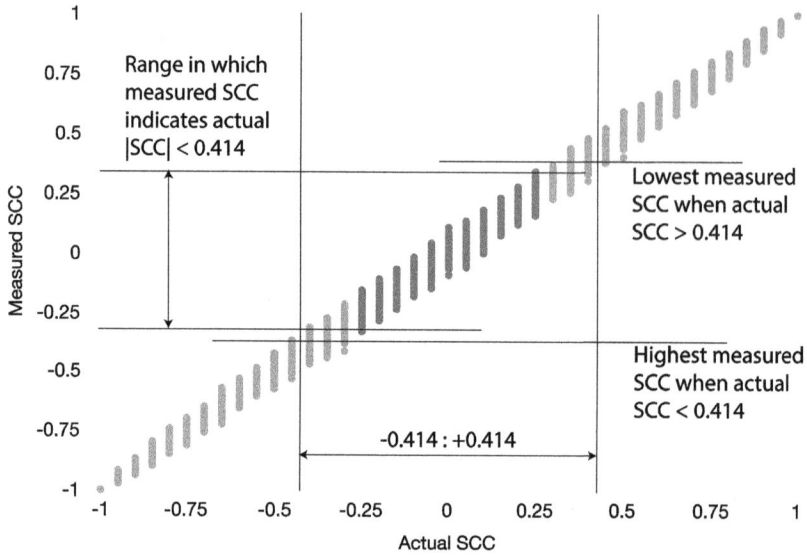

**Figure 9.7:** Constrained Range for SCC Against Measured SCC for 1024-Bit Blocks.

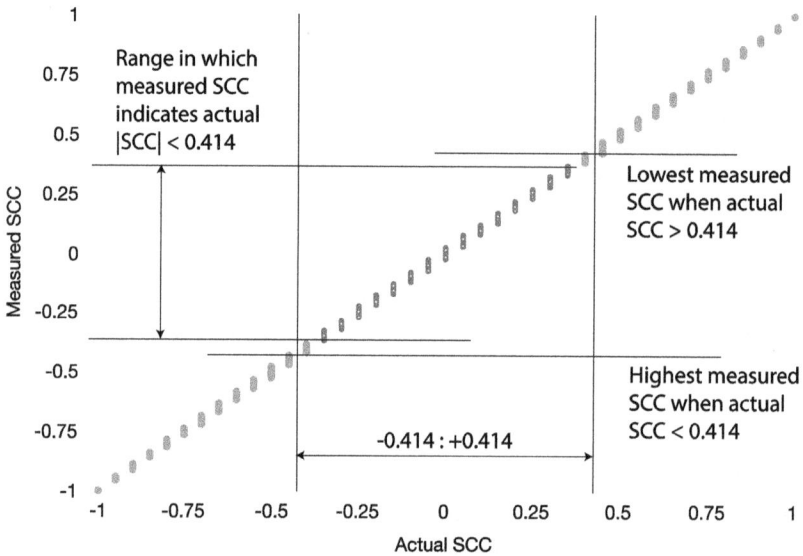

**Figure 9.8:** Constrained Range for SCC Against Measured SCC for 16384-Bit Blocks.

In a working source that uses feedback to keep the bias even, we can expect the bias to be close to 0. The SCC test will ensure the feedback is not introducing too much serial correlation. However, our goal is to detect failures in the source, and a failure in the feedback circuit will most likely lead to a very high bias. So, we also need to test for high bias. It is not appropriate to equate bias to min-entropy, since these tests are aimed at a serially correlated source. The worst case acceptable bias is typically going to be determined by the design. The tighter the feedback, the lower the bias.

Measuring bias is simpler. Counting the number of ones in a 256-block yields the bias as

$$\text{bias} = \frac{\text{ones}}{256}.$$

The mean of the bias should be 0.5. We might for example test for bias within the range 0.4 to 0.6. That equates a ones count between 103 and 153. In the Intel DRNG Pattern Counting online health test, we see the range determined empirically for a health entropy source was 96 to 159, which is a slightly larger range.

## 9.9 Online Source Independence Test

In Section 3.10, a class of algorithm is explained which is called a "multiple-input extractor". This is an algorithm that requires multiple entropy source inputs, typically 2 or 3, and requires those inputs to be statistically independent of each other. So, in an RNG using a multiple-input extractor, it would be appropriate to test that the entropy sources are independent.

A method similar to the SCC test can be used, only instead of testing correlation between successive bits, test the correlation between simultaneous bits from the entropy sources.

In Section 8.8.4, we started with the equation for the standard correlation coefficient:

$$c = \frac{n(\sum_{i=0}^{n-1} x_i y_i) - (\sum_{i=0}^{n-1} x_i)(\sum_{i=0}^{n-1} y_i)}{\sqrt{(n \sum_{i=0}^{n-1} x_i^2 - (\sum_{i=0}^{n-1} x_i)^2)(n \sum_{i=0}^{n-1} y_i^2 - (\sum_{i=0}^{n-1} y_i)^2)}}.$$

This can be computed directly. For example, the Python snippet 9.6 computes the correlation coefficient between two arrays of numbers of length $n$, X[i] and y[i].

**Listing 9.6:** Direct Serial Correlation Coefficient Measurement

```
sumxiyi = 0.0
sumxi = 0.0
sumyi = 0.0
sumxi2 = 0.0
sumyi2 = 0.0

for i in range(n): # Add up the summation terms
    sumxiyi += x[i]*y[i]
    sumxi   += x[i]
    sumyi   += y[i]
    sumxi2  += x[i]*x[i]
    sumyi2  += y[i]*y[i]
```

```
# Compute the correlation coefficient
top = (n*sumxiyi) - (sumxi*sumyi)
bottom = (n*sumxi2 - (sumxi*sumxi))*((n*sumyi2)- (sumyi*sumyi))
c = float(top)/math.sqrt(float(bottom))
```

In the case of binary data, the correlation coefficient is equivalent to the Pearson $\phi$ statistic.

When comparing pairs of bits, there are only four combinations of x[i] and y[i]: 00, 01, 10, and 11. We can count the occurrence of these combinations and call the counts $n_{00}$, $n_{01}$, $n_{10}$, and $n_{11}$. Also, count the frequency of the 1s and 0s in X[i] and Y[i] as x1, x0, y0, and y1. The Pearson $\phi$ can be expressed as

$$\phi = \frac{n11 \cdot n00 - n10 \cdot n01}{\sqrt{x1 \cdot x0 \cdot y1 \cdot y0}}.$$

The code snippet in Listing 9.7 below, operating over the same x[i] and y[i] bit lists, computes the correlation, using the equation for the Pearson $\phi$ coefficient.

**Listing 9.7:** Pearson Phi Compared to SCC

```
n11 = 0
n10 = 0
n01 = 0
n00 = 0
y1 = 0
y0 = 0
x1 = 0
x0 = 0

for i in range(n):
    if x[i] == 1 and y[i] == 1:
        n11 += 1
    if x[i] == 1 and y[i] != 1:
        n10 += 1
    if x[i] != 1 and y[i] == 1:
        n01 += 1
    if x[i] != 1 and y[i] != 1:
        n00 += 1

    if y[i] == 1:
        y1 += 1
    if y[i] != 1:
        y0 += 1
    if x[i] == 1:
        x1 += 1
    if x[i] != 1:
        x0 += 1

top = n11*n00 - n10*n01
```

```
bottom = math.sqrt(float(y1*y0*x1*x0))
c = float(top)/bottom
```

When the bits are unbiased, but correlated, the correlation coefficient, Pearson $\phi$, and $2P(x[i] = y[i]) - 1$ are all the same. In the list below we see the three computations computed over the same data, for 10 different random sequences x[i] and y[i] of 10 000 bits each. The data is unbiased but has been generated with correlation of about 0.1.

| Correlation Coeff, | Pearson Phi, | (2*P(x[i]=x[y]))-1 |
|---|---|---|
| 0.098347 | 0.098347 | 0.098400 |
| 0.110764 | 0.110764 | 0.110800 |
| 0.088655 | 0.088655 | 0.088800 |
| 0.088027 | 0.088027 | 0.088200 |
| 0.100057 | 0.100057 | 0.100000 |
| 0.102376 | 0.102376 | 0.102400 |
| 0.090503 | 0.090503 | 0.090800 |
| 0.109026 | 0.109026 | 0.109000 |
| 0.093808 | 0.093808 | 0.093800 |
| 0.082916 | 0.082916 | 0.083000 |

We can see that the simpler probability equation closely follows the Pearson $\phi$ and correlation coefficient.

The difference between the probability sum, and the other two values, is the result of the random variation of the bias around 0.5. The generated data is unbiased. However, each sample has some bias due to random variation.

If the data are significantly biased, then the probability sum is not equivalent to the Pearson $\phi$ or correlation coefficient. In the following test, the same methods were used, but the generated data had bias of about 0.3 introduced, as well as correlation.

| Correlation Coeff, | Pearson Phi, | (2*P(x[i]=x[y]))-1, | X mean, | Y mean |
|---|---|---|---|---|
| 0.079313 | 0.079313 | 0.231000 | 0.296600 | 0.297500 |
| 0.103685 | 0.103685 | 0.246800 | 0.298800 | 0.301600 |
| 0.098188 | 0.098188 | 0.240000 | 0.298900 | 0.304500 |
| 0.086859 | 0.086859 | 0.225600 | 0.306200 | 0.304000 |
| 0.117691 | 0.117691 | 0.257800 | 0.299900 | 0.301600 |
| 0.086518 | 0.086518 | 0.225800 | 0.302900 | 0.306600 |
| 0.087925 | 0.087925 | 0.234000 | 0.300700 | 0.299100 |
| 0.097780 | 0.097780 | 0.237200 | 0.299500 | 0.307300 |
| 0.091585 | 0.091585 | 0.241600 | 0.298900 | 0.294700 |
| 0.115425 | 0.115425 | 0.255200 | 0.304900 | 0.297500 |

We see that the probability computation is now completely different.

So, if you have an active mean test, which is rejecting biased samples of data, so that the subsequent correlation test is rejecting correlated samples, then the probability sum

$$\phi = \frac{2 \times \text{count}_{x[i]=y[i]}}{n}$$

is computationally simpler and sufficiently close to the actual correlation coefficient to be useful for testing. If the data may be significantly biased, then the probability sum should not be used, and the Pearson $\phi$ computed instead.

The benefit of using the probability sum is that, in hardware, it is much simpler to compute. The value of $n$ can be set to a power of 2, and then the divide by $n$ is simply a bit-shift in hardware. If computing the correlation between sequences being generated at gigabits per second, the hardware for the Pearson $\phi$ (with multiplies, divides, and square roots) may be challenging to implement in an efficient circuit. If the entropy source runs at kilobits per second (as is common with some ring oscillator circuits), then, it is trivial to test in software with the Pearson $\phi$.

# 10 SP800-22 Distinguishability Tests

SP800-22 Rev1a is the current revision of a NIST PRNG testing standard. This chapter focuses on the implementation of the standard. Details on using the tests are covered in Chapter 8.

The tests are as follows:
1. Monobit.
2. Frequency Test Within a Block.
3. Discrete Fourier Transform.
4. Nonoverlapping Template Matching.
5. Overlapping Template Matching.
6. Longest Run of Ones in a Block.
7. Binary Matrix Rank.
8. Random Excursion.
9. Random Excursion Variant.
10. Maurer's Universal Statistical.
11. Linear Complexity.
12. Serial.
13. Cumulative Sums.
14. Approximate Entropy.

## 10.1 First, Do not Assume the Contrapositive

The specification SP800-22rev1a contains a number of statements to the effect that "If P > threshold, conclude the data is random." This is simply wrong, and the users of these tests should be conscious of not assuming the contrapositive of the thing the test does not show.

If the $P$ value lands in the good range, that is, does not land in the range that shows the data is not random, then this does not mean that the test showed the data to be nonrandom. All you can know is that the test failed to show that the data is nonrandom. All tests are testing for something in particular, and there may be some other way in which the data is nonrandom. A good example being the output of a Linear Congruential Generator (LCG), where they will pass most statistical tests presented here, but are clearly deterministic. An algorithm designed to compute the internal state of an LCG from its output would have no problem distinguishing the data from random data, and the Linear Complexity Test has proven effective at distinguishing LCG output from random.

The specification includes a number of tests, and the procedure is to test output data from a PRNG with all the tests. If none of the tests indicate the data is indistinguishable from random, then we presume the data to be indistinguishable from ran-

https://doi.org/10.1515/9781501506062-010

dom, although there is some possibility that there is a way to distinguish the output of a PRNG from random.

## 10.2 SP800-22rev1a Monobit Test

The monobit test is a test of bias.[1] It runs over a series of bits and generates a $P$ value. Random data should achieve a high $P$ value. For example, to establish a 99% confidence level, you would check for $P \geq 0.01$.

If $P > 0.01$, then the test fails to show that the data is not random.

If $P \leq 0.01$, then the test shows that the data is not random with a confidence of 99%, meaning that truly random data would be below this threshold 1% of the time.

### 10.2.1 Application

The monobit test is a test whether a sequence of bits was generated with no bias. It is not sensitive to the order of bits. So, 1111100000 would be measured the same as 1010101010. Unlike the Chi-Square test, it always treats less bias as better, though some bias in a truly uniformly generated data set is more likely than it having no bias.

### 10.2.2 Procedure

Start with a string of $n$ bits, e. g., $0, 1, 0, 1, 0, 0, 1, 0, 1, 0, 1, 0, \ldots$.

Convert each 0 into $-1$, and 1 into $+1$: $X_i = -1, +1, -1, +1, -1, -1, +1, -1, +1, -1, \ldots$.

Compute

$$P = \text{erfc}\left(\frac{|\sum_{i=1}^{n} X_i|}{\sqrt{n} \cdot \sqrt{2}}\right).$$

If $P <$ confidence, then the data is not random.

### 10.2.3 Monobit Test Python Implementation

Listing 10.1: sp800_22_monobit_test.py

```
import math

def monobit(bits):
    ones = 0
```

---

1 The monobit test is described in Section 2.1 of [19].

```
zeroes = 0
n = len(bits)
for bit in bits:
    if (bit == 1):
        ones += 1
    else:
        zeroes += 1
s = abs(ones-zeroes)

p = math.erfc(float(s)/(math.sqrt(float(n)) * math.sqrt(2.0)))
return p
```

## 10.3 SP800-22rev1a Frequency Test Within a Block

The Frequency Test Within a Block is an improvement on the monobit test, in that by splitting the data into blocks and checking the bias within each block, the test is sensitive to nonstationarity within the data.

The data is split into blocks of a chosen size, and a Chi-square goodness of fit test is performed over the bias in each block, comparing against a 50/50 bias, which is expected from uniform data. So, variation of bias through the data will be detected.

### 10.3.1 Application

The Frequency Test Within a Block tests that data does not have a bias, and that the data is stationary in terms of bias.

### 10.3.2 Procedure

- Start with a string of $n$ bits, e. g., $0, 1, 0, 1, 0, 0, 1, 0, 1, 0, 1, 0, \ldots$.
- Choose a block-size of $M$ bits. SP800-22 recommends that the block-size be greater than 19 bits, also greater than 1% of the total number of bits, the total amount of data be at least 100 bits, and that the number of blocks be less than 100.
- Split the bit string into blocks of size $M$, throw away the remaining $n \mod M$ bits to get $n$ blocks, where

$$n = \frac{n - (n \mod M)}{M}.$$

- Compute the bias in each block by dividing the number of ones in each block by the size $M$. Call the bias for each block $b_i$.

- Compute the Chi-Square statistic

$$\chi^2 = 4M \sum_{i=1}^{n} \left( b_i - \frac{1}{2} \right)^2.$$

- Compute the $P$ value using the lower incomplete gamma function

$$P = \text{igamc}\left( \frac{n}{2}, \frac{\chi^2}{2} \right).$$

- If $P <$ confidence, then the data is not random.

### 10.3.3 Frequency Test Within a Block Python Implementation

**Listing 10.2:** sp800_22_frequency_within_block_test.py

```python
import math
from fractions import Fraction
from scipy.special import gamma, gammainc, gammaincc

#ones_table = [bin(i)[2:].count('1') for i in range(256)]
def count_ones_zeroes(bits):
    ones = 0
    zeroes = 0
    for bit in bits:
        if (bit == 1):
            ones += 1
        else:
            zeroes += 1
    return (zeroes, ones)

def frequency_within_block_test(bits):
    n = len(bits)
    M = 20
    N = int(math.floor(n/M))
    if N > 99:
        N=99
        M = int(math.floor(n/N))

    if len(bits) < 100:
        print "Too␣little␣data␣for␣test.␣Supply␣at␣least␣100␣bits"
        return False

    print "␣␣n␣=␣%d" % len(bits)
    print "␣␣N␣=␣%d" % N
    print "␣␣M␣=␣%d" % M

    num_of_blocks = N
```

```
block_size = M #int(math.floor(len(bits)/num_of_blocks))
#n = int(block_size * num_of_blocks)

proportions = list()
for i in xrange(num_of_blocks):
    block = bits[i*(block_size):((i+1)*(block_size))]
    zeroes,ones = count_ones_zeroes(block)
    proportions.append(Fraction(ones,block_size))

chisq = 0.0
for prop in proportions:
    chisq += 4.0*block_size*((prop - Fraction(1,2))**2)

p = gammaincc((num_of_blocks/2.0),float(chisq)/2.0)
success = (p >= 0.01)
return success
```

## 10.4 SP800-22rev1a Discrete Fourier Transform (DFT) Test

The Discrete Fourier Transform (DFT) Test computes a spectrograph of the binary input data and establishes that there are no frequency components that are outside the bounds of what would be expected for truly random data.

Specifically, the test determines if the number of points on the DFT plot that exceed the 95% threshold is statistically significantly distant from 5%.

Repetitive behaviors, such as repeating patterns of nonstationary properties that are oscillating will be detected easily by the DFT test.

An FFT plot has the benefit that humans are very good at being able to see features indicative of nonrandomness in a spectrogram. Regardless of the details of this test, if you are building an RNG or testing an RNG, it is always appropriate to plot the FFT of output data to see if anything is visible. This test only provides an algorithmic way to look at the plot, but the human eye is more flexible.

### 10.4.1 Application

This test is particularly applicable to directly testing circuits with feedback that may lead to oscillating behavior or algorithms that may exhibit oscillating behavior, such as LCGs or PCGs.

It does not directly detect bias, but biased data will cause an increase in low-frequency components, which would be picked up if the bias is too great.

### 10.4.2 Notes on the DFT Algorithm

The Discrete Fourier Transform is typically computed using the Cooly–Tukey Fast Fourier Transform algorithm. Computing an $N$-point DFT takes $O(N^2)$ operations. Computing an $N$-point DFT with an FFT algorithm takes $O(N \log_2^N)$ operations and so is computationally feasible for large data sizes.

The input data we use is bits, where 1 is treated as 1, and 0 is treated as −1. The input and output data to and from the DFT is defined as a string of complex numbers. It is a property of the DFT that, if all the input data are real, that is, have no imaginary components, then there will be conjugate symmetry in the output data. This means that the first half of the output data is mirrored in the second half, except that each value in the second half is the complex conjugate of the value it mirrors. This is the reason that the test below throws away the latter half of the output data of the DFT. It contains no information, since the input data has no imaginary components.

### 10.4.3 Procedure

– Start with an even $n$-bit string $\epsilon$ of $n$ bits, e. g., $\epsilon = [\epsilon_0, \epsilon_1, \ldots, \epsilon_{n-1}] =$
  ```
  1, 1, 0, 0, 1, 0, 0, 1, 0, 0, 0, 0, 1, 1, 1, 1, 1, 1, 0, 1, 1, 0, 1, 0, 1,
  0, 1, 0, 0, 0, 1, 0, 0, 0, 1, 0, 0, 0, 0, 1, 0, 1, 1, 0, 1, 0, 0, 0, 1, 1,
  0, 0, 0, 0, 1, 0, 0, 0, 1, 1, 0, 1, 0, 0, 1, 1, 0, 0, 0, 1, 0, 0, 1, 1, 0,
  0, 0, 1, 1, 0, 0, 1, 1, 0, 0, 0, 1, 0, 1, 0, 0, 0, 1, 0, 1, 1, 1, 0, 0, 0
  ```

– Map it to a sequence $X = [x_0, x_1, \ldots, x_n - 1]$, where the bits of the input string are mapped so that 0 becomes −1 and 1 remains 1. This can be expressed as $x_i = 2\epsilon_i - 1$, so that $X =$
  ```
   1, 1,-1,-1, 1,-1,-1, 1,-1,-1,-1,-1, 1, 1, 1, 1, 1, 1,-1, 1, 1,-1, 1,-1, 1,
  -1, 1,-1,-1,-1, 1,-1,-1,-1, 1,-1,-1,-1,-1, 1,-1, 1, 1,-1, 1,-1,-1,-1, 1, 1,
  -1,-1,-1,-1, 1,-1,-1,-1, 1, 1,-1, 1,-1,-1, 1, 1,-1,-1,-1, 1,-1,-1, 1, 1,-1,
  -1,-1, 1, 1,-1,-1, 1, 1,-1,-1,-1, 1,-1, 1,-1,-1,-1, 1,-1, 1, 1, 1,-1,-1,-1
  ```

– Perform a discrete Fourier transform on $F = \text{DFT}(X)$. $F$ is a sequence of $n$ complex points. In the example, we get 100 complex points $F =$

```
-1.60000000e+01  +0.00000000e+00j,  +5.93862039e+00  -2.51539444e+00j,
-2.67589879e+00  -6.42256599e+00j,  -7.08376213e+00  +3.96738305e-01j,
-2.66438749e+00  +1.15624349e+01j,  +1.03349947e+01  +5.00000000e+00j,
+2.21512214e-01  +7.01089753e+00j,  +4.80136072e+00  -2.33036129e+00j,
-7.08062561e-01  -3.47762970e+00j,  -6.07996540e+00  -4.58172901e+00j,
-1.76393202e+00  -5.42882455e+00j,  -1.04911374e+01  +6.32981777e-01j,
+5.38693388e-03  +4.94980090e+00j,  -4.45823263e+00  -9.14169471e+00j,
+8.83787442e+00  -1.89755975e+00j,  +9.77996556e+00  -5.00000000e+00j,
+2.12292945e+00  -3.91264653e+00j,  +1.30371632e+01  -1.00012101e+01j,
-1.27633802e+00  +6.15715429e+00j,  -1.85336692e+00  -5.05706260e+00j,
+7.08203932e-01  +5.98385365e+00j,  +7.47461730e-01  -2.08388548e+01j,
+1.01747096e+01  +3.55251685e+00j,  +1.06384517e+01  +1.30180170e+01j,
```

```
-1.84936134e+00  +4.02764591e+00j,  +2.00000000e+00  -1.00000000e+01j,
+1.80734114e+01  +4.90546547e+00j,  +6.11845184e+00  -2.11016158e+00j,
-3.98650175e+00  -4.36021675e+00j,  +4.22002842e+00  +1.19866926e+01j,
-6.23606798e+00  -4.53076859e+00j,  +7.54439506e+00  -8.55837499e+00j,
-3.46002141e+00  -1.16687747e+01j,  +2.25345739e+00  -5.60720949e+00j,
-3.88006878e+00  -6.32467522e+00j,  -5.77996556e+00  -5.00000000e+00j,
+8.92857353e+00  -1.84918391e+00j,  -4.46210268e+00  +2.30915929e+00j,
-9.21893143e+00  +2.33411587e-01j,  +2.89296768e-01  -1.14296886e+00j,
-1.27082039e+01  +1.15841916e+01j,  +1.43885532e+01  +1.22325737e+00j,
-1.27405117e+00  -3.88266279e+00j,  +3.74810245e+00  -1.26093110e+00j,
-3.44758420e+00  -8.56410452e-02j,  -6.33499466e+00  +5.00000000e+00j,
+6.01778056e+00  +1.12767224e+00j,  -4.59288985e+00  -1.39739164e+01j,
+5.90288463e-02  -1.20244051e+01j,  +5.29611413e+00  +6.78094342e+00j,
+1.60000000e+01  -2.08721929e-14j,  +5.29611413e+00  -6.78094342e+00j,
+5.90288463e-02  +1.20244051e+01j,  -4.59288985e+00  +1.39739164e+01j,
+6.01778056e+00  -1.12767224e+00j,  -6.33499466e+00  -5.00000000e+00j,
-3.44758420e+00  +8.56410452e-02j,  +3.74810245e+00  +1.26093110e+00j,
-1.27405117e+00  +3.88266279e+00j,  +1.43885532e+01  -1.22325737e+00j,
-1.27082039e+01  -1.15841916e+01j,  +2.89296768e-01  +1.14296886e+00j,
-9.21893143e+00  -2.33411587e-01j,  -4.46210268e+00  -2.30915929e+00j,
+8.92857353e+00  +1.84918391e+00j,  -5.77996556e+00  +5.00000000e+00j,
-3.88006878e+00  +6.32467522e+00j,  +2.25345739e+00  +5.60720949e+00j,
-3.46002141e+00  +1.16687747e+01j,  +7.54439506e+00  +8.55837499e+00j,
-6.23606798e+00  +4.53076859e+00j,  +4.22002842e+00  -1.19866926e+01j,
-3.98650175e+00  +4.36021675e+00j,  +6.11845184e+00  +2.11016158e+00j,
+1.80734114e+01  -4.90546547e+00j,  +2.00000000e+00  +1.00000000e+01j,
-1.84936134e+00  -4.02764591e+00j,  +1.06384517e+01  -1.30180170e+01j,
+1.01747096e+01  -3.55251685e+00j,  +7.47461730e-01  +2.08388548e+01j,
+7.08203932e-01  -5.98385365e+00j,  -1.85336692e+00  +5.05706260e+00j,
-1.27633802e+00  -6.15715429e+00j,  +1.30371632e+01  +1.00012101e+01j,
+2.12292945e+00  +3.91264653e+00j,  +9.77996556e+00  +5.00000000e+00j,
+8.83787442e+00  +1.89755975e+00j,  -4.45823263e+00  +9.14169471e+00j,
+5.38693388e-03  -4.94980090e+00j,  -1.04911374e+01  -6.32981777e-01j,
-1.76393202e+00  +5.42882455e+00j,  -6.07996540e+00  +4.58172901e+00j,
-7.08062561e-01  +3.47762970e+00j,  +4.80136072e+00  +2.33036129e+00j,
+2.21512214e-01  -7.01089753e+00j,  +1.03349947e+01  -5.00000000e+00j,
-2.66438749e+00  -1.15624349e+01j,  -7.08376213e+00  -3.96738305e-01j,
-2.67589879e+00  +6.42256599e+00j,  +5.93862039e+00  +2.51539444e+00j
```

- Compute the magnitude of the first half of the points to form a sequence $S$:

$$i \in \left\{0, 1, \ldots, \frac{n}{2} - 1\right\} S_i = |X_i|,$$

where $X_i$ is a complex variable $a + ib$. The magnitude $|X_i|$ is computed using the Pythagorean theorem

$$|X_i| = \sqrt{a^2 + b^2}.$$

The example sequence of magnitudes is $S =$

| | | | | |
|---|---|---|---|---|
| 16.0 | 6.44937372 | 6.95771429 | 7.09486343 | 11.86544822 |
| 11.48094572 | 7.01439604 | 5.33700745 | 3.54898027 | 7.61302962 |
| 5.70820393 | 10.51021547 | 4.94980383 | 10.17086134 | 9.03928964 |
| 10.98397589 | 4.4514753 | 16.43142808 | 6.28805118 | 5.38598655 |
| 6.02561676 | 20.85225568 | 10.77706319 | 16.81206172 | 4.43193738 |
| 10.19803903 | 18.7273007 | 6.47211209 | 5.90793418 | 12.70784956 |
| 7.70820393 | 11.4089298 | 12.17095111 | 6.04308435 | 7.42000339 |
| 7.6425128 | 9.11805387 | 5.02419914 | 9.2218858 | 1.17901248 |
| 17.19569547 | 14.4404578 | 4.0863525 | 3.95451883 | 3.44864774 |
| 8.07044964 | 6.12252624 | 14.70935 | 12.02455003 | 8.60406989 |

Plotting these values, we can see the spectrograph of the data as in Figure 10.1.

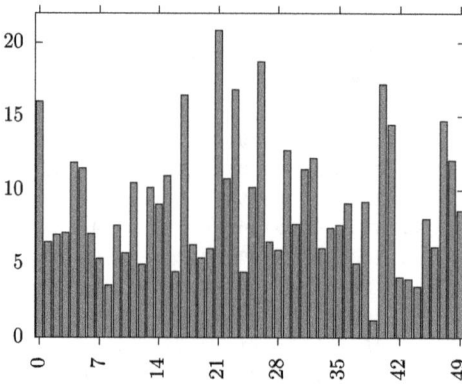

**Figure 10.1:** DFT Test Magnitudes.

- Compute the 95% threshold

$$T = \sqrt{\log \frac{1}{0.05} n}.$$

In the example, $T = 17.30818382602285$.
- Compute

$$N_0 = \frac{0.95n}{2}.$$

In the example, $N_0 = \frac{0.95 \cdot 100}{2} = 47.5$.
- Count $N_1 =$ the number of values in $S$ that are less than the threshold $T$.
In the example, $N_1 = 48$.
Compute

$$d = \frac{N_1 - N_0}{\sqrt{n(0.95)(0.125)}}.$$

– Compute the $P$ value

$$P = \text{erfc}\left(\frac{|d|}{\sqrt{(2)}}\right).$$

In the example, $P = 0.884635668537$.

– If $P \leq 0.01$, then the data is not random.

In the example, since $P \gg 0.01$, the test fails to show that the data is nonrandom.

### 10.4.4 DFT Test Example Code

The following example code takes a list of bits as its input parameter and performs the DFT test.

**Listing 10.3:** sp800_22_dft_test.py

```python
import numpy
import math

def dft_test(bits):
    n = len(bits)
    if (n % 2) == 1:                    # Make it an even number
        raise ValueError("The_list_length_is_not_even")

    # Convert to +1,-1
    ts = list()
    for bit in bits:
        if bit == 0:
            ts.append(-1.0)
        else:
            ts.append(1.0)

    # Compute DFT
    ts_np = numpy.array(ts)
    fs = numpy.fft.fft(ts_np)

    # Compute magnitudes of first half of sequence
    mags = abs(fs)[:n/2]

    # Compute upper threshold
    T = math.sqrt(math.log(1.0/0.05)*n)
    # Compute N0
    N0 = 0.95*n/2.0

    # Count the peaks above the upper threshold
    N1 = 0.0
    print "N0_=_",N0
```

```
for mag in mags:
    if mag < T:
        N1 += 1.0

# Compute d
d = (N1 - N0)/math.sqrt((n*0.95*0.5)/4) # Compute the P value

# Compute p
p = math.erfc(abs(d)/math.sqrt(2))

return p
```

## 10.5 SP800-22rev1a Nonoverlapping Template Matching Test

The Nonoverlapping Template Matching Test counts occurrences of a pattern within blocks of the data being tested. If the data is random, there is an expectation of the number of occurrences of each pattern in each block. A Chi-Square test of the measured occurrence rate against the expected occurrence rate is performed to get a $P$ value for the probability that the measured pattern occurrence rate would happen at random.

The pattern count is computed with a block of data using a sliding window bit-pattern matching window. Starting at the first position, the pattern is matched with the data in the sliding window.

Since this is a nonoverlapping test, when there is no match, the window slides one bit right and repeats. When it finds a match, it slides right past the pattern that was matched. So, it will not detect overlapping occurrences of the pattern.

Compared to the DFT test, this test does not rely on periodicity of the patterns being detected. It is capable of detecting defects that would lead to specific patterns occurring more often or less often than expected in random data. For example, positively biased data would favor bit strings with more bits set than less. Negatively serially correlated data would have fewer bit patterns, containing long strings of the same bit value compared to random data. Physical errors in a generator could lead to stuck bits or repeating behavior that this test could detect.

### 10.5.1 Application

This test is mostly useful as a means to detect defects in PRNG algorithms or entropy sources that claim to be full-entropy. As discussed above, various defects can lead to increased or decreased pattern frequencies that this test would detect.

It is not useful in measuring the degree that entropy sources do not achieve full entropy, since nonfull-entropy sources are not expected to pass this test.

## 10.5.2 Procedure

- Set $n$ = the length of the input data $X_0 \ldots X_{n-1}$ in bits.
- With the provided list of 7 sets of templates of different lengths from 2 to 8 bits, select one of the sets. For example, choose at random or repeat the test 7 times, iterating through every set.

  The templates are given in Listing 10.4.
- From the chosen set, choose one of the elements in the set. This element will be called $B$.
- Split the data bits into $N$ blocks of $M$ bits. If the number of bits is not divisible by $M$, then discard the left over bits. The specification does not say this, but it does not say what to do in this situation. So, discarding the additional bits is consistent with other tests in the same specification.

  Set $m = \text{len}(B)$

  Set $N$ = the number of blocks. The example code chooses $N = 8$.

  Compute the number of blocks

$$M = \left\lfloor \frac{n}{N} \right\rfloor.$$

  Set the number of bits to be used $n = M \cdot N$.

  Split the data into $N$-bit blocks $\text{BLOCK}_0 \ldots \text{BLOCK}_{M-1}$.
- Count the number of matches in each block $W_j$.

  For each block $\text{BLOCK}_j$
  - Set count = 0
  - For each starting position $i$ from 0 to $M - n - 1$
    - If bits numbered $i \ldots i + m - 1$ of $\text{BLOCK}_j$ match the template $B$, then increment count and move $i$ forward to the end of the matched block $i = i + m$.

    Record the count $W_j$ = count.
- Compute $\mu$ and $\sigma$:

$$\mu = \frac{M - n + 1}{2^m},$$

$$\sigma = M\left(\frac{1}{2^m}\right) - \left(\frac{2^m - 1}{2^{2m}}\right).$$

- Compute the $\chi^2$ statistic

$$\chi^2 = \sum_0^{N-1} \frac{(W_j - \mu)^2}{\sigma^2}.$$

- Compute the $P$ value

$$P = \text{igamc}\left(\frac{N}{2}, \frac{\chi^2}{2}\right).$$

- If $P < 0.01$, then the data is nonrandom.

### 10.5.3 Nonoverlapping Template Matching Test Example Code

**Listing 10.4:** sp800_22_non_overlapping_template_matching_test.py

```python
import math
from scipy.special import gamma, gammainc, gammaincc
import random

def non_overlapping_template_matching_test(bits):
    # The templates provided in SP800-22rev1a
    templates = [None for x in xrange(7)]
    templates[0] = [[0,1],[1,0]]
    templates[1] = [[0,0,1],[0,1,1],[1,0,0],[1,1,0]]
    templates[2] = [[0,0,0,1],[0,0,1,1],[0,1,1,1],
                    [1,0,0,0],[1,1,0,0],[1,1,1,0]]
    templates[3] = [[0,0,0,0,1],[0,0,0,1,1],[0,0,1,0,1],[0,1,0,1,1],
                    [0,0,1,1,1],[0,1,1,1,1],[1,1,1,0,0],[1,1,0,1,0],
                    [1,0,1,0,0],[1,1,0,0,0],[1,0,0,0,0],[1,1,1,1,0]]
    templates[4] = [[0,0,0,0,0,1],[0,0,0,0,1,1],[0,0,0,1,0,1],
                    [0,0,0,1,1,1],[0,0,1,0,1,1],[0,0,1,1,0,1],
                    [0,0,1,1,1,1],[0,1,0,0,1,1],[0,1,0,1,1,1],
                    [0,1,1,1,1,1],[1,0,0,0,0,0],[1,0,1,0,0,0],
                    [1,0,1,1,0,0],[1,1,0,0,0,0],[1,1,0,0,1,0],
                    [1,1,0,1,0,0],[1,1,1,0,0,0],[1,1,1,0,1,0],
                    [1,1,1,1,0,0],[1,1,1,1,1,0]]
    templates[5] = [[0,0,0,0,0,0,1],[0,0,0,0,0,1,1],[0,0,0,0,1,0,1],
                    [0,0,0,0,1,1,1],[0,0,0,1,0,0,1],[0,0,0,1,0,1,1],
                    [0,0,0,1,1,0,1],[0,0,0,1,1,1,1],[0,0,1,0,0,1,1],
                    [0,0,1,0,1,0,1],[0,0,1,0,1,1,1],[0,0,1,1,0,1,1],
                    [0,0,1,1,1,0,1],[0,0,1,1,1,1,1],[0,1,0,0,0,1,1],
                    [0,1,0,0,1,1,1],[0,1,0,1,0,1,1],[0,1,0,1,1,1,1],
                    [0,1,1,0,1,1,1],[0,1,1,1,1,1,1],[1,0,0,0,0,0,0],
                    [1,0,0,1,0,0,0],[1,0,1,0,0,0,0],[1,0,1,0,1,0,0],
                    [1,0,1,1,0,0,0],[1,0,1,1,1,0,0],[1,1,0,0,0,0,0],
                    [1,1,0,0,0,1,0],[1,1,0,0,1,0,0],[1,1,0,1,0,0,0],
                    [1,1,0,1,0,1,0],[1,1,0,1,1,0,0],[1,1,1,0,0,0,0],
                    [1,1,1,0,0,1,0],[1,1,1,0,1,0,0],[1,1,1,0,1,1,0],
                    [1,1,1,1,0,0,0],[1,1,1,1,0,1,0],[1,1,1,1,1,0,0],
                    [1,1,1,1,1,1,0]]
    templates[6] = [[0,0,0,0,0,0,0,1],[0,0,0,0,0,0,1,1],[0,0,0,0,0,1,0,1],
                    [0,0,0,0,0,1,1,1],[0,0,0,0,1,0,0,1],[0,0,0,0,1,0,1,1],
                    [0,0,0,0,1,1,0,1],[0,0,0,0,1,1,1,1],[0,0,0,1,0,0,1,1],
                    [0,0,0,1,0,1,0,1],[0,0,0,1,0,1,1,1],[0,0,0,1,1,0,0,1],
                    [0,0,0,1,1,0,1,1],[0,0,0,1,1,1,0,1],[0,0,0,1,1,1,1,1],
                    [0,0,1,0,0,0,1,1],[0,0,1,0,0,1,0,1],[0,0,1,0,0,1,1,1],
                    [0,0,1,0,1,0,1,1],[0,0,1,0,1,1,0,1],[0,0,1,0,1,1,1,1],
                    [0,0,1,1,0,1,0,1],[0,0,1,1,0,1,1,1],[0,0,1,1,1,0,1,1],
                    [0,0,1,1,1,1,0,1],[0,0,1,1,1,1,1,1],[0,1,0,0,0,0,1,1],
                    [0,1,0,0,0,1,0,1],[0,1,0,0,0,1,1,1],[0,1,0,0,1,0,1,1],
                    [0,1,0,1,0,0,1,1],[0,1,0,1,0,1,0,1],[0,1,0,1,0,1,1,1],
                    [0,1,0,1,1,1,1,1],[0,1,1,0,0,1,1,1],[0,1,1,0,1,1,1,1],
                    [0,1,1,1,1,1,1,1],[1,0,0,0,0,0,0,0],[1,0,0,1,0,0,0,0],
                    [1,0,0,1,1,0,0,0],[1,0,1,0,0,0,0,0],[1,0,1,0,0,1,0,0],
                    [1,0,1,0,1,0,0,0],[1,0,1,0,1,1,0,0],[1,0,1,1,0,0,0,0],
                    [1,0,1,1,0,1,0,0],[1,0,1,1,1,1,0,0],[1,0,1,1,1,1,0,0],
                    [1,1,0,0,0,0,0,0],[1,1,0,0,0,0,1,0],[1,1,0,0,0,1,0,0],
                    [1,1,0,0,1,0,0,0],[1,1,0,0,1,0,1,0],[1,1,0,1,0,0,0,0],
                    [1,1,0,1,0,0,1,0],[1,1,0,1,0,1,0,0],[1,1,0,1,1,0,0,0],
                    [1,1,0,1,1,0,1,0],[1,1,0,1,1,1,0,0],[1,1,1,0,0,0,0,0],
                    [1,1,1,0,0,0,1,0],[1,1,1,0,0,1,0,0],[1,1,1,0,0,1,1,0],
```

```
                    [1,1,1,0,1,0,0,0],[1,1,1,0,1,0,1,0],[1,1,1,0,1,1,0,0],
                    [1,1,1,1,0,0,0,0],[1,1,1,1,0,0,1,0],[1,1,1,1,0,1,0,0],
                    [1,1,1,1,0,1,1,0],[1,1,1,1,1,0,0,0],[1,1,1,1,1,0,1,0],
                    [1,1,1,1,1,1,0,0],[1,1,1,1,1,1,1,0]]

n = len(bits)
r = random.SystemRandom()    # Choose the template B
template_list = r.choice(templates)
B = r.choice(template_list)
m = len(B)
N = 8
M = int(math.floor(len(bits)/8))
n = M*N

blocks = list() # Split into N blocks of M bits
for i in xrange(N):
    blocks.append(bits[i*M:(i+1)*M])

W=list()                    # Count the number of matches of
for block in blocks:        # the template in each block Wj
    position = 0
    count = 0
    while position < (M-m):
        if block[position:position+m] == B:
            position += m
            count += 1
        else:
            position += 1
    W.append(count)

mu = float(M-m+1)/float(2**m) # Compute mu and sigma
sigma = M * ((1.0/float(2**m))-(float((2*m)-1)/float(2**(2*m))))

chisq = 0.0   # Compute Chi-Square
for j in xrange(N):
    chisq += ((W[j] - mu)**2)/(sigma**2)

p = gammaincc(N/2.0, chisq/2.0) # Compute P value

success = ( p >= 0.01)
return (success,p,None)
```

## 10.6 Overlapping Template Matching Test

The Overlapping Template Matching Test is similar to the Nonoverlapping Template Test in that it counts the frequency of the number of matches of a pattern within a number of blocks.

The difference with this measurement is that when a match is made, the pattern-matching algorithm moves along by one bit position, so it can match the same pattern in an overlapping position.

A $\chi^2$ test is performed against the number of times the patterns are matched 0, 1, 2, 3, 4, and 5 or more times.

The reference probabilities $\pi_0$ through $\pi_5$, stated in Section 2.8 of the specification, are presented in a very confusing fashion. The example in the test presents the following probabilities:

$$\pi_0 = 0.364091,$$
$$\pi_1 = 0.185659,$$
$$\pi_2 = 0.139381,$$
$$\pi_3 = 0.100571,$$
$$\pi_4 = 0.070432,$$
$$\pi_5 = 0.139865.$$

The text of the specification then goes on to say that those values were just for example, and the actual values are:

$$\pi_0 = 0.324652,$$
$$\pi_1 = 0.182617,$$
$$\pi_2 = 0.142670,$$
$$\pi_3 = 0.106645,$$
$$\pi_4 = 0.077147,$$
$$\pi_5 = 0.166269.$$

Section 3.8 provides the mathematical basis for the test, but confusingly lists the first set of probabilities above as the correct ones. So, it is not clear which set of probabilities the test specification is requiring.

By looking at the C implementation of the test in the NIST statistical test suite sts-2.1.2, we find that it also uses the first set, which is identified as being incorrect in Section 2.8 of the specification.

So, to investigate the right probabilities, we can run the test multiple times over uniform random data and see what the frequencies actually are. The plot in Figure 10.2 is a boxplot of the distribution of frequency of blocks in which the pattern was matched

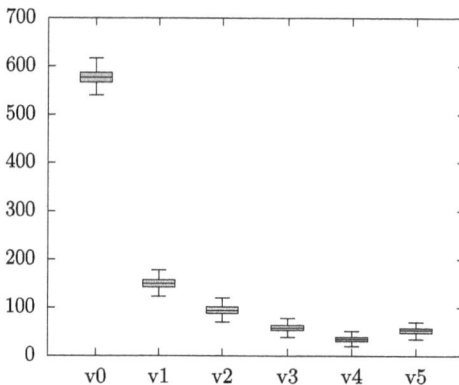

**Figure 10.2:** Frequency of Pattern Matched in the Overlapping Pattern Matching Test.

0, 1, 2, 3, 4, and 5 or more times in 800 runs of the test, each over the recommended 1,028,016 bits of data.

This does not appear to match the reference probabilities in the specification at all. If we compute the probabilities from the data, then we get a set of probabilities that is substantially different.

**Table 10.1:** Measured $x^2$ Probabilities from 800 runs of the Overlapping Pattern Matching Test.

|  | $v_0$ | $v_1$ | $v_2$ | $v_3$ | $v_4$ | $v_5$ |
|---|---|---|---|---|---|---|
| Mean | 576.91625 | 150.3025 | 94.2275 | 58.3075 | 35.355 | 52.89125 |
| Frequency | 0.595988 | 0.155271 | 0.097342 | 0.060235 | 0.036524 | 0.054640 |

So, when implementing this test, you may want to consider using the probabilities from Table 10.1, instead of the probabilities specified in SP800-22Rev1a.

### 10.6.1 Application

Like the nonoverlapping template matching test, the overlapping template matching test counts the frequencies of patterns in data and compares it against the expected frequencies for full-entropy data, using a $x^2$ test. The sliding template approach used may make it more sensitive to effects that have some periodicity in the data, which might not be picked up by the nonoverlapping test. It is questionable whether there is any purpose for the nonoverlapping test, given that we have the overlapping test.

### 10.6.2 Procedure

The data will be processed in blocks.
- Set $n$ = the length of the input data $\epsilon_0 \ldots \epsilon_{n-1}$ in bits. The length $n$ must be at least $10^6$, and preferably a divisible by $M$ and $N$.
- Choose a window template size $m$ = 9 or 10. The specification suggests picking "Various values of $m$," but it does not give a definitive rule on which sizes or how many sizes.
- Set $M$ = 1062. The specification states that the example code uses a value of 1032. This does not meet the $10^6$ lower data size bound in the specification. So, setting it to 1062 will meet that bound, while not being too far from the suggested value.
- Set $N$ = the number of blocks in which to divide $n$. The example code chooses $N$ = 968. This is a contrived number that leads to the test data size being close to $10^6$ bits. If the input data is longer, this value should probably be computed as

$\lfloor \frac{n}{N} \rfloor$, although the specification does not say this. The example code in Listing 10.5 simply truncates the data to $M \times N$ bits.

- Split the data bits into $N$ blocks of $M$ bits. If the number of bits is not divisible by $M$, discard the left over bits. The specification does not say this, but it does not say what to do in this situation. So, discarding the additional bits is consistent with other tests in the same specification.
- Set $B$ to an $m$-bit string to be matched. The specification is not clear on what pattern to use, but it is sufficient to pick any random value.
- Set $m = \text{len}(B)$.
- Initialize six counters $v_i = 0$ for $i \in \{0, 1, 2, 3, 4, 5\}$.
- Use a sliding window to find the number of matches of the pattern $B$ in each of the $n$ blocks. In a block, there are $x$ matches, where $x < 5$, increment $v_x$. Otherwise, when $x > 4$, increment $v_5$. Repeat for all the $N$ blocks.
- Compute

$$\lambda = \frac{M - m + 1}{2^m},$$

$$\mu = \frac{\lambda}{2}.$$

- Compute

$$\chi^2(\text{obs}) = \sum_{i=0}^{5} \frac{(v_i - N\pi_i)^2}{N\pi_i}.$$

Whereas, if using the values in the specification

$$\pi_0 = 0.364091,$$
$$\pi_1 = 0.185659,$$
$$\pi_2 = 0.139381,$$
$$\pi_3 = 0.100571,$$
$$\pi_4 = 0.070432,$$
$$\pi_5 = 0.139865,$$

or if using the corrected values from this book:

$$\pi_0 = 0.595988,$$
$$\pi_1 = 0.155271,$$
$$\pi_2 = 0.097342,$$
$$\pi_3 = 0.060235,$$
$$\pi_4 = 0.036524,$$
$$\pi_5 = 0.054640.$$

– Compute

$$\chi^2(\text{obs}) = \frac{(0 - 5\pi_0)^2}{5\pi_0} + \sum_{i=1}^{5} \frac{(1 - 5\pi_i)^2}{5\pi_i}.$$

– Compute the $P$ value

$$P = \text{igamc}\left(2.5, \frac{\chi^2(\text{obs})}{2}\right).$$

– If $P \leq 0.01$, then the data is nonrandom.

## 10.6.3 Overlapping Template Matching Test Example Code

**Listing 10.5:** sp800_22_overlapping_template_matching_test.py

```python
import math
from scipy.special import gamma, gammainc, gammaincc

def lgamma(x):
    return math.log(gamma(x))

def Pr(u, eta):
    if ( u == 0 ):
        p = math.exp(-eta)
    else:
        sum = 0.0
        for l in xrange(1,u+1):
            inner = -eta-u*math.log(2)
            inner = inner + l*math.log(eta)-lgamma(l+1)
            inner = inner + lgamma(u)-lgamma(l)-lgamma(u-l+1)
            sum += math.exp(inner)
        p = sum
    return p

def overlapping_template_matching_test(bits,blen=6):
    n = len(bits)

    m = 10
    # Build the template B as a list of 1s
    B = [1 for x in xrange(m)]

    N = 968
    K = 5
    M = 1062
    if len(bits) < (M*N):
        print "Insufficient_data._%d_bit_provided." % len(bits)
        print "___1,028,016_bits_required"
```

```
        return False

    blocks = list() # Split into N blocks of M bits
    for i in xrange(N):
        blocks.append(bits[i*M:(i+1)*M])

    # Count the distribution of matches of the template across blocks: Vj
    v=[0 for x in xrange(K+1)]
    for block in blocks:
        count = 0
        for position in xrange(M-m):
            if block[position:position+m] == B:
                count += 1

        if count >= (K):
            v[K] += 1
        else:
            v[count] += 1

    chisq = 0.0  # Compute Chi-Square
    # Chi-Req reference frequencies mandated in SP800-22
    #pi = [0.324652,0.182617,0.142670,0.106645,0.077147,0.166269]
    # Empirically derived values
    #pi = [0.595988, 0.155271, 0.097342, 0.060235, 0.036524, 0.054640]
    # Values used in STS-2.1.2 and chapter 3 of SP800-22 Rev1a
    pi = [0.364091, 0.185659, 0.139381, 0.100571, 0.0704323, 0.139865]
    piqty = [int(x*N) for x in pi]

    lambd = (M-m+1.0)/(2.0**m)
    eta = lambd/2.0
    sum = 0.0
    for i in xrange(K): #  Compute Probabilities
        pi[i] = Pr(i, eta)
        sum += pi[i]
    pi[K] = 1 - sum;

    sum = 0
    chisq = 0.0
    for i in xrange(K+1):
        chisq += ((v[i] - (N*pi[i]))**2)/(N*pi[i])
        sum += v[i]

    p = gammaincc(5.0/2.0, chisq/2.0) # Compute P value

    print "__chisq_=_",chisq
    print "__P_=_",p

    success = ( p >= 0.01)
    return success
```

## 10.7 SP800-22rev1a Longest Runs of Ones in a Block Test

The Longest Runs of Ones in a Block Test performs a $\chi^2$ test of the frequency of the longest run of ones in blocks of the data. It splits the data into blocks, finds the length of longest run of ones in each block, and assembles a frequency table of the lengths. A $\chi^2$ metric is computed against the expected distribution for random data.

### 10.7.1 Application

This test is most obviously sensitive to serial correlation between bits in the data. Negative serial correlation would lead to reduced number of longer runs and increased number of shorter runs, relative to random. Positive serial correlation would lead to an increased number of longer runs and reduce number of shorter runs.

For example, generating 2 KiB of random data with serial correlation of −0.1 and running it through NIST tests, we find it fails this test, but the monobit test (for frequency within a block) runs, and DFT tests all pass. So, those tests are failing to pick up on a fairly large and simple deviation from random.

A common symptom of a circuit failure in entropy sources is high serial correlation. So, this test may be useful for entropy sources that have particularly high-entropy per bit, but for which exhibit higher serial correlation when they fail. This failure mode is common with stepped update metastable sources and ring oscillators.

An odd feature of this test is that it only takes certain sizes of data in. Additional bits past its chosen block-size, and the chosen number of blocks are simply thrown away. So, it is possible to fool the test with data that are clearly nonrandom at the end, which is ignored by the test.

The largest number of bits this algorithm takes is 75 blocks of 10 000 bits. Any more data after that are ignored.

### 10.7.2 Procedure

This test is a little longer and more complex than some of the others because of the lookup tables it uses, instead of computed values.

With $n$ bits of data, find the block size $M$, the constant $K$, and the number of blocks $N$ by indexing into Table 10.2.

Compute 7 frequency variables $v_0 \ldots v_6$, and then compute a $P$ value with the following algorithm:

For each $M$-bit block, count the length $l$ of the longest run of 1s in the block.

$v_0 \ldots v_6$ are set to the frequency of the different longest lengths. The lengths that are assigned to bins vary according to the three values of $M$. Table 10.3 gives the assignments.

**Table 10.2:** Table To Compute $M$, $N$, and $K$ From the Number of Bits.

| $n$ | $M$ | $K$ | $N$ |
|---|---|---|---|
| $n < 128$ | Too Little Data | | |
| $n < 6272$ | 8 | 3 | 16 |
| $n < 750000$ | 128 | 5 | 49 |
| $n \geq 750000$ | 10000 | 6 | 75 |

**Table 10.3:** Longest Runs Frequency Bins.

| | $M = 8$ | $M = 128$ | $M = 10000$ |
|---|---|---|---|
| $v_0$ | number of runs of $\leq 1$ bit | number of runs of $\leq 4$ bits | number of runs of $\leq 10$ bits |
| $v_1$ | number of runs of 2 bits | number of runs of 5 bits | number of runs of 11 bits |
| $v_2$ | number of runs of 3 bits | number of runs of 6 bits | number of runs of 12 bits |
| $v_3$ | number of runs of $\geq 3$ bits | number of runs of 7 bits | number of runs of 13 bits |
| $v_4$ | | number of runs of 8 bits | number of runs of 14 bits |
| $v_5$ | | number of runs of $\geq 9$ bits | number of runs of 15 bits |
| $v_6$ | | | number of runs of $\geq 16$ bits |

Define the series or reference probabilities $\pi_i$:

- if $M = 8$, $\pi_0 \ldots \pi_3 = 0.2148, 0.3672, 0.2305, 0.1875$;
- if $M = 128$, $\pi_0 \ldots \pi_5 = 0.1174, 0.2430, 0.2493, 0.1752, 0.1027, 0.1124$;
- if $M = 512$, $\pi_0 \ldots \pi_5 = 0.1170, 0.2460, 0.2523, 0.1755, 0.1027, 0.1124$;
- if $M = 1000$, $\pi_0 \ldots \pi_5 = 0.1307, 0.2437, 0.2452, 0.1714, 0.1002, 0.1088$;
- if $M = 10000$, $\pi_0 \ldots \pi_6 = 0.0882, 0.2092, 0.2483, 0.1933, 0.1208, 0.0675, 0.0727$.

Compute

$$\chi^2 = \sum_{i=0}^{K} \frac{(v_i - N\pi_i)^2}{N\pi_i}.$$

Compute

$$P = \mathrm{igamc}\left(\frac{K}{2}, \frac{\chi^2}{2}\right).$$

If $P \leq 0.01$, then the data are nonrandom.

### 10.7.3 Longest Runs of Ones in a Block Test Example Code

Listing 10.6 code implements the Longest Runs of Ones in a Block Test:

**Listing 10.6:** sp800_22_longest_run_ones_in_a_block_test.py

```python
#!/usr/bin/env python

import math
from scipy.special import gamma, gammainc, gammaincc

def probs(M,i):
    M8    =     [0.2148, 0.3672, 0.2305, 0.1875]
    M128  =     [0.1174, 0.2430, 0.2493, 0.1752, 0.1027, 0.1124]
    M512  =     [0.1170, 0.2460, 0.2523, 0.1755, 0.1027, 0.1124]
    M1000 =     [0.1307, 0.2437, 0.2452, 0.1714, 0.1002, 0.1088]
    M10000 =    [0.0882, 0.2092, 0.2483, 0.1933, 0.1208, 0.0675, 0.0727]
    if (M == 8): return M8[i]
    elif (M == 128):   return M128[i]
    elif (M == 512):   return M512[i]
    elif (M == 1000):  return M1000[i]
    else:              return M10000[i]

def longest_run_ones_in_a_block_test(bits):
    n = len(bits)

    if n < 128:
        return 0
    elif n<6272:
        M = 8
    elif n<750000:
        M = 128
    else:
        M = 10000

    # compute new values for K & N
    if M==8:
        K=3
        N=16
    elif M==128:
        K=5
        N=49
    else:
        K=6
        N=75

    # Table of frequencies
    v = [0,0,0,0,0,0,0]

    for i in xrange(N): # over each block
        #find longest run
        block = bits[i*M:((i+1)*M)] # Block i

        run = 0
```

```
        longest = 0
        for j in xrange(M): # Count the bits.
            if block[j] == 1:
                run += 1
                if run > longest:
                    longest = run
            else:
                run = 0

    if M == 8:
        if longest <= 1:      v[0] += 1
        elif longest == 2:    v[1] += 1
        elif longest == 3:    v[2] += 1
        else:                 v[3] += 1
    elif M == 128:
        if longest <= 4:      v[0] += 1
        elif longest == 5:    v[1] += 1
        elif longest == 6:    v[2] += 1
        elif longest == 7:    v[3] += 1
        elif longest == 8:    v[4] += 1
        else:                 v[5] += 1
    else:
        if longest <= 10:     v[0] += 1
        elif longest == 11:   v[1] += 1
        elif longest == 12:   v[2] += 1
        elif longest == 13:   v[3] += 1
        elif longest == 14:   v[4] += 1
        elif longest == 15:   v[5] += 1
        else:                 v[6] += 1

# Compute Chi-Sq
chi_sq = 0.0
for i in range(K+1):
    p_i = probs(K,M,i)
    upper = (v[i] - N*p_i)**2
    lower = N*p_i
    chi_sq += upper/lower
print "  n = "+str(n)
print "  K = "+str(K)
print "  M = "+str(M)
print "  N = "+str(N)
print "  chi_sq = "+str(chi_sq)
p = gammaincc(K/2.0, chi_sq/2.0)

success = (p >= 0.01)
return success
```

## 10.8 SP800-22rev1a Binary Matrix Rank Test

This test looks for linear dependence between strings of bits in the data. This might typically be a feature of bad PRNG algorithms, such as LGCs, which explicitly output data with linear dependence.

Linear dependence is measured by splitting the data into blocks of 1024 bits and arranging those bits in each block into a 32-by-32 matrix; then computing the rank of the matrix, which gives the number of linearly independent values in the matrix. If the matrix is full-rank, that is, the rank is equal to the number of rows, then there is no linear dependence between the rows.

The rank can be found by performing Gaussian elimination on the matrix https://en.wikipedia.org/wiki/Gaussian_elimination. The linearly dependent pairs will be zeroed out. The rank can then be counted as the number of non zero rows.

The test performs a $\chi^2$ test between the distribution of ranks and the expected distribution of the ranks, given uniform random data.

### 10.8.1 Application

This test is most appropriate for simple PRNGs, which might introduce linear dependence between bits where subsequent bits can be expressed as a simple polynomial of previous bits.

A weakness of this test is that it is defined for only 32-by-32 entry matrices. This would make sense for algorithms using 32-bit arithmetic. However, the suitability of this test would be for all sizes of $n$-by-$m$ matrices, which would pick up on a broader class of PRNG algorithms. The reference test code only gives weightings for the 32-by-32 case, but somewhat confusingly, the spec goes on to give an example with 3-by-3 matrices, while not indicating if the weightings are the ones for a 32-by-32 case or not.

### 10.8.2 Procedure

- Choose the size of the $M$ row by $Q$ column matrix. The specification provides weightings for a 32×32 matrix. So, set $M = 32$ and $Q = 32$. The number of bits of input data is $n$. There must be sufficient data for at least 38 matrices. So, $N \geq 38MQ$. With $32 \times 32$ matrices, the minimum number of bits is 38912.
- Set the number of matrices

$$N = \left\lfloor \frac{n}{MQ} \right\rfloor.$$

- Create $N$ matrices from the input data. Place the first 32 bits in the top row and subsequent bits in subsequent rows. For example, with a $4 \times 4$ matrix, if the first

16 bits were 0010 0111 0010 1111, then the matrix would be

$$
\begin{bmatrix}
0 & 0 & 1 & 0 \\
0 & 1 & 1 & 1 \\
0 & 0 & 1 & 0 \\
1 & 1 & 1 & 1
\end{bmatrix}.
$$

- Compute the rank $R_l$ of each matrix.
- Count the number of full-rank matrices $F_M$, where $R_l = M$.
- Count the number matrices $F_{M-1}$, where $R_l = M - 1$.
- Compute the $\chi^2$ statistic. For $32 \times 32$ matrices, the weightings are $\pi_1 = 0.2888$, $\pi_2 = 0.5776$, and $\pi_3 = 0.1336$.

$$
\chi^2 = \frac{(F_M - \pi_1 N)^2}{\pi_1 N} + \frac{(F_{M-1} - \pi_2 N)^2}{\pi_2 N} + \frac{(N - F_M - F_{M-1} - \pi_3 N)^2}{\pi_3 N}.
$$

- Compute the $P$ value

$$
P = e^{-\frac{\chi^2}{2}}.
$$

- If $P < 0.01$, then the data are nonrandom.

To use other matrix sizes, the weightings $\pi_{1,2,3}$ can be computed. The equations are in Section 3.5 of the specification. Table 10.4 gives the weightings for all square matrices with $M$ and $Q$ between 3 and 41. As can be seen in the table, after 39, the weightings remain constant.

For an $M \times Q$ matrix with $r$ from 0 to $\min(M, Q)$, the equation for $P_r$, the probability that an $M \times Q$ matrix filled with uniformly random bits has rank $r$ is

$$
P_r = 2^{r(Q+M-r)-MQ} \prod \frac{(1 - 2^{i-Q})(1 - 2^{i-M})}{1 - 2^{i-r}}.
$$

The weights for the $\chi^2$ test are as follows:

$$
\pi_1 = P_M,
$$
$$
\pi_2 = P_{M-1},
$$
$$
\pi_3 = 1.0 - P_M - PM - 1.
$$

The following code generates the table:

**Listing 10.7:** binary_rank_weights.py

```
#!/usr/bin/env python

print "M⎵⎵⎵Q⎵⎵⎵Pi_1⎵⎵⎵⎵⎵⎵⎵⎵⎵⎵Pi_2⎵⎵⎵⎵⎵⎵⎵⎵⎵⎵Pi_3"
for x in range(3,42):
```

**Table 10.4:** Binary Matrix Rank Test Weightings.

| M | Q | $\pi_1$ | $\pi_2$ | $\pi_3$ |
|---|---|---|---|---|
| 3 | 3 | 0.328125 | 0.57421875 | 0.09765625 |
| 4 | 4 | 0.3076171875 | 0.576782226563 | 0.115600585937 |
| 5 | 5 | 0.298004150391 | 0.577383041382 | 0.124612808228 |
| 6 | 6 | 0.293347835541 | 0.577528551221 | 0.129123613238 |
| 7 | 7 | 0.291056055576 | 0.577564360283 | 0.131379584142 |
| 8 | 8 | 0.289919117859 | 0.577573242609 | 0.132507639533 |
| 9 | 9 | 0.289352869581 | 0.577575454516 | 0.133071675902 |
| 10 | 10 | 0.28907029842 | 0.577576006413 | 0.133353695167 |
| 11 | 11 | 0.288929150813 | 0.577576144252 | 0.133494704935 |
| 12 | 12 | 0.28885861147 | 0.577576178695 | 0.133565209835 |
| 13 | 13 | 0.288823350409 | 0.577576187304 | 0.133600462287 |
| 14 | 14 | 0.28880572203 | 0.577576189456 | 0.133618088514 |
| 15 | 15 | 0.288796908379 | 0.577576189994 | 0.133626901627 |
| 16 | 16 | 0.288792501688 | 0.577576190128 | 0.133631308184 |
| 17 | 17 | 0.288790298376 | 0.577576190162 | 0.133633511462 |
| 18 | 18 | 0.288789196729 | 0.57757619017 | 0.133634613101 |
| 19 | 19 | 0.288788645907 | 0.577576190173 | 0.133635163921 |
| 20 | 20 | 0.288788370497 | 0.577576190173 | 0.13363543933 |
| 21 | 21 | 0.288788232792 | 0.577576190173 | 0.133635577035 |
| 22 | 22 | 0.288788163939 | 0.577576190173 | 0.133635645888 |
| 23 | 23 | 0.288788129513 | 0.577576190173 | 0.133635680314 |
| 24 | 24 | 0.2887881123 | 0.577576190173 | 0.133635697527 |
| 25 | 25 | 0.288788103693 | 0.577576190173 | 0.133635706134 |
| 26 | 26 | 0.28878809939 | 0.577576190173 | 0.133635710437 |
| 27 | 27 | 0.288788097238 | 0.577576190173 | 0.133635712589 |
| 28 | 28 | 0.288788096162 | 0.577576190173 | 0.133635713664 |
| 29 | 29 | 0.288788095625 | 0.577576190173 | 0.133635714202 |
| 30 | 30 | 0.288788095356 | 0.577576190173 | 0.133635714471 |
| 31 | 31 | 0.288788095221 | 0.577576190173 | 0.133635714606 |
| 32 | 32 | 0.288788095154 | 0.577576190173 | 0.133635714673 |
| 33 | 33 | 0.28878809512 | 0.577576190173 | 0.133635714707 |
| 34 | 34 | 0.288788095103 | 0.577576190173 | 0.133635714723 |
| 35 | 35 | 0.288788095095 | 0.577576190173 | 0.133635714732 |
| 36 | 36 | 0.288788095091 | 0.577576190173 | 0.133635714736 |
| 37 | 37 | 0.288788095089 | 0.577576190173 | 0.133635714738 |
| 38 | 38 | 0.288788095088 | 0.577576190173 | 0.133635714739 |
| 39 | 39 | 0.288788095087 | 0.577576190173 | 0.13363571474 |
| 40 | 40 | 0.288788095087 | 0.577576190173 | 0.13363571474 |
| 41 | 41 | 0.288788095087 | 0.577576190173 | 0.13363571474 |

```
M = x
Q = x

r = M
outside = 2.0 ** ((r*(Q+M-r)) -M*Q)
mult = 1.0
for i in range(0,r):
    mult = mult * (1.0 - (2.0**(i-Q))) * (1-2.0**(i-M))
    mult = mult / (1-2.0**(i-r))

prob_m = outside * mult

r = M-1
outside = 2.0 ** ((r*(Q+M-r)) -M*Q)
mult = 1.0
for i in range(0,r):
    mult = mult * (1.0 - (2.0**(i-Q))) * (1-2.0**(i-M))
    mult = mult / (1-2.0**(i-r))

prob_mm = outside * mult
prob_remain = 1.0 - prob_m - prob_mm

print str(M).ljust(4) + str(Q).ljust(4) + str(prob_m).ljust(15)
       + str(prob_mm).ljust(15) + str(prob_remain).ljust(15)
```

### 10.8.3 SP800-22rev1a Binary Matrix Rank Test Example Code

In the example code below, the library gf2matrix is used for computing matrix ranks. This library code is not shown, but the full code is available at https://github.com/dj-on-github/sp800_22_tests.

**Listing 10.8:** sp800_22_binary_matrix_rank_test.py

```
import math
import copy
import gf2matrix

def binary_matrix_rank_test(bits,M=32,Q=32):
    n = len(bits)
    N = int(math.floor(n/(M*Q))) #Number of blocks
    print "  Number of blocks %d" % N
    print "  Data bits used: %d" % (N*M*Q)
    print "  Data bits discarded: %d" % (n-(N*M*Q))

    if N < 38:
        print "  Number of blocks must be greater than 37"
        p = 0.0
```

```
    return False,p,None

# Compute the reference probabilities for FM, FMM and remainder
r = M
product = 1.0
for i in xrange(r):
    upper1 = (1.0 - (2.0**(i-Q)))
    upper2 = (1.0 - (2.0**(i-M)))
    lower = 1-(2.0**(i-r))
    product = product * ((upper1*upper2)/lower)
FR_prob = product * (2.0**((r*(Q+M-r)) - (M*Q)))

r = M-1
product = 1.0
for i in xrange(r):
    upper1 = (1.0 - (2.0**(i-Q)))
    upper2 = (1.0 - (2.0**(i-M)))
    lower = 1-(2.0**(i-r))
    product = product * ((upper1*upper2)/lower)
FRM1_prob = product * (2.0**((r*(Q+M-r)) - (M*Q)))

LR_prob = 1.0 - (FR_prob + FRM1_prob)

FM = 0        # Number of full rank matrices
FMM = 0       # Number of rank -1 matrices
remainder = 0
for blknum in xrange(N):
    block = bits[blknum*(M*Q):(blknum+1)*(M*Q)]
    # Put in a matrix
    matrix = gf2matrix.matrix_from_bits(M,Q,block,blknum)
    # Compute rank
    rank = gf2matrix.rank(M,Q,matrix,blknum)

    if rank == M: # count the result
        FM += 1
    elif rank == M-1:
        FMM += 1
    else:
        remainder += 1

chisq =  (((FM-(FR_prob*N))**2)/(FR_prob*N))
chisq += (((FMM-(FRM1_prob*N))**2)/(FRM1_prob*N))
chisq += (((remainder-(LR_prob*N))**2)/(LR_prob*N))
p = math.e **(-chisq/2.0)
success = (p >= 0.1)

print "  Full Rank Count  = ",FM
print "  Full Rank -1 Count = ",FMM
print "  Remainder Count = ",remainder
```

```
print "␣␣Chi-Square␣=␣",chisq

return success
```

## 10.9 SP800-22rev1a Random Excursion Test

The Random excursion test builds a one-dimensional random walk (as discussed in Section 18.5) from the data, treating bit=0 as a move to the left (pos = pos − 1), and a bit = 1 as a move to the right (pos = pos + 1). The walk can be expected to revisit the start point a number of times if the data is uniformly random. The test tests the hypothesis that the data is random, by counting the number of times the start point is visited. The test actually considers how many times the data revisits 8 different points, from −4 to +4 not including 0.

The test is a $\chi^2$ test, computing the $\chi^2$ statistic and comparing against the expected distribution of revisiting the 8 points when using random data.

### 10.9.1 Application

This test is particularly sensitive to mean reverting behavior in data, for example as would be found in data from an entropy source, using negative feedback to maintain an even bias, or in a PRNG that erroneously outputs equal numbers of 1s and 0s. So, it is appropriate as a PRNG test and a test of entropy sources claiming to have full-entropy output.

It is not useful on entropy sources that are biased or have negative or positive serial correlation, since those sources would be expected to always fail this test.

### 10.9.2 Procedure

We start similarly to the DFT test, with an $n$-bit string $\epsilon$ of $n$ bits, e.g., $\epsilon = [\epsilon_1, \epsilon_2, \ldots, \epsilon_n] =$

```
1, 1, 0, 0, 1, 0, 0, 1, 0, 0, 0, 0, 1, 1, 1, 1, 1, 1, 0, 1, 1, 0, 1, 0, 1,
0, 1, 0, 0, 0, 1, 0, 0, 0, 1, 0, 0, 0, 0, 1, 0, 1, 1, 0, 1, 0, 0, 0, 1, 1
```

Map it to a sequence $X = [x_1, x_2, \ldots, x_n]$, where the bits of the input string are mapped so that 0 becomes −1, and 1 remains 1. This can be expressed as $x_i = 2\epsilon_i - 1$, or we have $X =$

```
 1,  1,-1,-1,  1,-1,-1,  1,-1,-1,-1,-1,  1,  1,  1,  1,  1,  1,-1,  1,  1,-1,  1,-1,  1,
-1,  1,-1,-1,-1,  1,-1,-1,-1,  1,-1,-1,-1,-1,  1,-1,  1,  1,-1,  1,-1,-1,-1,  1,  1
```

Compute the list of partial sums $S = S_i$, where

$$S_i = \sum_{i=1}^{i} x_i,$$

which is equivalent to computing

$$S_1 = x_1,$$
$$S_2 = x_1 + x_2,$$
$$S_3 = x_1 + x_2 + x_3,$$
$$\vdots$$
$$S_n = x_1 + x_2 + \cdots + x_n.$$

Make a new list $S'$, equivalent to sticking a 0 on each end of $S$: $S' = 0, S_0, S_1, \ldots,$ $S_n, 0$; $S'$ now contains the record of the random walk as shown in Figure 10.3.

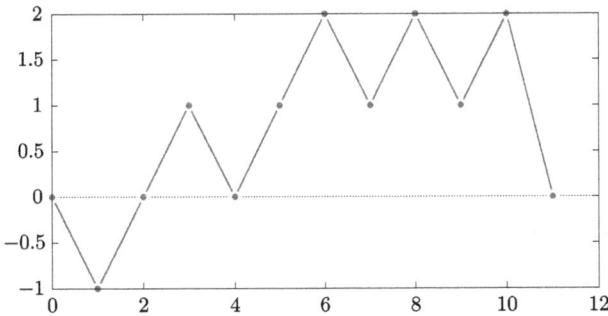

**Figure 10.3:** Plot of Partial Sums in Random Excursion Test.

A cycle is a sequence that starts from 0 and returns to 0. Count the number of cycles $J$, by counting the number of times the 0 point is visited, not including the first 0 in $S'$.

In Figure 10.3, we can see there are seven cycles. For the test results to be reliable, enough data needs to be fed into the test algorithm that $J$ is at least 500. The test specification requires that the test be discontinued if $J < 500$.

The specification recommends that at least 1 million bits are used. However, when $n = 1\,000\,000$, $J$ tends to be less than 500 most of the time. $10^7$ bits is a quantity, where $J$ will usually be greater than 500.

The next step is written in the specification in a particularly unclear way. So, hopefully, this description is a bit more clear.

For each of the eight values $x$ in $-4, -3, -2, -1, 1, 2, 3, 4$:

    for each of the values $k$ in $0, 1, 2, 3, 4, 5$:

    If $k < 5$:

    $v_k(x) = $ The count of the cycles in which $x$ occurs $k$ times else if $k = 5$:

$v_5(x)$ = The count of the cycles in which $x$ occurs > 4 times.

This gives you a 6-by-8 table of integer values. $\pi_k(x)$ is the table of equivalent probabilities for random data.

Note that there is an error in the specification, where they index into rows of this table, with $x$ being between $-5$ and $+5$. The rows are numbered 1 to 7. In reality, these probabilities are symmetric around 0. So, where the specification says to index into column $x$, actually, index into $|x|$ as indicated in Table 10.5.

**Table 10.5:** Table of $\pi_x(k)$ For Random Excursion Test.

| $|x|$ | $\pi_0(x)$ | $\pi_1(x)$ | $\pi_2(x)$ | $\pi_3(x)$ | $\pi_4(x)$ | $\pi_5(x)$ |
|---|---|---|---|---|---|---|
| 1 | 0.5 | 0.25 | 0.125 | 0.0625 | 0.0312 | 0.0312 |
| 2 | 0.75 | 0.0625 | 0.0469 | 0.00352 | 0.0264 | 0.0791 |
| 3 | 0.8333 | 0.0278 | 0.0231 | 0.0193 | 0.0161 | 0.0804 |
| 4 | 0.875 | 0.0156 | 0.0137 | 0.012 | 0.0105 | 0.0733 |
| 5 | 0.9 | 0.01 | 0.009 | 0.0081 | 0.0073 | 0.0656 |
| 6 | 0.9167 | 0.0069 | 0.0064 | 0.0058 | 0.0053 | 0.0588 |
| 7 | 0.9286 | 0.0051 | 0.0047 | 0.0044 | 0.0041 | 0.0531 |

For each of eight values $x$ in $-4, -3, -2, -1, 1, 2, 3, 4$, using the set of computed values $v_k(x)$ and the table $\pi_k(x)$, compute

$$\chi_x^2(\text{obs}) = \sum_{k=0}^{5} \frac{(v_k(x) - J\pi_k(x))^2}{J\pi_k(x)}.$$

This yields 8 $\chi_x^2(\text{obs})$ values for $x$ in $-4, -3, -2, -1, 1, 2, 3, 4$.
For each of the 8 $\chi_x^2(\text{obs})$ statistics, compute a $P_x$ value

$$P_x = \text{igamc}\left(\frac{5}{2}, \frac{\chi_x^2(\text{obs})}{2}\right).$$

If any of the 8 $P_x$ values are < 0.01, then the sequence is nonrandom.

### 10.9.3 Random Excursion Test Example Code

Listing 10.9: sp800_22_random_excursion_test.py

```
import math
from fractions import Fraction
from scipy.special import gamma, gammainc, gammaincc
import random
```

```python
def random_excursion_test(bits):
    n = len(bits)

    x = list()                  # Convert to +1,-1
    for bit in bits:
        if bit == 0:
            x.append((bit*2)-1)

    # Build the partial sums
    pos = 0
    s = list()
    for e in x:
        pos = pos+e
        s.append(pos)
    sprime = [0]+s+[0] # Add 0 on each end

    # Build the list of cycles
    pos = 1
    cycles = list()
    while (pos < len(sprime)):
        cycle = list()
        cycle.append(0)
        while sprime[pos]!=0:
            cycle.append(sprime[pos])
            pos += 1
        cycle.append(0)
        cycles.append(cycle)
        pos = pos + 1

    J = len(cycles)
    print "J="+str(J)

    vxk = [['a','b','c','d','e','f'] for y in [-4,-3,-2,-1,1,2,3,4] ]

    # Count Occurances
    for k in xrange(6):
        for index in xrange(8):
            mapping = [-4,-3,-2,-1,1,2,3,4]
            x = mapping[index]
            cyclecount = 0
            #count how many cycles in which x occurs k times
            for cycle in cycles:
                oc = 0
                #Count how many times x occurs in the current cycle
                for pos in cycle:
                    if (pos == x):
                        oc += 1
                # If x occurs k times, increment the cycle count
                if (k < 5):
```

```
                    if oc == k:
                        cyclecount += 1
                else:
                    if k == 5:
                        if oc >=5:
                            cyclecount += 1
            vxk[index][k] = cyclecount

    # Table for reference random probabilities
    pixk=[[0.5      ,0.25   ,0.125  ,0.0625  ,0.0312 ,0.0312],
          [0.75     ,0.0625 ,0.0469 ,0.0352  ,0.0264 ,0.0791],
          [0.8333   ,0.0278 ,0.0231 ,0.0193  ,0.0161 ,0.0804],
          [0.875    ,0.0156 ,0.0137 ,0.012   ,0.0105 ,0.0733],
          [0.9      ,0.01   ,0.009  ,0.0081  ,0.0073 ,0.0656],
          [0.9167   ,0.0069 ,0.0064 ,0.0058  ,0.0053 ,0.0588],
          [0.9286   ,0.0051 ,0.0047 ,0.0044  ,0.0041 ,0.0531]]

    success = True
    for index in xrange(8):
        mapping = [-4,-3,-2,-1,1,2,3,4]
        x = mapping[index]
        chisq = 0.0
        for k in xrange(6):
            top = float(vxk[index][k]) - (float(J) * (pixk[abs(x)-1][k]))
            top = top*top
            bottom = J * pixk[abs(x)-1][k]
            chisq += top/bottom
        p = gammaincc(5.0/2.0,chisq/2.0)
        if p < 0.01:
            err = " Not Random"
            success = False
        else:
            err = ""
        print "x = %1.0f\tchisq = %f\tp = %f %s"  % (x,chisq,p,err)
    if (J < 500):
        print "J too small (J < 500) for result to be reliable"
    elif success:
        print "PASS"
    else:
        print "FAIL: Data not random"
    return success
```

## 10.10 SP800-22rev1a Random Excursion Variant Test

The Random Excursion Variant Test is similar to the Random Excursion Test, except that instead of counting the frequency of occurrence of values within cycles, it treats the sequence as one big cycle and counts the occurrence over a wider range of numbers (from −9 to +9).

### 10.10.1 Application

As with the Random Excursion Test, this test is sensitive to mean-reverting behavior in data, for example, as would be found in data from an entropy source using negative feedback to maintain an even bias, or in a PRNG that erroneously outputs exactly equal numbers of 1s and 0s. So, it is appropriate as a PRNG test and a test of entropy sources claiming to have full-entropy output.

It is not useful on entropy sources that are biased or have negative or positive serial correlation, since those sources would be expected to always fail this test.

Unlike the Random Excursion Test, there is no limit on $J$, and so all random samples will be accepted for analysis.

The specification recommends the data size be at least 1 million bits.

### 10.10.2 Procedure

The Random Excursion Variant Test starts with the same four steps as the random excursion test as follows:

- Convert the bits to +1 and −1.
- Build the partial sums of the random walk (see Section 18.5).
- Append 0 to the start and end to get $S'$.
- Count the number of cycles $J$ by counting the 0s in $S'$, not including the first 0.

At this point, the procedure diverges from the random excursion test.

- For each of the 18 values $v$ in $-9, -8, \ldots, -1, 1, 2, \ldots, 9$ (note that 0 is omitted from this list), compute the count of the occurrences $\text{count}_v$ of each value $v$ in $S'$.
- Compute 18 $P_v$ values from the $\text{count}_v$ and $J$ with

$$P_v = \text{erfc}\left( \frac{|\text{count}_v - J|}{\sqrt{2J(|4v| - 2)}} \right).$$

- If any of the 18 $P_v$ values are $< 0.01$, then the sequence is nonrandom.

### 10.10.3 Random Excursion Variant Test Example Code

Listing 10.10: sp800_22_random_excursion_variant_test.py

```
import math
import random

def random_excursion_variant_test(bits):
    n = len(bits)
```

```
x = list()                     # Convert to +1,-2
for bit in bits:
    if bit == 0:
        x.append(-1)
    else:
        x.append(1)

# Build the partial sums
pos = 0
s = list()
for e in x:
    pos = pos+e
    s.append(pos)
sprime = [0]+s+[0] # Add 0 on each end

# Count the number of cycles J
J = 0
for value in sprime[1:]:
    if value == 0:
        J += 1

# Build the counts of offsets
count = [0 for x in xrange(-9,10)]
for value in sprime:
    if (abs(value) < 10):
        count[value] += 1

# Compute P values
success = True
for x in xrange(-9,10):
    if x != 0:
        top = abs(count[x]-J)
        bottom = math.sqrt(2.0 * J *((4.0*abs(x))-2.0))
        p = top/bottom

        if p < 0.01:
            err = " Not Random"
            success = False
        else:
            err = ""
        print "x = %1.0f\t count=%d\tp = %f %s" % (x,count[x],p,err)

if success:
    print "PASS"
else:
    print "FAIL: Data not random"
return success
```

## 10.11 SP800-22rev1a Maurer's Universal Statistical Test

Maurer's Universal Statistical Test is a compression test. It attempts to establish if the data is compressible. If it is sufficiently compressible, the conclusion is that the data is nonrandom.

### 10.11.1 Application

This test constitutes a good general-purpose distinguishability test that is sensitive to a nonuniform distribution of symbols, repetition of data, and correlations and biases.

In a previous version of SP800-22, there was a test called the Lempel–Ziv Compression Test. This test was flawed in the assumed output distribution, which was wrong, and in such a way that the Lempel–Ziv's mathematical properties do not allow for mathematical analysis, and so the conclusions of the test were not sound.

This test effectively replaces the Lepel–Ziv Compression Test with an algorithm that has a sound mathematical basis.

### 10.11.2 Procedure

The test divides the data into blocks and divides the data blocks into two parts, the first sequence of blocks being the initialization sequence and the remaining blocks being the test blocks.

- Choose the parameters:
  $L$, the length of each block in bits;
  $Q$, the number of blocks in the initialization sequence.
  The input data $\varepsilon$ is the string of $n$ bits $\varepsilon_{1...n}$.
  There will be $K$ remaining blocks, where $K = \lfloor \frac{n}{L} \rfloor - Q$.
- Split the data bits $\varepsilon$ into $Q$ initialization blocks and $K$ test blocks, each of $L$ bits. Discard the final $n - L(Q + K)$ bits that remain.
  For example, $\varepsilon = 01011010011101010111$, and so $n = 20$. Choosing the block-size $L = 2$ and 4 initialization blocks, so $Q = 4$ means $K = \lfloor \frac{20}{2} \rfloor - 4 = 6$.
  In this example, the initialization blocks, numbered 1 to 4, are binary 01, 01, 10, and 10. The test blocks, numbered 5 to 10, are binary 01, 11, 01, 01, 01, and 11.
  For a proper test, there should at least 387 840 bits. The value of $L$ should be between 6 and 16 and set according to Table 10.6.
  Compute
  $$Q = 10 \cdot 2^L.$$
- Construct a table of the position of the last instance of the $2^L$ possible values of the blocks in the initialization blocks. Denote these as $T_0 \ldots T_{2^L-1}$. If there are no such values of, for example, $x$, then set $T_x = 0$.

**Table 10.6:** Value of $L$ for Maurer's Universal Test.

| $n$ | $L$ |
|---|---|
| $n \geq 387840$ | 6 |
| $n \geq 904960$ | 7 |
| $n \geq 2068480$ | 8 |
| $n \geq 4654080$ | 9 |
| $n \geq 10342400$ | 10 |
| $n \geq 22753280$ | 11 |
| $n \geq 49643520$ | 12 |
| $n \geq 107560960$ | 13 |
| $n \geq 231669760$ | 14 |
| $n \geq 496435200$ | 15 |
| $n \geq 1059061760$ | 16 |

In the example, there are no instances of 00, so $T_0 = 0$. The last instance of 01 is at position 2. So $T_1 = 2$. The last instance of 10 is at position 4. So $T_3 = 4$, and there are no instances of 11. So $T_3 = 0$.

- Iterate over the table updating $T_j$ on each round and compute a running sum. First set sum $= 0$.

  Then, for each $L$-bit pattern in the test sequence at position $i$, starting at the start of the test block, that is, $i = Q + 1$
  - Compute $j$, the decimal value of the binary pattern.
  - Compute

$$\text{distance} = i - T_j.$$

  - Set

$$T_j = i.$$

  - Set

$$\text{sum} = \text{sum} + \log_2(\text{distance}).$$

- Compute the test statistic

$$f_n = \frac{\text{sum}}{K}.$$

- Compute the $P$ value.
  Define the ExpectedValue($L$) table (Table 10.7).
  Define the variance($L$) table (Table 10.8).
  Compute

$$\sigma = \sqrt{\text{variance}(L)}.$$

**Table 10.7:** ExpectedValue($L$) Table.

| $L$ | ExpectedValue($L$) |
|---|---|
| 1 | 0.73264948 |
| 2 | 1.5374383 |
| 3 | 2.40160681 |
| 4 | 3.31122472 |
| 5 | 4.25342659 |
| 6 | 5.2177052 |
| 7 | 6.1962507 |
| 8 | 7.1836656 |
| 9 | 8.1764248 |
| 10 | 9.1723243 |
| 11 | 10.170032 |
| 12 | 11.168765 |
| 13 | 12.168070 |
| 14 | 13.167693 |
| 15 | 14.167488 |
| 16 | 15.167379 |

**Table 10.8:** variance($L$) Table.

| $L$ | variance($L$) |
|---|---|
| 1 | 0.690 |
| 2 | 1.338 |
| 3 | 1.901 |
| 4 | 2.358 |
| 5 | 2.705 |
| 6 | 2.954 |
| 7 | 3.125 |
| 8 | 3.238 |
| 9 | 3.311 |
| 10 | 3.356 |
| 11 | 3.384 |
| 12 | 3.401 |
| 13 | 3.410 |
| 14 | 3.416 |
| 15 | 3.419 |
| 16 | 3.421 |

Compute

$$P = \text{erfc}\left(\left|\frac{f_n - \text{ExpectedValue}(L)}{\sigma\sqrt{2}}\right|\right).$$

– If $P < 0.1$, then the data are nonrandom.

## 10.11.3 Maurer's Universal Statistical Test Example Code

**Listing 10.11:** sp800_22_maurers_universal_test.py

```python
#!/usr/bin/env python

import math

def pattern2int(pattern):
    l = len(pattern)
    n = 0
    for bit in (pattern):
        n = (n << 1) + bit
    return n

def maurers_universal_test(bits,patternlen=None, initblocks=None):
    n = len(bits)

    # Step 1. Choose the block size
    if patternlen != None:
        L = patternlen
    else:
        ns = [904960,2068480,4654080,10342400,
              22753280,49643520,107560960,
              231669760,496435200,1059061760]
        L = 6
        if n < 387840:
            print "Error._Need_at_least_387840_bits._Got_%d." % n
            exit()
        for threshold in ns:
            if n >= threshold:
                L += 1

    # Step 2 Split the data into Q and K blocks
    nblocks = int(math.floor(n/L))
    if initblocks != None:
        Q = initblocks
    else:
        Q = 10*(2**L)
    K = nblocks - Q

    # Step 3 Construct Table
    nsymbols = (2**L)
    T=[0 for x in xrange(nsymbols)] # zero out the table
    for i in xrange(Q):                     # Mark final position of
        pattern = bits[i*L:(i+1)*L] # each pattern
        idx = pattern2int(pattern)
        T[idx]=i+1          # +1 to number indexes 1..(2**L)+1
                            # instead of 0..2**L
    # Step 4 Iterate
```

```
sum = 0.0
for i in xrange(Q,nblocks):
    pattern = bits[i*L:(i+1)*L]
    j = pattern2int(pattern)
    dist = i+1-T[j]
    T[j] = i+1
    sum = sum + math.log(dist,2)
print "␣␣sum␣=", sum

# Step 5 Compute the test statistic
fn = sum/K
print "␣␣fn␣=",fn

# Step 6 Compute the P Value
# Tables from https://static.aminer.org/pdf/PDF/000/120/333/
# a_universal_statistical_test_for_random_bit_generators.pdf
ev_table =   [0,0.73264948,1.5374383,2.40160681,3.31122472,
             4.25342659,5.2177052,6.1962507,7.1836656,
             8.1764248,9.1723243,10.170032,11.168765,
             12.168070,13.167693,14.167488,15.167379]
var_table = [0,0.690,1.338,1.901,2.358,2.705,2.954,3.125,
             3.238,3.311,3.356,3.384,3.401,3.410,3.416,
             3.419,3.421]

a = fn - ev_table[L]
b = (math.sqrt(var_table[L]))*math.sqrt(2))
mag = abs(a/b)

P = math.erfc(mag)
success = (P >= 0.01)
return success
```

## 10.12 SP800-22rev1a Linear Complexity Test

The linear complexity test runs the Berlekamp–Massey algorithm over blocks of data from the input data; the algorithm (Berlekamp–Massey) computes the shortest LFSR that can output the block. Over uniform data, the algorithm should not be able to find LFSRs that have a linear complexity significantly shorter than the input data block.

The Berlekamp–Massey algorithm is a standard algorithm, which will not be explained in detail here. The source code for the algorithm below is one simple implementation over a binary field. Given an input bitstring, it computes the smallest LFSR polynomial, which will reproduce the string. It can be considered a form of compression, since a polynomial, which is shorter than the string it produces, is a compressed form of the string. So, the Linear Complexity test can be considered to be a compression test.

### 10.12.1 Application

Certain examples of PRNGs, for example LCGs, will be compressible by the Berlekamp–Massey algorithm. Linear complexity tests have proven effective over time at detecting nonuniformities in such PRNGs.

### 10.12.2 Procedure

– Choose the block-size $M$ and split the $n$ databits into $N$ blocks of length $M$ bits. $M$ must be between 500 and 5000 bits. The number of input bits $n$ must be at least $10^6$. The number of blocks $N$ must be at least 200. The specification gives no guidance as to which values of $M$ are appropriate. From the smallest to longest $M$ (from 500 to 5000), the number of blocks $N = \lfloor \frac{n}{M} \rfloor$ varies from 2000 down to 200. So, for the code below, we chose to default $M = 512$.
– Compute the number of blocks

$$N = \left\lfloor \frac{n}{M} \right\rfloor.$$

– Choose the degrees of freedom. The specification suggests setting $K = 6$.
– Compute the linear complexity $L_i$ of each block numbered from $i = 1$ to $i = N$ by running the Berlekamp–Massey algorithm over each of the blocks

$$L_i = \text{BerlekampMassey}(\text{block}_i).$$

– Compute the mean

$$\mu = \frac{M}{2} + \frac{9 + (-1)^{M+1}}{36} - \frac{\frac{M}{3} + \frac{2}{9}}{2^M}.$$

– Compute a value $T_i$ for each block:

$$T_i = (-1)^M \cdot (L_i - \mu) + \frac{2}{9}.$$

– Compute a histogram $v_j$ with 6 bins over all the values of $T_i$:
  $v_0 = $ The number of $Ti$ such that $Ti \leq -2.5$,
  $v_1 = $ The number of $Ti$ such that $-2.5 < Ti \leq -1.5$,
  $v_2 = $ The number of $Ti$ such that $-1.5 < Ti \leq -0.5$,
  $v_3 = $ The number of $Ti$ such that $-0.5 < Ti \leq 0.5$,
  $v_4 = $ The number of $Ti$ such that $0.5 < Ti \leq 1.5$,
  $v_5 = $ The number of $Ti$ such that $1.5 < Ti \leq 2.5$,
  $v_6 = $ The number of $Ti$ such that $Ti > 2.5$.

- Compute the $\chi^2$ value.
  Define
  $\pi_0 = 0.010417$,
  $\pi_1 = 0.0325$,
  $\pi_2 = 0.125$,
  $\pi_3 = 0.5$,
  $\pi_4 = 0.25$,
  $\pi_5 = 0.0625$,
  $\pi_6 = 0.020833$.
  Compute

$$\chi^2 = \sum_{i=0}^{K} \frac{(v_i - N\pi_i)^2}{N\pi_i}.$$

- Compute the $P$ value

$$P = \text{igamc}\left(\frac{K}{2}, \frac{\chi^2}{2}\right).$$

- If $P < 0.01$, then the data are nonrandom.


### 10.12.3 Linear Complexity Test Example Code

Listing 10.12: sp800_22_linear_complexity_test.py

```
#!/usr/bin/env python

import math
from scipy.special import gamma, gammainc, gammaincc

def berelekamp_massey(bits):
    n = len(bits)
    b = [0 for x in bits]    #initialize b and c arrays
    c = [0 for x in bits]
    b[0] = 1
    c[0] = 1

    L = 0
    m = -1
    N = 0
    while (N < n):
        #compute discrepancy
        d = bits[N]
        for i in xrange(1,L+1):
            d = d ^ (c[i] & bits[N-i])
        if (d != 0):    # If d is not zero, adjust poly
```

```
         t = c[:]
         for i in xrange(0,n-N+m):
             c[N-m+i] = c[N-m+i] ^ b[i]
         if (L <= (N/2)):
             L = N + 1 - L
             m = N
             b = t
    N = N +1
    # Return length of generator and the polynomial
    return L , c[0:L]

def linear_complexity_test(bits,patternlen=None):
    n = len(bits)
    # Step 1. Choose the block size
    if patternlen != None:
        M = patternlen
    else:
        if n < 1000000:
            print "Error._Need_at_least_10^6_bits"
            exit()
        M = 512
    K = 6
    N = int(math.floor(n/M))
    print "__M_=_", M
    print "__N_=_", N
    print "__K_=_", K

    # Step 2 Compute the linear complexity of the blocks
    LC = list()
    for i in xrange(N):
        x = bits[(i*M):((i+1)*M)]
        LC.append(berelekamp_massey(x)[0])

    # Step 3 Compute mean
    a = float(M)/2.0
    b = (((((-1)**(M+1))+9.0))/36.0
    c = ((M/3.0) + (2.0/9.0))/(2**M)
    mu =  a+b-c

    T = list()
    for i in xrange(N):
        x = ((-1.0)**M) * (LC[i] - mu) + (2.0/9.0)
        T.append(x)

    # Step 4 Count the distribution over Ticket
    v = [0,0,0,0,0,0,0]
    for t in T:
        if t <= -2.5:
            v[0] += 1
```

```
    elif t <= -1.5:
        v[1] += 1
    elif t <= -0.5:
        v[2] += 1
    elif t <= 0.5:
        v[3] += 1
    elif t <= 1.5:
        v[4] += 1
    elif t <= 2.5:
        v[5] += 1
    else:
        v[6] += 1

# Step 5 Compute Chi Square Statistic
pi = [0.010417,0.03125,0.125,0.5,0.25,0.0625,0.020833]
chisq = 0.0
for i in xrange(K+1):
    chisq += ((v[i] - (N*pi[i]))**2.0)/(N*pi[i])
print "␣␣chisq␣=␣",chisq
# Step 6 Compute P Value
P = gammaincc((K/2.0),(chisq/2.0))
print "␣␣P␣=␣",P
success = (P >= 0.01)
return success
```

## 10.13 SP800-22rev1a Serial Test

The serial test counts the frequency of overlapping bit-patterns within the bitseries. Three lengths of pattern $m$, $m - 1$, and $m - 2$ are used, and all possible $2^{m-(1,2,3)}$ bit-patterns are counted. A $\chi^2$ test is performed against the expected counts for random data.

The correctness of this test is in some doubt, since the equations in the specification and the equations in the examples do not agree, and the numerical results in the examples in the specification are simply wrong.

For example, there are three equations in step (3) on page 2-27 (page 49 of the PDF) that state

$$\psi_m^2 = \frac{2^m}{n} \sum_{i_1...i_m} \left( v_{i_1...i_m} - \frac{n}{2^m} \right)^2 = \frac{2^m}{n} \sum_{i_1...i_m} v_{i_1...i_m}^2 - n,$$

$$\psi_{m-1}^2 = \frac{2^{m-1}}{n} \sum_{i_1...i_{m-1}} \left( v_{i_1...i_{m-1}} - \frac{n}{2^{m-1}} \right)^2 = \frac{2^{m-1}}{n} \sum_{i_1...i_{m-1}} v_{i_1...i_{m-1}}^2 - n,$$

$$\psi_{m-2}^2 = \frac{2^{m-2}}{n} \sum_{i_1...i_{m-2}} \left( v_{i_1...i_{m-2}} - \frac{n}{2^{m-2}} \right)^2 = \frac{2^{m-2}}{n} \sum_{i_1...i_{m-2}} v_{i_1...i_{m-2}}^2 - n.$$

In all three cases, the right side of the equation is ambiguous. Also, it is not clear whether the $-n$ exponent is inside the sum or outside the sum. Also, the vertical position of the $-n$ is somewhere between where it should be for an exponent and for a subtraction. So, it could be one or the other. Below is a bitmap picture (see Figure 10.4) from the actual specification showing how the typography and lack of parentheses can make the expression so confusing.

$$\frac{2^m}{n} \sum_{i_1\ldots i_m} v^2_{i_1\ldots i_m} - n$$

**Figure 10.4:** Ambiguous Expression From SP800-22 Serial Test.

Experimenting with all four possible interpretations of the order of operation, and whether it is a subtraction or an exponent, shows that it is a subtraction outside the summation. This interpretation matches the results of the middle part of the equation. So, the final expression would be better be written as

$$\left( \frac{2^m}{n} \sum_{i_1\ldots i_m} v^2_{i_1\ldots i_m} \right) - n.$$

Next, the final computation step in the specification states

$$P\_value1 = igamc(2^{m-2}, \Delta\psi^2_m)$$

and

$$P\_value2 = igamc(2^{m-3}, \Delta^2\psi^2_m).$$

The computed example values for $\Delta\psi^2_m$ and $\Delta^2\psi^2_m$ are 1.6 and 0.8. Yet, the values plugged into igamc are $\frac{\Delta\psi^2_m}{2}$ and $\frac{\Delta^2\psi^2_m}{2}$.

Section 3.11 of the specification gives information on the mathematical background of the serial test. It gives

$$P\_value1 = igamc\left( 2^{m-2}, \frac{\Delta\psi^2_m}{2} \right)$$

and

$$P\_value2 = igamc\left( 2^{m-3}, \frac{\Delta^2\psi^2_m}{2} \right),$$

which is consistent with the example, but not with the normative specification.

Further, the final result is simply wrong. The specification example states that

$$P\_value1 = igamc\left( 2, \frac{1.6}{2} \right) = 0.9057$$

and

$$P\_value2 = igamc\left( 1, \frac{0.8}{2} \right) = 0.8805,$$

whereas in reality

$$\mathrm{igamc}\left(2, \frac{1.6}{2}\right) = 0.0.80879$$

and

$$\mathrm{igamc}\left(1, \frac{0.8}{2}\right) = 0.67032.$$

Therefore, it is difficult to tell what the specification intends when it contains basic numerical errors and inconsistencies. The procedure below is the most likely correct interpretation of the specification, consistent with Section 3.11 and the referenced sources in the specification.

### 10.13.1 Application

Like the other pattern-counting tests, this test is sensitive to biases and correlations in the data that affect the frequency of bit-patterns and to flaws in a PRNG, which cause it to repeat values.

### 10.13.2 Procedure

- Input an $n$-bit string $\epsilon$ of bits $\epsilon_{1\ldots n}$.
- Choose $m$ such that $m < \lfloor \log_2(n) \rfloor - 2$.
- Append the first $m - 1$ bits $\epsilon_{1\ldots n-1}$ to the end of the bit string $\epsilon$.
- For each of the possible $2^m$ bit strings of length $m$, count the occurrences of that pattern starting at each position in $\epsilon$. Each number is denoted as $v_i$, where $i$ is the index into the $2^m$ values of the $m$ bit-pattern being counted.
- Compute

$$\psi_m^2 = \left(\frac{2^m}{n} \sum_{i_1\ldots i_m} v_{i_1\ldots i_m}^2\right) - n,$$

$$\psi_{m-1}^2 = \left(\frac{2^{m-1}}{n} \sum_{i_1\ldots i_{m-1}} v_{i_1\ldots i_{m-1}}^2\right) - n,$$

$$\psi_{m-2}^2 = \left(\frac{2^{m-2}}{n} \sum_{i_1\ldots i_{m-2}} v_{i_1\ldots i_{m-2}}^2\right) - n.$$

- Compute

$$\Delta \psi_m^2 = \psi_m^2 - \psi_{m-1}^2,$$
$$\Delta^2 \psi_m^2 = \psi_m^2 - 2\psi_{m-1}^2 + \psi_{m-1}^2.$$

– Compute

$$P\_value1 = \text{igamc}\left(2^{m-2}, \frac{\Delta\psi_m^2}{2}\right),$$

$$P\_value2 = \text{igamc}\left(2^{m-3}, \frac{\Delta^2\psi_m^2}{2}\right).$$

– If either $P\_value1 < 0.01$ or $P\_value2 < 0.01$, then the sequence is nonrandom.

### 10.13.3 Serial Test Example Code

**Listing 10.13:** sp800_22_serial_test.py

```
#!/usr/bin/env python

import math
from scipy.special import gamma, gammainc, gammaincc

def int2patt(n,m):
    pattern = list()
    for i in xrange(m):
        pattern.append((n >> i) & 1)
    return pattern

def countpattern(patt,bits,n):
    thecount = 0
    for i in xrange(n):
        match = True
        for j in xrange(len(patt)):
            if patt[j] != bits[i+j]:
                match = False
        if match:
            thecount += 1
    return thecount

def psi_sq_mv1(m, n, padded_bits):
    counts = [0 for i in xrange(2**m)]
    for i in xrange(2**m):
        pattern = int2patt(i,m)
        count = countpattern(pattern,padded_bits,n)
        counts.append(count)

    psi_sq_m = 0.0
    for count in counts:
        psi_sq_m += (count**2)
    psi_sq_m = psi_sq_m * (2**m)/n
    psi_sq_m -= n
```

```
    return psi_sq_m

def serial_test(bits,patternlen=None):
    n = len(bits)
    if patternlen != None:
        m = patternlen
    else:
        m = int(math.floor(math.log(n,2)))-2

        if m < 4:
            print "Error._Not_enough_data_for_m_to_be_4"
            return False,0,None
        m = 4

    # Step 1
    padded_bits=bits+bits[0:m-1]

    # Step 2
    psi_sq_m   = psi_sq_mv1(m, n, padded_bits)
    psi_sq_mm1 = psi_sq_mv1(m-1, n, padded_bits)
    psi_sq_mm2 = psi_sq_mv1(m-2, n, padded_bits)

    delta1 = psi_sq_m - psi_sq_mm1
    delta2 = psi_sq_m - (2*psi_sq_mm1) + psi_sq_mm2

    P1 = gammaincc(2**(m-2),delta1/2.0)
    P2 = gammaincc(2**(m-3),delta2/2.0)

    print "__psi_sq_m___=_",psi_sq_m
    print "__psi_sq_mm1_=_",psi_sq_mm1
    print "__psi_sq_mm2_=_",psi_sq_mm2
    print "__delta1_____=_",delta1
    print "__delta2_____=_",delta2
    print "__P1_____=_",P1
    print "__P2_____=_",P2

    success = (P1 >= 0.01) and (P2 >= 0.01)
    return success, None, [P1,P2]
```

## 10.14 SP800-22rev1a Cumulative Sums Test

The cumulative sums test computes the maximum excursion of a random walk over the cumulative sums over the bits in the sequence. It does this by first running through the data forwards, then again running through the data backwards.

Two *P* values are computed from the two maxima.

### 10.14.1 Application

The idea with this test is that, if the excursion grows large, then, there is some non-stationarity in the data (where bias varies with time), or there is some bias in the data. This may yield different values when running through forwards and backwards.

### 10.14.2 Procedure

The cumulative sums test tests the $P$ value twice, once running forward through the data and once running backwards. The procedure is as follows:

- Convert the $n$ bits $bit_i$ to +1, −1: $x_i = (2bit_i) - 1$.
- Build the forward partial sums $FS_n = \sum_{k=1}^{n} x_k$ of the random walk (see Section 18.5).
- Build the backward partial sums $BS_n = \sum_{k=1}^{n} x_{n-k+1}$ of the random walk (see Section 18.5).
- Find the largest absolute value forward_$z = |FS_i|$.
- Find the largest absolute value backward_$z = |BS_i|$.
- Compute the $P$ value twice, once with $z = $ forward_$z$ and once with $z = $ backward_$z$:

$$P = 1 - \sum_{\lfloor \frac{-n}{4}+1 \rfloor}^{\lfloor \frac{\frac{n}{z}-1}{4} \rfloor} \left[ \Phi\left( \frac{(4k+1)z}{\sqrt{n}} \right) - \Phi\left( \frac{(4k-1)z}{\sqrt{n}} \right) \right]$$

$$+ \sum_{k=\lfloor \frac{\frac{-n}{z}-3}{4} \rfloor}^{\lfloor \frac{\frac{n}{z}-1}{4} \rfloor} \left[ \Phi\left( \frac{(4k+3)z}{\sqrt{n}} \right) - \Phi\left( \frac{(4k+1)z}{\sqrt{n}} \right) \right].$$

Note that there is an error in the equation in the SP800-22 specification. The bounds of the summations are missing the floor symbol, and so imply a sum from a fractional number to a fractional number. With the floor symbol added, the results match the example results given in the specification.
- If $P < 0.01$ for either the forward or backward $P$ value, then the data are not random.

### 10.14.3 Cumulative Sums Test Example Code

Listing 10.14: sp800_22_cumulative_sums_test.py

```
#!/usr/bin/env python

import math
from scipy.special import gamma, gammainc, gammaincc
```

```python
import scipy.stats

def p_value(n,z):
    sum_a = 0.0
    startk = int(math.floor(((((float(-n)/z)+1.0)/4.0)))
    endk   = int(math.floor(((((float(n)/z)-1.0)/4.0)))
    for k in xrange(startk,endk+1):
        c = (((4.0*k)+1.0)*z)/math.sqrt(n)
        d = scipy.stats.norm.cdf(c)
        c = (((4.0*k)-1.0)*z)/math.sqrt(n)
        e = scipy.stats.norm.cdf(c)
        sum_a = sum_a + d - e

    sum_b = 0.0
    startk = int(math.floor(((((float(-n)/z)-3.0)/4.0)))
    endk   = int(math.floor(((((float(n)/z)-1.0)/4.0)))
    for k in xrange(startk,endk+1):
        c = (((4.0*k)+3.0)*z)/math.sqrt(n)
        d = scipy.stats.norm.cdf(c)
        c = (((4.0*k)+1.0)*z)/math.sqrt(n)
        e = scipy.stats.norm.cdf(c)
        sum_b = sum_b + d - e

    p = 1.0 - sum_a + sum_b
    return p

def cumulative_sums_test(bits):
    n = len(bits)
    # Step 1
    x = list()                  # Convert to +1,-1
    for bit in bits:
        #if bit == 0:
        x.append((bit*2)-1)

    # Steps 2 and 3 Combined
    # Compute the partial sum and records the largest excursion.
    pos = 0
    forward_max = 0
    for e in x:
        pos = pos+e
        if abs(pos) > forward_max:
            forward_max = abs(pos)
    pos = 0
    backward_max = 0
    for e in reversed(x):
        pos = pos+e
        if abs(pos) > backward_max:
            backward_max = abs(pos)
```

```
# Step 4
p_forward  = p_value(n, forward_max)
p_backward = p_value(n,backward_max)

success = ((p_forward >= 0.01) and (p_backward >= 0.01))
plist = [p_forward, p_backward]

if success:
    print "PASS"
else:
    print "FAIL:_Data_not_random"
return success, None, plist
```

## 10.15 SP800-22rev1a Approximate Entropy Test

The approximate entropy test counts the frequency of all patterns of a certain bit-length $m$ and all the patterns of bit-length $m+1$, then performs a $\chi^2$ test on the expected difference between the two counts and the actual difference.

The test specifies that $m < \log_2(n) - 6$, where $n$ is the number of bits in the data. However, it does not say how small m can be. The runtime of the test increases exponentially with $m$ and linearly with $n$. So, for large $n$, choosing the largest $m$ that meets the above bound results in a runtime that is too long to be useful. Running this test over 1 mibyte of data results in a largest possible $m$ of 17, which results in $2^{17} + 2^{18}$ runs through $n$-bit positions, which for 8 megabits is a very long runtime. Therefore, in the reference code, $m$ is limited to be no bigger than 4, so the tests can compete.

### 10.15.1 Application

This test is sensitive to RNGs that produce repeating patterns or have any bias or correlation that would affect the distribution of $m$-bit patterns. So, it is a fairly effective test, except for the very long runtimes, which limit the amount of data that can usefully be run through it.

### 10.15.2 Procedure

The approximate entropy test runs the main loop of the algorithm twice, once using a pattern length of $m$ and a second time replacing $m$ with $m + 1$.

- Choose $m$ such that $m < \log_2(n) - 5$, where $n$ is the number of bits in the data. In practice, limiting $m$ to be 2 or 3 seems to be necessary for performance reasons when analyzing a 1 mibyte file.
- Repeat twice with $x = m$, followed by $x = m + 1$, using the following 4 steps:
  - To the end of the string of bits, append the first $x - 1$ of the string of bits so that there are $n$ starting positions for $x$ bit sequences.

- Count the number of occurrences of all $2^x$ patterns within the string of bits at each bit position from 0 to $n$. We will call these counts $C_i^x$, where $x$ is the length of the pattern, and $i$ takes on each of the $2^x$ possible binary patterns.
- Build a list of values by dividing each value of $C_i^x$ by $n$, that is, $D_i^x = \frac{C_i^x}{n}$.
- Compute $\varphi(x) = \sum (D_i^x \log(\frac{D_i^x}{10}))$.
- Compute $a = \varphi(m) - \varphi(m-1)$.
- Compute $\chi^2 = 2n(\log_e(2) - a)$.
- Compute $p = \text{igamc}(2^{m-1}, \frac{\chi^2}{2})$.
- If $p < 0.01$, then the sequence is not random.

## 10.15.3 Approximate Entropy Test Example Code

**Listing 10.15:** sp800_22_approximate_entropy_test.py

```python
#!/usr/bin/env python

import math
from scipy.special import gamma, gammainc, gammaincc

def bits_to_int(bits):
    theint = 0
    for i in xrange(len(bits)):
        theint = (theint << 1) + bits[i]
    return theint

def approximate_entropy_test(bits):
    n = len(bits)

    m = int(math.floor(math.log(n,2)))-6
    if m < 2:
        m = 2
    if m >3 :
        m = 3

    print "  n          = ",n
    print "  m          = ",m

    Cmi = list()
    phi_m = list()
    for iterm in xrange(m,m+2):
        # Step 1
        padded_bits=bits+bits[0:iterm-1]

        # Step 2
        counts = list()
        for i in xrange(2**iterm):
```

```python
        #print "  Pattern #%d of %d" % (i+1,2**iterm)
        count = 0
        for j in xrange(n):
            if bits_to_int(padded_bits[j:j+iterm]) == i:
                count += 1
        counts.append(count)
        print "  Pattern %d of %d, count =%d" % (i+1,2**iterm, count)

    # step 3
    Ci = list()
    for i in xrange(2**iterm):
        Ci.append(float(counts[i])/float(n))

    Cmi.append(Ci)

    # Step 4
    sum = 0.0
    for i in xrange(2**iterm):
        sum += Ci[i]*math.log((Ci[i]/10.0))
    phi_m.append(sum)
    print "  phi(%d)    =%f" % (m,sum)

# Step 5
appen_m = phi_m[0] - phi_m[1]
print "  AppEn(%d)  =%f" % (m,appen_m)
chisq = 2*n*(math.log(2) - appen_m)
print "  ChiSquare = ",chisq

# Step 6
p = gammaincc(2**(m-1),(chisq/2.0))

success = (p >= 0.01)
return success, p, None
```

# 11 Software Tools

In this chapter, we look at a number of software tools related to random numbers and some ways of using them.

hex2bin and bin2hex: Utility programs to convert between hex and binary formats.

dec2hex: A program to convert decimal format data to hex format.

cleanhex: A program to clean up nonhex data from files of hex data, such as 0x prefixes and all nonhex characters.

djenrandom: A program to generate random data with controllable statistical properties.

quickrdrand: A program to quickly generate large amounts of uniform random data using the on-chip RNG available on some Intel and AMD CPUs.

ent: A program to measure statistical properties of data.

djent: An improved rewrite of ent.

dieharder: A program to apply a number of tests of PRNG distinguishability from random.

nist_22_tests: A program to apply the NIST SP800-22rev1a tests of PRNG distinguishability from random.

nist_90b_tests: A program to apply the NIST SP800-90B tests of entropy.

First, we look at the data format utilities, because they are used later in the examples of the random data tools.

## 11.1 hex2bin

hex2bin is a simple program that converts hexadecimal data to binary data.

hex2bin can be downloaded from https://github.com/dj-on-github/hexbinhex, which also includes bin2hex.

Starting with some random hexadecimal data in a file hexfile.hex:

```
$ cat hexfile.hex
F17E48A852F23C7AB66563CC1101193F75ED4D5FD50D4DBD70B0952CE0AE0E9C
36BD7F6F52B2C8AD3ECB43751E318EF0F8FB0E73293100A6D68D5ED8BD11B7F8
2D84AAB9D7F836A08D7BE8BFA84477CE7129CB078E4372600EC5353FA78F5610
3FB55F71C33FF7FDF5E523403A337B5A20A241A30EB5B7FC51DC122E3D32841D
5CDD489AAB079DB7070857A47CE2E3B3CB3E9EEF48B63229CFF450ADBB283245
94BDE6E6FBDF32DAC8F4A4B249C5E08F5D652EC57F196AA018A5F64CBBDD40E0
608D5121FFF1B13B6350C5D5B0DB8D23A0084FAC9522A2E01E098B533ED546C2
D22FDC5860C7D420AB669277E3F2E5055A0116953CDCCA7B4724398523ECCE4A
110582D729E7EC423E88BC8B64B2D198645FCBE6B0C1B9A837CE8BACCBCFD887
CA7DAC58C35B86BA32F3B78C4C00D9E057141A42260B249A0C55
```

https://doi.org/10.1515/9781501506062-011

We can convert it to binary. The -o option is used to name the output file

```
$ hex2bin hexfile.hex -o binfile.bin.
```

Using the standard unix utility hexdump, we can see that the binary file contains a binary version of the hexdata as follows:

```
$ hexdump binfile.bin
0000000 f1 7e 48 a8 52 f2 3c 7a b6 65 63 cc 11 01 19 3f
0000010 75 ed 4d 5f d5 0d 4d bd 70 b0 95 2c e0 ae 0e 9c
0000020 36 bd 7f 6f 52 b2 c8 ad 3e cb 43 75 1e 31 8e f0
0000030 f8 fb 0e 73 29 31 00 a6 d6 8d 5e d8 bd 11 b7 f8
0000040 2d 84 aa b9 d7 f8 36 a0 8d 7b e8 bf a8 44 77 ce
0000050 71 29 cb 07 8e 43 72 60 0e c5 35 3f a7 8f 56 10
0000060 3f b5 5f 71 c3 3f f7 fd f5 e5 23 40 3a 33 7b 5a
0000070 20 a2 41 a3 0e b5 b7 fc 51 dc 12 2e 3d 32 84 1d
0000080 5c dd 48 9a ab 07 9d b7 07 08 57 a4 7c e2 e3 b3
0000090 cb 3e 9e ef 48 b6 32 29 cf f4 50 ad bb 28 32 45
00000a0 94 bd e6 e6 fb df 32 da c8 f4 a4 b2 49 c5 e0 8f
00000b0 5d 65 2e c5 7f 19 6a a0 18 a5 f6 4c bb dd 40 e0
00000c0 60 8d 51 21 ff f1 b1 3b 63 50 c5 d5 b0 db 8d 23
00000d0 a0 08 4f ac 95 22 a2 e0 1e 09 8b 53 3e d5 46 c2
00000e0 d2 2f dc 58 60 c7 d4 20 ab 66 92 77 e3 f2 e5 05
00000f0 5a 01 16 95 3c dc ca 7b 47 24 39 85 23 ec ce 4a
0000100 11 05 82 d7 29 e7 ec 42 3e 88 bc 8b 64 b2 d1 98
0000110 64 5f cb e6 b0 c1 b9 a8 37 ce 8b ac cb cf d8 87
0000120 ca 7d ac 58 c3 5b 86 ba 32 f3 b7 8c 4c 00 d9 e0
0000130 57 14 1a 42 26 0b 24 9a 0c 55
000013a
```

Without an input filename, it will take input from stdin.

Without an output filename, it will send binary data to stdout.

There is one additional option, that is, -s <n> that directs it to skip the first n lines of text. This is to allow header lines to be skipped.

Nonhex data in a file will be ignored. Also, any prefix 0x will be ignored.

## 11.2 bin2hex

bin2hex is a simple program that converts binary data to hexadecimal data.

bin2hex can be downloaded from https://github.com/dj-on-github/hexbinhex, which also includes hex2bin.

Starting with the random binary data in the file generated above binfile.bin, we can convert it back to hex. Unlike hexdump, note that the output has no spaces.

```
$ bin2hex binfile.bin
F17E48A852F23C7AB66563CC1101193F75ED4D5FD50D4DBD70B0952CE0AE0E9C
36BD7F6F52B2C8AD3ECB43751E318EF0F8FB0E73293100A6D68D5ED8BD11B7F8
2D84AAB9D7F836A08D7BE8BFA84477CE7129CB078E4372600EC5353FA78F5610
```

```
3FB55F71C33FF7FDF5E523403A337B5A20A241A30EB5B7FC51DC122E3D32841D
5CDD489AAB079DB7070857A47CE2E3B3CB3E9EEF48B63229CFF450ADBB283245
94BDE6E6FBDF32DAC8F4A4B249C5E08F5D652EC57F196AA018A5F64CBBDD40E0
608D5121FFF1B13B6350C5D5B0DB8D23A0084FAC9522A2E01E098B533ED546C2
D22FDC5860C7D420AB669277E3F2E5055A0116953CDCCA7B4724398523ECCE4A
110582D729E7EC423E88BC8B64B2D198645FCBE6B0C1B9A837CE8BACCBCFD887
CA7DAC58C35B86BA32F3B78C4C00D9E057141A42260B249A0C55
```

There is a width option to allow any number of bytes per line.

```
$ bin2hex binfile.bin -w 24
F17E48A852F23C7AB66563CC1101193F75ED4D5FD50D4DBD
70B0952CE0AE0E9C36BD7F6F52B2C8AD3ECB43751E318EF0
F8FB0E73293100A6D68D5ED8BD11B7F82D84AAB9D7F836A0
8D7BE8BFA84477CE7129CB078E4372600EC5353FA78F5610
3FB55F71C33FF7FDF5E523403A337B5A20A241A30EB5B7FC
51DC122E3D32841D5CDD489AAB079DB7070857A47CE2E3B3
CB3E9EEF48B63229CFF450ADBB28324594BDE6E6FBDF32DA
C8F4A4B249C5E08F5D652EC57F196AA018A5F64CBBDD40E0
608D5121FFF1B13B6350C5D5B0DB8D23A0084FAC9522A2E0
1E098B533ED546C2D22FDC5860C7D420AB669277E3F2E505
5A0116953CDCCA7B4724398523ECCE4A110582D729E7EC42
3E88BC8B64B2D198645FCBE6B0C1B9A837CE8BACCBCFD887
CA7DAC58C35B86BA32F3B78C4C00D9E057141A42260B249A
0C55
$ bin2hex binfile.bin -w 2
F17E
48A8
52F2
3C7A
B665
63CC
1101
...
```

The -o option can be used to specify an output file.
Without an input filename, it will take input from stdin.
Without an output filename, it will send binary data to stdout.

## 11.3 cleanhex

The program cleanhex will cleanup hexadecimal data in a file by removing nonhex characters, spaces and 0x prefixes. Lines where the first nonwhitespace character is # will also be ignored.

```
$ ./cleanhex -h
Usage: cleanhex [options] [filename]
```

```
Options:
  -h, --help              show this help message and exit
  -o FILE, --output=FILE
                          Write output to <filename> instead of stdout
  -v, --verbose           Show many internal gory details
```

Many hex-files output from logging programs and other tools contain header data, commas, comments, and 0x prefixes. For example, you may have the following file:

```
$ cat dirtyhex.hex
# Some logged data
55DD76FD
0xA02E1933

9B,0x79, 0xC4, 0xDF
34 02 B3 60
477F 64BD

# more logged data
E89512 22
B5620xA944
433FC6B1
A5896DC7
70671810
```

Clean this up by running it through cleanhex.

```
$ cleanhex dirtyhex.hex
55DD76FD
A02E1933
9B79C4DF
3402B360
477F64BD
E8951222
B562A944
433FC6B1
A5896DC7
70671810
```

## 11.4 djenrandom

djenrandom is available at https://github.com/dj-on-github/djenrandom.

djenrandom implements a number of models of random sources and options to output data from those sources in various formats.

It was originally developed in order to test entropy testing algorithms, by being enabled to feed data into the test algorithms with known entropy and statistical values. The results of the tests could then be compared with the known statistics to establish the correctness of the test.

### djenrandom Models

Following are the models implemented:

**pure:** The pure model generates uniform random data using an SP800-90A AES-CTR-DRBG algorithm.

**SUMS:** The SUMS (Step Update Metastable Source) models the family of meta-stable sources that have feedback to center the source in the metastable curve. This approximates the entropy source used in Intel chips and some others. By manipulating the parameters, it is possible to generate data with both bias and serial correlation.

**biased:** Generates data with a defined constant bias (probability of 1) per bit.

**correlated:** Generates data with a defined serial correlation coefficient.

**LCG:** Generates data with a Linear Congruential Generator. The parameters of the LCG can be controlled.

**PCG:** Generates data with a Permuted Congruential Generator. The parameters of the PCG can be controlled.

**normal:** Generates normally distributed data in floating point form, using the provided values for $\mu$ and $\sigma$.

**file:** Takes random data directly from a file. This allow djenrandom to be used for formatting conversion and for applying the built-in processing options to the data.

### Output formats

By default djenrandom outputs 1 KiB of data using the pure model, in hex format, with 32 bytes per line.

```
$ djenrandom
FE590E658B6AFAFADD3CC5050FCCA736B1D2D97A177C24212E796F483656E04D
3AD47970FA138E97B15A509A39949070CCDABDF0B2F20D224FF76DCD08A9D80B
1DBD592FA4835FD36D9374C9527AFF3F82890068AF531469823C67A8EB2BD7C6
7C185C5AFCE896C53A4F6D783C0711E887BB358F83CAEE1F6C8376C301D05018
578242DEAF34791FF13F64176CF73A53F697BCFF63DC5CF2C78A68EDAC2DC867
6C95AA4B9756EFC56E831E3B5FECE42FF406B6FAE51E27394C9CAABBFE95EF53
F17E48A852F23C7AB66563CC1101193F75ED4D5FD50D4DBD70B0952CE0AE0E9C
36BD7F6F52B2C8AD3ECB43751E318EF0F8FB0E73293100A6D68D5ED8BD11B7F8
2D84AAB9D7F836A08D7BE8BFA84477CE7129CB078E4372600EC5353FA78F5610
3FB55F71C33FF7FDF5E523403A337B5A20A241A30EB5B7FC51DC122E3D32841D
5CDD489AAB079DB7070857A47CE2E3B3CB3E9EEF48B63229CFF450ADBB283245
94BDE6E6FBDF32DAC8F4A4B249C5E08F5D652EC57F196AA018A5F64CBBDD40E0
E36722FE460F3ABF3CCF31FD8C02BF2975491E4956F995B66620D74BF56D20D0
B3912522390460F59A54031AB9D812A5281B9E61C968D68E0AED22D0B56A591A
51EC6895F9A4016957C9EDA5F40D59F6057909A5666C7F37BBF5F9BD55BC1C58
1401BED44FA8C2886007131373841D511EA49E74B965724273849D84E1AF39AB
BC75172C714847123AAFA6D9BE457864B9E0391345667D68C494DA49AAA08341
5A37233D69C1BA02E04BDDAD60485A949BD23CD985E5421124C316386BC2FDD6
6ED9E95D8AA76E63DCEAD026C31C4B2DB4C9F282296CE66A066CFCFAD8CB2181
78EED7BDB7D58795CF01C5481396088B866696E70DD6C1128B8EBC3E16FC8E29
BD290B47CA79275D66E7B139091C8F44D647EDFF30FA5958374F330BD6E3023F
```

```
7360A83AEE19F916D785AC2E9AA6AFE0943171CCB15F393D81254E6E8EC99701
1FBC5AD80B5A2806CB98EBCB32E56109DB275C6F7880EF67B6BE108381F64847
6DF6662068618D98D477E193E756C21798EF90EB95F5EF3887BC8EF9659A61E8
8904E05105EBE14F85869E720F4ADDBB7D218D4EE9D25450ED395B27736EFEFB
344320A19CB05CD049B98110D55210F430378CECAD2FC432426507B1BC1D74E1
219F43056025DE55880184C62A6E6D5D8E5BE923BE2D95A20CE4926641A8E2CA
F626F307869A0D91C2C02D7938BC414FC36257A9D750927399F78FFFAB303C5B
608D5121FFF1B13B6350C5D5B0DB8D23A0084FAC9522A2E01E098B533ED546C2
D22FDC5860C7D420AB669277E3F2E5055A0116953CDCCA7B4724398523ECCE4A
110582D729E7EC423E88BC8B64B2D198645FCBE6B0C1B9A837CE8BACCBCFD887
34F6D57031E3CA7DAC58C35B86BA32F3B78C4C00D9E057141A42260B249A0C55
```

The -v option will display additional information.

```
$ djenrandom -v
Format=Hex
model=pure
size = 1 kilobytes
XOR mode off
XOR range mode off
Output to STDOUT
Hardware Random Seeding off. Deterministic mode.
  Restir c_max=511
FE590E658B6AFAFADD3CC5050FCCA736B1D2D97A177C24212E796F483656E04D
3AD47970FA138E97B15A509A39949070CCDABDF0B2F20D224FF76DCD08A9D80B
1DBD592FA4835FD36D9374C9527AFF3F82890068AF531469823C67A8EB2BD7C6
...
110582D729E7EC423E88BC8B64B2D198645FCBE6B0C1B9A837CE8BACCBCFD887
34F6D57031E3CA7DAC58C35B86BA32F3B78C4C00D9E057141A42260B249A0C55
Total Entropy = 0.000000
Per bit Entropy = 0.000000 %
```

The "Total Entropy" and "Per bit Entropy" values at the end give entropy values for the statistical models SUMS, biased, and correlated.

The additional information output is sent to STDERR, whereas the random data go to STDOUT or to the file if file output is used. So, if outputting to the file, the information is visible on the command line, whereas the random data end up in the file.

To output to a file, instead of STDOUT, add -o <filename>.

The -b option outputs data in binary. For example,

```
$ djenrandom -b -o randomdata.binary
```

With -b, one would typically use -o <filename> or pipe the output to another program, since outputting random binary data to the command line is not very useful.

The number of bytes per line can be altered with -w <bytes>. That is,

```
$ djenrandom -w 4
FE590E65
8B6AFAFA
DD3CC505
0FCCA736
...

$ djenrandom -w 24
FE590E658B6AFAFADD3CC5050FCCA736B1D2D97A177C2421
2E796F483656E04D3AD47970FA138E97B15A509A39949070
CCDABDF0B2F20D224FF76DCD08A9D80B1DBD592FA4835FD3
...
```

The data generated will be the same everytime by default.

```
$ djenrandom | head -1
FE590E658B6AFAFADD3CC5050FCCA736B1D2D97A177C24212E796F483656E04D
$ djenrandom | head -1
FE590E658B6AFAFADD3CC5050FCCA736B1D2D97A177C24212E796F483656E04D
$ djenrandom | head -1
FE590E658B6AFAFADD3CC5050FCCA736B1D2D97A177C24212E796F483656E04D
```

To make the output nondeterministic, use the -s option.

```
$ djenrandom -s | head -1
65E63EBE3868ADD770BB72B4F864D9E08802E6DE65AF1F2C9386E4701D5CF5C0
$ djenrandom -s | head -1
FBF44858CD1BAC77431F98FD00C5AD1AD33F24256E6334BE14038394F56A1954
$ djenrandom -s | head -1
066027040C9B866CF98D5644765C01DA20FDB9184A87587B2976245E9BE5422A
```

For more data, request a number of KibiBytes of data with -k <KiBytes>. The following example writes 1 MiByte to a file 1MiByteRandom.bin. The stat command is used to show the size of the resulting file.

```
$ djenrandom -b -k 1024 -o 1MiByteRandom.bin
$ stat -f "%z" 1MiByteRandom.bin
1048576
```

## 11.4.1 Pure Model

The pure model is the default. To explicitly invoke it, use -m pure.

```
$ djenrandom -m pure
FE590E658B6AFAFADD3CC5050FCCA736B1D2D97A177C24212E796F483656E04D
3AD47970FA138E97B15A509A39949070CCDABDF0B2F20D224FF76DCD08A9D80B
...
```

### 11.4.2 SUMS – Step Update Metastable Source Model

The SUMS model models a metastable digital latch that has a feedback network to balance the two sides of the latch, so the probability of outputting a 0 or 1 remains close to $\frac{1}{2}$.

This closely models the entropy source used in Intel chips and entropy sources used by some other manufacturers.

The latch model is based on two back-to-back inverters, where the two sides are labeled NodeA and NodeB. There are two stable states, where $NodeA, NobeB = 0, 1$ or $1, 0$. By turning off the circuit, both sides are forced to converge to the same value, either $0, 0$ or $1, 1$; then releasing both sides by releasing the force or turning on the circuit, the latch has to choose between converging to the $0, 1$ state or the $1, 0$ state. Noise drives the circuit to randomly choose either of the two stable states. This yields one bit of random data.

The curve that describes the probability of NodeA resolving to one state, that is, $P(1)$, given the feedback state variable $t$ for one side of the curve is

$$P(1) = \frac{1}{2}\left(1 + \text{erf}\left(\frac{t}{\sqrt{2}}\right)\right).$$

When NodeA resolves to 1, we move the feedback left by decreasing $t$ by one step, thus increasing the probability of getting a 0.

When NodeA resolves to 0, we move the feedback right by increasing $t$ by one step, thus increasing the probability of getting a 1.

The stepsize when moving left can be different than the stepsize moving right, which models asymmetry in the feedback circuit. If they are different, then the output will be biased, because it takes more steps in the direction of the smaller feedback step.

With larger stepsize, the serial correlation coefficient increases. With smaller stepsize, the serial correlation coefficient decreases.

The stepsizes are controlled by the -l <left stepsize> and -r <right stepsize> options. In addition, noise can be added to the stepsize using the --stepnoise=<noise on step> option.

All the values for the stepsize options and the stepnoise options are relative to $\sigma_m$, which is the standard deviation of the variation of the curve.

If we make the right stepsize twice as big as the left stepsize, then we find that the output is biased. Here, we are using the program ent to measure the mean.

```
$ djenrandom -m sums -1 0.1 -r 0.2 -b | ent -b | grep mean
Arithmetic mean value of data bits is 0.3335 (0.5 = random).
```

Following, we can see the serial correlation vary as we increase the stepsize:

```
$ djenrandom -m sums -l 0.01 -r 0.01 -b | ent -b | grep Serial
Serial correlation coefficient is -0.012697 (totally uncorrelated = 0.0).

$ djenrandom -m sums -l 0.05 -r 0.05 -b | ent -b | grep Serial
Serial correlation coefficient is -0.017100 (totally uncorrelated = 0.0).

$ djenrandom -m sums -l 0.1 -r 0.1 -b | ent -b | grep Serial
Serial correlation coefficient is -0.027832 (totally uncorrelated = 0.0).

$ djenrandom -m sums -l 0.5 -r 0.5 -b | ent -b | grep Serial
Serial correlation coefficient is -0.108887 (totally uncorrelated = 0.0).
```

## 11.4.3 Biased Model

Invoke the biased model with -m biased - -bias=<bias>. The bias should be written as a positive decimal between 0 and 1, describing the probability of each bit being 1.

The following example creates data with a 10% probability of a bit being 1:

```
$ djenrandom -m biased --bias=0.1
008000100081000020000000020000040020004040C00180C0008000250021158
80000008058020000002A0000042400803004002080010000000100212040440
...
```

The following example creates data with a 30% probability of a bit being 1:

```
$ djenrandom -m biased --bias=0.3
01A2111A4085050122821AE8A033504802290685E0019AD0108400B540A91FB0
8402860D0588610042A5AB208643410B132142074C095218A0089222334606D0
...
```

The following example creates data with a 90% probability of a bit being 1:

```
$ djenrandom -m biased --bias=0.9
FFB7FDFFFFFFFFEDFFDFBEFEF57FFFFD6F6FE6EDFFF7FFFFD5CFFBBFFFFFFFFA
FF7FE6FFEFFFFFFDEEBFBF7DFFEBFFFFF73FFF1FFFDDFBFDFFFEFF7EFF7F7FFF
...
```

## 11.4.4 Correlated Model

Invoke the correlated model with -m correlated - -correlation=<SCC>. The correlation should be written as a decimal between −1.0 and +1.0, describing the serial correlation coefficient of the data.

Below, we see how data with a high positive SCC tends to have long runs of the same value, 0 or 1:

```
$ djenrandom -m correlated --correlation=0.8
FF8FFC000000001C003F81FE0CFFFFFCE0E011E3FFF0000033DFF87FFFFFFFF9
FF0011FFE0000003E1807F03FFE7FFFFF08000BFFFC3F803FFFE00FE00FF0000
18019FFCC0FFEC0200001FFE1FFFFFFFFCF0000F01800000000FF8F0400383FF
...
```

Next, we see how data with a high negative SCC tends to have long runs of alternating bit values, which lead to 0x55 and 0xAA values in the hex representation:

```
$ djenrandom -m correlated --correlation=-0.8
AA55554AAA54AAAA955555556AAAAAD556AAAD522AABAA2AAA55556CAA94B3AA
5555555AAC556AAAAA926AAAAAD6D55AA8AAD556A5554AAAAAAAB556B6AD52D5
AAAA912AAAD2556AA955556AAAAD552AAAD5AAAAD552554AB555552B55555AAB
...
```

### 11.4.5 LCG Model

The LCG model generates data with a Linear Congruential Generator algorithm. The standard parameters, the multiplier $a$, adder $c$, and modulus $m$ can be set with

```
--lcg_a=<multiplier>,  --lcg_c=<adder> and --lcg_m=<multiplier>
```

A subset of the output bits can be selected. The number of bits in each output selected with

```
--lcg_outbits=<number of output bits>
```

and the number of lower-order bits to discard is selected with

```
--lcg_truncate=<number of bits to discard>
```

For example, one set of parameters from ISO/IEC 9899 for a 31-bit generator, with 15 bits of output per iteration, is $m = 2^{31}$, $a = 1103515245$, and $c = 12345$. Bits 30-16 of the LCG state are output.

Using djenrandom the invocation would be as follows:

```
$ djenrandom -m lcg --lcg_a=1103515245 --lcg_c=12345 --lcg_m=2147483648\
                --lcg_outbits=15 --lcg_truncate=16
338BD6665342B7044FD05F2068882FF46D98636C8CC3852FD93EFD94B23F4C6B
59412151CB469039AC15A20ED0AAC292297252170801D4FBD9E142D7F92056CA
F724456A8F758C3B649860F2EBA86AB31C662B1638EBBDCE867B67B79C4A22BD
...
```

The verbose output tells you the subfield that is selected for output in the output bit-field line. Here, it is shown to be bits 30:16 that are output.

```
$ ./djenrandom -m lcg --lcg_a=1103515245 --lcg_c=12345 --lcg_m=2147483648\
                --lcg_outbits=15 --lcg_truncate=16 -v
Format=Hex
model=linear congruential generator
```

```
a   = 0x41c64e6d
c   = 0x3039
m   = 0x80000000
start x = 0x2682b002
Output bit field = 30:16
...
```

### 11.4.6 PCG Model

The PCG model generates data with a Permuted Congruential Generator algorithm. A PCG has a generator function and an output function. The options for the generator function are MCG or LCG. It is selected with

```
--pcg_generator=<MCG|LCG>
```

The output function can either be XSH-RS or XSH-RR. It is selected with

```
--pcg_of=<XSH_RS|XSH_RR>
```

The state size of the PCG is one of 16, 32, or 64 bits. This is set with

```
--pcg_state_size=<16|32|64>
```

The default PCH is given in the verbose information

```
$ djenrandom -m pcg -v
Format=Hex
model=permuted congruential generator
  state size = 32
  State update algorithm LCG
  Output function XSH_RR
```

To set a different PCG, for example, an MCG generator with 64 bits of state and the XSH-RR output function, do the following:

```
$ djenrandom -m pcg --pcg_generator=MCG --pcg_of=XSH_RR --pcg_state_size=64
F31D04995E9FA5229B313785E6A314877983F6B980AA641F2F573592C1E94DD9
CFB606E6961720D78FF3A217B2C59E314EC9CFCDFCA74A70E17DE073906F5D13
8F61E5EAE7F0DFA73BC24A3D481D61F83E543D857F0DB1657A345C5A9B44D0F3
...
```

### 11.4.7 XorShift Model

The XorShift model generates data with the XorShift algorithm. There is only one option, that is, setting the state size to either 32 or 128 bits.

```
$ djenrandom -m xorshift --xorshift_size=32
5D2CE5AF9BF5BC05142467438A5E96052A9492F143C0EFA06CD5319F24FF1EB7
226E31A7F755076DF914E8206C2FC365E3A3426EC97E9666E98F9CFC41B7CE52
```

AF608190F41BD90E70E4959CD4B816A1F8833009ABFEF9F51151703AA64ABB7E
...

or

```
$ djenrandom -m xorshift --xorshift_size=128
```
97ED5F523CE8B72B60AA04638BB65AF8DB5597724B101D1ECEBD6A35CA7BFD1D
1F760F08BA9E00BFA72676E248C1B95FE59B12D1919B3D84F05EA85247CA0A54
A83523E92B993CD2668C341DCF938E42F54BEFEBB752417C33DE135401CB638A
...

### 11.4.8 Normal Model

The normal model, unlike the other models, which produce binary data, produces floating point data, one value per line. The distribution of the floating point data generated is Gaussian.

By default, $\mu = 0$ and variance = 1.0.

```
$ djenrandom -m normal
0.04824939
-0.02096109
-0.05418924
-0.07950429
0.26449034
-0.05494280
0.22212504
```
...

To set $\mu$, use the --mean=<$\mu$> parameter.

```
$ djenrandom -m normal --mean=-2.0
-1.95175061
-2.02096109
-2.05418924
-2.07950429
-1.73550966
-2.05494280
-1.77787496
-1.97058693
-1.90170746
-2.41556001
-1.88998102
```
...

To set the variance, use the --variance=<variance> parameter. Usually, -s would also be used to get nondeterministic output.

```
$ djenrandom -m normal --variance=8.0 -s
2.19209003
```

```
4.23611682
0.92638181
3.56629611
3.33895153
-3.01737664
3.22425511
-1.83711188
2.71901470
-4.35196221
-3.60943845
-0.91653128
1.92246792
...
```

Both mean and variance can be used at the same time.

```
$ djenrandom -m normal --mean=4.0 --variance=8.0 -s
5.71228791
0.58107807
2.53044721
9.15961510
4.61019086
3.49908462
0.54303397
0.84727537
0.73356252
5.21475989
9.54801986
6.32223486
3.85988004
5.17018972
4.09864550
...
```

Here, we set the mean to 2.0 and the variance to 0.5, and create 100 KiSamples of data.

```
$ djenrandom -m normal --mean=2.0 --variance=0.5 -k 100 > normal_model_example.dat
```

A plot of the resulting histogram is shown in Figure 11.1.

### 11.4.9 File Model

The file model does not generate any random data, it reads it from a file and then outputs it through the normal output functions of djenrandom.

File input can take hex format data, binary format data, or ASCII binary data, which is data representing each bit with an ASCII 0 or ASCII 1.

By default the input format is hex.

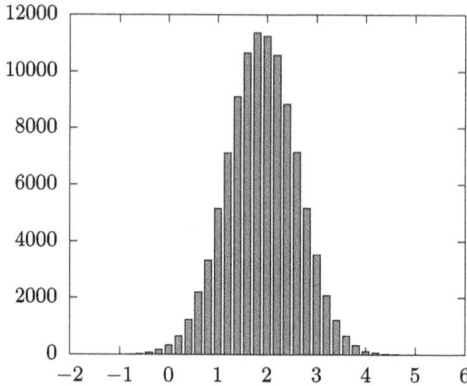

**Figure 11.1:** Histogram of 102 400 Numbers From the djenrandom Normal Model.

Set the input filename using -i <filename>

In this example, hexfile.hex is a file containing ASCII hex characters.

```
$ cat hexfile.hex
FE590E658B6AFAFADD3CC5050FCCA736B1D2D97A177C24212E796F483656E04D
3AD47970FA138E97B15A509A39949070CCDABDF0B2F20D224FF76DCD08A9D80B
36BD7F6F52B2C8AD3ECB43751E318EF0F8FB0E73293100A6D68D5ED8BD11B7F8
BD290B47CA79275D66E7B139091C8F44D647EDFF30FA5958374F330BD6E3023F
7360A83AEE19F916D785AC2E9AA6AFE0943171CCB15F393D81254E6E8EC99701
1FBC5AD80B5A2806CB98EBCB32E56109DB275C6F7880EF67B6BE108381F64847
F626F307869A0D91C2C02D7938BC414FC36257A9D750927399F78FFFAB303C5B
608D5121FFF1B13B6350C5D5B0DB8D23A0084FAC9522A2E01E098B533ED546C2
D22FDC5860C7D420AB669277E3F2E5055A0116953CDCCA7B4724398523ECCE4A
110582D729E7EC423E88BC8B64B2D198645FCBE6B0C1B9A837CE8BACCBCFD887
34F6D57031E3CA7DAC58C35B86BA32F3B78C4C00D9E057141A42260B249A0C55
```

By inputting into djenrandom with the file model, we can see that the data is simply read in and then printed back out.

```
$ djenrandom -m file -i hexfile.hex
FE590E658B6AFAFADD3CC5050FCCA736B1D2D97A177C24212E796F483656E04D
3AD47970FA138E97B15A509A39949070CCDABDF0B2F20D224FF76DCD08A9D80B
36BD7F6F52B2C8AD3ECB43751E318EF0F8FB0E73293100A6D68D5ED8BD11B7F8
BD290B47CA79275D66E7B139091C8F44D647EDFF30FA5958374F330BD6E3023F
7360A83AEE19F916D785AC2E9AA6AFE0943171CCB15F393D81254E6E8EC99701
1FBC5AD80B5A2806CB98EBCB32E56109DB275C6F7880EF67B6BE108381F64847
F626F307869A0D91C2C02D7938BC414FC36257A9D750927399F78FFFAB303C5B
608D5121FFF1B13B6350C5D5B0DB8D23A0084FAC9522A2E01E098B533ED546C2
D22FDC5860C7D420AB669277E3F2E5055A0116953CDCCA7B4724398523ECCE4A
110582D729E7EC423E88BC8B64B2D198645FCBE6B0C1B9A837CE8BACCBCFD887
34F6D57031E3CA7DAC58C35B86BA32F3B78C4C00D9E057141A42260B249A0C55
```

The other input formats are selected with -f <hex|binary|01>.

We can input the data in hex format and convert it back to binary, with -f hex to set the input format and -b to set the binary output. Here, we use a utility program to view the binary output.

```
$ djenrandom -m file -f hex -i hexfile.hex -o binfile.bin -b
$ bin2hex binfile.bin
FE590E658B6AFAFADD3CC5050FCCA736B1D2D97A177C24212E796F483656E04D
3AD47970FA138E97B15A509A39949070CCDABDF0B2F20D224FF76DCD08A9D80B
36BD7F6F52B2C8AD3ECB43751E318EF0F8FB0E73293100A6D68D5ED8BD11B7F8
BD290B47CA79275D66E7B139091C8F44D647EDFF30FA5958374F330BD6E3023F
7360A83AEE19F916D785AC2E9AA6AFE0943171CCB15F393D81254E6E8EC99701
1FBC5AD80B5A2806CB98EBCB32E56109DB275C6F7880EF67B6BE108381F64847
F626F307869A0D91C2C02D7938BC414FC36257A9D750927399F78FFFAB303C5B
608D5121FFF1B13B6350C5D5B0DB8D23A0084FAC9522A2E01E098B533ED546C2
D22FDC5860C7D420AB669277E3F2E5055A0116953CDCCA7B4724398523ECCE4A
110582D729E7EC423E88BC8B64B2D198645FCBE6B0C1B9A837CE8BACCBCFD887
34F6D57031E3CA7DAC58C35B86BA32F3B78C4C00D9E057141A42260B249A0C55
```

We can read in binary and output as hex.

```
$ djenrandom -m file -i binfile.bin -f binary
FE590E658B6AFAFADD3CC5050FCCA736B1D2D97A177C24212E796F483656E04D
3AD47970FA138E97B15A509A39949070CCDABDF0B2F20D224FF76DCD08A9D80B
36BD7F6F52B2C8AD3ECB43751E318EF0F8FB0E73293100A6D68D5ED8BD11B7F8
BD290B47CA79275D66E7B139091C8F44D647EDFF30FA5958374F330BD6E3023F
7360A83AEE19F916D785AC2E9AA6AFE0943171CCB15F393D81254E6E8EC99701
1FBC5AD80B5A2806CB98EBCB32E56109DB275C6F7880EF67B6BE108381F64847
F626F307869A0D91C2C02D7938BC414FC36257A9D750927399F78FFFAB303C5B
608D5121FFF1B13B6350C5D5B0DB8D23A0084FAC9522A2E01E098B533ED546C2
D22FDC5860C7D420AB669277E3F2E5055A0116953CDCCA7B4724398523ECCE4A
110582D729E7EC423E88BC8B64B2D198645FCBE6B0C1B9A837CE8BACCBCFD887
34F6D57031E3CA7DAC58C35B86BA32F3B78C4C00D9E057141A42260B249A0C55
```

With the file model, one can limit the amount of data read in using the -k <KibiBytes> option. However, if you do not set a data quantity with the -k <KiBytes> option, the file model will read to the end of the file.

## 11.5 quickrdrand

Quickrdrand is a simple program to output pure random data very quickly. It uses the RdRand instruction available on most Intel CPUs and recent AMD CPUs.

The output of RdRand is always nondeterministic, so the output of quickrdrand is always nondeterministic.

```
$ ./quickrdrand -h
quickrdrand [-b][-c][-h][-k <KiBytes>]
      -b       Output in binary, otherwise outputs in hex
      -c       Output continuously
```

```
-k <k>    Output k KiBytes of random data
-h        Print this message
```

### 11.5.1 Quickrdrand Output Formats

The default output is 1 kibyte of hex format data.

```
$ ./quickrdrand
af8041a779dde2bf 1f19de5e13e0f13b 7cdd7cd9c6478197 ebfe067a4d79a497
95fae2ef69d1ea19 1a93016c91faf622 45fb675f17924a82 15260e5bb2023d5b
216df2620770e1c6 4d8eee70a3e2b840 48020f43e98198f2 2d7f8506f364fa58
ebf14459516cde54 af76284cefea12ff abac817132fc8110 cb2542683e9c3da1
e3a17b5d55edd1eb db52abff554bf09f d966ee1dcd028bdd baed29a15db63ec4
5549995ef7707626 1208771bddc25096 36d343511e909921 3ab7772b068178a9
f2048da6476b9803 78c69b624f18689a 588c365c055c968d 87f55ec44c2153d1
db7723c19ef3f466 3e404bcddd3a2508 5df218653023beb3 ea7351d8e7055706
19afee0d5b05d08a 9094bcc408d1ae84 2b7af5f461f0cb78 1882a4cd5162635d
c2a9a5078a2edad7 a882d30955e7caa3 4face453a7d7052f c0b7bb96459cdb95
93933bebe0cd1fba 7ecec475690af157 72da9036320fc518 966d36baabd1e5fe
394bbf80cb6960f4 f0604732b02596cd ba8e554e537d41aa 3eac1b64ac4291d1
717582c0e4d53766 7c35532327083b7a 4aa42511eddbbfbb 79e3fd71d7a6527d
4cd3737a8c41b396 530b26a3f249bdea 523427772c19623f 7f7c6e111921d4ba
e53cdff00ddcef27 e3d1ba480e713892 12cd459a7110e32d 97c09a8242e31d72
b3688861805b51df e51527a9a45c30ee 684bf7061162b5ac 7f9cec6b0d6d7cd5
93d8723a9ce1a68b c9324dc5ef0226a1 63480cdd5fc10d3f 38d5162e6d2f2e4a
3548b80d7a5d676b 2b2b1bbcf2cb1bcd 5e38e0c1cf971954 2c783e5386c11bab
b35c561bd3d8ea39 11d3d8f5795e693e a5aae58b6c3c323b c41530722dc930ed
4e0d6648a4e9f42e eadc09075aa3b4d7 1d68d37b3eb9d395 cf1a159f6e73bc67
23724b2991720b6a 6c82d811d6e47b2b 3c4a965c9c3393e0 84420f06894c0c3c
9ac1c25625cc104a 3b31839f4f06cb60 ff2b207462824571 9f5e145db54dcd84
271642c769b4f1a0 954cde5f4a12798f d6c83b27214bea1e 578a81b69edd24db
3652668021f41619 14f78f47fabc3dfc b51b3f508b219170 20b7d663c1abd756
6566d50830193f66 aba0bbdc65adc802 f3dbbe8ab6e4d92b 14cb2f85272770a4
b0d27e92f2ebbe5a 99b632c155b3ba9b 5017747d29a92532 63868733597c9772
0eb405bc0fba3136 fc103f3ec43b5ee9 d23daf6b084d0315 5eca913744e699e1
b17498c205fc4518 fa6e86a38fea4496 f71ecfd20c6c461f bda2aee5d201ad19
f3c5e6014388efa5 cf27058d425138a4 c3a0e1b96afc5ff7 82f84a01e756fd1c
a0cf111e23436fd9 08b051d5670981cf eb177db023e1e204 ddf27c9960aeb5d4
2bd6a760912da5fd 802f89aaadbc0129 344feb5cb933daf0 ae695fda89b43268
de783a0c6cc55ac1 412c22091ad11a4c b8872636a5b99ef9 b7c83a30b7f891a7
```

To get binary output, use the -b option.

```
$ ./quickrdrand -b > binfile.bin
$ bin2hex binfile.bin | head
BEC41D89FA8A0282F28EB36498A9D87987E452BFD5DA26EAE921C5299CE8CB56
C680D7540E3212497F1DE17AF778BD5F22C3173F2D8E1C573FCBA0DA3F4825E8
6DC9D82B836DD4BA1437D65FE8EE0132533C23869E3C8EB931E0D4A4FC7011E6
```

```
1021DCE656E385B5EEBFE6D18E6B29936B6C09658769F1250F46FCBDAA683475
7D38213B284B627C03D9AAB5A8924EC311FA4413B24563965DA0CF707ED79CD8
B2EBEF63DAD9740412B7584214412FE5FA7DD49E22DC0FE9A4E4B98877813810
E3F1E4DBD48144F228C6F38A79B3340C7586A9A2E4CFC1A1B78E21A8921AF620
0070A992142F8BABC600739F2BEF4B73416BCD176C932D6F2F876B6FC5253E31
0060A7EE30BA8514EA3A404F29176D77584BFAEFF59FB1514CF7CE786C548356
873EA05E9ECE3B8A3F910A5BF7A8449381F10C88A116275438A25603FF386577
```

### 11.5.2 Quickrdrand data output size

To request more data, use the -k <KiBytes> option, for example, to get a 100 kibyte binary file.

```
$ ./quickrdrand -k 100 -b > binfile.bin
$ stat -f "%z" binfile.bin
102400
```

## 11.6 ent

ent calculates statistics over random data.

```
$ ent -u
ent --   Calculate entropy of file.   Call
         with ent [options] [input-file]

         Options:   -b   Treat input as a stream of bits
                    -c   Print occurrence counts
                    -f   Fold upper to lower case letters
                    -t   Terse output in CSV format
                    -u   Print this message

By John Walker
   http://www.fourmilab.ch/
   January 28th, 2008
```

### 11.6.1 Ent Output Formatting

The default output format of ent, as demonstrated here, is verbose:

```
$ djenrandom -m biased --bias=0.8 -k 100 -b | ent -b
Entropy = 0.722053 bits per bit.

Optimum compression would reduce the size
```

of this 819200 bit file by 27 percent.

Chi square distribution for 819200 samples is 294789.61, and randomly would exceed this value less than 0.01 percent of the times.

Arithmetic mean value of data bits is 0.7999 (0.5 = random).
Monte Carlo value for Pi is 0.723309504 (error 76.98 percent).
Serial correlation coefficient is 0.000127 (totally uncorrelated = 0.0).

The output can be formatted in a terse CSV format using the -t option:

```
$ djenrandom -m biased --bias=0.8 -k 100 -b | ent -b -t
0,File-bits,Entropy,Chi-square,Mean,Monte-Carlo-Pi,Serial-Correlation
1,819200,0.722053,294789.612700,0.799938,0.723310,0.000127
```

Unfortunately, ent does not take multiple-input file names. Therefore, to combine the output of tests of multiple files into a CSV file, one needs to execute ent multiple times, once for each file, then strip the header from all but the first file before concatenating the files together into one CSV file.

### 11.6.2 Ent Symbol Size Options

The -b option is used to tell ent to treat the data as bits instead of bytes. So, for example, the $\chi^2$ test will have 256 bins for bytewise data and 2 bins for bitwise data.

The various tests in ent behave differently in binary mode. In binary mode they generally treat the data as having only two symbols, 0 and 1. In nonbinary mode they treat the data as having 256 symbols, 0 to 255, each made from 8 bits.

### 11.6.3 Ent Occurrence Counts

The -c option causes ent to output the frequency of each symbol. This illustrates well the difference between binary mode and the default bytewise mode. First, in binary mode, it gives the occurrence count for the two symbols 0 and 1:

```
$ djenrandom   -k 100 -b | ent -c -b
Value Char Occurrences  Fraction
  0             410216   0.500752
  1             408984   0.499248

Total:          819200   1.000000
...
```

If we input the same command line, but omit the -b binary flag from ent, it outputs the occurrences of each of the 256 8-bit symbols.

```
$ djenrandom  -k 100 -b | ent -c
Value Char Occurrences Fraction
    0              445   0.004346
    1              400   0.003906
    2              408   0.003984
    3              380   0.003711
    4              376   0.003672
    5              398   0.003887
  ... [values from 6 to 249 omitted]
  250              389   0.003799
  251              426   0.004160
  252              395   0.003857
  253              373   0.003643
  254              368   0.003594
  255              396   0.003867

Total:          102400   1.000000
...
```

### 11.6.4 Ent Statistical Metrics

The statistics that are output in the normal mode of ent are entropy, compression, the $\chi^2$ test of randomness, the mean, the Monte Carlo value for $\pi$, and the serial correlation coefficient.

For example, running ent over the Latex file for this chapter gives:

```
$ ent  5_software_tools.tex
Entropy = 5.360299 bits per byte.

Optimum compression would reduce the size
of this 29237 byte file by 32 percent.

Chi square distribution for 29237 samples is 209344.73, and randomly
would exceed this value less than 0.01 percent of the times.

Arithmetic mean value of data bytes is 76.6648 (127.5 = random).
Monte Carlo value for Pi is 4.000000000 (error 27.32 percent).
Serial correlation coefficient is 0.363767 (totally uncorrelated = 0.0).
```

For most purposes, the interesting results are from the mean, SCC, and $\chi^2$ tests. The entropy number is mostly useless. For instance, it will give a near perfect entropy result on data with high serial correlation coefficient.

Here, we generate 100 kibytes of data with a serial correlation coefficient of 0.2, and run the ent tests over it. Ent reports effectively perfect entropy of 0.99997 bits.

```
$. djenrandom -m correlated --correlation=0.2 -k 100 -b | ent -b
Entropy = 0.999997 bits per bit.
```

This is because it computes the Shannon Entropy $H_1(X)$ for a memoryless channel, which assumes all symbols to be independent.

```
Optimum compression would reduce the size
of this 81920 bit file by 0 percent.
```

The compression result is computed directly from the measured entropy. There is no additional information in the compression number that is not already in the entropy result. In this example, we see the compression test reports a perfect result of 0%. This is because it is treating the binary data as having only two symbols, 0 or 1, which are equally probable, rather than a larger multibit symbol set, where the bitstrings of the same value are more likely than strings of alternating bits. In general, the compression test result varies nonlinearly with min-entropy, which makes the compression result hard to interpret.

```
Chi square distribution for 819200 samples is 3.26, and randomly
would exceed this value 7.10 percent of the times.
```

The $\chi^2$ test passes. This is to be expected since the $\chi^2$ test of randomness tests only bias and is insensitive to correlation.

```
Arithmetic mean value of databits is 0.4990 (0.5 = random).
```

Similarly, as we would expect, the mean is close to 0.5.

```
Monte Carlo value for Pi is 2.984882222 (error 4.99 percent).
```

The Monte Carlo Pi value is significantly off. This reflects the nonuniform distribution of multibit values in serially correlated data. However, it is not clear what constitutes a good or bad result.

```
The serial correlation coefficient is 0.201169 (totally uncorrelated = 0.0).
```

The serial correlation of 0.201169 is close to the 0.2 as we would expect, since we generated data with SCC=0.2. If we increased the quantity of data, we would expect this value to get closer to 0.2. So, the data quantity is increased by 10, and we see the measured SCC reduced from 0.201169 down to 0.20019, which is very close to a 10× reduction in the discrepancy of the measured value.

```
$ djenrandom -m correlated --correlation=0.2 -k 1000 -b  | ent -b | grep Serial
Serial correlation coefficient is 0.200190 (totally uncorrelated = 0.0).
```

### 11.6.5 Uses of ent

Since the useful outputs from ent give normal statistics rather than special RNG tests, it is primarily useful for testing entropy sources. Running ent over data from most PRNGs, whether secure or not, will give perfect results. For example, with an insecure LCG output, we get the following result:

```
$ djenrandom  -m lcg -k 100 -b | ent
Entropy = 7.998185 bits per byte.

Optimum compression would reduce the size
of this 102400 byte file by 0 percent.

Chi square distribution for 102400 samples is 257.17, and randomly
would exceed this value 45.02 percent of the times.

Arithmetic mean value of data bytes is 127.2796 (127.5 = random).
Monte Carlo value for Pi is 3.151294972 (error 0.31 percent).
Serial correlation coefficient is -0.003767 (totally uncorrelated = 0.0).
```

Compare this with the same amount of secure uniform random data, and we see very similar values characteristic of perfectly random bits.

```
$ djenrandom  -m pure -k 100 -b | ent
Entropy = 7.998165 bits per byte.

Optimum compression would reduce the size
of this 102400 byte file by 0 percent.

Chi square distribution for 102400 samples is 261.47, and randomly
would exceed this value 37.69 percent of the times.

Arithmetic mean value of data bytes is 127.7526 (127.5 = random).
Monte Carlo value for Pi is 3.131372319 (error 0.33 percent).
Serial correlation coefficient is 0.000810 (totally uncorrelated = 0.0).
```

Many entropy sources have serial correlation and bias, and so ent is good for measuring those values. Here, we run it against the SUMS entropy source model with an excessively large stepsize and stepsize asymmetry that should lead to detectable bias and correlation.

```
$ djenrandom  -m sums -l 0.3 -r 0.2 -k 100 -b | ent
Entropy = 7.717876 bits per byte.

Optimum compression would reduce the size
of this 102400 byte file by 3 percent.

Chi square distribution for 102400 samples is 35539.88, and randomly
would exceed this value less than 0.01 percent of the times.

Arithmetic mean value of data bytes is 153.2162 (127.5 = random).
Monte Carlo value for Pi is 2.494784953 (error 20.59 percent).
Serial correlation coefficient is -0.082369 (totally uncorrelated = 0.0).
```

The numbers are much worse. The Shannon entropy is significantly less than a perfect 8 bits per byte. The compression ratio is 3% instead of 0%. The $\chi^2$ test fails instead of passing. The mean is 153.2162 instead of 127.5. The value for the Monte

Carlo computed $\pi$ is 20.59% away from $\pi$, instead of 0.33%. The serial correlation is −0.082369 rather than 0.00081.

Thus, ent is a useful tool for detecting nonrandom artifacts in the output of physical circuits. It is not appropriate for detecting more subtle flaws in PRNGs.

## 11.7 djent

The program djent is a reimplementation of ent written for this book. It has a number of improvements over ent. So, we will only cover the differences here rather than revisiting the ent features.

It can be downloaded from github at https://github.com/dj-on-github/djent.

```
djent -h
Usage: djent [-brpcuhfts] [-l <n>] [-i <input file list filename>] [filenames]

Compute statistics of random data.
  Author: David Johnston, dj@deadhat.com

  -i <filename>   --inputfilelist=<filename> Read list of filenames from <filename>
  -p              --parse_filename          Extract CID, Process, Voltage and
                                            Temperature from filename.
                                            The values will be included in
                                            the output.
  -l <n>          --symbol_length=<n>       Treat incoming data symbols as
                                            bitlength n. Default is 8.
  -b              --binary                  Treat incoming data as binary.
                                            Default bit length will be -l 1
  -r              --byte_reverse            Reverse the bit order in
                                            incoming bytes
  -c              --occurrence              Print symbol occurrence counts
  -w              --scc_wrap                Treat data as cyclical in SCC
  -n <n>          --lagn=<n>                Lag gap in SCC. Default=1
  -f              --fold                    Fold uppercase letters to lower case
  -t              --terse                   Terse output
  -s              --suppress_header         Suppress the header in terse output
  -h or -u        --help                    Print this text
```

The principal improvements with respect to ent are:
- Multiple filenames can be passed in on the command line. This works well with terse CSV output, where the results for each file appear on one line each.
- Instead of putting filenames on the command line, the -i FILENAME option will direct djent to read a list of file names from the file indicated.
- -h can be used to get the help information in addition to -u.
- The filename is included in the terse CSV output.
- ent processes data as symbols of 1 bit or 8 bits. djent can process symbol sizes from 1 bit to 32 bits.
- The SCC test is not wrap-around as with ent. Random data typically are not cyclical. So, comparing the last data with the first is not correct. The -w option will restore the wrap-around behavior.

- The Lag-N correlation coefficient can be computed with the -n LAG option.
- Data are read with the most significant bit in each byte being the first.
- Test conditions can be parsed from the filename and included in the output. This is particularly useful when testing batches of raw data samples that have been taken at various voltages and temperatures. The four parameters parsed are component ID, process information, voltage, and temperature. These are included in the output so can be easily read into other tools that read CSV.

## 11.7.1 Parseable Filenames

For example, to analyze a series of measurements from a chip identified as X10, with typical silicon parameters (in semiconductor design denoted as TTTT for 4 typical parameters) at 25 Centigrade, and voltages varying from 1 V to 1.7 V, the filenames might be written as:

```
rawdata_CID-X10_PROC-TTTT_1p0V_25p0C_.bin,
rawdata_CID-X10_PROC-TTTT_1p2V_25p0C_.bin,
rawdata_CID-X10_PROC-TTTT_1p4V_25p0C_.bin, and
rawdata_CID-X10_PROC-TTTT_1p7V_25p0C_.bin.
```

The format for the four parseable parameters are: _CID-<chip ID>_, _PROC-<process info>_, _<x>p<y>V_ for volts, and _<x>p<y>C_ for temperature. The fields must be delimited with underscores. The p is used in place of the decimal point. For example, 1.,V would be written _1p4V_ .

Here, the output columns have been split into three to fit on the page but the actual output is one line per file. The -p option requests the filename parsing. The -t option requests terse CSV output.

```
djent -b -t -p rawdata*
  0,  File-bytes,     CID, Process, Voltage,   Temp,    Entropy,
  1,       10240,     X10,    TTTT,    1.00,  25.00,   0.999996,
  2,       10240,     X10,    TTTT,    1.20,  25.00,   0.999987,
  3,       10240,     X10,    TTTT,    1.40,  25.00,   1.000000,
  4,       10240,     X10,    TTTT,    1.70,  25.00,   0.999991,

  Chi-square,  Entropy,  Chi-square,     Mean, Monte-Carlo-Pi,
  52.711574, 0.999996,   52.711574, 0.498895,       3.076202,
  22.138648, 0.999987,   22.138648, 0.497864,       3.050410,
  96.655747, 1.000000,   96.655747, 0.499927,       3.059789,
  31.767705, 0.999991,   31.767705, 0.501746,       3.073857,

  Serial-Correlation,  Filename
            0.047363,  rawdata_CID-X10_PROC-TTTT_1p0V_25p0C_.bin
            0.079904,  rawdata_CID-X10_PROC-TTTT_1p2V_25p0C_.bin
            0.111708,  rawdata_CID-X10_PROC-TTTT_1p4V_25p0C_.bin
            0.144364,  rawdata_CID-X10_PROC-TTTT_1p7V_25p0C_.bin
```

We see the measured serial correlation clearly increasing with temperature. This is a contrived result, but it is a pattern that mirrors similar results in real silicon entropy sources, where feedback increases with voltage.

### 11.7.2 Measuring Lag-N Correlation Coefficient

The Lag-N feature lets us see how correlation drops off with increasing separation between bits. Lag-N correlation is explored further in Section 8.8.5.

Starting with a serially correlated file with −0.7 serial correlation

```
$ djenrandom -b -m correlated --correlation=-0.7 -k 100 > corrm0p7.bin,
```

we see the Lag-N serial correlation coefficient reduce with increasing $N$

```
$ djent -b -n 1 corrm0p7.bin | grep Serial
    Serial Correlation = -0.699993.
$ djent -b -n 2 corrm0p7.bin | grep Serial
    Serial Correlation = -0.344864
$ djent -b -n 3 corrm0p7.bin | grep Serial
    Serial Correlation = 0.242280
$ djent -b -n 4 corrm0p7.bin | grep Serial
    Serial Correlation = -0.169406
$
```

### 11.7.3 Changing Symbol Size

The data can be treated as having a symbol size other than 1 or 8. For example, to divide the data in the above file into 4-bit symbols, use the -l 4 option. For instance, since the data is bit-serially correlated, and it is treated as a multibit symbol, the distribution of 4-bit patterns is no longer uniform; 0101 and 1010 are more likely than 0000 or 1111 in negatively correlated data. So, it fails the Chi-Sq test, and the measured Shannon entropy reduces accordingly with the distribution.

```
$ djent -b -l 4 corrm0p7.bin
 opening corrm0p7.bin as binary
 Symbol Size(bits) = 4
    Shannon IID Entropy = 2.830821 bits per symbol
    Optimal compression would compress by 29.229482 percent
    Chi square: symbol count=204798, distribution=472115.69, randomly
                exceeds 0.00 percent of the time
    Mean = 7.495513
    Monte Carlo value for Pi is 3.697410 (error 17.69 percent).
    Serial Correlation = 0.121606
```

## 11.8 Dieharder

Dieharder is designed as a PRNG test program. It implements a large battery of hypothesis tests for distinguishability from random.

```
$ dieharder -h
#=============================================================================#
#                 dieharder version 3.31.1 Copyright 2003 Robert G. Brown      #
#=============================================================================#

Usage:

dieharder [-a] [-d dieharder test number] [-f filename] [-B]
          [-D output flag [-D output flag] ... ] [-F] [-c separator]
          [-g generator number or -1] [-h] [-k ks_flag] [-l]
          [-L overlap] [-m multiply_p] [-n ntuple]
          [-p number of p samples] [-P Xoff]
          [-o filename] [-s seed strategy] [-S random number seed]
          [-n ntuple] [-p number of p samples] [-o filename]
          [-s seed strategy] [-S random number seed]
          [-t number of test samples] [-v verbose flag]
          [-W weak] [-X fail] [-Y Xtrategy]
          [-x xvalue] [-y yvalue] [-z zvalue]
```

The help information given with the -h option is too long to show here, but right at the end, it gives the entirely sensible guidance on how to interpret the $P$ values that the tests generate. The guidance is a very concise summary of the explanation of $P$ values given in Chapter 8.

```
NOTE WELL:  The assessment(s) for the rngs may, in fact, be completely
incorrect or misleading.  In particular, ``Weak'' P values should occur
one test in a hundred, and ``Failed'' P values should occur one test in
a thousand -- that is what P MEANS.  Use them at your Own Risk!  Be Warned!
```

The list of tests can be displayed using the -l option.

```
$ dieharder -l
#=============================================================================#
#                 dieharder version 3.31.1 Copyright 2003 Robert G. Brown      #
#=============================================================================#
Installed dieharder tests:
 Test Number                   Test Name                Test Reliability
===============================================================================
   -d 0                   Diehard Birthdays Test              Good
   -d 1                     Diehard OPERM5 Test               Good
   -d 2              Diehard 32x32 Binary Rank Test           Good
   -d 3               Diehard 6x8 Binary Rank Test            Good
   -d 4                   Diehard Bitstream Test              Good
```

| -d 5 | Diehard OPSO | Suspect |
|---|---|---|
| -d 6 | Diehard OQSO Test | Suspect |
| -d 7 | Diehard DNA Test | Suspect |
| -d 8 | Diehard Count the 1s (stream) Test | Good |
| -d 9 | Diehard Count the 1s Test (byte) | Good |
| -d 10 | Diehard Parking Lot Test | Good |
| -d 11 | Diehard Minimum Distance (2d Circle) Test | Good |
| -d 12 | Diehard 3d Sphere (Minimum Distance) Test | Good |
| -d 13 | Diehard Squeeze Test | Good |
| -d 14 | Diehard Sums Test | Do Not Use |
| -d 15 | Diehard Runs Test | Good |
| -d 16 | Diehard Craps Test | Good |
| -d 17 | Marsaglia and Tsang GCD Test | Good |
| -d 100 | STS Monobit Test | Good |
| -d 101 | STS Runs Test | Good |
| -d 102 | STS Serial Test (Generalized) | Good |
| -d 200 | RGB Bit Distribution Test | Good |
| -d 201 | RGB Generalized Minimum Distance Test | Good |
| -d 202 | RGB Permutations Test | Good |
| -d 203 | RGB Lagged Sum Test | Good |
| -d 204 | RGB Kolmogorov-Smirnov Test Test | Good |
| -d 205 | Byte Distribution | Good |
| -d 206 | DAB DCT | Good |
| -d 207 | DAB Fill Tree Test | Good |
| -d 208 | DAB Fill Tree 2 Test | Good |
| -d 209 | DAB Monobit 2 Test | Good |

Note the test reliability column. The reliability of a test is high when it reliably gives the same results over multiple tests on data of the same quality. Those tests that are listed as suspect and Do Not Use are unreliable and likely to report good data as having a low $P$ value, indicating it is distinguishable from random.

Since dieharder is principally intended to test PRNGs, it includes a generator code for a number of PRNGs. The program will generate enough data from the PRNG being tested to meet the needs of each test. If you are inputting file data to dieharder, using the -f option, then, you need to ensure that the data file is big enough to meet the requirements of the tests. If you have a new algorithm, an option is to incorporate the algorithm into dieharder so that it will run for as long as needed to provide the necessary data.

Passing -g n, selects generator $n$, -g -1, gets it to list out the set of built-in generators and the file input options.

```
$ dieharder -g -1
#=============================================================================#
#            dieharder version 3.31.1 Copyright 2003 Robert G. Brown          #
#=============================================================================#
```

| # | Id Test Name | | Id Test Name | | Id Test Name | # |
|---|---|---|---|---|---|---|
| | 000 borosh13 | |001 cmrg | |002 coveyou | |
| | 003 fishman18 | |004 fishman20 | |005 fishman2x | |
| | 006 gfsr4 | |007 knuthran | |008 knuthran2 | |
| | 009 knuthran2002 | |010 lecuyer21 | |011 minstd | |
| | 012 mrg | |013 mt19937 | |014 mt19937_1999 | |
| | 015 mt19937_1998 | |016 r250 | |017 ran0 | |
| | 018 ran1 | |019 ran2 | |020 ran3 | |
| | 021 rand | |022 rand48 | |023 random128-bsd | |
| | 024 random128-glibc2 | |025 random128-libc5 | |026 random256-bsd | |
| | 027 random256-glibc2 | |028 random256-libc5 | |029 random32-bsd | |
| | 030 random32-glibc2 | |031 random32-libc5 | |032 random64-bsd | |
| | 033 random64-glibc2 | |034 random64-libc5 | |035 random8-bsd | |
| | 036 random8-glibc2 | |037 random8-libc5 | |038 random-bsd | |
| | 039 random-glibc2 | |040 random-libc5 | |041 randu | |
| | 042 ranf | |043 ranlux | |044 ranlux389 | |
| | 045 ranlxd1 | |046 ranlxd2 | |047 ranlxs0 | |
| | 048 ranlxs1 | |049 ranlxs2 | |050 ranmar | |
| | 051 slatec | |052 taus | |053 taus2 | |
| | 054 taus113 | |055 transputer | |056 tt800 | |
| | 057 uni | |058 uni32 | |059 vax | |
| | 060 waterman14 | |061 zuf | | | |
| | 200 stdin_input_raw | |201 file_input_raw | |202 file_input | |
| | 203 ca | |204 uvag | |205 AES_OFB | |
| | 206 Threefish_OFB | |207 XOR (supergenerator) | |208 kiss | |
| | 209 superkiss | | | | |
| | 400 R_wichmann_hill | |401 R_marsaglia_multic. | |402 R_super_duper | |
| | 403 R_mersenne_twister | |404 R_knuth_taocp | |405 R_knuth_taocp2 | |
| | 500 /dev/random | |501 /dev/urandom | | | |

## 11.8.1 Running Dieharder Against Internal Generators

To test with all tests against an internal generator, use -a to select all tests and -g n to select the generator.

For example, to test the Fishman20 PRNG, use dieharder -a -g 004. The output is too long to show here. So, we skip a number of the passed tests and focus on the expected failures from a low-quality PRNG, such as Fishman20. The weak and fail results are marked with an arrow.

```
$ dieharder -a -g 004
#=============================================================================#
#            dieharder version 3.31.1 Copyright 2003 Robert G. Brown          #
#=============================================================================#
   rng_name    |rands/second|  Seed   |
     fishman20|  1.33e+08  |1531898547|
#=============================================================================#
        test_name   |ntup| tsamples |psamples|  p-value  |Assessment
#=============================================================================#
    diehard_birthdays|  0|      100|   100|0.56304220|  PASSED
      diehard_operm5|  0|  1000000|   100|0.70060434|  PASSED
  diehard_rank_32x32|  0|    40000|   100|0.39200732|  PASSED
    diehard_rank_6x8|  0|   100000|   100|0.42031706|  PASSED
    diehard_bitstream|  0|  2097152|   100|0.88590673|  PASSED
        diehard_opso|  0|  2097152|   100|0.00821109|  PASSED
        diehard_oqso|  0|  2097152|   100|0.15638108|  PASSED
         diehard_dna|  0|  2097152|   100|0.00000000|  FAILED <--
 diehard_count_1s_str|  0|   256000|   100|0.76010402|  PASSED
 diehard_count_1s_byt|  0|   256000|   100|0.36828192|  PASSED


    [Skip many tests]


        diehard_craps|  0|   200000|   100|0.72937259|  PASSED
        diehard_craps|  0|   200000|   100|0.40345011|  PASSED
 marsaglia_tsang_gcd|  0| 10000000|   100|0.00000000|  FAILED <--
 marsaglia_tsang_gcd|  0| 10000000|   100|0.54159731|  PASSED
         sts_monobit|  1|   100000|   100|0.99781199|   WEAK  <--
            sts_runs|  2|   100000|   100|0.00236854|   WEAK  <--
          sts_serial|  1|   100000|   100|0.60771417|  PASSED
          sts_serial|  2|   100000|   100|0.12253685|  PASSED


    [skip several repetitions of sts_serial]


          sts_serial| 16|   100000|   100|0.69782414|  PASSED
          sts_serial| 16|   100000|   100|0.81858989|  PASSED
         rgb_bitdist|  1|   100000|   100|0.04910746|  PASSED
         rgb_bitdist|  2|   100000|   100|0.40843886|  PASSED
         rgb_bitdist|  3|   100000|   100|0.12487242|  PASSED


    [skip several passed rgb_bitdist tests]


         rgb_bitdist| 11|   100000|   100|0.07316657|  PASSED
         rgb_bitdist| 12|   100000|   100|0.37861888|  PASSED
 rgb_minimum_distance|  2|    10000|  1000|0.00029813|   WEAK   <--
 rgb_minimum_distance|  3|    10000|  1000|0.00000033|  FAILED <--
 rgb_minimum_distance|  4|    10000|  1000|0.00000000|  FAILED <--
 rgb_minimum_distance|  5|    10000|  1000|0.00000364|   WEAK   <--
     rgb_permutations|  2|   100000|   100|0.88894260|  PASSED
     rgb_permutations|  3|   100000|   100|0.55647323|  PASSED
```

```
  rgb_permutations|   4|    100000|     100|0.95729286|  PASSED
  rgb_permutations|   5|    100000|     100|0.17068216|  PASSED
    rgb_lagged_sum|   0|   1000000|     100|0.47589634|  PASSED
    rgb_lagged_sum|   1|   1000000|     100|0.58095745|  PASSED


[Skipped several passed rgb_lagged_sum tests]

    rgb_lagged_sum|  31|   1000000|     100|0.29267055|  PASSED
    rgb_lagged_sum|  32|   1000000|     100|0.79058158|  PASSED
    rgb_kstest_test|  0|     10000|    1000|0.27240874|  PASSED
    dab_bytedistrib|  0|  51200000|       1|0.76581784|  PASSED
           dab_dct| 256|     50000|       1|0.35792137|  PASSED
Preparing to run test 207.  ntuple = 0
       dab_filltree|  32|  15000000|       1|0.40228986|  PASSED
       dab_filltree|  32|  15000000|       1|0.32009900|  PASSED
Preparing to run test 208.  ntuple = 0
      dab_filltree2|   0|   5000000|       1|0.05815773|  PASSED
      dab_filltree2|   1|   5000000|       1|0.51960969|  PASSED
Preparing to run test 209.  ntuple = 0
       dab_monobit2|  12|  65000000|       1|0.68393001|  PASSED
```

So, we see three tests that are listed as being reliable can distinguish data from the Fishman20 PRNG from random. The next step, to ensure that the *P* value is not just a rare outlier, is to focus on each of the tests that failed, running them multiple times. In the example below, we use -d 17 to select the marsaglia_tsang_gcd test that failed. We would do this multiple times to confirm the validity of the result.

```
$ dieharder -d 17 -g 004
#=============================================================================#
#            dieharder version 3.31.1 Copyright 2003 Robert G. Brown          #
#=============================================================================#
   rng_name    |rands/second|   Seed    |
     fishman20|  1.31e+08  |2580229865|
#=============================================================================#
        test_name   |ntup| tsamples |psamples|  p-value |Assessment
#=============================================================================#
  marsaglia_tsang_gcd|  0|  10000000|     100|0.00000000|  FAILED
  marsaglia_tsang_gcd|  0|  10000000|     100|0.88905238|  PASSED
```

## 11.8.2 Running Dieharder Against Stdin

To test data from a running program that outputs random data, we can tell dieharder to take the data from stdin, using the -g 200 option to input from raw binary. Then, pipe in the data from the program. For example, here we run a single test against the RdRand output using a quickrdrand in binary mode -b with the continuous output option -c.

```
$ quickrdrand -b -c | dieharder -d 3 -g 200
#=============================================================================#
#            dieharder version 3.31.1 Copyright 2003 Robert G. Brown        #
#=============================================================================#
   rng_name    |rands/second|   Seed   |
stdin_input_raw|   1.74e+07  |2977565777|
#=============================================================================#
         test_name   |ntup| tsamples |psamples|  p-value |Assessment
#=============================================================================#
    diehard_rank_6x8|   0|   100000|    100|0.73147361|  PASSED
```

### 11.8.3 Running Dieharder Against File Input

If you have data in a file to test, then the principle issue is making sure that the file is big enough to meet the needs of the tests. Here, djenrandom is used with standard input, with increasing amounts of data, until we stop getting an EOF (end of file) error.

```
$ djenrandom -b -k 100 | dieharder -d 3 -g 200
# stdin_input_raw(): Error: EOF
$ djenrandom -b -k 1000 | dieharder -d 3 -g 200
# stdin_input_raw(): Error: EOF
$ djenrandom -b -k 10000 | dieharder -d 3 -g 200
# stdin_input_raw(): Error: EOF
$ djenrandom -b -k 100000 | dieharder -d 3 -g 200
# stdin_input_raw(): Error: EOF
$ djenrandom -b -k 1000000 | dieharder -d 3 -g 200
#=============================================================================#
#            dieharder version 3.31.1 Copyright 2003 Robert G. Brown        #
#=============================================================================#
   rng_name    |rands/second|   Seed   |
stdin_input_raw|   5.54e+05  |3100298057|
#=============================================================================#
         test_name   |ntup| tsamples |psamples|  p-value |Assessment
#=============================================================================#
    diehard_rank_6x8|   0|   100000|    100|0.41090496|  PASSED
```

As we can see, the test does not run until a gigabyte of data is available. Some tests take more data than others.

Raw file input is selected with -g 201. -f <filename> is used to the indicate the file name to dieharder.

For example, first we make a 1 gigabyte binary file of random data

```
$ quickrdrand -b -k 1048576 > GigRand.bin
```

then we test the file with dieharder.

```
$ dieharder -d 3 -g 201 -f GigRand.bin
#=============================================================================#
#            dieharder version 3.31.1 Copyright 2003 Robert G. Brown          #
#=============================================================================#
   rng_name    |           filename          |rands/second|
 file_input_raw|                     GigRand.bin|  1.74e+07  |
#=============================================================================#
        test_name   |ntup| tsamples |psamples|  p-value |Assessment
#=============================================================================#
    diehard_rank_6x8|   0|    100000|     100|0.70545937|  PASSED
```

## 11.9 NIST STS 2.1.2

NIST has published a test suite for the NIST SP800-22Rev1a statistical test specification. Just as Dieharder, this is a battery of hypothesis tests for distinguishability from
random. There is some overlap between NIST's STS and the Dieharder tests.

The code can be downloaded from http://csrc.nist.gov/groups/ST/toolkit/rng/
documents/sts-2.1.2.zip.

Unfortunately, the NIST STS software has some significant flaws. Rather than being command-line driven, it has an interactive text mode user-interface that is hard to
use, and also there are significant bugs.

For example, we start here with a 1 mibibyte binary uniform random file
megrand.bin and try to test it with the STS. The command is assess.

It starts with unclear parameter requirements.

```
$ ./assess
Usage: ./assess <stream length>
   <stream length> is the length of the individual bit stream(s) to be processed
```

If we try 1, the program starts up in the following manner:

```
$ ./assess 1
          G E N E R A T O R    S E L E C T I O N
          ----------------------------------------

   [0] Input File              [1] Linear Congruential
   [2] Quadratic Congruential I   [3] Quadratic Congruential II
   [4] Cubic Congruential       [5] XOR
   [6] Modular Exponentiation   [7] Blum-Blum-Shub
   [8] Micali-Schnorr           [9] G Using SHA-1

   Enter Choice: 0
```

We select 0, because we want to read from the file.

```
User Prescribed Input File: megrand.bin

          S T A T I S T I C A L   T E S T S
          ------------------------------------

[01] Frequency                        [02] Block Frequency
[03] Cumulative Sums                   [04] Runs
[05] Longest Run of Ones               [06] Rank
[07] Discrete Fourier Transform        [08] Nonperiodic Template Matchings
[09] Overlapping Template Matchings    [10] Universal Statistical
[11] Approximate Entropy               [12] Random Excursions
[13] Random Excursions Variant         [14] Serial
[15] Linear Complexity

   INSTRUCTIONS
       Enter 0 if you DO NOT want to apply all of the
       statistical tests to each sequence and 1 if you DO.

Enter Choice: 1
```

We go with 1 to run all the tests.

```
    P a r a m e t e r   A d j u s t m e n t s
    ------------------------------------------
[1] Block Frequency Test - block length(M):         128
[2] NonOverlapping Template Test - block length(m): 9
[3] Overlapping Template Test - block length(m):    9
[4] Approximate Entropy Test - block length(m):     10
[5] Serial Test - block length(m):                  16
[6] Linear Complexity Test - block length(M):       500

Select Test (0 to continue): 0
```

Next, we are asked "How many bitstreams?" Presumably it is one, since we have only one file.

```
How many bitstreams? 1

Input File Format:
  [0] ASCII - A sequence of ASCII 0's and 1's
  [1] Binary - Each byte in data file contains 8 bits of data

Select input mode:   1

  Statistical Testing In Progress........
```

```
igam: UNDERFLOW
      Statistical Testing Complete!!!!!!!!!!!!!

Segmentation fault: 11
```

And the program crashes with a segfault; a fine example of quality government software.

This time we make a guess that it wants to be given the number of bits in the file. The file is 1 mibibyte, which is $1024 \cdot 1024 \cdot 8 = 8388608$ bits.

```
$ ./assess 8388608
```

We then run through the same sequence of questions, and it appears to run.

```
How many bitstreams? 1

Input File Format:
  [0] ASCII - A sequence of ASCII 0's and 1's
  [1] Binary - Each byte in data file contains 8 bits of data

Select input mode:  1

  Statistical Testing In Progress.........

  Statistical Testing Complete!!!!!!!!!!!!!
```

However, there is no result printed. Maybe no result indicates no failures, but this is not clear, and there is no manual. So, to see what happens with a test failure, this run will use correlated data with SCC=0.2 of exactly the same size. This should fail the tests, so we can see what the software returns when given data that should fail the tests.

```
$ djenrandom -b -k 1024 -m correlated --correlation=0.2 > badmegrand.bin
$ ls -l *.bin
-rw-r--r--  1 dj  staff  1048576 Apr  1 17:39 badmegrand.bin
-rw-r--r--  1 dj  staff  1048576 Apr  1 17:09 megrand.bin
$
```

And run it through assess.

```
$ ./assess 8388608
            G E N E R A T O R    S E L E C T I O N
            ------------------------------------------
[... Skipping through the same steps]
  Input File Format:
    [0] ASCII - A sequence of ASCII 0's and 1's
```

```
[1] Binary - Each byte in data file contains 8 bits of data

Select input mode:  1

    Statistical Testing In Progress.........
```
```
igamc: UNDERFLOW
igamc: UNDERFLOW
igamc: UNDERFLOW
igamc: UNDERFLOW
igamc: UNDERFLOW
igamc: UNDERFLOW
```

The code appears to get stuck in an endless loop reporting igamc: UNDERFLOW. Cancelling it and restarting, we end up with yet another crash.

```
Select input mode:  1

    Statistical Testing In Progress.........
```
```
igamc: UNDERFLOW
igamc: UNDERFLOW
Segmentation fault: 11
```

So, the NIST STS 2.1.2 test suite appears to have significant bugs and cannot be recommended. The Python implementations of all the SP800-22 tests written to accompany this book do work and so can be used in place of the NIST STS. They are available at https://github.com/dj-on-github/sp800_22_tests.

## 11.10 NIST SP800-90B Entropy Assessment Suite

The draft specification NIST SP800-90B includes a number of statistic metric tests to measure the entropy of unprocessed random data from an entropy source.

It can be downloaded from github at https://github.com/usnistgov/SP800-90B_EntropyAssessment.

Fortunately, this NIST software, unlike the NIST STS, comes with a user manual. The specification distinguishes between IID (Independent and Identically Distributed) entropy source and non-IID entropy source. There is a suite to measure the entropy of non-IID sources and a suite to test IID sources.

With an entropy source, a common failure is that while the data looks random, the data may be similar or the same as previous outputs, when the entropy source is restarted, typically, by powering the source off and on again. For this, there is a restart test, which is fed restart sequences taken from multiple restarts of the source.

First impressions are not encouraging:

```
./noniid_main.py: line 17: import: command not found
from: can't read /var/mail/util90b
from: can't read /var/mail/mostCommonValue
from: can't read /var/mail/noniid_collision
from: can't read /var/mail/markov
from: can't read /var/mail/maurer
from: can't read /var/mail/SP90Bv2_predictors
from: can't read /var/mail/tuple
from: can't read /var/mail/LRS
./noniid_main.py: line 35: syntax error near unexpected token `('
./noniid_main.py: line 35: `    args = get_parser('non-IID').parse_args()'
```

This turns out to be because the code does not include a hash-bang line at the start to tell the system to run the program as Python. To fix this, add #!/usr/r/bin/env python to the first line of noniid_main.py or invoke it with python noniid_main.py.

```
$ python ./noniid_main.py -h
usage: noniid_main.py [-h] [-u use_bits] [-v] datafile bits_per_symbol

Run the Draft NIST SP 800-90B (January 2016) non-IID Tests

positional arguments:
  datafile              dataset on which to run tests
  bits_per_symbol       number of bits used to represent sample output values

optional arguments:
  -h, --help            show this help message and exit
  -u use_bits, --usebits use_bits
                        use only the N lowest order bits per sample
  -v, --verbose         verbose mode: show detailed test results
```

We will start with some serially correlated data SCC = −0.2. Serially correlated data is non-IID, because bits are not independent. Since the correlation is negative, the most likely values are 01010101 or 10101010, which are equiprobable.

Using the method in Section 8.8.4, we compute the probability of 1 following 0 as $0.5 + \frac{0.2}{2} = 0.6$. Similarly, the probability of 0 following 1 is 0.6. So, the probability of 10101010 or 01010101 is $0.5 \cdot 0.6^7$. The first bit is equiprobable, and the subsequent bits have the correlated probability of 0.6. So, the min-entropy per byte is

$$-\log_2(0.5 \cdot 0.6^7) \approx 6.89572$$

bits of entropy per byte, or approximately 86% entropy per bit. This assumes that we are ignorant of the previous output. If we know the previous output bit, then the probability of the first bit is 0.6 not 0.5. So, the probability of 10101010 or 01010101 from an

RNG, where we know the previous outputs, is

$$-\log_2(0.6^8) \approx 5.89572$$

bits of entropy per byte, or approximately 74% entropy per bit. We can run this data through the non-IID tool to see how accurate the test is.

Since the data is generated bit-by-bit, and the dependency is purely between adjacent bits, the noniid_main.py program is invoked with a symbol length of 1 bit.

```
$ python noniid_main.py -v corrm0p2.bin 1
reading 1048576 bytes of data
Read in file corrm0p2.bin, 1048576 bytes long.
Dataset: 1048576 1-bit symbols, 2 symbols in alphabet.
Output symbol values: min = 0, max = 1

Running entropic statistic estimates:
 - Most Common Value Estimate: p(max) = 0.501991, min-entropy = 0.994266
 - Collision Estimate: p(max) = 0.537109, min-entropy = 0.896712
 - Markov Estimate: p(max) = 4.41646e-39, min-entropy = 0.995409
 - Compression Estimate: p(max) = 0.5, min-entropy = 1
 - t-Tuple Estimate: p(max) = 0.526897, min-entropy = 0.924408
 - LRS Estimate: p(max) = 0.501736, min-entropy = 0.994999

Running predictor estimates:
Computing MultiMCW Prediction Estimate: 99 percent complete
        Pglobal: 0.501316
        Plocal: 0.443529
MultiMCW Prediction Estimate: p(max) = 0.501316, min-entropy = 0.996209

Computing Lag Prediction Estimate: 99 percent complete
        Pglobal: 0.501481
        Plocal: 0.388154
Lag Prediction Estimate: p(max) = 0.501481, min-entropy = 0.995732

Computing MultiMMC Prediction Estimate: 99 percent complete
        Pglobal: 0.500885
        Plocal: 0.407621
MultiMMC Prediction Estimate: p(max) = 0.500885, min-entropy = 0.997449

Computing LZ78Y Prediction Estimate: 99 percent complete
        Pglobal: 0.500980
        Plocal: 0.426059
LZ78Y Prediction Estimate: p(max) = 0.50098, min-entropy = 0.997176
-----------------------
min-entropy = 0.896712

Don't forget to run the sanity check on a restart dataset using H_I = 0.896712
```

Our best case min-entropy for a signal guess was 86%. The min-entropy for the general case was 74%, yet the tool is giving an estimate of over 89%.

So, we can try this with 8-bit symbols to see what we get.

```
$ python noniid_main.py -v corrm0p2.bin 8
reading 1048576 bytes of data
Read in file corrm0p2.bin, 1048576 bytes long.
Dataset: 1048576 8-bit symbols, 256 symbols in alphabet.
Output symbol values: min = 0, max = 255

Running entropic statistic estimates:
- Most Common Value Estimate: p(max) = 0.0143485, min-entropy = 6.12296
- Collision Estimate: p(max) = 0.0473854, min-entropy = 4.39941
- Markov Estimate (map 6 bits): p(max) = 1.79968e-180, min-entropy = 4.66484
- Compression Estimate: p(max) = 0.0728725, min-entropy = 3.77848
- t-Tuple Estimate: p(max) = 0.0158071, min-entropy = 5.98329
- LRS Estimate: p(max) = 0.00592078, min-entropy = 7.4

Running predictor estimates:
Computing MultiMCW Prediction Estimate: 99 percent complete
        Pglobal: 0.013927
        Plocal: 0.009897
MultiMCW Prediction Estimate: p(max) = 0.0139273, min-entropy = 6.16595

Computing Lag Prediction Estimate: 99 percent complete
        Pglobal: 0.005343
        Plocal: 0.002119
Lag Prediction Estimate: p(max) = 0.00534252, min-entropy = 7.54826

Computing MultiMMC Prediction Estimate: 99 percent complete
        Pglobal: 0.014999
        Plocal: 0.009897
MultiMMC Prediction Estimate: p(max) = 0.0149989, min-entropy = 6.059

Computing LZ78Y Prediction Estimate: 99 percent complete
        Pglobal: 0.014998
        Plocal: 0.009897
LZ78Y Prediction Estimate: p(max) = 0.0149981, min-entropy = 6.05907
-----------------------
min-entropy = 3.77848

Don't forget to run the sanity check on a restart dataset using H_I = 3.77848
```

Now the result of the measurement is dramatically worse than the actual min-entropy. 3.77848 bits of entropy per 8 bits is approximately 47% entropic.

So, the min-entropy estimates of these tests appear to be problematic for serially correlated entropy sources.

There was an earlier version of the Markov test that allowed the group size and number of steps in the Markov chain to be controlled. This gives results that are closer to the actual min-entropy.

```
$entropyTest -t markov -i 1 -o 1 -s 9 -g 10 -b corrm0p2.bin
Warning: steps = 9 (10 samples)
Warning: groupLength = 10
Filename: corrm0p2.bin
Test name: markov
Number of samples: 16777216
Number of events: 0
Mean score: 0.000000
Adjusted mean score: 0.000000
Standard deviation: 0.000000
Entropy type: min-entropy
Entropy estimate: 7.910299
```

Since that result is 7.91 bits of entropy per 10 bits, that is 79% entropy.

Doing a frequency histogram of the 256-byte values in the data, we find that the values 0xAA and 0x55 (10101010 and 01010101 in binary, respectively) were the most frequent values, as expected; and taking the negative log base 2 and dividing by 8 bits yield approximately 76.969% entropy, which is a very close to the actual 74% entropy of the generated data.

So, a lesson to learn from this is to not trust the non-IID min-entropy estimation tools until you have tested the tools. Use programs, such as djenrandom to create data with known entropy, and use that to calibrate the min-entropy estimation tools, before you run them on the data. Use models that generate data with statistical properties similar to the entropy source. Create a model, if necessary. The SUMS model in djenrandom was created to model a class of metastable entropy sources with feedback and was effective in showing that the simulation model results matched predicted results of a mathematical model and the measured results of the entropy source circuit, thus giving confidence in the entropy result.

# 12  RdRand and RdSeed Instructions in x86 CPUs

## 12.1  Intel DRNG

The Intel DRNG (Digital Random Number Generator) is included in all Intel CPUs since the Ivy Bridge models in 2011. It is accessed through the RdRand instruction. The RdSeed instruction has been available since the release of the Broadwell architecture in Desktop CPUs, and the CherryView architecture in low power SoCs (System on Chip).

The design is based on the SP800-90 specification. However, at the time, that specification only defined DRBG (Deterministic Random Bit Generator) algorithms (more commonly termed PRNGs). The entropy source and entropy extractor was left for the implementer to work out, so Intel developed a metastable entropy source and CBC-MAC-based extractor design.

Later, SP800-90 was renamed SP800-90A, and drafts of SP800-90B and C were released. The original SP800-90B draft did not include the AES-CBC-MAC extractor. We made a submission to NIST asking it to be included and proposing text, and they did include it in the later drafts along with CMAC and HMAC options. The B and C drafts remain draft standards at the time of writing.

The entropy source is based on metastability of a latch with a differential feedback circuit. It was mostly made from logic gates, and so was manufacturable in normal semiconductor processes. This was the enabling technology that precipitated the rest of the development.

The entropy extractor algorithm chosen was AES-CBC-MAC. Since CBC MAC can be built with an AES block cipher at its core, and the SP800-90 CTR DRBG algorithm can also be built with an AES block cipher at its core, the extractor and DRBG could be designed to share the same AES block cipher.[1]

To meet the requirements for RNGs in FIPS 140-2, the design also needed to exclude scan chain test from the logic, because it could be used as an attack vector, to shift in known state or shift out keys. So instead, a BIST (Built In Self Test) system was added that tested the integrity of the logic, both during manufacture and every time the chip powers on.

Also needed was an online self test for the entropy source. The pattern counting test described in Section 9.7 was developed for the online test. This was a tagging test as described in Section 9.1 that tagged the blocks of data going into the extractor as healthy or unhealthy.

---

[1] A paper [7] by Yvgenny Dodis, Rosario Gennaro, Johan Håstad, Hugo Krawczyk, and Rabin Tal, which proved that the CBC MAC algorithm was a secure entropy extractor.

https://doi.org/10.1515/9781501506062-012

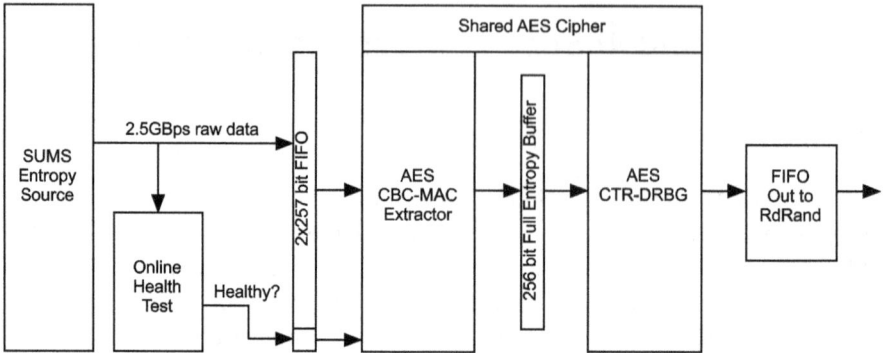

**Figure 12.1:** Ivy Bridge Intel DRNG Architecture.

The resulting structure is shown in Figure 12.1.

The buffer that takes in the 256-bit chunks of data from the entropy source also takes in the health tag from the online health test. This health tag travels with the data through the buffer.

Since the output of AES is only 128 bits, the output of AES-CBC-MAC is also 128 bits. However, the number of bits to reseed the SP800-90 AES-CTR-DRBG is equal to the key size (128) plus the AES data block size (128), meaning 256 bits were needed from the extractor for each reseed. So, a 256-bit intermediate buffer was included to take in the full-entropy data from the entropy extractor. Once the 256 bits of extractor data are available in the buffer, the DRBG will reseed. At other times, the DRBG will be filling the output buffer by generating data. If the output buffers are all full and the reseed buffer was full, the whole RNG sleeps to save power. An incoming bus read to read in data will wake up the RNG, a value will be pulled from the FIFO, and so the DRBG will then push out another random number and reseed.

The entropy extractor takes in data 128 bits at a time, and for each 128 bits it computes one round of the AES-CBC-MAC algorithm. In practice, it performs this process in pairs, once for the lower half of the 256-bit seed, and once for the upper half. This is due to the health tag from the OHT, which is attached to the 256-bit input data chunk, whereas each round of AES-CBC-MAC consumes 128 bits. So, two rounds of CBC-MAC can happen for each chunk of 256 bits of raw data from the OHT.

The number of rounds of CBC-MAC is counted, and a seed is issued to the DRBG for reseeding, when the counter reaches 3, resulting in 4 rounds. However, if the health tag is 0, indicating the input data failed the online health test, then the data will still be entered into the CBC-MAC calculation, but the counter will not increment. So, all unhealthy tagged data is still mixed into to the seed, but it is not counted. The extractor requires 4 healthy tagged samples before it will issue a seed.

### 12.1.1 RdRand Instruction

The RdRand instruction is encoded within 3 or 4 bytes. The encoding is described in the Intel Instruction Reference at https://www.intel.com/content/dam/www/public/us/en/documents/manuals/64-ia-32-architectures-software-developer-instruction-set-reference-manual-325383.pdf.

If it has a 16- or 32-bit destination register, the encoding in the Intel instruction reference is "0F C7 /6". This means 0x0f, 0xc7 followed by a ModR/M byte, which specifies the destination register.

For 16-bit and 64-bit destinations, there is a prefix byte added to indicate the size.

The full encoding for 16-, 32-, and 64-bit destinations is shown in Tables 12.1, 12.2, and 12.3.

| 16-Bit Destination Register | Hex RdRand Encoding |
|---|---|
| ax | 66 0F C7 F0 |
| cx | 66 0F C7 F1 |
| dx | 66 0F C7 F2 |
| bx | 66 0F C7 F3 |
| sp | 66 0F C7 F4 |
| bp | 66 0F C7 F5 |
| si | 66 0F C7 F6 |
| di | 66 0F C7 F7 |

Table 12.1: Instruction Encodings for RdRand with 16-Bit Destination Registers.

| 32-Bit Destination Register | Hex RdRand Encoding |
|---|---|
| eax | 0F C7 F0 |
| ecx | 0F C7 F1 |
| edx | 0F C7 F2 |
| ebx | 0F C7 F3 |
| esp | 0F C7 F4 |
| ebp | 0F C7 F5 |
| esi | 0F C7 F6 |
| edi | 0F C7 F7 |

Table 12.2: Instruction Encodings for RdRand with 32-Bit Destination Registers.

| 64-Bit Destination Register | Hex RdRand Encoding |
|---|---|
| rax | 48 0F C7 F0 |
| rcx | 48 0F C7 F1 |
| rdx | 48 0F C7 F2 |
| rbx | 48 0F C7 F3 |
| rsp | 48 0F C7 F4 |
| rbp | 48 0F C7 F5 |
| rsi | 48 0F C7 F6 |
| rdi | 48 0F C7 F7 |

Table 12.3: Instruction Encodings for RdRand with 64-Bit Destination Registers.

### 12.1.2 RdSeed

The RdSeed instruction has the same structure as the RdRand instruction, but the ModR/M field is in a different range.

The full encoding for 16-, 32-, and 64-bit destinations is shown in Tables 12.4, 12.5, and 12.6.

| 16-Bit Destination Register | Hex RdSeed Encoding |
|---|---|
| ax | 66 0F C7 F8 |
| cx | 66 0F C7 F9 |
| dx | 66 0F C7 FA |
| bx | 66 0F C7 FB |
| sp | 66 0F C7 FC |
| bp | 66 0F C7 FD |
| si | 66 0F C7 FE |
| di | 66 0F C7 FF |

**Table 12.4:** Instruction Encodings for RdSeed with 16-Bit Destination Registers.

| 32-Bit Destination Register | Hex RdSeed Encoding |
|---|---|
| eax | 0F C7 F8 |
| ecx | 0F C7 F9 |
| edx | 0F C7 FA |
| ebx | 0F C7 FB |
| esp | 0F C7 FC |
| ebp | 0F C7 FD |
| esi | 0F C7 FE |
| edi | 0F C7 FF |

**Table 12.5:** Instruction Encodings for RdSeed with 32-Bit Destination Registers.

| 64-Bit Destination Register | Hex RdSeed Encoding |
|---|---|
| rax | 48 0F C7 F8 |
| rcx | 48 0F C7 F9 |
| rdx | 48 0F C7 FA |
| rbx | 48 0F C7 FB |
| rsp | 48 0F C7 FC |
| rbp | 48 0F C7 FD |
| rsi | 48 0F C7 FE |
| rdi | 48 0F C7 FF |

**Table 12.6:** Instruction Encodings for RdSeed with 64-Bit Destination Registers.

The publication of the draft SP800-90C draft specification came after the first release of the RdRand instruction in Intel products. The RdSeed instruction implements a feature in this specification, the XOR construction NRBG.

The SP800-90C draft specification describes two structures for full-entropy outputs, the Oversampling Construction and the XOR construction.

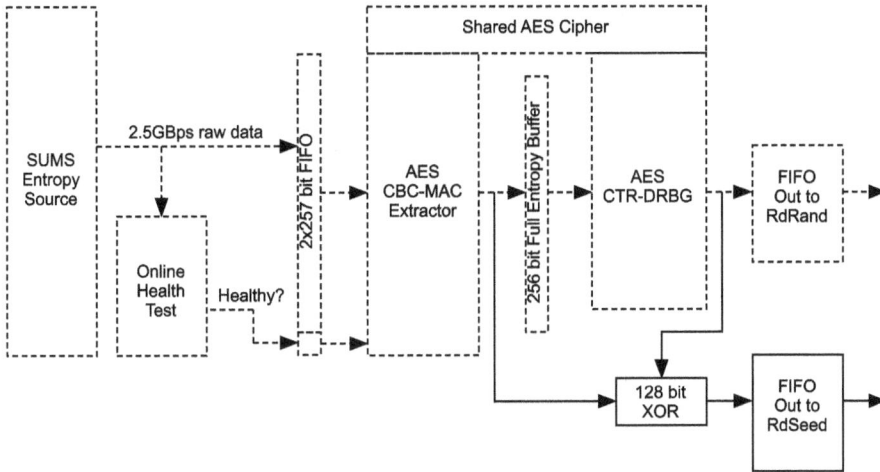

**Figure 12.2:** RdSeed NRBG Addition.

An XOR construction NRBG (Nondeterministic Random Bit Generator) was added to the DRNG design to comply with the draft specification.

In this structure, a seed from the extractor is taken and XORed with an output from the DRBG, and the result is passed into the NRBG output FIFO. The full-entropy seed data from the extractor can either go to reseed the DRBG or it can go to the NRBG output. A round robin scheduler decides where it will go when both the NRBG queue is not full and the DRBG wants to be reseeded.

The highlighted additional logic for the NRBG path is shown in Figure 12.2.

The NRBG output data go to a register from which the CPU reads when the RdSeed instruction is executed.

### 12.1.3 AMD Support for RdRand and RdSeed

In recent AMD CPUs, support for the RdRand and RdSeed instructions was added. However, I have been unable to find detailed information or audit reports that describe the RNG design or the entropy quality.

# 13 Accessing RNGs from Software

In this chapter, we look at ways to access RNGs in software on various platforms and languages. Some CPUs offer built-in RNGs. Some platforms include RNGs that are accessible by the CPU. Some languages offer ways of accessing RNGs, and some operating systems offer API interfaces or file system interfaces to access RNGs.

The cases we look at here are:

- The MacOS and BSD getentropy() syscall;
- The Linux getrandom() syscall;
- The Unix and Linux /dev/random and /dev/urandom services;
- The Intel RdRand and RdSeed CPU Instructions;
- The Python Random Library;
- The Windows CryptRand API.

## 13.1 MacOS and BSD getentropy()

The MacOSX operating system available on Apple computers provides a syscall getentropy() that writes secure random numbers to a buffer. The function prototype is in the sys/random.h header.

getentropy() takes two arguments; first a pointer to the destination of the random numbers, and second, a size_t value, giving the number of bytes of random data to fetch.

If the call is successful, then 0 is returned, otherwise, –1 is returned.

The C example below was compiled with the LLVM clang C compiler on MacOS 10.12.6.

**Listing 13.1:** getentropy.c

```
#include <stdio.h>
#include <stdint.h>
#include <sys/random.h>

int main() {
    uint32_t buffer[64];
    int i;
    int result;
    result = getentropy(buffer, 64*sizeof(uint32_t));

    if (result == 0) {
        for(i=0;i<64;i++) printf("%08x\n",buffer[i]);
    }
    return result;
}
```

https://doi.org/10.1515/9781501506062-013

The BSD operating system also supports the same getentropy() call. However, unlike MacOSX, the header file is unistd.h. So, the BSD version below is different from the MacOSX version only in the include line that includes unistd.h instead of random.h

**Listing 13.2:** bsd_getentropy.c

```
#include <stdio.h>
#include <stdint.h>
#include <unistd.h>

int main() {
    uint32_t buffer[64];
    int i;
    int result;
    result = getentropy(buffer, 64*sizeof(uint32_t));

    if (result == 0) {
        for(i=0;i<64;i++) printf("%08x\n",buffer[i]);
    }
    return result;
}
```

## 13.2 Linux getrandom() Syscall

The Linux operating system Kernel has supported a getrandom() syscall in kernel versions since 3.17. glibc has supported the function interface since version 2.25.

Details are available at http://man7.org/linux/man-pages/man2/getrandom.2.html.

getentropy() takes three arguments; first, a pointer to the destination of the random numbers; second, a size_t value, giving the number of bytes of random data to fetch, and third, a flags value.

The function returns –1 if no data was written to the buffer; otherwise, the function returns the number of bytes written to the buffer, which may be less than the requested number.

Two flags are here defined:

- GRND_RANDOM. By default getrandom() will pull data from the same source as /dev/urandom. With the GRND_RANDOM flag set, getrandom() will pull from the same source as /dev/random. With this option, there is a likelihood that the requested bytes are not available, and so the function will either block or return with no data, based on the GRND_NONBLOCK flag.
- GRND_NONBLOCK. If no data is available from the source, getrandom, by default, will block until data becomes available. If the GRND_NONBLOCK flag is set, then when data is not available from the source, getrandom() will return –1 immediately, instead of blocking.

The function is a system call; so instead of calling getrandom() as implied in the documentation, the function needs to be called through the syscall() interface. The C code below shows this.

This was compiled using gcc on a Fedora Core 23 Linux Operating System.

**Listing 13.3:** getrandom.c

```
#include<stdio.h>
#include<stdint.h>
#include<unistd.h>
#include<syscall.h>
#include<errno.h>
#include<linux/random.h>

int main() {

    unsigned char buffer[64];
    int i;
    int result;
    result = syscall(SYS_getrandom, buffer, 64, 0);

    if (result > 0) {
        printf("%d_bytes_returned\n",result);
        for(i=0;i<result;i++) {
            printf("%02x",buffer[i]);
            if ((i > 0) && (((i+1) % 4) == 0)) printf("\n");
        }
        if ((i%4) != 0) printf("\n");
    }
    else {
        printf("Error._getrandom()_returned_errno_%d\n",errno);
        return -1;
    }
    return 0;
}
```

Since the length of the data returned from getrandom() may be any number of bytes, up to the requested number, the output printing routing needs to cope with printing the final newline at the end of the final line if the total number of bytes is not a multiple of the line length. This is the reason for the more complicated output routing compared to the MacOSX and BSD getentropy() function example.

## 13.3 /dev/random and /dev/urandom

Unix-based operating systems, such as SysV Unix, Linux, and MacOSX all provide access to an operating system based software RNG. This access is through two synthetic files at /dev/random and /dev/urandom and an IOCTL API interface.

The code below uses the unix standard open() and read() calls to access /dev/u-random.

**Listing 13.4:** devrandom.c

```c
#include <stdio.h>
#include <stdint.h>
#include <sys/stat.h>
#include <fcntl.h>
#include <unistd.h>

int main() {
    uint32_t buffer[64];
    int f;
    int result;
    int i;

    f = open("/dev/urandom", O_RDONLY);
    if (f < 0) {
        printf("Error:_open()_failed_to_open_/dev/random_for_reading\n");
        return -1;
    }

    result = read(f, buffer, 64*sizeof(uint32_t));

    if (result < 0) {
        printf("error,_failed_to_read_%lu_bytes\n",64*sizeof(uint32_t));
        return -1;
    }

    for(i=0;i<64;i++) printf("%08x\n",buffer[i]);
    return 0;
}
```

Alternatively, this can be done with ANSI C standard file IO.

**Listing 13.5:** devrandom2.c

```c
#include <stdio.h>
#include <stdint.h>

int main() {
    uint32_t buffer[64];
    FILE *f;
    int result;
    int i;

    f = fopen("/dev/urandom", "r");
    if (f == NULL) {
        printf("Error:_open()_failed_to_open_/dev/random_for_reading\n");
        return 1;
```

```
}

result = fread(buffer, sizeof(uint32_t), 64,f);

if (result < 1) {
    printf("error,_failed_to_read_and_words\n");
    return 1;
}

printf("Read_%d_words_from_/dev/urandom\n",result);
for(i=0;i<result;i++) printf("%08x\n",buffer[i]);
return 0;
}
```

## 13.4 RdRand and RdSeed

The RdRand and RdSeed instructions are two instructions available on Intel X86 CPUs and recent AMD CPUs. The underlying physical RNGs on Intel and AMD CPUs are not the same, but both claim to conform to SP800-90.

Access from C is typically done through inline assembly. This is simple. However, the details vary between windows and Linux, because the calling conventions are different. In addition, the CPUID instruction should be used to identify whether or not the instructions are available, and this involves additional assembly.

The RdRand instruction returns a value into the destination register and, if a value was returned, then the carry flag is set. If no value was returned, then the carry flag will be clear.

The Intel Software Developer's Guide indicates that the correct procedure is to retry RdRand up to 10 times until the carry flag indicates a value was returned, or 10 retries occur without a value being returned, and the program should infer that an error has occurred. In practice, RdRand always returns a value. This is true in all Intel products released before 2018. However, the rationale is that in the future this may not remain true, and transitory underflow errors might occur in future products. What Intel is guaranteeing is that, if the RNG is working, then 10 retries will always return a value.

The reason RdRand always returns a value, regardless of how many threads are simultaneously executing the RdRand instruction, is that the RNG is designed to output data faster than the on-chip bus to which it is attached. So, instead of underflowing, accesses to the RNG's bus port queue up and the instructions take longer under high load, rather than leading to underflows.

The maximum throughput of RdRand varies between platforms. Low power embedded Intel CPUs run as slow as 200 mibytes/s. The fastest Intel server CPUs can provide up to 2 gibytes/s at the time of writing.

While I have not measured it directly, the Bulldozer performance is reported to be substantially slower, while more recent AMD CPUs somewhat improve the speed.

Intel gives no upper iteration limit for the RdSeed instruction. The rate of random values available for RdSeed from the RNG is slower than for RdRand, because RdSeed returns full-entropy values from the extractor output instead of outputs from the hardware DRBG. A guide for the available throughput is given for RdSeed, and the instruction may underflow under heavy load. Nevertheless, RdSeed is a faster RNG than most other available RNGs.

The code below is from the rdrand_stdint library that I have maintained for a number of years for personal use. This is the current version of C code, first developed for accessing RdRand with C code compiled with GCC on Linux. It has been extended to work on Windows under visual studio, Linux with GCC, and MacOSX with CLang. It has also been updated to use the stdint types uint16_t, uint32_t, and uint64_t, so that data sizes are explicit.

Variations on this code have been published by Intel in reference libraries for RdRand and RdSeed. However, I find this code to be more convenient to compile and link with code than a pre-compiled library.

The library defines 13 functions:

- int rdrand16_step(uint16_t *therand)
  This executes a single RdRand instruction with a 16-bit destination and places the result in the location given in the parameter. On success, it returns 1; on underflow it returns 0.
- int rdseed16_step(uint16_t *therand)
  This executes a single RdSeed instruction with a 16-bit destination and places the result in the location given in the parameter. On success, it returns 1; on underflow, it returns 0.
- int rdrand32_step(uint32_t *therand)
  This executes a single RdRand instruction with a 32-bit destination and places the result in the location given in the parameter. On success, it returns 1; on underflow, it returns 0.
- int rdseed32_step(uint32_t *therand)
  This executes a single RdSeed instruction with a 32-bit destination and places the result in the location given in the parameter. On success, it returns 1; on underflow, it returns 0.
- int rdrand64_step(uint64_t *therand)
  This executes a single RdRand instruction with a 64-bit destination and places the result in the location given in the parameter. On success, it returns 1; on underflow, it returns 0.
- int rdseed64_step(uint64_t *therand)
  This executes a single RdSeed instruction with a 64-bit destination and places the result in the location given in the parameter. On success, it returns 1; on underflow, it returns 0.

- int rdrand_get_uint32_retry(uint32_t retry_limit, uint32_t *dest);
  This executes the RdRand instruction with a 32-bit destination inside a retry loop for up to retry_limit iterations. The resulting data is written to the location pointed to by dest.
- int rdrand_get_uint32_retry(uint32_t retry_limit, uint32_t *dest);
  This executes the RdRand instruction with a 32 bit destination inside a retry loop for up to retry_limit iterations. The resulting data is written to the location pointed to by dest.
  If it is successful, then 1 is returned. In the case of underflow, 0 is returned.
- int rdseed_get_uint32_retry(uint32_t retry_limit, uint32_t *dest);
  This executes the RdSeed instruction with a 32 bit destination inside a retry loop for up to retry_limit iterations. The resulting data is written to the location pointed to by dest.
  If it is successful, then 1 is returned. In the case of underflow, 0 is returned.
- int rdrand_get_uint64_retry(uint32_t retry_limit, uint64_t *dest);
  This executes the RdRand instruction with a 64 bit destination inside a retry loop for up to retry_limit iterations. The resulting data is written to the location pointed to by dest.
  If it is successful, then 1 is returned. In the case of underflow, 0 is returned.
- int rdseed_get_uint64_retry(uint32_t retry_limit, uint64_t *dest);
  This executes the RdSeed instruction with a 64 bit destination inside a retry loop for up to retry_limit iterations. The resulting data is written to the location pointed to by dest.
  If it is successful, then 1 is returned. In the case of underflow, 0 is returned.
- int rdrand_check_support()
  This returns 1 if the RdRand instruction is available. Otherwise 0 is returned.
- int rdseed_check_support()
  This returns 1 if the RdSeed instruction is available. Otherwise, 0 is returned.

The lower level _step functions are useful when composing your own loops that may fetch specific amounts of data, or include custom error handling. The _retry functions perform the retry loop in accordance with Intel recommendations.

The C example below first checks for RdRand support, then fetches 32 64-bit random numbers with RdRand. It uses a retry limit of 10 consistent with the guidelines.

**Listing 13.6:** rdrandlibtest.c

```
#include <stdio.h>
#include <stdint.h>
#include "rdrand_stdint.h"

int main() {

    int i;
```

```
    uint64_t buffer[32];

    i = 0;

    if (rdrand_check_support() == 1) {
        for(i=0;i<32;i++) rdrand_get_uint64_retry(10,&buffer[i]);

        for(i=0;i<32;i++) printf("%01611x\n",buffer[i]);
    }
    else printf("RdRand␣instruction␣not␣supported\n");

}
```

This second example uses RdSeed. Since RdSeed can underflow, this checks the return value and keeps calling until enough random numbers are retrieved. The retry limit is set at 1000.

**Listing 13.7:** rdseedlibtest.c

```
#include <stdio.h>
#include <stdint.h>
#include "rdrand_stdint.h"

int main() {

    int i;
    uint64_t buffer[32];
    int result;
    i = 0;

    if (rdseed_check_support() == 1) {
        for(i=0;i<32;i++) {
            do result = rdseed_get_uint64_retry(1000,&buffer[i]);
            while (result == 0);
        }
        for(i=0;i<32;i++) printf("%01611x\n",buffer[i]);
    }
    else printf("RdRand␣instruction␣not␣supported\n");

}
```

Here, we look at lower-level codes to directly access RdRand and RdSeed and check the CPUID bits for RdRand and RdSeed support.

The CPUID instruction returns data about the CPU. It has multiple leaves, which are selected with the EAX register. Put the leaf numbers into the EAX register, then execute the CPUID instruction, and the information will be returned in EAX, EBX, ECX, and EDX.

The manufacturer ID is in leaf 0.

The RdRand support bit is in bit 30 of leaf 1.

The RdSeed support bit is bit 18 of leaf 7.

On Windows, to execute the CPUID instruction from within C, using the MinGW GCC compiler, the following code can be used with minGW:

**Listing 13.8:** minGW CPUID Code

```
void get_cpuid_windows(int leaf, CPUIDinfo *info) {
uint32_t a;
uint32_t b;
uint32_t c;
uint32_t d;

asm("\n\
    mov %4, %%eax\n\
    cpuid\n\
    mov %%eax,%0\n\
    mov %%ebx,%1\n\
    mov %%ecx,%2\n\
    mov %%edx,%3":"=r"(a),"=r"(b),"=r"(c),"=r"(d):"r"(leaf):
    "%eax","%ebx","%ecx","%e    dx");
    info->EAX = a;
    info->EBX = b;
    info->ECX = c;
    info->EDX = d;
}
```

On current versions of Visual Studio, there is no support for inline assembly for 64-bit targets, so the intrinsics library needs to be used.

First:

```
#include <intrin.h>
```

Then to use CPUID, use:

```
    int regs[4];
    __cpuid(regs, leaf);
```

where leaf chooses what CPUID data to return, and the data will be returned in the 4 regs values.

For Linux and MacOSX, the following code can be used:

**Listing 13.9:** GCC and Clang CPUID Code

```
/* GAS format to make both clang and GCC happy*/
void get_cpuid_linux(CPUIDinfo *info, const uint32_t func, const uint32_t subfunc)
{
asm(".intel_syntax noprefix;\n\
mov r8, rdi;\n\
mov r9, rsi;\n\
mov r10, rdx;\n\
push rax;\n\
push rbx;\n\
push rcx;\n\
```

```
push_rdx;\n\
mov_eax,_r9d;\n\
mov_ecx,_r10d;\n\
cpuid;\n\
mov_DWORD_PTR_[r8],_eax;\n\
mov_DWORD_PTR_[r8+4],_ebx;\n\
mov_DWORD_PTR_[r8+8],_ecx;\n\
mov_DWORD_PTR_[r8+12],_edx;\n\
pop_rdx;\n\
pop_rcx;\n\
pop_rbx;\n\
pop_rax;\n\
.att_syntax_prefix\n");
}
```

For cross platform code for Linux, MacOS, and minWG on Windows, the following will use one or the other routine according to the platform:

```
void get_cpuid(CPUIDinfo *info, const uint32_t func, const uint32_t subfunc) {
    #if defined(WIN32) || defined(_WIN32) || defined(__WIN32)
        && !defined(__CYGWIN__    )
        get_cpuid_windows(func, info);
    #else
        get_cpuid_linux(info, func, subfunc);
    #endif
}
```

Writing cross platform CPUID code that will also compile in Visual Studio is left as an exercise for the interested programmer.

The following sequence of routines tests for Intel or AMD CPUs (the two families of CPUs that support the RdRand and RdSeed instructions) and then checks for the RdRand and RdSeed bits to check if the instructions are supported:

**Listing 13.10:** Detecting AMD and Intel Signatures

```
typedef uint32_t DWORD;

int check_is_intel() {
    CPUIDinfo info;

    get_cpuid(&info,0,0);
    if(memcmp((char *)(&info.EBX), "Genu", 4) == 0 &&
        memcmp((char *)(&info.EDX), "ineI", 4) == 0 &&
        memcmp((char *)(&info.ECX), "ntel", 4) == 0) {
            return 1;
    }

    return 0;
}

int check_is_amd() {
    CPUIDinfo info;
```

```
        get_cpuid(&info,0,0);

        if( memcmp((char *)(&info.EBX), "Auth", 4) == 0 &&
            memcmp((char *)(&info.EDX), "enti", 4) == 0 &&
            memcmp((char *)(&info.ECX), "cAMD", 4) == 0) {
                return 1;
        }
        return 0;
}

int check_rdrand() {
    CPUIDinfo info;

    get_cpuid(&info,1,0);

    if ((info.ECX & 0x40000000)==0x40000000) return 1;
    return 0;
}

int check_rdseed() {
    CPUIDinfo info;

    get_cpuid(&info,7,0);

    if ((info.EBX & 0x00040000)==0x00040000) return 1;
    return 0;
}

int rdrand_check_support() {
    if ((check_is_intel()==1) || (check_is_amd()==1)){
        if (check_rdrand()==1) return 1;
    }
    return 0;
}

int rdseed_check_support() {
    if ((check_is_intel()==1) || (check_is_amd()==1)){
        if (check_rdseed()==1) return 1;
    }
    return 0;
}
```

Finally, to get random numbers with RdRand and RdSeed, the following inline assembly routines can be used for 16-, 32-, and 64-bit destinations, respectively:

**Listing 13.11:** RdRand and RdSeed Inline Assembly

```
int rdrand16_step(uint16_t *therand) {
uint16_t foo;
```

```
int cf_error_status;
asm("\n\
          rdrand %%ax;\n\
          mov $1,%%edx;\n\
          cmovae %%ax,%%dx;\n\
          mov %%edx,%1;\n\
          mov %%ax, %0;":"=r"(foo),"=r"(cf_error_status)::"%ax","%dx");
        *therand = foo;
    return cf_error_status;

}


int rdseed16_step(uint16_t *therand) {
uint16_t foo;
int cf_error_status;
asm("\n\
          rdseed %%ax;\n\
          mov $1,%%edx;\n\
          cmovae %%ax,%%dx;\n\
          mov %%edx,%1;\n\
          mov %%ax, %0;":"=r"(foo),"=r"(cf_error_status)::"%ax","%dx");
        *therand = foo;
    return cf_error_status;
}


int rdrand32_step(uint32_t *therand) {
int foo;
int cf_error_status;
asm("\n\
          rdrand %%eax;\n\
          mov $1,%%edx;\n\
          cmovae %%eax,%%edx;\n\
          mov %%edx,%1;\n\
          mov %%eax,%0;":"=r"(foo),"=r"(cf_error_status)::"%eax","%edx");
        *therand = foo;
    return cf_error_status;
}


int rdseed32_step(uint32_t *therand) {
int foo;
int cf_error_status;
asm("\n\
          rdseed %%eax;\n\
          mov $1,%%edx;\n\
          cmovae %%eax,%%edx;\n\
          mov %%edx,%1;\n\
          mov %%eax,%0;":"=r"(foo),"=r"(cf_error_status)::"%eax","%edx");
        *therand = foo;
    return cf_error_status;
```

```
}

int rdrand64_step(uint64_t *therand) {
uint64_t foo;
int cf_error_status;
asm("\n\
          rdrand %%rax;\n\
          mov $1,%%edx;\n\
          cmovae %%rax,%%rdx;\n\
          mov %%edx,%1;\n\
          mov %%rax, %0;":"=r"(foo),"=r"(cf_error_status)::"%rax","%rdx");
        *therand = foo;
return cf_error_status;
}

int rdseed64_step(uint64_t *therand) {
uint64_t foo;
int cf_error_status;
asm("\n\
          rdseed %%rax;\n\
          mov $1,%%edx;\n\
          cmovae %%rax,%%rdx;\n\
          mov %%edx,%1;\n\
          mov %%rax, %0;":"=r"(foo),"=r"(cf_error_status)::"%rax","%rdx");
        *therand = foo;
return cf_error_status;
}
```

The library files (rdrand_stdint.c and rdrand_stdint.h) that include this code are available at https://github.com/dj-on-github/rdrand_stdint.

On Visual Studio, the rdrand16_step(), rdrand32_step(), and rdrand64_step() functions are available from the intrinsics library as _rdrand16_step(), _rdrand32_step(), and _rdrand64_step. Note that the rdrand and rdseed intrinsics have one underscore prefix, whereas the __cpuid() intrinsic has a two underscore prefix. I have no idea why.

So, in Visual Studio, the basic routines for using CPUID to check for Intel or AMD CPUs, and then checking for RdRand or RdSeed support could be implemented as follows:

**Listing 13.12:** Windows CPUID Check

```
#include <stdio.h>
#include "stdafx.h"
#include <string.h>
#include <stdlib.h>
#include <intrin.h>

#define BUFFERSZ 128
```

```c
int check_is_intel() {
        int regs[4];

        __cpuid(regs, 0);

        if (memcmp((char *)(&regs[1]), "Genu", 4) == 0 &&
                memcmp((char *)(&regs[2]), "ineI", 4) == 0 &&
                memcmp((char *)(&regs[3]), "ntel", 4) == 0) {
                return 1;
        }
        return 0;
}

int check_is_amd() {
        int regs[4];

        __cpuid(regs, 0);

        if (memcmp((char *)(&regs[1]), "Auth", 4) == 0 &&
                memcmp((char *)(&regs[2]), "enti", 4) == 0 &&
                memcmp((char *)(&regs[3]), "cAMD", 4) == 0) {
                return 1;
        }
        return 0;
}

int check_rdrand() {
        int regs[4];

        __cpuid(regs, 1);

        if ((regs[2] & 0x40000000) == 0x40000000) return 1;
        return 0;
}

int check_rdseed() {
        int regs[4];

        __cpuid(regs, 7);

        if ((regs[1] & 0x00040000) == 0x00040000) return 1;
        return 0;
}
```

The intrinsic _rdrand64_step() routine in a loop that fills a buffer and also performs the retry could be implemented as follows:

**Listing 13.13:** get_qints.c

```c
int _rdrand_get_n_qints_retry(unsigned int n, unsigned int retry_limit,
                              unsigned long long int *dest)
{
        int success;
        unsigned int count;
        unsigned int i;

        for (i = 0; i<n; i++)
        {
                count = 0;
                do
                {
                        success = _rdrand64_step(dest);
                } while ((success == 0) && (count++ < retry_limit));
                if (success == 0) return 0;
                dest = &(dest[1]);
        }
        return 1;
}
```

For the RdSeed case, substitute rdseed for rdrand in the above code.

## 13.5 The Python Random Library

Python provides a class Random, which provides a wide variety of methods for seed-ing and running PRNGs, and returning data in various forms, including floating point, bounded integers, and strings of bits.

In addition to the basic Random class, there is a SystemRandom subclass, which provides the same methods, but sources data from the operating system random num-ber service, including on Windows and Linux. So, this provides a fitting cross platform solution to accessing operating system random numbers.

The default RNG in Python is a seedable PRNG with multiple-output formatters. This is not suitable for cryptographic purposes. We will look at this first, and then look at three cryptographically secure options in Python (os.urandom, SystemRan-dom, and the RdRand library).

The basic random class can be called with several methods. The random() method returns a floating-point number between 0 and less than 1.

The getstate() and setstate() methods allow the state of the RNG to be saved and replayed from that point later on. The code in Listing 13.14 does this. The random class is used. s=getstate() saves the starting state in s. Three numbers are generated. The state is pushed back into the RNG with setstate(s), and the three numbers are repeated in the second output.

**Listing 13.14:** python_random.py

```python
#!/usr/bin/env python

import random
r = random
s = r.getstate()

print "random.random()_Returns_floating_point_numbers_in_[0,1)"
for i in xrange(3):
    x = r.random()
    print "_",x

r.setstate(s)

print "Reseeding_with_the_starting_state_causes_it_to_repeat"
for i in xrange(3):
    x = r.random()
    print "_",x
```

We see the sequence repeated in the output.

```
random.random() Returns floating point numbers in [0,1)
    0.900977983956
    0.0187926260625
    0.828115387666
Reseeding with the starting state causes it to repeat
    0.900977983956
    0.0187926260625
    0.828115387666
```

The getrandbits(n) method returns an integer made of *n* random bits.

**Listing 13.15:** python_random2.py

```python
#!/usr/bin/env python

import random
r = random

for i in xrange(1,17):
    x = r.getrandbits(i)
    print "__bits:_%2d_random_value:_0x%04x" % (i,x)
```

The output gives 16 random numbers of 1 bit through 16 bits.

```
    bits:   1 random value: 0x0001
    bits:   2 random value: 0x0001
    bits:   3 random value: 0x0005
    bits:   4 random value: 0x0004
    bits:   5 random value: 0x000f
    bits:   6 random value: 0x000c
```

```
bits:    7 random value: 0x0079
bits:    8 random value: 0x0077
bits:    9 random value: 0x01be
bits:   10 random value: 0x0042
bits:   11 random value: 0x00b8
bits:   12 random value: 0x0c8d
bits:   13 random value: 0x1d4f
bits:   14 random value: 0x0c80
bits:   15 random value: 0x665a
bits:   16 random value: 0xb834
```

For integers between a range, we can use the randint(a,b) function, which will return a number between *a* and *b*, inclusive.

**Listing 13.16:** python_random3.py

```
#!/usr/bin/env python

import random
r = random

x = [r.randint(10,15)   for y in range(20)]
print x
```

We see the output in the range [10,15].

```
[12,  13,  14,  15,  10,  12,  15,  15,  11,  13,
 13,  14,  15,  10,  10,  14,  11,  13,  13,  11]
```

A similar function randrange() is available, which uses the same parameters as the range function. So, random.randrange(x) returns random numbers between 0 and $x-1$. random.randrange(a,b) returns numbers between *a* and $b-1$. The step parameter can also be used. random.randrange(0,101,10) random chooses numbers from the set: $0, 10, 20, \ldots, 80, 90, 100$.

**Listing 13.17:** python_random4.py

```
#!/usr/bin/env python

import random
r = random

x = [r.randrange(0,101,10)   for y in range(20)]
print x
```

The output, as described above, is made of random numbers from 0 to 100, in steps of 10.

```
[50,  90,  10,  40,  70,  20,  50,  90,  10,  0,
 70,  30,  100,  80,  60,  70,  80,  50,  90,  80]
```

There are many other functions in the Python random library to generate random numbers from a variety of distributions.

### 13.5.1 Python Cryptographically Secure Random Numbers

The os.urandom() method will return a string of bytes from the system random number service. On Unix-like operating systems, such as Linux and OSX, it will return bytes from the system's /dev/urandom RNG. On Windows, it will use the system's CryptGenRandom() call.

The example below gets 10 random bytes on an OSX platform using Python 2.7.12.

**Listing 13.18:** python_random5.py

```python
#!/usr/bin/env python

import os

k = 0
bytes = os.urandom(16)
for byte in bytes:
    k = (k << 8) + ord(byte)
print "%032x" % k,
```

which outputs a 256-bit random number

```
921a0f9c4d60803ebb44237cfcc259c7.
```

The random.SystemRandom class works similar to the random class described above. However, it pulls random data from the system random service. This means that reseeding functions will not work, and so sequences cannot be repeated.

The code below calls the SystemRandom class to get 5 256-bit keys.

**Listing 13.19:** python_random6.py

```python
#!/usr/bin/env python

import random
r = random.SystemRandom()

for i in range(5):
    key = r.getrandbits(256)
    print "  %064x" % key
```

As we would expect, the output consists of 5 random numbers, each 256 bits in length.

```
86d8e833c9567d1cc0b256b0d030a3ca9fe4a978d4f2961b3d7032575b225def
7bc0c553f3c45e3320b3b8417966ce4605f3a0be056ecabe714e77aed9d5ed34
d468e907564021f914471d97c45e7d489f5d68508d93145a22411416b619e0c6
95cc5b4eb92cc55f43aea0a7408992cf2d884cc469dd3c8f87eea2d86fdca610
3ad3e12bd92663d3d84de123a1f8d34a7e9e4616c6aadcae7c62614eabbc35cb
```

To use RdRand directly in Python, you can install the RdRand library. This is available as a Python package that can be installed with the easy_install utility. The sources are available on github at https://github.com/stillson/rdrand.

To install:

```
$easy_install RdRand
$
```

We can then import RdRandom from the rdrand library and use it like the normal random library, with all the usual functions available.

**Listing 13.20:** python_random7.py

```
#!/usr/bin/env python

from rdrand import RdRandom

r = RdRandom()
for i in xrange(5):
    print "%f" % r.random()
print
for i in xrange(5):
    print "%032X" % r.getrandbits(256),
```

which gives the expected results of five random floating point numbers between 0 and 1, followed by five 256-bit hexadecimal numbers.

```
0.579644
0.991523
0.982102
0.225253
0.328945

ECE36304DD6887BFD831B5AA034CE5E07E7EB9C90BFA30B279CF1A51BE425B3A
7EB534012D49ACA61AC7102103A6F1DDBAC743CE729EF2B9B3F7503EBEF89E1C
474BCBBD01ACDEFF5777CE1A0041D94A1BBF041C978A76F1A99F729C82AF6644
1160F5EE8C1CEAE39D25EAD761C923F4BE4ACE9C5916D52662B4F73E2780B0CC
50E7EA22314C087D62627F7D2FCEDEF181779F53F6E0FCCEBB7727B445CEB053
```

A limitation with this library is that it only supports RdRand on Intel CPUs. The AMD RdRand instruction is not supported. RdSeed is supported neither on AMD nor on Intel CPUs.

I added support for both instructions RdRand and RdSeed on both AMD and Intel CPUs. The code is available on github at https://github.com/dj-on-github/rdrand.

This has been accepted upstream by the developer, so support for RdRand and RdSeed on both Intel and AMD CPUs may be in the standard Python PyPi package by the time you read this.

To use RdSeed, simply import RdSeedom in place of RdRandom.

**Listing 13.21:** python_random8.py

```python
#!/usr/bin/env python

from rdrand import RdSeedom

r = RdSeedom()
for i in xrange(5):
    print "%f" % r.random()
print
for i in xrange(5):
    print "%032X" % r.getrandbits(256)
```

## 13.6 The Windows CryptGenRand() API

Windows includes a cryptography service, which includes a random number service. At the time of writing, the internal PRNG is a 256-bit SP800-90 HMAC-DRBG, which uses available entropy sources, including RdRand or RdSeed.

The example below follows the C++ examples in the Microsoft documentation, which is much more complete. The code below does the minimum to get a random number. It sets up a cryptographic context, which is required in order to call Crypt-GenRandom(), and then calls CryptGenRandom() to yield random numbers. The setting up of a basic C++ program in Visual Studio includes large amounts of boilerplate code, which is not shown here.

I experimented with calling CryptGenRandom(), using C instead of C++, but was unsuccessful, because the required libraries did not appear to be available in Microsoft Visual Studio.

**Listing 13.22:** windows_cryptgenrandom.cpp

```cpp
HCRYPTPROV hCryptProv = NULL;  // CSP Handle
LPCSTR name = "AKeyContainer";
BYTE          pbData[16];
int           success = 0;

// Acquire a context
if(CryptAcquireContext(
   &hCryptProv,
   name,
   NULL,      // NULL indicates the default provider
   PROV_RSA_FULL,
   0))
{
    success = 1;
}
else {
```

```
    // Failed to get the default context, so try to make one

    if (GetLastError() == NTE_BAD_KEYSET) {
        if(CryptAcquireContext(&hCryptProv, UserName,
        NULL, PROV_RSA_FULL, CRYPT_NEWKEYSET)) {
            success = 1;
        }
    }
    else {
        printf("Error._Failed_to_get_or_make_new_Crypto_Context.\n");
        exit(1);
    }
}

if (success == 1) {
    if(CryptGenRandom(hCryptProv, 8, pbData)) {
        for (i=0;i<8;i++) printf("%02x",pbData[i]);
    }
    else {
        printf("CryptGenRandom()_did_not_return_random_numbers\n");
    }
    // Release the handle
    CryptReleaseContext(hCryptProv,0);
}
```

# 14 Floating-Point Random Numbers

Generating uniformly distributed floating-point random numbers is a standard problem in computer science. We have explored many ways to generate uniformly distributed random bits. However, if we populate a floating-point number with uniformly distributed random bits,[1] then the result will be highly nonuniform.

The following code generates the data for Figure 14.1, which is a histogram of 10 000 000 random floating-point numbers between 0.0 and 1.0, where the bits of the exponent field and mantissa field were populated with uniformly distributed random bits.

The code takes random bits from the RdRand instruction and puts them in the exponent and mantissa fields. If the exponent turns out to be greater than 1022, then it tries again until it gets an exponent equal to or less than 1022, so that all the resulting floating-point numbers are between 0.0 and 1.0.

**Listing 14.1:** float_bad_dist.c

```
#include <stdio.h>
#include <stdint.h>
#include <math.h>
#include "rdrand_stdint.h"

#define BINS 10
#define ITERATIONS 10000000
uint64_t histogram[BINS];

uint64_t get_random_bits() {
    uint64_t x;
    rdrand_get_uint64_retry(10,&x);
    return x;
}

void add_to_histogram(double f) {
    double x;
    int i;
    x = f * BINS;
    for (i=0;i<BINS;i++) {
        if (x <= ((double)(i+1))) {
            histogram[i] += 1;
            break;
        }}
    return;
}
int main() {
    uint64_t mantissa;
    uint64_t exponent;
    uint64_t sign;
    uint64_t x;
    double *fp;
    double f;
```

---

**1** For example, an IEEE 754-1985 [22] 64 bit binary floating-point number.

https://doi.org/10.1515/9781501506062-014

```
int i;
for (i=0;i<BINS;i++) histogram[i]=0;
for (i=0;i<ITERATIONS;i++) {
    mantissa = get_random_bits() & 0x0fffffffffffff; // mask to 56 bits
    do {
        exponent = get_random_bits() & 0x3ff; // mask to 10 bits
    } while (exponent > 1022);
    sign = 0;
    x = (sign << 63) | ((exponent & 0x7ff) << 52) | mantissa;
    fp = (double *)&x;
    f = *fp;
    add_to_histogram(f);
}
for (i=0;i<BINS;i++) printf("%d\t%1.1f\t%d\n",i, ((double)i)/BINS, histogram[i]);
}
```

The resulting histogram is shown in Figure 14.1.

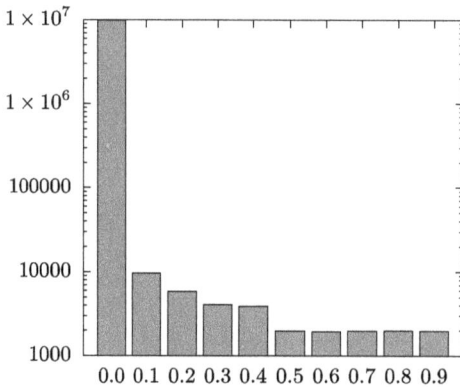

**Figure 14.1:** Nonuniform Distribution of Randomized Bits in 64-Bit Floating-Point Numbers.

To make the smaller bars visible, a logarithmic scale was needed. We can see that almost all the values land in the smallest bin, between 0.0 and 0.1. We can see that the upper half of the bins with values between 0.5 and 1.0 all have a similar frequency. This is because they all have the same exponent, 1022. The numbers in the bins below 0.5 have exponents between 1021 and 0. So, numbers between 0.0 and 0.5 occur, on average, 1022 times more often than numbers between 0.5 and 1.0.

We need algorithms that generate uniformly distributed floating-point numbers rather than merely putting random bits into a floating-point number. We will look at three such algorithms:

- Fixed Exponent Method;
- Exponent Distribution Compensation;
- Dividing by Largest Random Integer.

Where there is no floating-point hardware support, for example, when implementing directly in logic, or on a microcontroller that does not have floating-point hardware, one of the first two methods would be appropriate, because they directly derive the bits of the floating-point value without performing floating-point operations. The final method assumes you have a floating-point hardware available to do multiplication and addition, and so is a reasonable method to use in a software implementation, running on a CPU with floating-point support.

## 14.1 The Floating-Point Number Distribution

The general floating-point format contains one sign bit, an exponent field, and a mantissa field. See Figure 14.2.

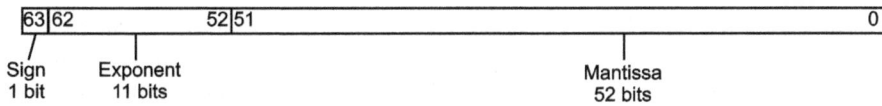

Figure 14.2: IEEE 754 Binary64 Floating-Point Format.

In the IEEE 754 binary64 format, the exponent is offset by −1023, so that negative exponents can be represented. The mantissa is treated as a fixed-point binary number, where bit 51 (the most significant bit) is valued at 0.5, bit 50 at 0.25, and so on. The mantissa is given an implicit +1.

So, the value represented by the sign $s$, exponent $e$, and mantissa $m$ is

$$(-1)^s(1 + (m \times 2^{-52}))2^{e-1023}.$$

The $(-1)^s$ part transforms $s = 0$ to 0 and $s = 1$ to −1.
The $2^{-52}$ part is to shift the mantissa right 52 bit positions.
The −1023 offset of the exponent is to allow smaller values to be represented.
So, for example, 1 would be represented as $s = 0$, $e = 1023$, and $m = 0$. Applying the transforms and shifts, that makes sign = 1, exponent = 0, and mantissa = 1.0, so is $1 \times 2^0 \times 1.0 = 1.0$.

The numbers in which the bits of the exponent are all zeroes are called the subnormal numbers. In this case, 1.0 is not added to the mantissa, so when $e = 0$, the number represented is

$$(-1)^s(m \times 2^{-52})2^{-1022}.$$

Some example values, with the fields decoded, are shown in Table 14.1.[2]

---

**2** The IEEE 754 [22] specification reserves the case of exponent being all ones to encode for positive and negative infinity and NaN (Not a Number). These are not relevant to the random number generation process (since we will be generating those numbers), but need to be understood to fully understand the IEEE 754 standard.

**Table 14.1:** Example Floating-Point Values.

| Value | Sign Bit | Exponent Field | Mantissa Field | $(-1)^s$ | $e - 1023$ | $1 + (m \times 2^{-52})$ |
|-------|----------|----------------|----------------|----------|------------|--------------------------|
| −3.0  | 1        | 0x00000400     | 0x8000000000000 | −1      | 1          | 1.5                      |
| 0.0   | 0        | 0x00000000     | 0x0000000000000 | +1      | −1022      | 0.0                      |
| 1.0   | 0        | 0x000003ff     | 0x0000000000000 | +1      | 0          | 1.0                      |
| 10.0  | 0        | 0x00000402     | 0x4000000000000 | +1      | 3          | 1.25                     |

The smallest positive and negative values are encoded with the exponent = 0 and mantissa = 1, which encodes for the number $2^{-1074}$.

For any specific fixed exponent, there are $2^{52}$ different representable values from the 52-bit value in the mantissa.

The largest mantissa is 52 ones or 0xfffffffffffff. The smallest is 0. We examine the range of positive values from the smallest to largest mantissa, for $e$ = 1021 through to $e$ = 1026, and measure the range of numbers for each exponent with the following code:

**Listing 14.2:** float_maxmin.py

```
#!/usr/bin/python

def makefloat(s,e,m):
    sign = (-1)**s

    mantissa = m * (2.0**(-52));
    if e!=0:
        mantissa = mantissa + 1;

    if e==0:
        exponent = -1022
    else:
        exponent = e-1023

    value = sign * mantissa * (2.0**exponent)

    return value

es = [1021,1022,1023,1024,1025,1026]

lowend = 0
highend = 0x0fffffffffffff
for e in es:
    smallest = makefloat(0,e,lowend)
    largest = makefloat(0,e,highend)

    print("e_=_%d,_from_:_%f___to__%f,_range_%f"
        % (e,smallest,largest,largest-smallest))
```

**Table 14.2:** Ranges for Adjacent Floating-Point Exponents.

| Exponent | Smallest | Largest | Range |
|---|---|---|---|
| 1021 | 0.25 | 0.5 | 0.25 |
| 1022 | 0.5 | 1.0 | 0.5 |
| 1023 | 1.0 | 2.0 | 1.0 |
| 1024 | 2.0 | 4.0 | 2.0 |
| 1025 | 4.0 | 8.0 | 4.0 |
| 1026 | 8.0 | 16.0 | 8.0 |

The results are shown in Table 14.2.

So, we see the range of values for each exponent covers a range on the number line that is twice as big as the next lower exponent. Within each exponent, there are the same number of mantissa values, so the granularity of the number representation doubles each time you decrease the exponents by 1.

The exception is the case where the exponent equals zero. Since 1 is not added to the mantissa, the size of the space and the granularity of the numbers representations is equal to the case where the exponent equals 1.

From this we can conclude that if we populate the exponent and mantissa of a floating-point number with uniform random bits, then we will not get a uniform distribution of random floating-point numbers. There are far more numbers packed in the small end of the distribution. Picking uniformly from the set of floating-point numbers will yield more small numbers than large numbers.

## 14.2 The Fixed-Exponent Method

The fixed-exponent method uses only a single exponent value. This way the values that can be represented are determined by different possible mantissa values.

A problem is that one exponent only has a limited range. For example, the exponent that gives the range that goes up to 1.0 can only be used to represent numbers down to 0.5.

An obvious solution is to subtract 0.5 from the value to turn it into a value in the range of 0 to 0.5, then, take one more random bit and assign it to the sign bit, so the range is now from −0.5 to +0.5, then adding 0.5 back to make it a range from 0.0 to 1.0. This method, therefore, requires hardware or software that can perform floating point addition and subtraction.

This method achieves floating-point random numbers that are uniform, such that the frequency of which the numbers appear in a range tends to be the same as the frequency with which the numbers land in any other equal-sized range, as the number of random numbers becomes large. In addition, the spacing between the representable numbers is uniform across the full range of 0.0 to 1.0.

This comes at the cost of limiting the total number of representable numbers to twice the size of the mantissa number space. For larger floating-point sizes this may be fine, but for the smallest IEEE 754 format, having the binary16 16-bit format and only 10 bits of mantissa, with this method there would be only 2048 total numbers that could be represented between 0.0 and 1.0.

The code below implements this algorithm and outputs 1000 floating-point random numbers. The main() routine fixes the exponent to 1022 and performs the above algorithm, subtracting 0.5, putting in the randomized sign bit, and adding 0.5.

**Listing 14.3:** float_fixed_exp.c

```c
#include <stdio.h>
#include <stdint.h>
#include <math.h>
#include "rdrand_stdint.h"

uint64_t get_random_bits() {
    uint64_t x;
    rdrand_get_uint64_retry(10,&x);
    return x;
}

int main() {
    uint64_t mantissa;
    uint64_t exponent;
    uint64_t sign;
    uint64_t x;
    double *f;

    int i;
    for (i=0;i<1000;i++) {
        x = get_random_bits();
        mantissa = x &  0x0fffffffffffffff;
        exponent = 1022;
        sign = (x >> 52) & 0x01;
        x = ((exponent & 0x7ff) << 52) | mantissa;
        f = (double *)&x;
        *f = *f - 0.5;
        x = x | (sign << 63);
        *f = *f + 0.5;
        printf("%f\n",*f);
    }
}
```

Running this, the output gives random numbers between 0.0 and 1.0.

```
0.907871
0.827061
0.613368
```

```
0.425238
0.185770
0.431664
0.634837
0.571471
0.221661
0.556650
0.045592
0.768600
0.659263
0.827613
0.398768
0.301094
0.891130
0.065346
0.593995
0.571065
0.648588
0.308043
0.986195
0.891395
0.520205
0.352134
0.013925
```

## 14.3 Exponent Distribution Compensation

This method makes uniform floating-point numbers by picking the larger exponents more frequently than the smaller exponents.

For example, if we are generating 64-bit floating-point numbers between 0 and 1.0, then we would use the exponents from 1022 down to 0, so the largest number available is 1.0, and the smallest is 0.

The random numbers should appear 50% of the time in the range 1.0 to 0.5, which is covered by the numbers with exponent = 1022. The numbers should appear 25% of the time in the range 0.5 down to 0.25, where the exponent = 1021. This continues with the frequency of numbers appearing in each exponent, reducing by half for each reduction of 1 in the exponent.

A simple algorithm to choose the exponent would be:

```
Set E=1022
While (E > 0)
    Generate a uniform random bit x
    If x==1 return E
    set E=E-1
return 0
```

The maximum number of random bits this would consume is 1022 bits. However, this will never actually happen. The probability of getting 1022 zeroes in a row of full-entropy bits is $2^{-1022}$, which is so small that it almost certainly will never happen.

The 52-bit mantissa can then be populated with uniform random bits, and if both positive and negative numbers are needed, then the sign bit takes one more random bit.

The C code below generates 64-bit floating-point random numbers using the above algorithm. The get_random_bits() function is the same as in the previous section. The choose_exponent() algorithm does exactly what the name says, using the above algorithm. The main function gets a random mantissa and an exponent and assembles them into a 64-bit double-precision floating-point value. It iterates 1000 times to generate 1000 values.

**Listing 14.4:** float_compensated_dist.c

```c
#include <stdio.h>
#include <stdint.h>
#include <math.h>
#include "rdrand_stdint.h"

uint64_t get_random_bits() {
    uint64_t x;
    rdrand_get_uint64_retry(10,&x);
    return x;
}

uint64_t choose_exponent(uint64_t start) {
    uint64_t e;

    e = start;
    do {
        if ((get_random_bits() & 0x01) == 1) return e;
        e = e-1;
    } while (e > 0);
    return ((uint64_t)0);
}

int main() {
    uint64_t start;
    uint64_t mantissa;
    uint64_t exponent;
    uint64_t sign;
    uint64_t x;
    double *f;

    start = 1022;
    int i;
    for (i=0;i<1000;i++) {
```

```
        mantissa = get_random_bits() & 0x0fffffffffffff;
        exponent = choose_exponent(start);
        sign = get_random_bits() & 0x01;
        x = (sign << 63) | ((exponent & 0x7ff) << 52) | mantissa;
        f = (double *)&x;
        printf("%f__exponent=%llu\n",*f,exponent);
    }
}
```

If we run this, we get an output of values between 0.0 and 1.0.

```
-0.725555   exponent=1022
-0.526681   exponent=1022
 0.252682   exponent=1021
 0.797492   exponent=1022
-0.708880   exponent=1022
 0.403246   exponent=1021
-0.409078   exponent=1021
-0.265515   exponent=1021
-0.588492   exponent=1022
 0.883815   exponent=1022
 0.450101   exponent=1021
 0.260649   exponent=1021
 0.488896   exponent=1021
-0.375821   exponent=1021
 0.260723   exponent=1021
-0.023976   exponent=1017
-0.097089   exponent=1019
 0.594970   exponent=1022
-0.333136   exponent=1021
...
```

## 14.4 Diving by the Largest Random Integer

This final method simply takes a uniform random binary integer and divides it by the largest possible random integer. The size of the random integer should be of similar size to the floating-point representation, so a good coverage of the available random floating-point numbers is achieved.

With an $n$-bit random integer $\text{RAND}_n$, the largest possible number is $2^n - 1$.

The random floating point number $f$ is computed with

$$f = \frac{1.0 \times \text{RAND}_n}{2^n - 1}.$$

In the case of Binary64 floating-point numbers that the C double type supports, this could be implemented in C as follows:

**Listing 14.5:** make_random_float.c

```c
double make_random_float(uint64_t random_int) {
    uint64_t random_max = 0xffffffffffffffff;
    double f;
    f = ((double)1.0) / random_max;
    f = f * random_int;
    return f;
}
```

The divide should happen before the multiply, because floating-point representations have much finer resolution at smaller numbers than at larger numbers.

The following program generates 10 000 000 floating-point numbers between 0.0 and 1.0, and outputs histogram data in 10 bins, just as the bad random distribution shown at the start of this chapter.

**Listing 14.6:** uniform_float_range.c

```c
#include <stdio.h>
#include <stdint.h>
#include <math.h>
#include "rdrand_stdint.h"

#define BINS 10
#define ITERATIONS 10000000

int histogram[BINS];

uint64_t get_random_bits() {
    uint64_t x;
    rdrand_get_uint64_retry(10,&x);
    return x;
}

void add_to_histogram(double f) {
    double x;
    int i;
    x = f * BINS;
    for (i=0;i<BINS;i++) {
        if (x <= ((double)(i+1))) {
            histogram[i] += 1;
            break;
        }}
    return;
}
int main() {
    double f;
    uint64_t random;
    uint64_t random_max;
    int i;

    random_max = 0xffffffffffffffff; // 64 bits
    for (i=0;i<ITERATIONS;i++) {
        random = get_random_bits();
        f = (((double)1.0) / random_max)*random;
        add_to_histogram(f);
    }
```

```
  for (i=0;i<BINS;i++) printf("%d\t%1.1f\t%d\n",i, ((double)i)/BINS, histogram[i]);
}
```

In the output, we can see that the data are uniformly distributed with the bins each holding a similar amount of numbers.

```
0       0.0     1000014
1       0.1     1000084
2       0.2     999238
3       0.3     1002345
4       0.4     1000176
5       0.5     1001394
6       0.6     999160
7       0.7     1000030
8       0.8     998724
9       0.9     998835
```

Plotted in the same manner as the first plot in this chapter, we can see the uniformity of the numbers. The x axis labels show the lower bound of each bin, so, for example, the 0.8 label refers to the 0.8–0.9 bin. See Figure 14.3.

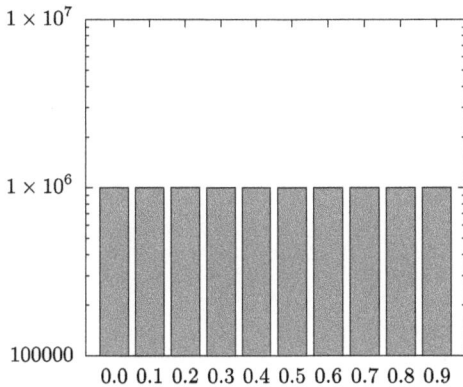

**Figure 14.3:** Uniform Distribution of Random Floating-Point Numbers Using Integer Division.

# 15 Making a Uniform Random Number Between Nonpower of Two Bounds

Making random numbers that are in a range between 0 and $2^n - 1$ is simple, because it only requires $n$ uniform random bits with a 50% probability of being 1, otherwise being 0. If the bounds are offset from zero, but still the range is a power of two, that is, between $0 + x$ and $2^n - 1 + x$, then it is still simple. Just make an $n$-bit random number and add $x$.

If, however, the random numbers need to be uniformly distributed between a range that is not a power of two in size, then other methods are needed to ensure the resulting distribution is uniform.

For example, if you require a random number between 0 and 10 inclusive, then taking a 4-bit random number modulo 11 will return numbers between 0 and 10, but the distribution will not be uniform. The 4-bit random number uniformly returns values between 0 and 15. The numbers 0 to 10 modulo 11 will return the same numbers 0 to 10. The numbers between 11 and 15 get mapped to the range 0 to 4 when taken modulo 11.

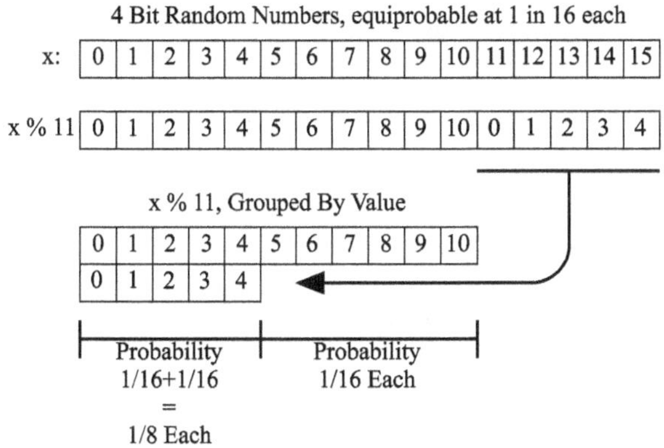

**Figure 15.1:** Nonuniform Wraparound Arising from the Modulo of a Random Number.

This is visualized in Figure 15.1. The five numbers equal to or larger than the modulo order get wrapped around to the 0 to 4 range. So, numbers in the range 0 to 4 have twice as many chances of being the random value returned as the numbers from 5 to 10.

The following code generates numbers between 0 and 200 by taking an 8-bit random number modulo 201. 1 000 000 numbers are generated, and the distribution is output as a histogram.

https://doi.org/10.1515/9781501506062-015

**Listing 15.1:** bad_wraparound.py

```python
#!/usr/bin/env python

import math
import random
rs = random.SystemRandom()

def rand_range(maxrand):
    number_of_bits = int(math.ceil(math.log(maxrand+1,2)))
    x = rs.getrandbits(number_of_bits)
    x = x % 12
    return x

histogram = [0 for x in range(16)]

for i in xrange(1000000):
    result = rand_range(11)
    histogram[result] = histogram[result]+1

print("Histogram")
for i in xrange(16):
    print("value␣:␣%2d␣␣frequency␣%d" % (i,histogram[i]))
```

The output shows that the frequency of the numbers that have the modulo values wrapped around them is twice as much as the other numbers:

```
Histogram
value :   0  frequency 125202
value :   1  frequency 124773
value :   2  frequency 124753
value :   3  frequency 125042
value :   4  frequency 62683
value :   5  frequency 62654
value :   6  frequency 62301
value :   7  frequency 62720
value :   8  frequency 62515
value :   9  frequency 62226
value :  10  frequency 62665
value :  11  frequency 62466
value :  12  frequency 0
value :  13  frequency 0
value :  14  frequency 0
value :  15  frequency 0
```

Here, we take a look at three common solutions that yield a uniform or close to uniform distribution of numbers in a nonpower of 2 range:
- The rejection method;
- Using a large random number with a small modulus;
- The floating-point method.

## 15.1 Rejection Method for Nonpower of 2 Bounds

The rejection method entails generating an $n$-bit random number, where $n$ is the smallest number of bits, where $2^n - 1 > m$, and where $m$ is the modulo order.

If the start of the desired range is not 0, then a number in the range 0 to the size of the desired range $-1$ is computed, and the start position added.

Then, for each random number produced, a uniform $n$-bit random number is generated. If the number is within the 0-based range, then that number is used and the offset added if necessary. If the number is outside the 0-based range, then the random number is discarded, and a new $n$-bit random number is generated, until one within the range is generated and used.

The following Python code is an example that implements this algorithm, generates 1 000 000 numbers in the range 5 to 14, and outputs the distribution as a histogram.

**Listing 15.2:** rejection_method.py

```python
#!/usr/bin/env python

import math
import random
rs = random.SystemRandom()

def rand_range(range_start, range_end):
    range_size = 1+range_end-range_start
    number_of_bits = int(math.ceil(math.log(range_size,2)))
    while True:
        x = rs.getrandbits(number_of_bits)
        if x < range_size:
            break

    result = x + range_start
    return result

range_start = 5
range_end = 14
number_of_numbers = 1000000

histogram = [0 for x in range(range_end+4)]

for i in xrange(number_of_numbers):
    result = rand_range(range_start, range_end)
    histogram[result] = histogram[result]+1

print("Histogram")
for i in xrange(range_end+3):
    print("value_:_%2d__frequency_%d" % (i,histogram[i]))
```

The output shows the distribution to be uniform across the desired range of 5 to 14, though not appearing at all outside that range.

```
Histogram
value :   0   frequency 0
value :   1   frequency 0
value :   2   frequency 0
value :   3   frequency 0
value :   4   frequency 0
value :   5   frequency 100080
value :   6   frequency 100530
value :   7   frequency 99447
value :   8   frequency 100088
value :   9   frequency 100191
value :  10   frequency 100175
value :  11   frequency 99871
value :  12   frequency 100080
value :  13   frequency 99715
value :  14   frequency 99823
value :  15   frequency 0
value :  16   frequency 0
```

A drawback of this algorithm is that it is not time-bounded. The number of iterations needed to get a number within the required range is not deterministic.

## 15.2 Large Number, Small Modulus Method for Nonpower of 2 Bounds

If we need a distribution that is close to uniform, but do not need it to be exactly uniform, then this method works and has the benefit of being a constant time algorithm.

The principle is that, if the random number used is in a range much greater than the size of the range being generated, then the nonuniformity is reduced.

In Figure 15.2, we see the effect of the random range being 6.4 times greater than the modulus, with the modulus being 5, and the random number being 5 bits, yielding random numbers from 0 to 31.

We can see that the difference between the probabilities is now much smaller. There are 6 opportunities to land in one of the 5 element groups and only one opportunity to land in the set of two values.

To make the nonuniformity vanishingly small, we need a random number with a range into which the output range size can divide many more times. For example, compute the number of bits needed to represent numbers in the output range size and add 64 bits to yield the number of bits in each random number to generate. Then, the difference between the most probable and least probable values is less than one in $2^{64}$.

x: | 0 | 1 | 2 | 3 | 4 | 5 | 6 | 7 | 8 | 9 | 10 | 11 | 12 | 13 | 14 | 15 | 16 | 17 | 18 | 19 | 20 | 21 | 22 | 23 | 24 | 25 | 26 | 27 | 28 | 29 | 30 | 31 |

x % 5 | 0 | 1 | 2 | 3 | 4 | 0 | 1 | 2 | 3 | 4 | 0 | 1 | 2 | 3 | 4 | 0 | 1 | 2 | 3 | 4 | 0 | 1 | 2 | 3 | 4 | 0 | 1 | 2 | 3 | 4 | 0 | 1 |

x % 5, Grouped By Value

| 0 | 1 | 2 | 3 | 4 |
|---|---|---|---|---|
| 0 | 1 | 2 | 3 | 4 |
| 0 | 1 | 2 | 3 | 4 |
| 0 | 1 | 2 | 3 | 4 |
| 0 | 1 | 2 | 3 | 4 |
| 0 | 1 | 2 | 3 | 4 |
| 0 | 1 |   |   |   |

Probability 7/32 Each    Probability 6/32 Each

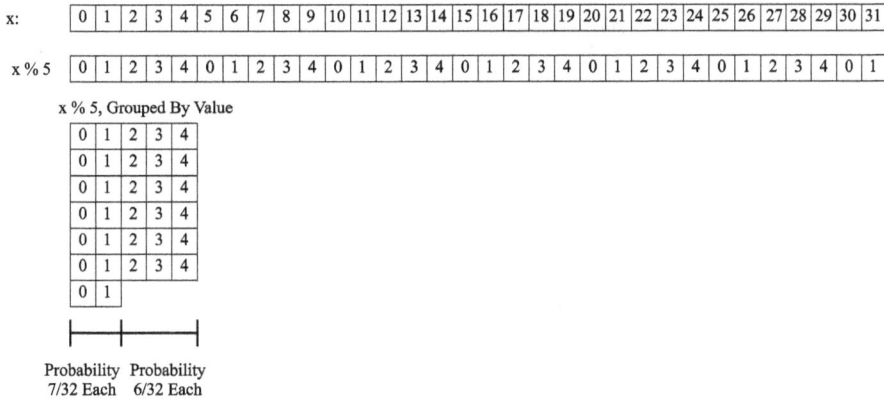

**Figure 15.2:** Large Random Number Modulo a Small Modulus.

The following Python code is an example of this algorithm. The code is identical to the nonuniform example in the introduction to this section, except that 64 is added to the number of bits in each of the random numbers generated on the 8th line.

**Listing 15.3:** small_modulus.py

```python
#!/usr/bin/env python

import math
import random
rs = random.SystemRandom()

def rand_range(maxrand):
    number_of_bits = int(math.ceil(math.log(maxrand+1,2))) + 64
    x = rs.getrandbits(number_of_bits)
    x = x % 12
    return x

histogram = [0 for x in range(16)]

for i in xrange(1000000):
    result = rand_range(11)
    histogram[result] = histogram[result]+1

print("Histogram")
for i in xrange(16):
    print("value_:_%2d__frequency_%d" % (i,histogram[i]))
```

We can see that the output appears random, since there are at least $2^{64}$ more uniform bins to land than in the single final nonuniform block of values.

```
Histogram
value :  0  frequency 83264
```

```
value :    1   frequency 83330
value :    2   frequency 83900
value :    3   frequency 83864
value :    4   frequency 83376
value :    5   frequency 82986
value :    6   frequency 83353
value :    7   frequency 83142
value :    8   frequency 83206
value :    9   frequency 83398
value :   10   frequency 82993
value :   11   frequency 83188
value :   12   frequency 0
value :   13   frequency 0
value :   14   frequency 0
```

## 15.3 Floating-Point Method for Nonpower of 2 Bounds

The floating-point method is another slightly imperfect method that yields close to uniform random numbers. The nonuniformity is a function of the small rounding errors involved in floating-point arithmetic.

It is principally useful in software implementations, where there is hardware support for floating-point arithmetic. If the resulting number is intended to be floating point, the final conversion back to integers can be dropped, and then, there is no more loss of uniformity than would be caused by the subsequent use of floating-point representation.

Section 14.4 describes a method for making uniformly distributed random floating-point numbers in the range [0, 1], using floating point support in C. This scheme is the same, except with the output offset and scaled to match the desired range.

```
Set range = range_end - range_start + 1
Set Random64 = n random bits as an integer //E.G. 64 bits
Set rand_max = 2^n-1
Convert range to floating point frange
Compute in floating point: Set f = (frange/rand_max)*Random64
Convert f to integer fint
Return fint+range_start
```

The following C code implements this algorithm, generates 1 000 000 numbers in the range 9 to 13, and outputs the resulting distribution as a histogram.

**Listing 15.4:** uniform_float_range.c

```c
#include <stdio.h>
#include <stdint.h>
#include <math.h>
```

```c
#include "rdrand_stdint.h"

#define RANGE_START 9
#define RANGE_END 13
#define ITERATIONS 1000000

int histogram[RANGE_END+3];

uint64_t get_random_bits() {
    uint64_t x;
    rdrand_get_uint64_retry(10,&x);
    return x;
}

int main() {
    double f;
    uint64_t random;
    uint64_t random_max;
    uint64_t range;
    uint64_t fint;
    int i;

    range = RANGE_END - RANGE_START + 1;

    for (i=0;i<RANGE_END+3;i++) histogram[i] = 0;

    random_max = 0xffffffffffffffff; // 64 bits
    for (i=0;i<ITERATIONS;i++) {
        random = get_random_bits();
        f = (((double)range) / random_max)*random;
        fint = (int)f + RANGE_START;
        histogram[fint] += 1;
    }
    for (i=0;i<RANGE_END+3;i++) printf("%d\t%d\n",i, histogram[i]);
}
```

The output shows the distribution within the specified range 9 to 13 to be uniform.

```
0        0
1        0
2        0
3        0
4        0
5        0
6        0
7        0
8        0
9        200069
10       199761
11       199658
```

| | |
|---|---|
| 12 | 200383 |
| 13 | 200129 |
| 14 | 0 |
| 15 | 0 |

This method is convenient in software implementations where floating-point is available and has the benefit of being constant time.

# 16 Generating Random Prime Numbers

In public key cryptography, randomly choosing large prime numbers is an essential component of the security of the system. Failing to choose a prime, or choosing the prime pairs in a way that makes their products easy to factor or easy to predict will undermine the security of the algorithm.

For example, an RSA key pair is made of two large prime numbers $p$ and $q$. The numbers should be on the order of 1024 bits or greater, and so the product $pq$ will be of the order of 2048 bits or greater. The private key is composed of $p$ and $q$ (although you only need to store one of them, because you can divide the public key to get the other), and the public key is the product $pq$ along with a public exponent $e$, which is decided upon or computed as part of the RSA specification.

When naming the length of an RSA key, we refer to the length of the public key, which is generally twice the length of the primes. A 2048-bit key has 1024 bit primes.

At the time of writing, 1024-bit keys are still in use, but have been deprecated for some time.

The distribution of primes is not uniform, with primes becoming rarer amongst larger integers.

The code in Listing 16.1 prints all the primes below $2^{17}$. It returns 12251 primes.

**Listing 16.1:** primedist.py

```python
#!/usr/bin/python
import math

def is_prime(n):
    if n==2 or n==3: return True
    if (n % 2 == 0) or (n < 2): return False # Reject even or negative
    limit = int(n**0.5)+1
    for i in xrange(3,limit,2): # list of odd numbers
        if (n % i == 0):
            return False
    return True

for n in xrange(2**17):
    if is_prime(n):
        print n
```

In Figure 16.1, we plot these prime numbers as a histogram with bins of size 8192. We can see the reducing frequency with larger numbers.

The prime counting function, usually denoted $\pi(n)$, gives an approximation for the number of primes less than or equal to $n$:

$$\pi(n) \approx \frac{n}{\log_e(n)}.$$

https://doi.org/10.1515/9781501506062-016

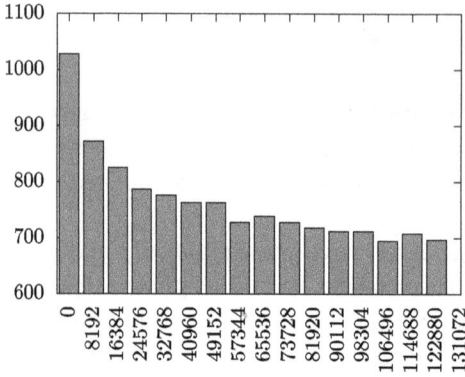

**Figure 16.1:** Histogram of Prime Distribution.

So, for a 1024-bit prime, we might choose to look for primes in the range $[2^{1023}, 2^{1024}-1]$. We want to avoid very small primes, and if we are choosing randomly from the primes, then we are more likely to get a smaller number of primes, due to the nonuniform distribution. So, we have to choose some cutoff.

Therefore, we can plug those limits into the prime-counting function to get an approximation for the number of primes in the range we are searching for:

$$n \approx \pi(2^{1024} - 1) - \pi(2^{1023})$$
$$\approx \frac{2^{1024} - 1}{\log_e(2^{1024} - 1)} - \frac{2^{1023}}{\log_e(2^{1023})}$$

Plugging these numbers into a normal computer arithmetic does not work, because the values are too large to convert to floats. But $\log_e(2^{1023})$ is approximately 709, and $\log_e(2^{1024} - 1)$ is approximately 710. So, we can proceed with integer arithmetic.

We find that the number of primes in the range $[2^{1023}, 2^{1024} - 1]$ is approximately $10^{305}$ or $2^{1023}$.

Therefore, to choose uniformly between all those primes in the range, we can expect to need to provide at least 1023 bits of entropy. In practice, the simple algorithms will take more, because they have to test multiple random numbers before finding a prime one.

Our goal in randomly selecting a prime is to select uniformly amongst the set of primes. It is not to select primes, uniformly distributed across the number line. So, a large set of primes generated by a good prime selection algorithm will have a distribution that matches closely to the distribution of all the primes in the range, as in Figure 16.1.

The simple algorithm that will select uniformly is to pick a random number in the range and test if it is prime. If it is not prime, then repeat until a prime is found. The average gap between the primes at around $2^{1024}$ is about 709:

$$\text{gap} = \lfloor 2^{1024} \log_e(2^{1024}) - (2^{1024} - 1) \log_e(2^{1024} = 1) \rfloor = 709.$$

Therefore, if we start picking random numbers in the range, then we can expect on average to find a prime number every 709 attempts.

To select a random number in the range, we can start with a 1024-bit string of random bits, then set the least significant bit to 1 to ensure we are selecting an odd number, and we can set the most significant bit to 1 so that the lowest possible number is $2^{1023}$, and the highest possible number is $2^{1024} - 1$.

However, we will find that the naive is_prime() function used in the previous listing will not work. The algorithm searches for divisors in every odd number up to the square root of the number we are testing for primality. If the number is $2^{1024}$, then the square root is $2^{512}$, and checking the $\frac{2^{512}}{2}$ odd divisors is not computationally feasible.

A commonly used, and much faster, example of a good primality test is the Miller–Rabin test. This is a probabilistic algorithm that, for each iteration, reduces the probability that the number is not prime or concludes the number is not prime. The computational complexity of the algorithm is $O(k \log^3(n))$. There are optimizations of this algorithm based on FFTs, which further reduce the complexity. The basic algorithm is given below in Python.

**Listing 16.2:** miller_rabin.py

```python
#!/usr/bin/python

import random
rand = random.SystemRandom()

def is_probably_prime(n,k):
    # The range doesn't handle the small primes well
    # So handle them first
    if (n == 2) or (n == 3) or (n==5):
        return True
    if (n < 7):
        return False

    # Separate the 2 factors from n-1
    # So n-1 = 2**r * d
    d = n-1
    r = 0
    while ((d % 2) == 0) and (d > 2):
        d = d >> 1
        r = r + 1
    # k is the chosen iteration count
    for i in xrange(k):
        a = rand.randint(2,n-2)
        x = pow(a,d,n)
        if (x==1) or (x == (n-1)):
            continue
```

```
    for j in xrange(r-1):
        x = pow(x,2,n)
        if x == 1:
            return False
        if x == (n-1):
            break
    if x == (n-1):
        continue
    return False
return True

for i in xrange(1,100):
    if is_probably_prime(i,10):
        print "%d__Prime" % i
    else:
        print "%d" % i
```

When the number of iterations is $k$, the probability that the algorithm erroneously declares a composite number to be prime is $4^{-k}$, and so, also $2^{-2k}$. So, for example, for an error probability of 1 in $2^{256}$, we would set $k = 128$.

However, we will be running this test on average 710 times per prime value tested in the order of $2^{1024}$. So, we are interested in the error probability of finding a composite and erroneously declaring it a prime, before we find a real prime. To do so, we can use the Bayes theorem.

The probability that $n$ is composite is $X$ and $P(X) = \frac{709}{710}$. The probability that $n$ is prime is $\bar{X}$ and $P(\bar{X}) = \frac{1}{710}$. The probability that the Miller–Rabin test declares $n$ probably prime is $Y$ and $P(Y) = \frac{1}{710}$. The probability that we declare $n$ probably prime after $k$ rounds given $n$ is composite is $P(Y|X) = 2^{-2k}$. The probability that we declare $n$ probably prime, after $k$ rounds, given $n$ is prime, is $P(Y|\bar{X}) = 1 - 2^{-2k}$.

We are interested in the error probability that $n$ is composite given that the Miller–Rabin test declared it to be probably prime, which is $P(X|Y)$.

Using the Bayes theorem, the probability $P(Y|X)$ can be computed. Here, we apply the Bayes theorem and plug in the numbers from the case of 1024-bit prime numbers:

$$P(Y|X) = \frac{P(Y|X)P(X)}{P(Y|X)P(X) + P(Y|\bar{X})P(\bar{X})}$$
$$= \frac{2^{-2k} \times \frac{709}{710}}{(2^{-2k} \times \frac{709}{710}) + ((1 - 2^{-2k}) \times \frac{1}{710})}.$$

If we choose $k = 10$ rounds, we find that $P(X|Y) = 9.5E^{-7}$. If we choose $k = 128$ rounds, we find that $P(X|Y) = 9.5E^{-7}$.

If we want the probability of error to be less than 1 in $2^{256}$, we need to find which value gives us the desired error probability below 1 in $2^{256}$.

Below we iterate this Bayes computation for $k$ from 100 to 140.

**Listing 16.3:** miller_rabin_bayes.py

```python
#!/usr/bin/python

import math

pxbar = 1.0/710.0
px = 709.0/710.0


for k in xrange(100,140):
    pygx = 2.0 ** (-2*k)
    pygxbar = 1.0-(2.0 ** (-2*k))

    top = pygx * px
    bottom = top + (pygxbar * pxbar)

    error_prob = top/bottom
    error_bits = math.log(error_prob,2)

    print "k=%d, error_prob = 1 in 2^%f" % (k,error_bits)
```

We find that the lowest $k$ giving an error probability below 1 in $2^{256}$ is $k = 133$.

```
k=100, error_prob = 1 in 2^-190.530358
k=101, error_prob = 1 in 2^-192.530358
k=102, error_prob = 1 in 2^-194.530358
k=103, error_prob = 1 in 2^-196.530358
k=104, error_prob = 1 in 2^-198.530358
k=105, error_prob = 1 in 2^-200.530358
k=106, error_prob = 1 in 2^-202.530358
k=107, error_prob = 1 in 2^-204.530358
k=108, error_prob = 1 in 2^-206.530358
k=109, error_prob = 1 in 2^-208.530358
k=110, error_prob = 1 in 2^-210.530358
k=111, error_prob = 1 in 2^-212.530358
k=112, error_prob = 1 in 2^-214.530358
k=113, error_prob = 1 in 2^-216.530358
k=114, error_prob = 1 in 2^-218.530358
k=115, error_prob = 1 in 2^-220.530358
k=116, error_prob = 1 in 2^-222.530358
k=117, error_prob = 1 in 2^-224.530358
k=118, error_prob = 1 in 2^-226.530358
k=119, error_prob = 1 in 2^-228.530358
k=120, error_prob = 1 in 2^-230.530358
k=121, error_prob = 1 in 2^-232.530358
k=122, error_prob = 1 in 2^-234.530358
k=123, error_prob = 1 in 2^-236.530358
k=124, error_prob = 1 in 2^-238.530358
k=125, error_prob = 1 in 2^-240.530358
k=126, error_prob = 1 in 2^-242.530358
```

```
k=127, error_prob = 1 in 2^-244.530358
k=128, error_prob = 1 in 2^-246.530358
k=129, error_prob = 1 in 2^-248.530358
k=130, error_prob = 1 in 2^-250.530358
k=131, error_prob = 1 in 2^-252.530358
k=132, error_prob = 1 in 2^-254.530358
k=133, error_prob = 1 in 2^-256.530358
k=134, error_prob = 1 in 2^-258.530358
k=135, error_prob = 1 in 2^-260.530358
k=136, error_prob = 1 in 2^-262.530358
k=137, error_prob = 1 in 2^-264.530358
k=138, error_prob = 1 in 2^-266.530358
k=139, error_prob = 1 in 2^-268.530358
```

The Python code below uses the Miller–Rabin primality test from above to find 1024-bit numbers, with $k = 133$, so that the error probability is less than 1 in $2^{256}$.

**Listing 16.4:** Find Prime Algorithm

```python
def find_prime(bits):
    n = rand.getrandbits(bits)
    n = n | 0x01 # set the lowest bit
    n = n | (1 << (bits-1)) # set the upper bit
    k = 133
    while not(is_probably_prime(n,k)):
        n = rand.getrandbits(bits)
        n = n | 0x01 # set the lowest bit
        n = n | (1 << (bits-1)) # set the upper bit
    return n


for i in xrange(4):
    x = find_prime(1024)
    print "Prime_%X" % x
```

The output is a list of four highly probable primes:

```
Prime 8A65A43056AB2A98BA444F640A81D55EEBFBFF4489FC30B90AC4459F4F2779B2
      1733A7049C25D3B55755E540C735C9C348DB804BCFE2EFCC0998F74B44DC135A
      FABED7AE2E3
Prime D32391E53D8D0CADAF30BE665EB1D4F69240B5811E8619DB1623275349548DEB
      B1F6B502D677053C55F31386DB654BE0A84CC7939970B4720A
      155F8606C0B08C3CB26D31897
Prime CE93360201485167D6196AD02AB1B771EC0483EA7705AB3C0E6B25ECA9B87FE6
      0EA16B6CF657960BB759EC4AABE6C46500E67C5E150D16A66B01E4738DC2E459
      933EE87B393
Prime F8991884F5A27100B958C551FF43DF63D1A741CE4868F4B764329ED7DF50F734
      E9AC804F69ACFD9AEA76287560491094FD956426D90F672E8A4DAAE60787345A
      C98C9EE09D9
```

Since it is written in interpreted Python, it takes a few seconds to find each prime. More efficient implementations can be found in most cryptographic libraries, written in C, or some other compiled language.

## 16.1 Safe and Strong Primes

There are primes for which there are algorithms that significantly reduce the computational effort of factoring the product of two primes, where one is of a specific form. For example, Pollard's $p - 1$ algorithm provides an efficient way to factor $pq$ if $p - 1$ does not have a large prime factor.

A safe prime is a prime that does not suffer this vulnerability. A way to test for a prime being safe is to check that $p - 1$ is twice a Sophie Germain prime. A Sophie Germain prime is a prime $p$ for which $2p + 1$ is also a prime.

So, once a prime $p$ is found, compute $q = \frac{p-1}{2}$, and then check that $q$ is also prime. If not, then keep searching for $p$ that meets this criteria. This slows down the prime search a lot and is largely unnecessary for public keys of 2048 bits or larger.

Another class of prime is the Strong Prime, for which there are different definitions. Typically, a prime is $p + 1$ strong if the largest prime factor of $p + 1$ is large.[1]

The reason for this is that a factoring method called the Elliptic Curve Method (ECM), developed by Lenstra and available in [11], is more efficient than the $p - 1$ factoring method; it does not require weak primes. The only defence against the ECM algorithm is its use of larger primes.[2]

---

[1] The paper "Are Strong Primes Needed for RSA?" [23] by Ron Rivest and Robert Silverman, https://people.csail.mit.edu/rivest/pubs/RS01.version-1999-11-22.pdf goes into detail on the definitions of weak keys and safe and strong primes. It concludes that strong and safe primes are not effective at increasing security and that the only defence is to make $p$ large enough.

[2] Efficient algorithms for finding strong primes are given in Section 5 of the Rivest and Silverman paper [23]. However, since with current key sizes, using strong primes is not necessary, we will not go into details regarding the implementation here.

# 17 Additive Distributions

Noise sources, also termed entropy sources, sample noise from the environment and usually turn that noise into partially random data. We find environmental noise, such as noise in circuits or radiated noise or many other natural sources of noise, follow a nonuniform distribution, and that distribution tends to follow a "Gaussian" or "Normal" distribution. This section shows, by example, why this is the case.

## 17.1 Dice

Standard dice, when thrown, returns a uniform random number between 1 and 6, assuming we have a fair, perfectly balanced dice. If we throw multiple dice at the same time and add the results, the distribution ceases to be uniform and takes on a bell curve shape.

Here is a simple program to roll groups of dice a number of times and build the histogram of the frequency of the different results.

**Listing 17.1:** dice.py

```
#!/usr/bin/env python

import sys
import random
randsource = random.SystemRandom() # nondeterministic random source

iterations = int(sys.argv[1])   # Number of throws
number_of_dice = int(sys.argv[2])    # Number of dice each throw

bins = [0 for _ in range((number_of_dice*6)+3)]   # Roll the dice
for i in xrange(iterations):
    throw=0
    for j in xrange(number_of_dice):
        throw = throw + randsource.randint(1,6)
    bins[throw] +=1

print "x_y" # Print the header

max=0             # Find the maximum so we can normalize it
for f in bins:
    if f > max:
        max = f

for i in xrange(0,(6*number_of_dice)+3): #Print out the histogram
    print "%d_%f" % (i, float(bins[i])/float(max))
```

https://doi.org/10.1515/9781501506062-017

Figure 17.1 shows the change of the distribution of the result as the number of dice thrown, and added together, change from 1, 3, 5, 7 to 10 dice. Each time, 100 000 rolls are made to build up the distribution curve.

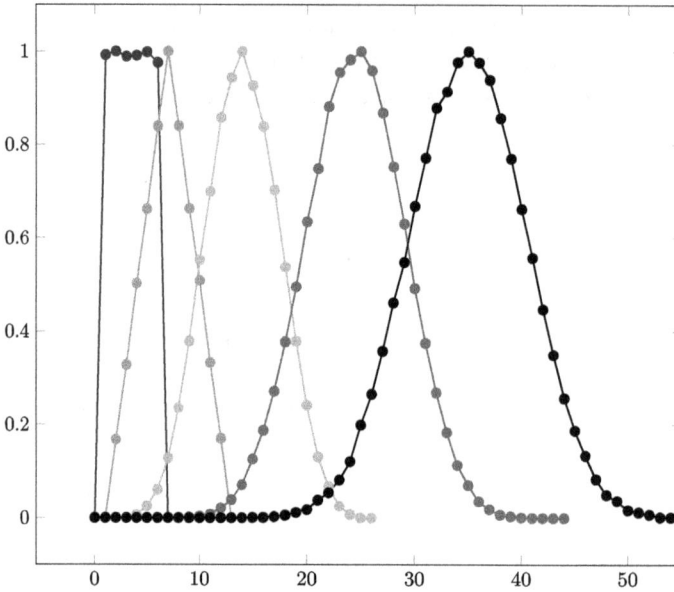

**Figure 17.1:** 100 000 Rolls of 1, 2, 4, 7 and 10 Dice.

We can see in Figure 17.1 how the distribution for 1 dice is close to uniform. As the number of dice per roll increases, the shape of the distribution starts to look more like a normal (or Gaussian) curve.

## 17.2 Unfair Dice

If we change the fair dice with unfair dice, we can see the nonuniform distribution of the dice in the leftmost plot that is formed by rolling 1 dice 100 000 times. As we add more unfair dice to the roll, we see the shape of the curve move toward being normally distributed, even though the dice has a nonuniform distribution. See Figure 17.2.

## 17.3 How the Normal Distribution Forms

We can now look at why the normal distribution seems to pop out whenever you add together a number of random events. To make things a little simpler, we will use coin tosses rather than dice, so there are only two outcomes that can map to binary bits.

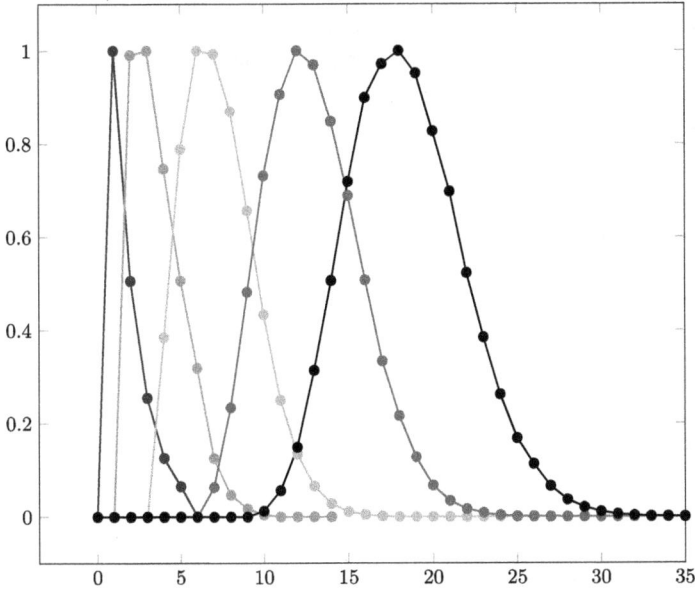

**Figure 17.2:** 100,000 Rolls of 1, 2, 4, 7 and 10 Unfair Dice.

Given a fair coin, the probability of heads is $\frac{1}{2}$, and the probability of tails is also $\frac{1}{2}$. So, we have a uniform distribution with two possible values. If we tread tails as 0 and heads as 1, we can add up multiple coin throws. That is, when throwing two coins and adding the result, we could end up with a result of either 0, 1, or 2.

However, for $n$ binary outcomes (in this case, $n = 2$), the number of possible combinations is $2^n$. So, for 2 coins, there are 4 combinations TT, TH, HT, HH, or 00, 01, 10, 11.

Those four combinations (see Table 17.1) of coin outcomes map to 3 end results, 0, 1, or 2.

As you can see, there is one way to get a 0, two ways to get a 1, and one way to get a 2. So $P(0) = \frac{1}{4}$, $P(1) = \frac{1}{2}$, $P(2) = \frac{1}{4}$. So, we no longer have a uniform distribution as with 1 coin. With two coins, we have a distribution with a bump in the middle.

**Table 17.1:** Result of Adding Two Coin Tosses.

| Coin Toss Outcome | Result |
|---|---|
| 0+0 | 0 |
| 0+1 | 1 |
| 1+0 | 1 |
| 1+1 | 2 |

We shall go on to see that "the number of ways" something can be, or can be arranged is both one of the ways of measuring entropy and also part of the reason we get normal distributions in nature.

If we go to three coins (see Table 17.2), then we find the distribution will have more states.

**Table 17.2:** Result of Adding Three Coin Tosses.

| Coin Toss Outcome | Result |
|---|---|
| 0+0+0 | 0 |
| 0+0+1 | 1 |
| 0+1+0 | 1 |
| 0+1+1 | 2 |
| 1+0+0 | 1 |
| 1+0+1 | 2 |
| 1+1+0 | 2 |
| 1+1+0 | 3 |

We now see one way to make 0, three ways to make 1, three ways to make 2, and one way to make 3.

If we write out a table (see Table 17.3) of the distributions for increasing numbers of coins in each toss, then we can see a pattern emerge that follows the normal curve. There are more ways to make the numbers in the middle of the distribution, and fewer as you move to the edges of the distribution, until you reach the largest and smallest values, which only have one way each.

**Table 17.3:** Distributions For Multiple Coin Tosses.

| Number of Coins | Combinations | Results | Distribution |
|---|---|---|---|
| 1 | 2 | 0, 1 | $\frac{1}{2}, \frac{1}{2}$ |
| 2 | 4 | 0, 1, 2 | $\frac{1}{4}, \frac{2}{4}, \frac{1}{4}$ |
| 3 | 8 | 0, ..., 3 | $\frac{1}{8}, \frac{3}{8}, \frac{3}{8}, \frac{1}{8}$ |
| 4 | 16 | 0, ..., 4 | $\frac{1}{16}, \frac{4}{16}, \frac{6}{16}, \frac{4}{16}, \frac{1}{16}$ |
| 5 | 32 | 0, ..., 5 | $\frac{1}{32}, \frac{5}{32}, \frac{10}{32}, \frac{10}{32}, \frac{5}{32}, \frac{1}{32}$ |
| 6 | 64 | 0, ..., 6 | $\frac{1}{64}, \frac{6}{64}, \frac{15}{64}, \frac{20}{64}, \frac{15}{64}, \frac{6}{64}, \frac{1}{64}$ |

# 18 Probability Distributions

In this chapter, we are looking at how the numbers drawn from random processes tend to be arranged. For example, the 6 numbers of a thrown dice may all be equally likely, and so have a uniform distribution. The intensity of light from a twinkling star varies about an average intensity and tends to have a Gaussian (also known as normal) distribution. The number of clicks from a Geiger counter, every second, might follow a distribution that looks Gaussian, but if the number is very low, that Gaussian curve gets squished against the left, which is called a Poisson curve.

The terminology for distributions is often used loosely. So, first, we take a look at the names of the various types of distributions we will encounter.

## 18.1 Names of Probability Distributions

While the term "probability distribution" is used to denote a general idea of how the probability of individual events is spread among those events; it is not a well-defined term. Those distributions may be discrete or continuous and may be cumulative or not. "Probability Distribution" is a general term; it can be made more specific by adding adjectives such as "cumulative", "continuous", or "discrete".

There are more specific names, such as PMF (Probability Mass Function), PDF (Probability Density Function), and the still ambiguous CDF (Cumulative Density Function).

|  | Discrete | Continuous |
|---|---|---|
| Not Cumulative | Probability Mass Function | Probability Density Function |
| Cumulative | Cumulative Distribution Function | Cumulative Distribution Function |

While there is some logic to the terms probability mass function and probability density function being used to denote the discrete and continuous cases, the term cumulative distribution function is used for both discrete and continuous distributions, and so may need to be clarified by adding "discrete" or "continuous" to the description.

Typically, terms are used loosely, and all these things will be called a "probability distribution", or PDF is used both in the discrete and continuous contexts, and the reader is supposed to infer from the context what is meant. The most obvious guide is the graphs.

If you are looking at something like Figure 18.1, then you have a continuous, non-cumulative PDF. The distribution goes up and back down again. A cumulative distribution is monotonic; it never goes back down again, so it is a PDF, not a CDF. The continuous line tells us that it is continuous.

https://doi.org/10.1515/9781501506062-018

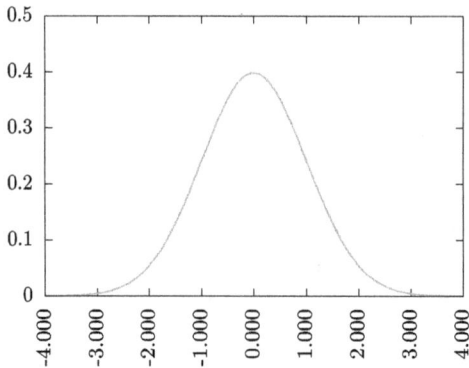

**Figure 18.1:** An Example PDF.

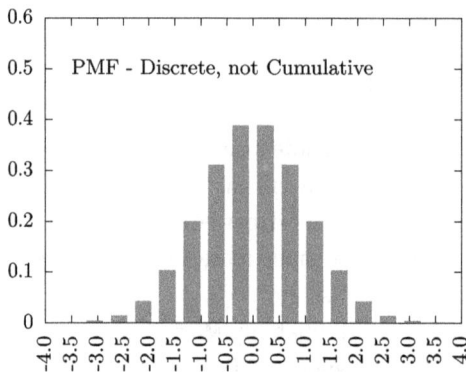

PMF - Discrete, not Cumulative

**Figure 18.2:** An Example PMF.

If you are looking at something like Figure 18.2, then you have a discrete, noncumulative PMF. The individual bars indicate that we are dealing with discrete points of ranges.

If you are looking at something like Figure 18.3, then you have a continuous, cumulative CDF. The distribution rises from left to right and never falls when moving from left to right, and so it is monotonic. Therefore, it is a CDF, not a PDF. The continuous line tells us that it is continuous.

If you are looking at something like Figure 18.4, you have a discrete, cumulative CDF. The distribution rises from left to right and never falls when moving from left to right, and so it is monotonic. This is a clue that it is a CDF, not a PDF. A CDF is the integral of a PDF, and the values in the PDF can never be negative. So, the CDF can only go up or stay the same as it goes from left to right. The individual bars indicate that we are dealing with discrete points of ranges.

In this book, we will use PDF, PMF, cCDF, and dCDF for Probability Density Function, Probability Mass Function, Continuous Cumulative Distribution Function, and Discrete Cumulative Distribution Function, respectively.

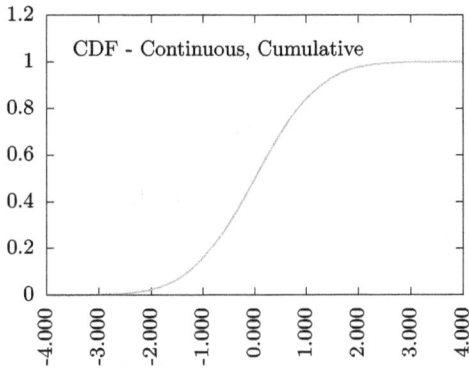

**Figure 18.3:** An Example Continuous CDF.

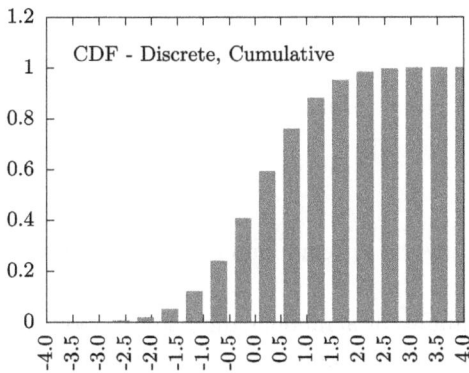

**Figure 18.4:** An Example Discrete CDF.

## 18.2 Properties of Distributions

All common types of distribution, including those used in this book, have some common properties.

First, the probabilities in PMF (continuous) or PDF (discrete) distributions add up to 1. For a discrete distribution $X$ with $n$ points,

$$\sum_{i=1}^{n} P(X = i) = 1.$$

For a PMF continuous distribution from 0 to $n$, the area under the curve is 1:

$$\int_{i=0}^{n} x(i) = 1.$$

## 18.3 Fair Dice and Uniform Random Numbers

Uniform random numbers generally take the form of a sequence of numbers picked from a range of numbers, where the chance of each number occurring is equal. Hence, the name "uniform" comes from the equal probability of each of the possible values.

If we have a normal 6-sided dice and throw it 18 times, we might get the following sequence of numbers between 1 and 6, picked at random:

```
[2, 2, 1, 6, 1, 1, 1, 2, 1, 1, 2, 1, 4, 1, 5, 3, 3, 6].
```

Since this book has a focus on RNGs in computers, rather than rolling actual dice, we will use computer programs. This sequence was created with the following Python program:

**Listing 18.1:** dice1.py

```
import sys, random
randsource = random.SystemRandom() # nondeterministic random source

throws = [randsource.randint(1,6) for x in xrange(18)]
print throws
```

This builds a list of 18 numbers, calling the system random service to return a random number between 1 and 6, inclusive.

Even though the numbers are picked uniformly at random, this does not look uniform. If the frequency of the numbers in the sequence were uniform, then the expected frequency of each value is $\frac{18}{6}$ = 3. The counts are:

```
We rolled 1 eight times.
We rolled 2 four times.
We rolled 3 twice.
We rolled 4 once.
We rolled 5 once.
We rolled 6 twice.
```

So while the numbers were picked uniformly, the numbers we ended up with are clearly not uniform. The distribution is uniform, the sequence generated from the distribution is (probably) not.

In a truly uniform randomly generated sequence, any short sequence can be expected to appear nonuniform. As the length of the sequence increases, the uniformity tends to increase, although if it is truly uniform, all possible sequences, including those that look very uniform and those that look completely nonuniform are in fact equally likely. The tendency for uniformly generated data to appear to be more uniform, the longer the sequence of numbers generated, results from there being many more uniform looking combinations than nonuniform looking combinations.

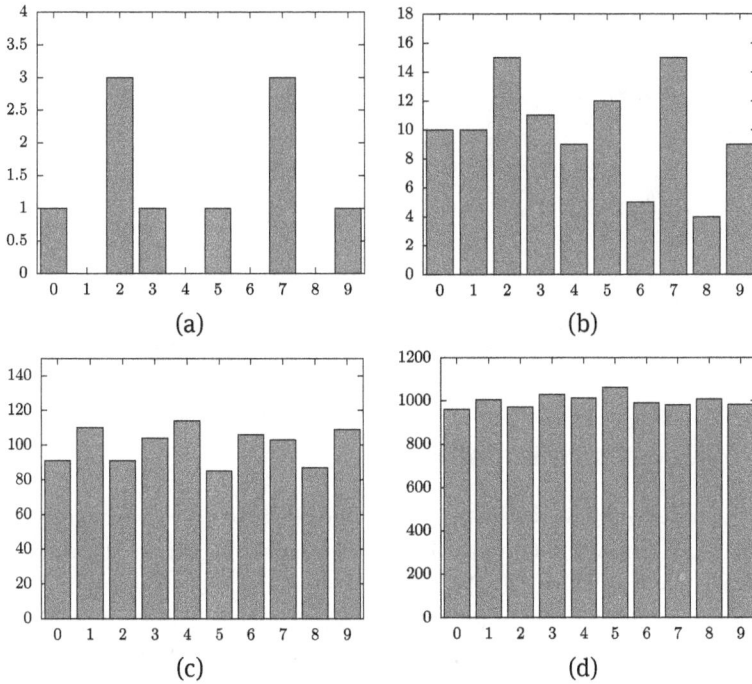

**Figure 18.5:** (a) Histogram of 10 Random Digits; (b) Histogram of 100 Random Digits; (c) Histogram of 1000 Random Digits; (d) Histogram of 10 000 Random Digits.

To make the diagrams prettier, we will switch to using a 10-sided dice, with the sides labeled from 0 to 9.

If we roll our 10-sided dice many more times, the output tends to look more uniform. Figures 18.5 (a), 18.5 (b), 18.5 (c), and 18.5 (d) show the distributions for 10, 100, 1000, and 10 000 digits, respectively. We can see that the distribution becomes more uniform as the number of numbers increases.

If we jump a couple of orders of magnitude and plot a frequency histogram of 10 000 000 rolls of the 10 sided dice, we get Figure 18.6.

As we can see, it is now hard to distinguish the distribution from a uniform distribution.

A conventional dice is an example of a device to generate uniform random numbers between 1 and 6. In practice, dice are never perfect. They often have some bias, where the different numbers are more or less likely to occur as a result of nonuniformity in the material or the construction of the dice. All RNGs suffer from this problem to a greater or lesser extent. In later chapters, we will explore ways to take imperfect random numbers and algorithmically transform them into another distribution, such as uniform or Gaussian.

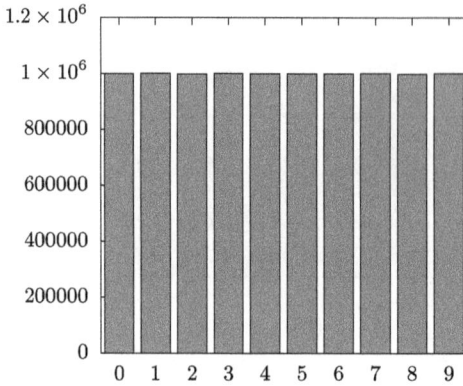

**Figure 18.6:** Histogram of 10 000 000 Random Digits.

## 18.4 Normal/Gaussian Distributions

Distributions of random data we find in nature are often distributed following the normal or Gaussian distribution. In Chapter 17, we look at how the normal distribution forms. Here, we will just see what it looks like and note some of its properties.

The normal probability density function (PDF) is described by the equation below. In engineering and some mathematical texts, the character $\varphi$ is used for the normal probability distribution function.

$$\text{normalpdf}(x) = \varphi(x) = \frac{e^{-\frac{1}{2}x^2}}{\sqrt{2\pi}}.$$

This looks like Figure 18.7.

This represents the shape of general normal distribution that many datasets take, but is scaled and positioned, such that the mean $\mu = 0$, the area under the curve is 1, and the standard deviation $\sigma = 1$, and hence the variance $\sigma^2 = 1$.

The cumulative distribution function (CDF) is the function describing the probability of an event drawn from the probability distribution to be less than the value $x$.

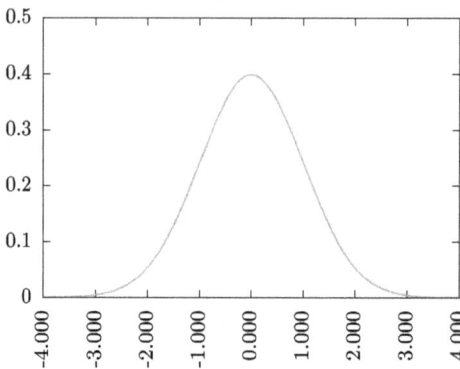

**Figure 18.7:** Curve of the Standard Normal Probability Density Function.

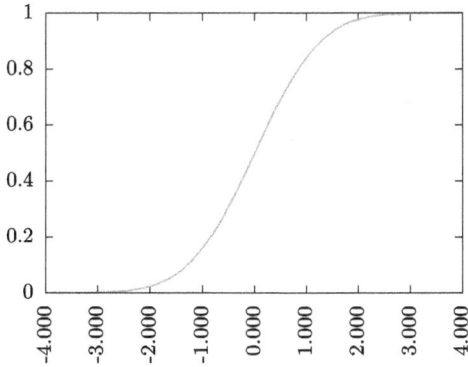

Mathematically, the CDF is the integral of the PDF. It is sometimes represented using the uppercase phi $\Phi$:

$$\text{normalcdf}(x) = \Phi(x) = \frac{1}{\sqrt{2\pi}} \int_{-\infty}^{x} e^{-\frac{1}{2}x^2} dx.$$

The standard normal CDF curve is shown in Figure 18.8. As we would expect, the function goes from 0 to 1, since the area under the standard normal PDF curve is 1.

There is no closed form equation for the normal CDF. It is usually computed using iterative numerical methods. Most computer languages have built-in or library functions that can efficiently compute the normal CDF curve.

There is a related function erf, which is

$$\text{erf}(x) = \frac{1}{\sqrt{\pi}} \int_{-x}^{x} e^{-t^2} dt.$$

Since the PDF function that is being integrated over is symmetrical, this can be simplified by integrating over half the area, and doubling the constant multiplier

$$\text{erf}(x) = \frac{2}{\sqrt{\pi}} \int_{0}^{x} e^{-t^2} dt.$$

By substituting this expression into the standard normal CDF equation, we get:

$$\Phi(x) = \frac{1 + \text{erf}\left(\frac{x}{\sqrt{2}}\right)}{2}.$$

The standard normal PDF is a special case of the general normal curves. The spread of the PDF is characterized as the standard deviation, represented by the $\sigma$ symbol.

The $x$ position of the mean of the distribution is represented by the $\mu$ symbol.

We can generalize the normal PDF function using $\mu$ and $\sigma$:

$$\text{normalpdf}(x, \sigma, \mu) = \frac{\varphi(\frac{x-\mu}{\sigma})}{\sigma} = \frac{1}{\sigma\sqrt{2\pi}}e^{-\frac{(x-\mu)^2}{2\sigma^2}}.$$

Likewise, the standard normal CDF generalized with $\mu$ and $\sigma$ is as follows:

$$\text{normalcdf}(x, \sigma, \mu) = \Phi(\frac{x-\mu}{\sigma}).$$

In the General Normal PDF, varying $\mu$ moves the peak of the density function to $\mu$ on the x axis. Figure 18.9 shows three normal distributions with $\sigma = 1$ and $\mu = 0$ (for the center curve), $\mu = -3$ (for the leftmost curve), and $\mu = 2$ (for the rightmost curve).

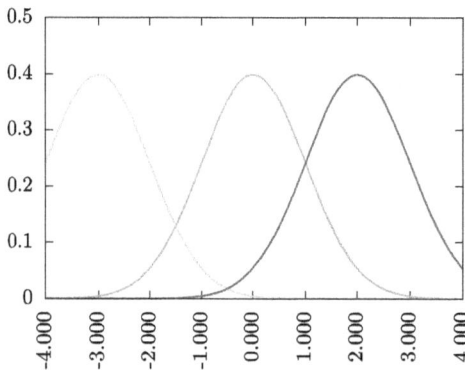

**Figure 18.9:** Normal Curves With $\mu = -3$, $\mu = 0, \mu = 2$.

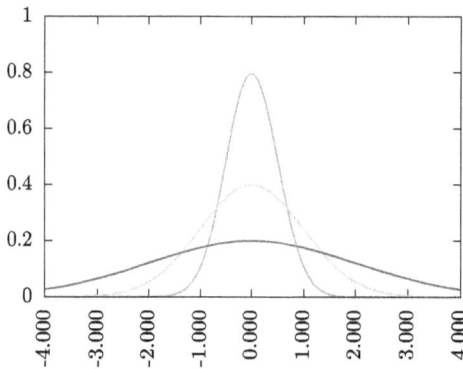

**Figure 18.10:** Normal Curves With $\sigma = 0.5$, $\sigma = 1, \sigma = 2$.

Varying $\sigma$ varies the spread of the curve. As $\sigma$ increases, the spread increases, and the amplitude decreases in order to maintain the area under the curve as 1. Figure 18.10 shows three normal distributions with $\mu = 1$ and $\sigma = 0.5$ (for the narrowest curve), $\sigma = 1$ (for the middle curve), and $\sigma = 2$ (for the widest curve).

Figure 18.11 shows three curves, where we vary both parameters. The leftmost curve has $\mu = -2$, $\sigma = 0.5$, the center curve has $\mu = 1$, $\sigma = 1$, and the rightmost curve has $\mu = 2$, $\sigma = 2$.

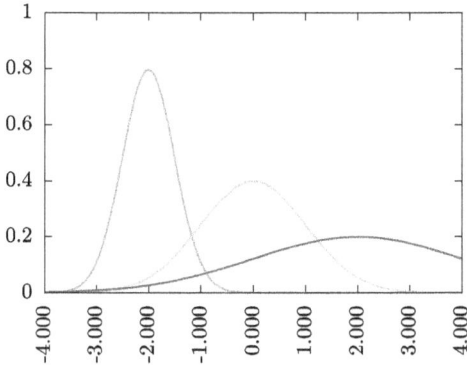

**Figure 18.11:** Normal Curves With $\mu = -2$, $\sigma = 0.5$; $\mu = 0$, $\sigma = 1$; and $\mu = 2$, $\sigma = 2$.

All continuous normal probability density curves can be completely described with just the two parameters $\mu$ and $\sigma$. These distributions are used in many fields of mathematics. In random number generators, PDFs and CDFs are primarily used to model some of the underlying physical phenomena that entropy sources are built on.

### 18.4.1 Normal PDFs and CDFs in Programming Languages

Here, we take a look at how to access functions related to normal distributions in computer languages. There are eight common types of functions for the normal distributions that we consider here. Some are supported directly in some languages, but in some languages we need to build these functions out of other functions. Following are examples of functions related to normal distributions in computer languages:

$\varphi(x)$ the standard normal PDF function.

normalpdf$(x, \mu, \sigma)$ the related general normal PDF function given $\mu$ and $\sigma$.

$\Phi(x)$ the standard normal CDF $\Phi(x)$.

$\Phi^{-1}(p)$ the inverse of $\Phi(x)$.

normalcdf$(x, \mu, \sigma)$ general normal CDF function given $\mu$ and $\sigma$.

erf$(x)$ the error function. This is the underlying function that needs to be computed using numerical approximation algorithms in order to implement CDF function. So, it is usually a good idea for a language to provide an efficient implementation of this either directly or within a library.

erf$^{-1}(x)$ is the inverse of the error function erf$(x)$. Like erf$(x)$, this function needs to be computed using numerical approximation methods.

qcdf (*p*) is the inverse function to the normal CDF, also called the percentile point function. This returns the *x* position on the normal CDF that would yield the probability *P*; that is, if $x = \text{qcdf}(p, \mu, \sigma)$, then $p = \Phi(x, \mu, \sigma)$.

normalrand($\mu$, $\sigma$) is the random deviate function that returns random numbers drawn from a normal distribution.

Most computational environments provide functions for working with normal distributions. Here, we examine examples in Gnuplot, Python, R, C, and Excel.

### 18.4.2 Gnuplot Normal Distribution Functions

| Function | Gnuplot Function | Comment |
|---|---|---|
| $\varphi(x)$ | Not Implemented | Define as phi(x) = (exp((-0.5)*x*x))/(sqrt(2.0*pi) |
| normalpdf($x, \mu, \sigma$) | Not Implemented | Define as normalpdf(x,mu,sigma) = phi((x-mu)/sigma)/sigma |
| $\Phi(x)$ | norm(x) | Directly Supported |
| $\Phi^{-1}(x)$ | invnorm(x) | Directly Supported |
| normalcdf($x, \mu, \sigma$) | Not Implemented | Define as normalcdf(x,mu,sigma) = norm((x-mu)/sigma) |
| erf ($x$) | erf(x) | Directly Supported |
| erf$^{-1}(x)$ | inverf(x) | Directly Supported |
| qcdf ($x, \mu, \sigma$) | Not Implemented | Define as qcdf(p,mu,sigma) = mu+(sigma*invnorm(p)) |
| normalrand($\mu, \sigma$) | Not Implemented | Usually source random variates from a file |

Gnuplot provides the norm(x) function. This returns the value of the standard normal CDF at position *x*.

The following Gnuplot program generates the plot of the standard normal CDF shown in Figure 18.8 using the norm(x) function.

```
set term png
set output '../img/normalcdf_curve.pdf'
set xrange [-4:4]
set yrange [0:1.0]
set format x "%2.3f"
set xtics rotate
set key off
set style line 1 lw 3
plot norm(x) with lines linestyle 1
```

Gnuplot does not have a direct function for the normal PDF, but unlike the CDF, the normal PDF function is simple to express as a closed form function. The Gnuplot code below plots the three normal PDFs shown in Figure18.11.

The function normalpdf(X) is created, which returns the value of the standard normal PDF at position *x*.

The function normalpdfms(x,mu,sigma) is created, which returns the value at position $x$ of a general normal PDF with parameters mu and sigma. It is defined in terms of normalpdf(x).

```
set term png
set output '../img/normalpdf_musigma_curve.pdf'
set xrange [-4:4]
set yrange [0:1.0]
set format x "%2.3f"
set xtics rotate
set key off
set style line 1 lw 3
set style line 2 lw 3
set style line 3 lw 3
normalpdf(x) = (exp((-0.5)*x*x))/(sqrt(2.0*pi))
normalpdfms(x,mu,sigma) = normalpdf((x-mu)/sigma)/sigma
plot normalpdfms(x,-2,0.5) with lines linestyle 1, \
        normalpdfms(x,0,1) with lines linestyle 2, \
        normalpdfms(x,2,2) with lines linestyle 3
```

Gnuplot also does not support the quantile function. It is necessary to define it as a function based on the built-in invnorm() function

```
qcdf(p,mu,sigma) = mu+(sigma*invnorm(p)).
```

### 18.4.3 Python Normal Distribution Functions

The Python SciPy library provides a set of functions for handling distributions, with all the functions described above and many more.

| Function | Python SciPy Function |
|---|---|
| $\varphi(x)$ | scipy.stats.norm.pdf(x) |
| normalpdf$(x, \mu, \sigma)$ | scipy.stats.norm.pdf(x,loc=mu,scale=sigma) |
| $\Phi(x)$ | scipy.stats.norm.cdf(x) |
| $\Phi^{-1}(x)$ | scipy.stats.norm.ppf(x) |
| normalcdf$(x, \mu, \sigma)$ | scipy.stats.norm.cdf(x,loc=mu,scale=sigma) |
| erf$(x)$ | scipy.special.erf(x) |
| erf$^{-1}(x)$ | scipy.special.erfinv(x) |
| qcdf$(p, \mu, \sigma)$ | scipy.stats.norm.ppf(p,loc=mu,scale=sigma) |
| normalrand$(\mu, \sigma)$ | scipy.stats.norm.rvs(mu,sigma) |

There are many more related functions described on the scipy website at https://docs.scipy.org/doc/scipy-0.16.1/reference/generated/scipy.stats.norm.html.

Python also supports the error function erf(x) in the math library but not the inverse error function.

```
import math
for i in xrange(8):
    print "erf(%f)␣=␣%f" % ((i-4.0)/2.0, math.erf(((i-4.0)/2.0)))
```

Output

```
erf(-2.000000) = -0.995322
erf(-1.500000) = -0.966105
erf(-1.000000) = -0.842701
erf(-0.500000) = -0.520500
erf(0.000000) = 0.000000
erf(0.500000) = 0.520500
erf(1.000000) = 0.842701
erf(1.500000) = 0.966105
```

Random Gaussian variates can by generated by calling the random.gauss(mu, sigma) function.

```
import random as r

for i in xrange(10):
    r.gauss(0,1)
```

Output

```
0.255924212351608
-2.563407082261902
0.005161255006346413
0.5554792171614131
1.6118922380580807
1.359738127117484
-0.5008807117968405
0.48083265035674355
-0.9303369735608747
0.6418591080114107
```

Using the equations shown above, it is easy to implement some of the functions directly in Python.

The following Python code computes the standard normal CDF $\Phi(x)$:

```
import math
def phi(x):
    return 0.5*(math.erf(x / math.sqrt(2.0))+1.0)
```

This python code computes the standard normal PDF:

```
import math
def normalpdf(x):
    return math.exp((-0.5)*x*x)/(math.sqrt(2.0*math.pi))
```

### 18.4.4 R Normal Distribution Functions

The R language provides a consistently named set of functions for statistical distributions, with a prefix d for the PDF, p for the PMF, q for the quantile function, and r for
random deviates. The prefix is followed by the distribution name, which for the normal
distribution is norm. The error functions $\operatorname{erf}(x)$ and $\operatorname{erf}^{-1}(x)$ are not directly available.
They can be built from the pnorm and qnorm functions, respectively. Various libraries
implement the error functions.

| Function | R Function |
|---|---|
| $\varphi(x)$ | dnorm(x) |
| normalpdf$(x, \mu, \sigma)$ | dnorm(q, mean, sd) |
| $\Phi(x)$ | pnorm(X) |
| $\Phi^{-1}(p)$ | qnorm(p) |
| normalcdf$(x, \mu, \sigma)$ | pnorm(x, mean, sd) |
| $\operatorname{erf}(x)$ | erf <- function(x) 2 * pnorm(x * sqrt(2)) - 1 |
| $\operatorname{erf}^{-1}(x)$ | erfinv <- function (x) qnorm((1 + x)/2)/sqrt(2) |
| qcdf $(p, \mu, \sigma)$ | qnorm(p, mean, sd) |
| normalrand$(\mu, \sigma)$ | rnorm(mean,sigma) |

The R documentation for the normal distribution functions is available at: https://
stat.ethz.ch/R-manual/R-devel/library/stats/html/Normal.html.
    The following R code generates a plot of the R pnorm() and dnorm() functions.

**Listing 18.2:** R Code to Plot pnorm() and dnorm() Functions

```
#!/usr/bin/env Rscript

# Output to PDF file r_normalplot.pdf
pdf("../img/r_normalplot.pdf")

x <- seq(-4, 4, length=100)
px <- pnorm(x)
dx <- dnorm(x)

plot(x, dx, type="l", lty=2, xlab="x",
   ylab="pnorm(x)_dnorm(x)", main="R_pnorm_and_dnorm_distribution",
   xlim=c(-4, 4), ylim=c(0, 1.1))

lines(x, px, lwd=2)
legend(-4,1, c("pnorm(x)","dnorm(x)"), lty=c(1,2))

dev.off()
q()
```

    The output is shown in Figure 18.12.

**R pnorm and dnorm distribution**

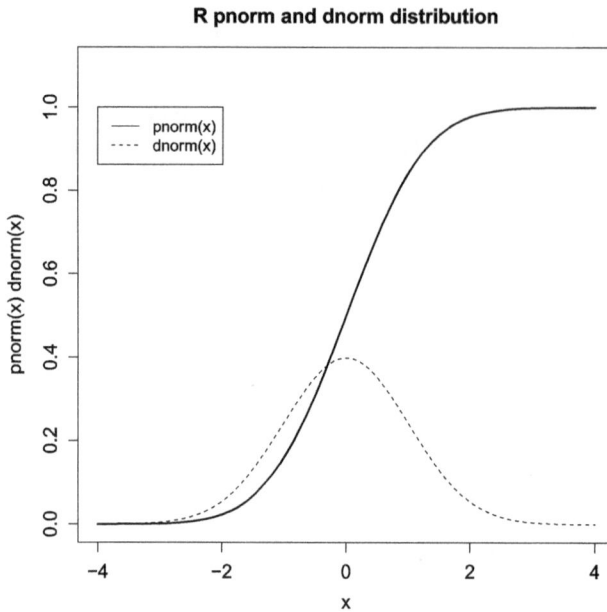

Figure 18.12: R pnorm(x) and dnorm(x) Functions.

### 18.4.5 C Normal Distribution Functions

The math library of C only provides the erf and gamma functions from our list of functions. The other distribution functions will need to be built from scratch. There is no normal random deviate function either, so we will look at the Box–Muller transform and Ziggurat algorithms for generating normally distributed random deviates from uniform random inputs.

| Function | C Function |
|---|---|
| $\varphi(x)$ | Not Supported |
| normalpdf$(x, \mu, \sigma)$ | Not Supported |
| $\Phi(x)$ | Not Supported |
| $\Phi^{-1}(p)$ | Not Supported |
| normalcdf$(x, \mu, \sigma)$ | Not Supported |
| erf $(x)$ | erf(x) in the math library |
| erf$^{-1}(x)$ | Not Supported |
| qcdf $(p, \mu, \sigma)$ | Not Supported |
| normalrand$(\mu, \sigma)$ | Not Supported |

The C code in Listing 18.3 implements the standard normal PDF, the normal PDF given $\mu$ and $\sigma$, the standard normal CDF, and the normal CDF given $\mu$ and $\sigma$. The main() routine outputs a few points along the curves, and we can see the results look about right in Figure 18.13.

**Listing 18.3:** C Code for Normal PDF

```c
#include <math.h>
#include <stdio.h>

double standard_normalpdf(double x) {
    double p;
    double pi = M_PI;
    p = (exp((-0.5)*x*x))/(sqrt(2.0*pi));
    return p;
}

double normalpdf(double x, double mu, double sigma) {
    double p;
    p = standard_normalpdf((x-mu)/sigma)/sigma;
    return p;
}

double standard_normalcdf(double x) {
    double p;

    p = (1.0 + erf(x/sqrt(2.0)))/2.0;
    return p;
}

double normalcdf(double x, double mu, double sigma) {
    double p;

    p = standard_normalcdf((x-mu)/sigma);;
    return p;
}

int main() {
    double x;

    for (x=-4.0; x <= 4.001; x+=0.1) {
        printf("%0.2f␣␣%1.8f\n",x,standard_normalpdf(x));
    }
    for (x=-4.0; x <= 4.001; x+=0.1) {
        printf("%0.2f␣␣%1.8f\n",x,normalpdf(x,-1.0,0.6));
    }
    for (x=-4.0; x <= 4.001; x+=0.1) {
        printf("%0.2f␣␣%1.8f\n",x,standard_normalcdf(x));
    }
    for (x=-4.0; x <= 4.001; x+=0.1) {
        printf("%0.2f␣␣%1.8f\n",x,normalcdf(x,1.0,0.25));
    }
}
```

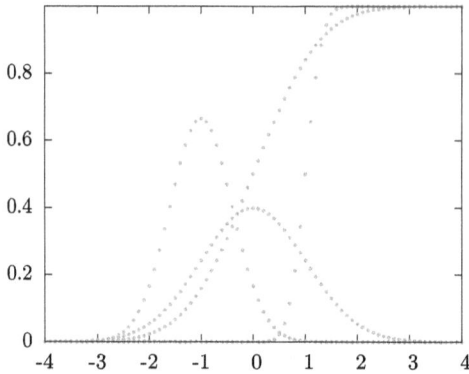

**Figure 18.13:** C Normal PDF and CDF Output Plot.

The inverse error function is not so simple to implement. The following code implements the series expansion equations described at http://mathworld.wolfram.com/InverseErf.html. The plot of the results is in Figure 18.14. However, this algorithm is only accurate to 8 decimal places. The principal problem is that the accuracy of the algorithm decreases as the parameter gets closer to –1 or 1, and so requires an increasing number of terms in the series expansion to maintain accuracy. To achieve 8 decimal places, 1000 iterations are used. So, for that level of accuracy, it is very inefficient.

**Listing 18.4:** C Code for Inverse Error Function

```c
#include <math.h>
#include <stdio.h>

// Compute erfinv using series expansion
// http://mathworld.wolfram.com/InverseErf.html

double erfinv(double p) {
    #define KMAX 1000 /* number of iterations */
    int k,m,n,i;
    long double c[KMAX];
    long double erfi, an, x, xpower;

    if (p <= -1.0) return -INFINITY;
    if (p >= 1.0) return INFINITY;

    // compute c_k
    c[0] = 1.0;
    c[1] = 1.0;
    for (k=2; k<KMAX;k++) {
        c[k] = 0.0;
        for (m=0; m<k;m++){
            c[k] += (c[m] * c[k-1-m])/((m+1.0)*((2.0*m)+1.0));
        }
```

```
    }

    x = p * (sqrt(M_PI)) / 2.0;
    xpower = x;
    erfi = x;

    for (n=1;n<KMAX;n++) {
        an = c[n] / ((2.0*n)+1);
        xpower = xpower * x * x;
        erfi += an*xpower;
    }

    return erfi;
}

int main() {
    double p;

    for (p=-1.0; p < 1.001; p+=0.01) {
        printf("%0.2f␣␣%1.8f\n",p,erfinv(p));
    }
}
```

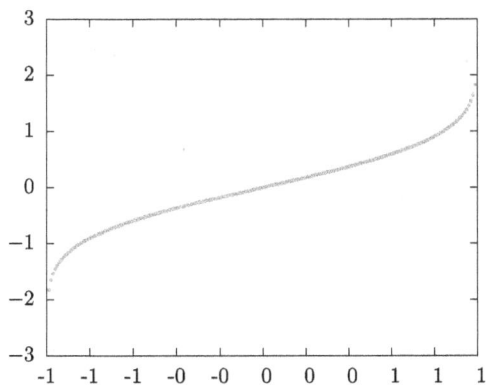

**Figure 18.14:** C Inverse Error Function Plot.

More efficient algorithms split the input into different ranges and implement different approximation algorithms for the different ranges. Two examples of efficient implementations can be seen in the boost C++ library at http://www.boost.org/doc/libs/1_37_0/boost/math/special_functions/detail/erf_inv.hpp and a Go language implementation here https://github.com/markthelaw/GoStatHelper/blob/master/StatUtil/StatUtil.go.

Unless our goal is to improve on the established piecewise algorithms, it is recommended to replicate or use existing library code.

For generating normally distributed random deviates, see the Box–Muller transform in Section 7.1 and the Ziggurat algorithm in Section 7.2.

### 18.4.6 Excel Normal Distribution Functions

The Microsoft Excel spreadsheet program supports all the functions here, except for the inverse error function, which can be built from the built-in gamma function.

| Function | C Function |
|---|---|
| $\varphi(x)$ | NORMDIST(x, 0, 1, False) |
| normalpdf$(x, \mu, \sigma)$ | NORMDIST(x, mean, standard_dev, False) |
| $\Phi(x)$ | NORMDIST(x, 0, 1, True) |
| $\Phi^{-1}(p)$ | NORMSINV(p) |
| normalcdf$(x, \mu, \sigma)$ | NORMDIST(x, mean, standard_dev, True) |
| erf$(x)$ | ERF(x) |
| erf$^{-1}(x)$ | SQRT(GAMMAINV(p,0.5,1)) |
| qcdf$(p, \mu, \sigma)$ | NORMINV(p, mean, standard_dev) |
| normalrand$(\mu, \sigma)$ | NORMINV(RAND(),mean,standard_dev) |

## 18.5 Random Walks and Degrees of Freedom

Here, we take a look at random walks, with the goal of clarifying the meaning and effect of degrees of freedom, which occur in a less obvious manner in many statistical tests, such as the Chi-Square test and the ANOVA test.

Random walks provide an easy way to visualize how some classes of distribution form. A random walk is modelled as a series of points. The state of the system is at one of the points, and each step will move to an adjacent point, choosing at random between the available adjacent points.

Figure 18.15 shows the path of 5 random walks on a 2D plane.

In Figure 18.16, each point shows the final position of each of 500 random walks, after 100 random steps in a 2D plane.

One notable feature of this plot is that while 100 steps are being taken, the endpoints cluster around the center and rarely get beyond a distance of 60.

We start by examining a simpler situation of a random walk moving along the line of integers by +1 or –1 each step, starting at 0. In this example, 30 steps are taken, so the final state will land somewhere between –30 and +30. Each step, left or right, is equally probable. We repeat the process 10 000 times and plot the distribution of the final position after 30 steps.

The following code computes the distribution of the final distance from the origin of 10 000 walks, each of 30 steps, along a line.

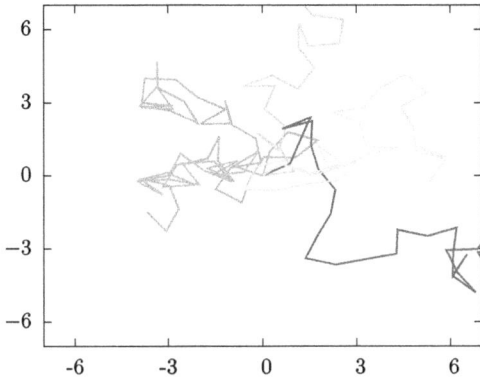

**Figure 18.15:** Random Walk Paths.

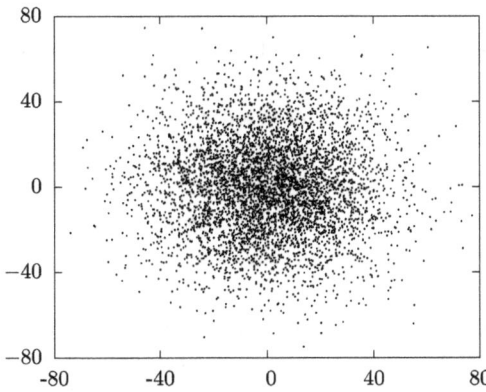

**Figure 18.16:** Random Walk Endpoints.

**Listing 18.5:** random_walk_1d.py

```python
#!/usr/bin/env python

import random
repetitions = 10000
steps = 30
finalstates = [0 for i in xrange(0,steps+1)]
for i in xrange(repetitions):
    state = 0
    for j in xrange(steps):
        if random.choice([True, False]):
            state += 1
        else:
            state -= 1
    finalstates[abs(state)] += 1
# Print out
for i in xrange(0,steps+1):
    print "%d_%d" % (i,finalstates[i])
```

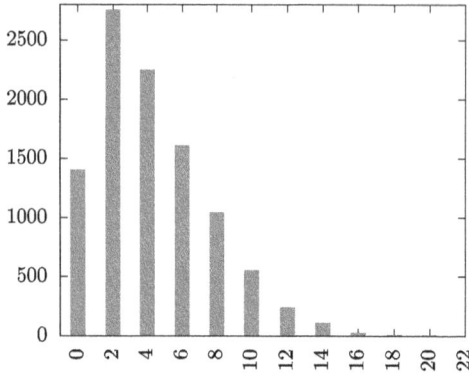

**Figure 18.17:** Random Walk Distribution of 10000 One-Dimensional Walks.

Plotting the output we get Figure 18.17.

We can see how the random walker is more likely to end up close to the center than further away. This logically arises from the random steps being uniformly distributed (50% left, 50% right), so, on average, the number of leftward steps is close to the number of rightward steps.

However, landing right on the center is not the most likely outcome. You can see it is about twice as likely that the walker ends up one unit away from the origin. One way of thinking of this is that there are twice as many places (2) that are one step away from the origin, but there is only 1 origin.

We can also see that the final distance from the origin is always even. This is because we are taking an even number of steps. Therefore, if we take the steps in pairs, either we are moving no distance (left + right, right + left), or we are moving a distance of two (left + left, right + right).

In the parlance of statistics, we would say our walker has "one degree of freedom". In other words, the freedom to move along a one-dimensional line.

We can take a look at what happens if we free our walker from the line and let her walk on a two-dimensional plane. So, now, the rules are that at each step taken, the walker randomly picks a direction on the plane and walks one step in that direction.

If we can go from 1 dimension to 2, obviously we can also try it in 3 or more dimensions. The following code computes the distribution of the final distance from the origin of 10 000 walks, each of 30 steps, in $n$ dimensions, where we can freely choose $n$.

**Listing 18.6:** random_walk_nd.py

```
#!/usr/bin/env python

import sys
import random
import math
repetitions = 10000
steps = 30
```

```
n = int(sys.argv[1])       # Number of dimensions
limit = int(sys.argv[2]) # Maximum bin number
if len(sys.argv) > 2:
    granularity = int(sys.argv[3])
else:
    granularity = 1

def random_unit_n_vector(n):
    v = [random.gauss(0, 1) for i in xrange(n)]
    m = math.sqrt(sum(x*x for x in v))
    return [x/m for x in v]

finaldistance = [0 for x in xrange(0,(granularity*steps)+1)]
for i in xrange(repetitions):
    state = [0.0 for x in xrange(n)]
    for j in xrange(steps):
        step = random_unit_n_vector(n)
        state2 = [a + b for a,b in zip(state, step)]
        state = state2
    distance = math.sqrt(sum(x*x for x in state))
    intdist = int(math.floor(distance*granularity))
    finaldistance[intdist]+=1

# Print out
for i in xrange((granularity*limit)+1):
    print "%2.1f_%d" % (float(i)/float(granularity),finaldistance[i])
```

We invoke this program as follows:

```
./random_walk_nd <number of dimensions> <maximum bin number> <granularity>
```

The granularity parameter determines how many bins to split the data into per unit distance. So granularity = 4 would lead to 4 bins that were $\frac{1}{4}$ of a unit distance wide.

Figures 18.18, 18.19 and 18.20 are the distributions for random walks in 2, 3, and 4 dimensions. The distance is now no longer an integer, and we divide them into fractional bins to plot the histogram with an adequate resolution.

We can see the curve tightens up (become more narrow) and takes on a shape closer to a Gaussian distribution as the number of dimensions increases. We might conclude that, if we add more dimensions, then it gets progressively closer to being a Gaussian distribution.

If we let our hyperdimensional walker walk freely in 100 dimension space, the distribution indeed looks gaussian. See Figure 18.21.

There are a number of statistical tests such as the Chi-Square test and the ANOVA test, where a parameter of the test is "degrees of freedom". The degrees-of-freedom parameter selects between a family of curves that become progressively more Gaussian

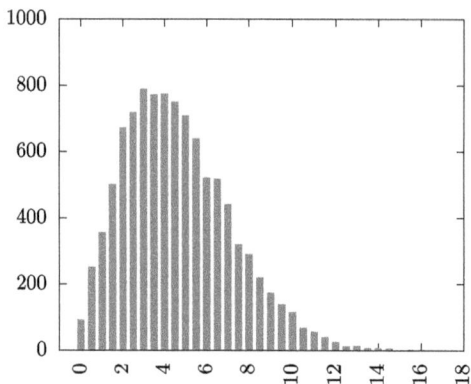

**Figure 18.18:** Random Walk Distribution of 10000 2 Dimensional Walks.

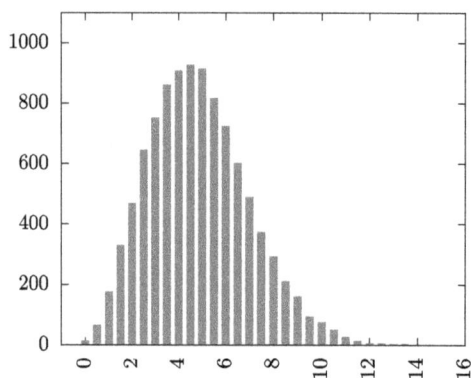

**Figure 18.19:** Random Walk Distribution of 10000 3 Dimensional Walks.

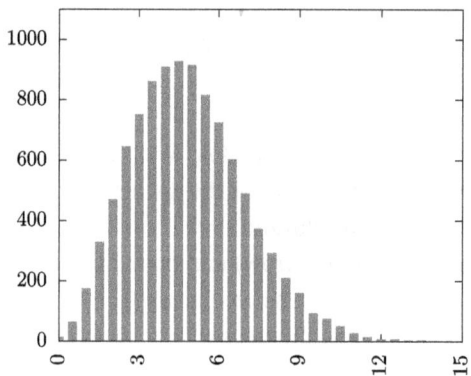

**Figure 18.20:** Random Walk Distribution of 10000 4 Dimensional Walks.

as the degrees of freedom increase. The behavior of random walks above is a direct example of the process by which these curves become closer to a Gaussian distribution as the number of variables increases.

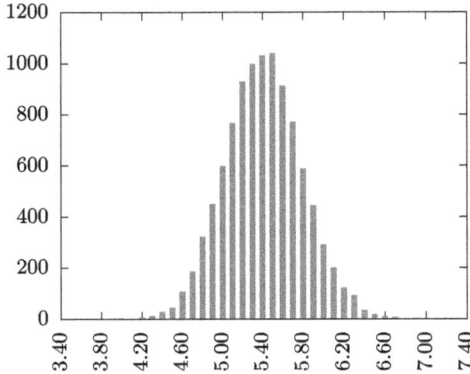

**Figure 18.21:** Random Walk Distribution of 10000 100-Dimensional Walks.

## 18.5.1 Expected Final Positions for Random Walks

If you take many walks of $N$ steps in a $d$-dimensional random walk, then the previous plots make it clear that the spread of the final distance distributions all have a peak, indicating the expected final distance.

For a one-dimensional random walk, the expected final distance is

$$E\left(\sqrt{\sum_{i=1}^{N} x_i}\right) = \sqrt{\frac{2N}{\pi}},$$

where $x_i$ is drawn from a uniform random distribution $X \in \{-1, +1\}$. The second part of the equation is for large $N$.

So, for the 30-step one-dimensional random walks, the equation states the expected distance is close to $\sqrt{\frac{60}{\pi}} \approx 4.37$. This is clearly inaccurate. Figure 18.17 shows the answer to be 2. However, for increasing $N$, the equation increases in accuracy.

For $d > 1$ dimensions, the expression for the expected distance becomes

$$\sqrt{\frac{2N}{d}} \frac{\Gamma(\frac{d+1}{2})}{\Gamma(\frac{d}{2})}.$$

In Python we would write this as:

**Listing 18.7:** Algorithm to Computed Expected Random Walk Distance

```
#!/usr/bin/python

import math

def expected_dist(N,d):
    if d == 1:
        e = math.sqrt((2.0*N)/math.pi)
```

```
    else:
        e = math.sqrt((2.0*N)/d)
        e = e*(math.gamma((d+1)/2.0)/math.gamma(d/2.0))
    return e

N = 1000
for d in xrange(1,11):
    print "%d_steps,_%dD,_expectation_=_%f" % (N,d,expected_dist(N,d))
```

As we would expect of an expression with an outer square root operation, this grows more slowly as $N$ increases.

```
1000 steps, 1D, expectation = 25.231325
1000 steps, 2D, expectation = 28.024956
1000 steps, 3D, expectation = 29.134625
1000 steps, 4D, expectation = 29.724955
1000 steps, 5D, expectation = 30.090111
1000 steps, 6D, expectation = 30.337905
1000 steps, 7D, expectation = 30.516943
1000 steps, 8D, expectation = 30.652296
1000 steps, 9D, expectation = 30.758187
1000 steps, 10D, expectation = 30.843278
```

## 18.6 Poisson Point Processes

The progressions of curves in the random walk results may look very familiar if you have studied Poisson point processes.

A Poisson point process is one where we count the number of events happening in a fixed window of time, or occurrences in a volume of space or some similar scenario, provided there is an average or expected rate.

For example, if you had a manufacturing line making circuit boards, which were then tested to see that they work, and the random errors in the machines led to there being a probability of making 10 defective circuit boards an hour, then the Poisson distribution would give you the probability that some number of defective boards would occur in a 1 hour window.

The Poisson processes are described by the Poisson distributions. The Poisson distributions have one parameter $\lambda$, which is the average number of events to occur in the window of time or space.

For the Poisson distribution to correctly represent the probability distribution of the Poisson process, the random events must occur independently of each other. So, for example, the Poisson process would not well represent the arrival of buses at a bus stop, because they are on a regular schedule.

Since you can only have a zero or positive integer number of events occurring, the equation for the distribution of $n$, the probability that $n$ equals the actual number of events, $N$ events occurring given the expected number of those events occurring, is $\lambda$. Such a scenario in a Poisson point process is

$$P(N = n|\lambda) = \frac{\lambda^n}{n!}e^{-\lambda}.$$

This distribution describes the probabilities of integer numbers of events, so the Poisson distributions are discrete; so they are PMFs.

Figure 18.22 shows the Poisson PMFs for values of $\lambda$ of 0.5, 1.0, 1.5, 2.0, and 2.5. We can see the curves moving rightward as $\lambda$ increases. Since there are multiple overlapping curves, they have been plotted with lines and points instead of a bar chart.

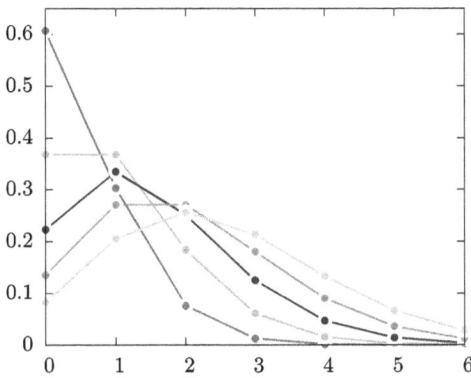

**Figure 18.22:** Poisson PMFs for $\lambda = 0.5, 1.0, 1.5, 2.0, 2.5$.

If we increase $\lambda = 30$, then we can see the distribution is now very close to the Gaussian distribution. See Figure 18.23.

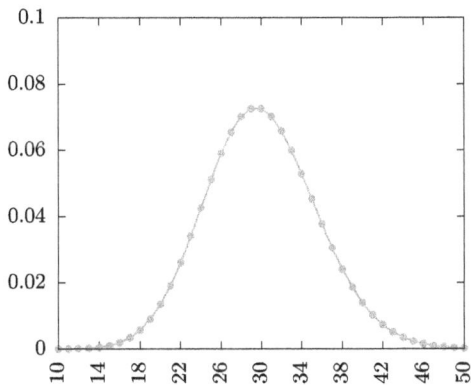

**Figure 18.23:** Poisson PMF for $\lambda = 30$.

## 18.7 The Binomial Distribution

The binomial distribution has many uses. In the context of random numbers, its use is mostly to do with testing random numbers, by checking if the frequency of some symbol is outside the expected bounds, determined by the binomial distribution.

### 18.7.1 The Binomial PMF

The binomial distribution is discrete. For a number of events with two outcomes (which we will describe as success or failure, and a probability of each outcome for each event, where $P(\text{success}) + P(\text{failure}) = 1$, the binomial distribution describes the probability of getting $k$ successes out of $n$ trials.

So, for any binomial curve, the shape of the curve is determined by only the two parameters, $n$, the number of trials (or events or tests or symbols etc.) and $p$, the probability of the event.

For example, if we have 256 uniformly random 4-bit numbers, then the probability of an individual symbol we are counting is $p = \frac{1}{2^4} = \frac{1}{16} = 0.0625$, and the number of symbols $n$ is 256.

For an integer value $k$ between 0 and $n$, the binomial probability of $k$ successes is written as

$$B(k; n, p) = \binom{n}{k} p^k (1 - p)^{n-k}.$$

The $\binom{n}{k}$ term is the number of ways to choose $k$ symbols from $n$ symbols and is computed with

$$\binom{n}{k} = \frac{n!}{k!(n - k)!}.$$

The following program computes the binomial PMF distribution with the above equations and plots the results. The parameters are $n$, $p$, and the maximum limit of the $x$ axis.

**Listing 18.8:** Binomial PMF program

```
#!/usr/bin/env python

import sys
import math
import matplotlib
import matplotlib.pyplot as plt

# Compute the PMF
def binom_pmf(n,p):
    xs = range(n+1)
```

```
    ys = [(math.factorial(n)/(math.factorial(k)*math.factorial(n-k))) \
          *(p**k) \
          *((1-p)**(n-k)) for k in range(n+1) ]
    return xs,ys

n = int(sys.argv[1])
p = float(sys.argv[2])

# Set the X limit
if len(sys.argv) > 3:
    xlimit = int(sys.argv[3])
    plt.xlim([0,xlimit])

xs,ys = binom_pmf(n,p)

# Plot the result
plt.plot(xs,ys,"o")
plt.ylabel("binom_pmf(n={},p={}".format(n,p))
plt.xlabel("k")
plt.grid(True)
plt.savefig('../img/binomial_pmf.pdf')
```

Executing this with $n = 512$, $p = 0.0625$ and setting the x axis to a maximum of 40:

```
> ./binomial_pmf.py 254 0.0625 40
>
```

This program generates the diagram shown in Figure 18.24.

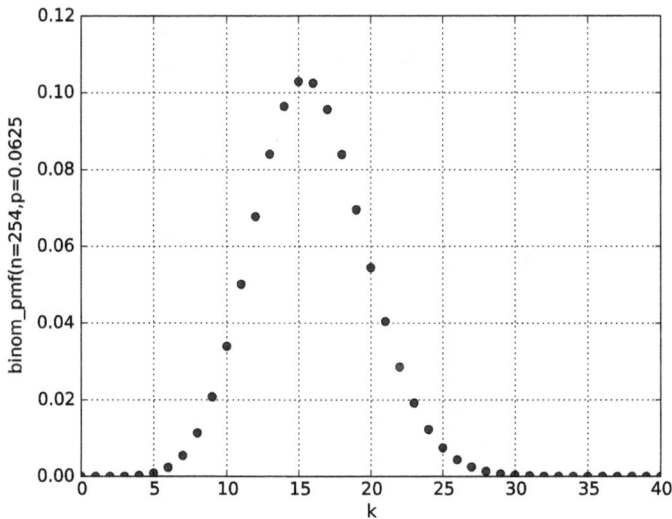

Figure 18.24: Binomial PMF for $n = 256$, $p = 0.625$.

We can see how it behaves like a discrete version of the normal distribution.

Textbooks often overlook the complexity of computing the binomial coefficients. For large $n$ and medium $k$, the numbers can grow extremely large. For example, the numerator of $\binom{n}{k}$ for $n = 1024$ is:

```
541852879605885728307692194468385473800155396353801344448287027
068321061207337660373314098413621458671907918845708980753931994
165770187368260454133333721939108367528012764993769768292516937
891165755680659663747947314518404886677672556125188694335251213
677274521963430770133713205796248433128870088436171654690237518
390452944732277808402932158722061853806162806063925435310822186
848239287130261690914211362251144684713888587881629252104046295
315949943900357882410243934315037444113890806181406210863953275
235375885018598451582229599654558541242789130902486944298610923
153307579131675745146436304024890820442907734561827369030502252
796926553072967370990758747793127635104702469889667961462133026
237158973227857814631807156427767644064591085076564783456324457
736853810336981776080498707767046394272605341416779125697733374
568037475186676265961665615884681450263337042522664141862157046
825684773360944326737493676674915098953768112945831626643856479
027816385730291542667725665642276826058264393884514911976419675
509290208592713156362983290989441052732125187249527501314071676
405516936190781821236701912295767363117054126589929916482008515
781751955466910902838729232224509906388638147771255227782631322
385756948819393658889908993670874516860653098411020299853816281
564334981847105777839534742531499622103488807584513705769839763
993103929665046046121166651345131149513657400869056334867859885
025601787284982567787314407216524272262997319791568603629406624
740101482697559533155736658800562921274680657285201570401940692
285557800611429055755324549794008939849146812639860750085263298
820224719585505344773711590656682821041417265040658600683844945
104354998812886801316551551714673388323340851763819713591312372
548673734783537316341517369387565212899726597964903241208727348
690699802996369265070088758384854547542272771024255049902319275
830918157448205196421072837204937293516175341957775422453152442
280391372407717891661203061040255830055033886790052116025408740
454620938384367637886658769912790922323717371343176067483352513
629123336288589362713229418356588401041872786935443907708527828 8
558308427090461075019007184933139915558212752392329879780649639
075333845719173822840501869570463626600235265587502335595489311
637509380219119860471335771652403999403296360245577257963673286
654348957325740999710567131623272345766761937651408103999193633
908286420510098577454524068106897392493138287362226257920000000
000000000000000000000000000000000000000000000000000000000000000
000000000000000000000000000000000000000000000000000000000000000
000000000000000000000000000000000000000000000000000000000000000
00000000000000000000000000000000000000000000000000000000000000
```

or, more compactly, approximately $5.41 \times 10^{2639}$.

The denominator $n!(n-k)!$ is

```
120915443054241974014999692604347303364104367551492210883029484
578088106956335569301640106321361650944599370299331096292036696 5
796246276409499345501290871546855317813330719832040921216714480
599428821407738724434139093236991088445996605848068552928847518
675072046411197225564396834502757734965389767188272929125721854
658954476725194811528635393661329705788800788265638581040293523
893373292326465911048854284868530692486737915649931973424624934
352967685216185498533031088815220890004271907315317586872782738
314230880193746938451544136433592936927782011380918989384392196
709601536899717348814875057318337553394369210270778682157174660
122198247939906760988267101403732009847824279757694073155829943
055112513060447166625675467023327892299123586261311967713833453
844630636686917512935957390731018620449200200696016436386320236
598419693868438278980925540237243447983210068223096310460832410
009409669736551270530769805338558526224170143234666021578814637
697558621145762633468458356748331692149875157892878589818410048
325502163533225126682514721069024356584016044499397503678621714
394802596995585017862601097855216005828794598442931610821699003
307815603642866531315924047105726007363064315544313871451389294
023836631591608181672211341573990212999136418041623683757000494
421057294527116698401147422874622854775019296292127326431001337
550394409809066992792087784888762193116307690974261739051961164
987574877687478822357741557577333588844403217723808229771898172
140038010074767348865423938485483098232428607329423391879476021
569331928265850664993728265184826635861053419167936667628220589
681714032878111756615586065990123566760785976237993707255890613
906707535858676189702904789578819274323154901183889080523102143
583826187545392893932109259149703326974810919992484014007251601
079797414411653627505266143878850941749385521752000589973600051
014731776556972580991118570265115329248701613638139858467314188
522020811723525326313721258962333084387863828514524736648131985
424489788530915072798376229073948996847803732060380665291736192
913967000187371829902890019493106759813561983493622717320083275
776000000000000000000000000000000000000000000000000000000000000
000000000000000000000000000000000000000000000000000000000000000
000000000000000000000000000000000000000000000000000000000000000
000000000000000000000000000000000000000000000000000000000000000
000
```

or approximately $1.2 \times 10^{2333}$.

Both these numbers are much larger than the 64-bit integer representation that is common in current computers.

Also, for small $p$ and large $k$ or large $(n-k)$, the $p^k$ and $p^{n-k}$ terms can grow extremely small, resulting in floating-point precision problems, for example, for $p = \frac{1}{100}$ and $k = 512$, $p^k = 10^{-1023}$, which is way below the 53-bit precision of standard or double-precision floating-point numbers in computers. So, attempting to compute the binomial coefficients can easily lead to numerical overflow or underflow in computers.

Binomial functions can be computed using the incomplete beta function. Therefore, it is possible to get around this problem. Appendix B describes a high precision implementation of the incomplete beta function and its use to compute the binomial PMF, CDF, and quantile functions.

### 18.7.2 The Binomial Discrete CDF

The CDF of the binomial PMF gives the probability that the number of successful results in $n$ trials with success probability $p$ is less than or equal to $k$. It is logically the sum of the values in the CDF from $x = 0$ to $= k$, or

$$\text{BCDF}(k; n, p) = \sum_{i=0}^{\lfloor k \rfloor} \binom{n}{i} p^i (1 - p)^{n-i}.$$

So, if computing a point in the PMF is going to be computationally hard, then computing the $\text{BCDF}(k; n, p)$ is going to be computationally $k$ times harder. See Figure 18.25.

An alternative and computationally feasible way to compute the binomial CDF is to use the regularized incomplete beta function, usually written as $I_x(a, b)$.

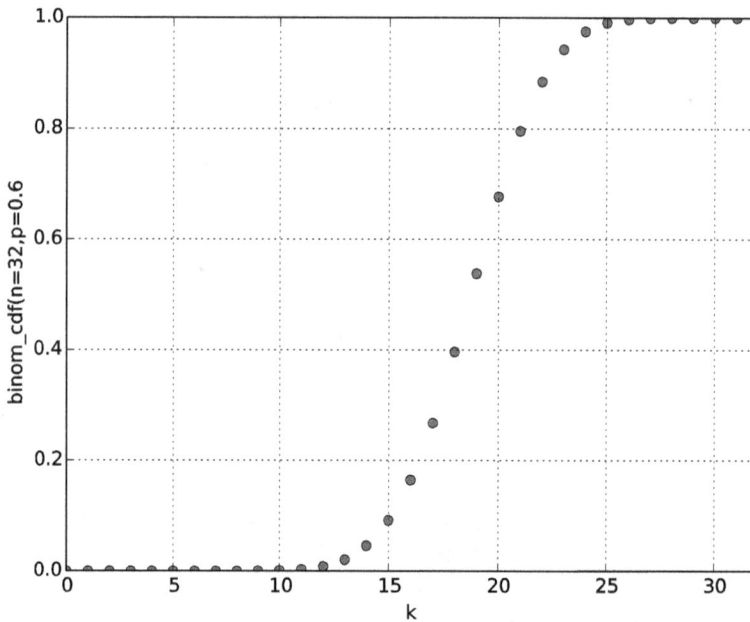

Figure 18.25: Binomial Cumulative Distribution Function for $n = 32$, $p = 0.6$.

The beta function $\beta(a, b)$ can be computed in terms of the gamma function:

$$\beta(a, b) = \frac{\Gamma(a)\Gamma(b)}{\Gamma(a) + \Gamma(b)}.$$

This is relevant because in the case of most computer mathematical libraries, the gamma function is generally available, and the beta function is less often available. In the case of the Python MPFR library, a high-precision gamma function is available, so we can compute the binomial CDF by taking advantage of this underlying function in the library.

The beta function is used by the regularized incomplete beta function $I_x(a, b)$:

$$I_x(a, b) = \frac{1}{\beta(a, b)} \int_0^x t^{a-1}(1 - t)^{b-1}dt.$$

Appendix B provides the Python code to compute the incomplete beta function with high precision using a continued fraction iterative computation.

With the regularized beta function available, using high-precision arithmetic, we are then able to compute the Binomial CDF in terms of the incomplete beta function without running into integer overflows or floating-point underflows:

This was used to build the tables in Appendix A, which could not be computed with standard precision arithmetic.

$$BCDF(k; n, p) = I_{1-p}(n - k, k + 1)$$

### 18.7.3 The Binomial Quantile Function

The binomial quantile function is the inverse of the binomial CDF. Since the CDF is discrete, there may not be an exact answer, so the quantile function finds the smallest $x$ in the binomial CDF that will return the probability greater than the provided probability $\alpha$, that is, find the smallest $x$ such that

$$\alpha \leq BCDF(x; n, p).$$

For example, with $n = 32$, $p = 0.4$, and $\alpha = 0.67$, we can see in Figure 18.26 how the quantile function indexes into the curve, finding the horizontal point that intersects with $\alpha$, and then returning the next higher integer if it lands between two integers. In this case the horizontal line at $BCDF(k; 32, 0.4) = \alpha$.

The code below uses the Python mpfr library that comes with the gmpy2 library for high-precision floating-point numbers.

The incomplete beta function algorithm is described in Appendix B and is used by the algorithm below, which computes the binomial quantile function.

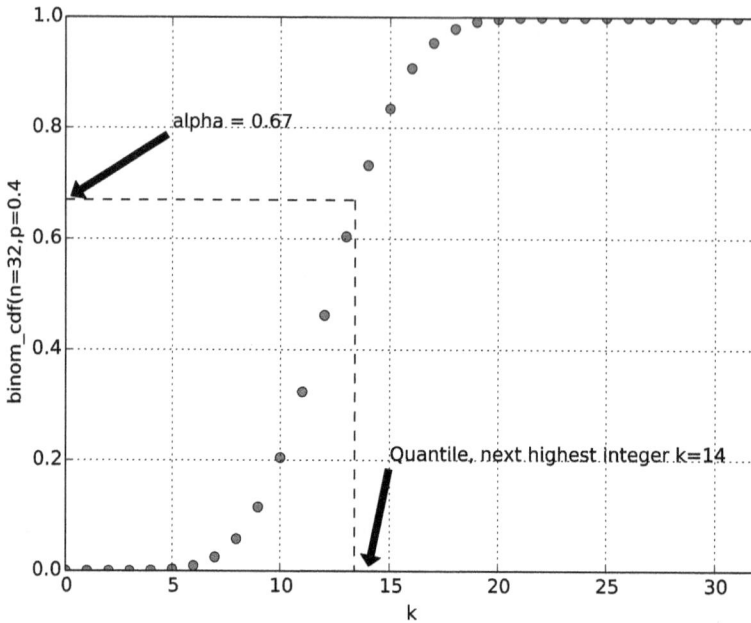

**Figure 18.26:** Binomial Quantile Function for $n = 32$, $p = 0.4$, $\alpha = 0.67$.

**Listing 18.9:** incomplete_beta.py

```python
#!/usr/bin/env python

import math
import gmpy2
from gmpy2 import mpfr
from incomplete_beta import *

# Binomial CDF
def BCDF(n, k, p):
    return mpfr('1.0') - ibeta(mpfr(k+1),mpfr(n-k),p)

# Find smallest k where B(n,k,p) > alpha
# using binary chop search
# Equivalent to Excel CRITBINOM function
def binomial_quantile(n, p, alpha):
    min = 0;
    max = n;
    mid = min + ((max-min) >> 1)
    keepgoing = True
    while (keepgoing):
        b = BCDF(n,mid,p)
        if (b > alpha):
            max = mid
```

```
    elif (b < alpha):
        min = mid
    elif (b == alpha):
        keepgoing = False

    newmid = min + ((max-min) >> 1)
    if (newmid == mid):
        keepgoing=False
    mid = newmid

if (b < alpha): # Make sure we have smallest b > alpha
    mid += 1
return mid
```

The algorithm performs a binary search for the $k$ that returns a value closest to $\alpha$, followed by a check at the end to increase the value by 1, if the indexed value turns out to be less than alpha, so that it returns the smallest $k$ that yields a value greater than $\alpha$, not less.

# 19 Quantifying Entropy

## 19.1 Rényi Entropy

*The first section of this chapter is entirely on the topic of the mathematics of Rényi Entropy. It involves single variable calculus. The working out of the special cases of Rényi Entropy is shown verbosely so that the interested reader can follow along. Feel free to skip this part if you are not comfortable with calculus.*[1]

Rényi [18] defined an expression for the entropy of order $\alpha$ of a distribution $X$, where $X$ is represented as a list of probabilities $X = (p_1, \ldots, p_n)$:

$$H_\alpha(X) = H_\alpha(p_1, \ldots, p_n) = \frac{1}{1-\alpha} \log_2 \left( \sum_{i=1}^{n} P_i^\alpha \right), \quad \alpha \geq 0, \alpha \neq 1.$$

The value of $\alpha$ determines the class of entropy being measured.

$\alpha = 0$ is equivalent to Hartly entropy, also known as max-entropy, which can be considered as a best case measure of entropy. The expressed $H_0(X)$ simplifies to

$$H_0(x) = H_0(p_1, \ldots, p_n) = \log_2 \left( \sum_{i=1}^{n} p_i^0 \right) = \log_2(n).$$

So, Hartley entropy considers each value in the distribution to be equally likely, and therefore the distribution is flat. The maximum possible entropy is, therefore, inferred.

$\alpha = 1$ is equivalent to Shannon entropy as described in [20]. The $\frac{1}{1-\alpha}$ term in the Rényi entropy equation prevents us directly plugging in $\alpha = 1$. So, instead, we define the Shannon entropy as a limit with $\alpha$ approaching 1:

$$H_1(X) = \lim_{\alpha \to 1} H_\alpha(X).$$

When the limit is evaluated, this gives

$$H_1(X) = H_1(p_1, \ldots, p_n) = - \sum_{i=1}^{n} p_i \log_2(p_i).$$

In other words, sum together the $\log_2$ of each value from the distribution multiplied by the probability of the value. This gives an average entropy for the distribution.

---

[1] I found a similar derivation of Shannon entropy from Rényi entropy to my derivation below at http://www.tina-vision.net/docs/memos/2004-004.pdf. I have not been able to find a published derivation of min-entropy from Rényi entropy, so the derivation that I worked out with a little help from a family member with a mathematics Ph. D. is the only derivation I am aware of.

https://doi.org/10.1515/9781501506062-019

$\alpha = 2$ is known as collision entropy. It computes the probability that any two values taken from the distribution are equal $P|X = Y|$:

$$H_2(X) = H_2(p_1,\ldots,p_n) = -\log_2 \sum_{i=1}^{n} p_i^2.$$

$\alpha = \infty$ is known as min-entropy. It can be considered the worst case measure of entropy, using the lowest possible entropy value from the distribution:

$$H_\infty(X) = H_\infty(p_1,\ldots,p_n) = -\log_2(\max(p_i)).$$

Min-entropy is the measure most commonly used in extractor theory. The input requirements for entropy extractors are usually expressed in terms of min-entropy.

### 19.1.1 Derivation of Shannon Entropy from Rényi Entropy

The derivation of the equation for Shannon entropy $H_1(X)$ from $H_1(X) = \lim_{\alpha \to 1} H_\alpha(X)$ is not obvious. Rényi's paper simply states that it can easily be seen. That may be true if you are Alfréd Rényi, but it certainly was not obvious to me.

A snippet from Rényi's article "On Measures of Entropy and Information" can be seen in Figure 19.1, in which he claims that the derivation can be easily seen.

(1.21) $\qquad H_a(p_1, p_2, \cdots, p_n) = \frac{1}{1-\alpha} \log_2 \left( \sum_{k=1}^{n} p_k^a \right),$

where $\alpha > 0$ and $\alpha \neq 1$ have these properties. The quantity $H_a(p_1, p_2, \cdots, p_n)$ defined by (1.21) can also be regarded as a measure of the entropy of the distribution $\mathcal{P} = (p_1, \cdots, p_n)$. In what follows we shall call

$$H_a(p_1, p_2, \cdots, p_n) = H_a[\mathcal{P}]$$

the *entropy of order* $\alpha$ of the distribution $\mathcal{P}$. We shall deal with these quantities in the next sections. Here we mention only that, as is easily seen,

(1.22) $\qquad \lim_{a \to 1} H_a(p_1, p_2, \cdots, p_n) = \sum_{k=1}^{n} p_k \log_2 \frac{1}{p_k}.$

Thus Shannon's measure of entropy is the limiting case for $\alpha \to 1$ of the measure of entropy $H_a[\mathcal{P}]$. In view of (1.22) we shall denote in what follows Shannon's measure of entropy (1.1) by $H_1(p_1, \cdots, p_n)$ and call it the measure of entropy of order 1 of the distribution. Thus we put

(1.23) $\qquad H_1[\mathcal{P}] = H_1(p_1, p_2, \cdots, p_n) = \sum_{k=1}^{n} p_k \log_2 \frac{1}{p_k}.$

**Figure 19.1:** Excerpt from Rényi paper "On Measures of Entropy and Information".

So that the derivation can be understood, it is shown here:

$$H_\alpha(X) = \frac{1}{1-\alpha} \log_2 \left( \sum_{i=1}^{n} p_i^\alpha \right),$$

$$H_1(X) = \lim_{\alpha \to 1} \frac{1}{1 - \alpha} \log_2 \left( \sum_{i=1}^{n} p_i^\alpha \right).$$

The divisor $1 - \alpha$ tends to 0 as $\alpha$ tends to 1. Also, $\sum_{i=1}^{n} p_i^\alpha$ tends to 0 as $\alpha$ tends to 1. So the whole equation tends to $\frac{0}{0}$.

We can use L'Hôpital's rule to evaluate this limit:

$$\lim_{x \to y} \frac{f(x)}{g(x)} = \lim_{x \to y} \frac{\frac{d}{dx} f(x)}{\frac{d}{dx} g(x)}.$$

To make the derivation easier, we rewrite this using the natural logarithm and placing $1 - \alpha$ below the sum:

$$H_1(X) = \lim_{\alpha \to 1} \frac{\ln(\sum_{i=1}^{n} p_i^\alpha)}{1 - \alpha}.$$

Now we can declare

$$f(\alpha) = \ln \left( \sum_{i=1}^{n} p_i^\alpha \right)$$

and

$$g(\alpha) = 1 - \alpha.$$

Finding the derivative of the denominator $g(\alpha)$ is easy:

$$\frac{d}{d\alpha} g(\alpha) = \frac{d}{d\alpha}(1 - \alpha) = -1.$$

Finding the derivative of the numerator $f(\alpha)$ requires the chain rule, since the outer function $v() \equiv \ln()$ and the inner function $w(\alpha) \equiv \sum_{i=1}^{n} p_i^\alpha$:

$$\frac{d}{d\alpha} f(\alpha) = \frac{d}{d\alpha} v(w(\alpha)) \frac{d}{d\alpha} w(\alpha),$$

$$\frac{d}{d\alpha} v(\alpha) = \frac{d}{d\alpha} \ln(\alpha) = \frac{1}{\alpha},$$

$$\frac{d}{d\alpha} w(\alpha) = \frac{d}{d\alpha} \sum_{i=1}^{n} p_i^\alpha = \sum_{i=1}^{n} (p_i^\alpha) \ln(p_i),$$

$$\frac{d}{d\alpha} f(\alpha) = \frac{d}{d\alpha} \ln \left( \sum_{i=1}^{n} p_i^\alpha \right) \sum_{i=1}^{n} (p_i^x) \ln(p_i)$$

$$= \frac{1}{\sum_{i=1}^{n} p_i^\alpha} \sum_{i=1}^{n} p_i \ln(p_i).$$

So, now, we have the derivatives of $f(\alpha)$ and $g(\alpha)$, and we can express the full limit as per L'Hôpital's rule:

$$\lim_{\alpha \to 1} \frac{\frac{d}{d\alpha}f(\alpha)}{\frac{d}{d\alpha}g(\alpha)} = \lim_{\alpha \to 1} \frac{\frac{1}{\sum_{i=1}^{n} p_i^{\alpha}} \sum_{i=1}^{n} p_i \ln(p_i)}{-1}.$$

We know that the sum of all probabilities in the distribution = 1. So,

$$\lim_{\alpha \to 1} \sum_{i=1}^{n} p_i^{\alpha} = \sum_{i=1}^{n} p_i = 1.$$

Substituting that back into the chain rule outcome gives

$$H_1(X) = -\sum_{i=1}^{n} p_i \ln(p_i),$$

which is the definition of Shannon entropy, measured in nats. Rebasing it into $\log_2$ gives the Shannon entropy measured in Shannons, which are more commonly referred to as bits:

$$H_1(X) = -\sum_{i=1}^{n} p_i \log_2(p_i).$$

### 19.1.2 Derivation of Min Entropy from Rényi Entropy

Min-entropy is defined as $H_\infty(X)$.

Min-entropy is a measure of the probability of correctly guessing a value taken from the distribution. So, when making a guess of what a random variable will turn out to be, the best guess is to choose the highest probability symbol. Therefore, we can define min-entropy as follows:

$$H_\infty(X) = H_\infty(p_1, \ldots, p_n) \doteq -\log_2(\max(p_i)).$$

Using the methods in Section 19.1.1 to try to derive this equation leads to a nonsensical answer. A solution is to borrow from $L^p$-norm theory.

We can derive the min-entropy expression by observing the relationship between Rényi entropy and the $L^p$-norm of probability distribution $\|x\|_p$, treated as a vector of probabilities:

$$H_\alpha(X) = \frac{\alpha}{1 - \alpha} \log_2(\|P\|_\alpha).$$

The $L^p$-norm of $(x_1, \ldots, x_n)$ is expressed as $\|x\|_p = (|x_1|^p + \cdots + |x_n|^p)^{\frac{1}{p}}$.
In the case where $p = \infty$, $\|x\|_\infty = \max(|x_1|, \ldots, |x_n|)$.

So, using that expression in the $L^p$-norm version of the Rényi entropy equation, we get

$$H_\infty(X) = \frac{\infty}{1-\infty}\log_2(\|X\|_\infty) = -\log_2(\max(|p_1|,\ldots,|p_n|))$$
$$= -\log_2(\max(p_i)).$$

## 19.2 Min-Entropy of Biased Binary Sources

For a purely biased, stationary source producing $n$ bits each, with bias $b$, where $b$ is the probability of any bit being 1, we can compute the min-entropy.

For $b > 0.5$, the most probable value is all ones. The joint probability of all the bits being 1 is $P(1)^n$.

For $b < 0.5$, the most probable value is all zeroes. The joint probability of all the bits being 1 is $P(0)^n$. Since $P(1) = 1 - P(0)$, we can express that as $(1 - P(0))^n$.

For $b = 0.5$, all values are equally likely. So the min-entropy per bit is 1.

The min-entropy curve will be symmetric around $P(1) = 0.5$. So, we can express it as a single equation by just checking for the more probable value:

$$H_\infty(X) = -\log_2(\max(P(1)^n, P(0)^n)).$$

Plotting this as a curve of min-entropy per bit against bias on the $x$ axis, we get Figure 19.2.

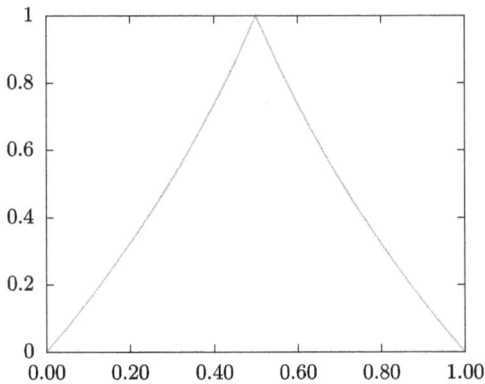

Figure 19.2: Per Bit Min-Entropy of Biased Binary Data.

## 19.3 Min-Entropy of Serially Correlated Binary Sources

As with the biased source, the scheme for finding the min-entropy of serially correlated data is to identify the most probable symbol. Since the nature of serial correlation is to alter the probability of each bit, based on its previous bit, then the symbols we consider need to include more than one bit.

A random bit series that is described completely by its serial correlation coefficient (SCC) has no bias. The probability of a bit is described by the value of the previous bit and the SCC:

$$P(x_{i+1} = x_i) = \frac{SCC}{2} + 0.5.$$

So, for positive SCC, $P(x_{i+1} = x_i) > 0.5$. For negative SCC, $P(x_{i+1} = x_i) < 0.5$. For SCC = 0, $P(x_{i+1} = x_i) = \frac{1}{2}$.

In other words, with negative SCC, each bit is more likely to be the opposite of its preceding bit than not. Therefore, the most probable symbols are 101010... and 010101....

With positive SCC each bit is more likely to be the same as its preceding bit than not. The most probable symbols are 000000... and 111111....

For SCC = 0.5, all symbols are equally probable. So, the per bit entropy in the $n$-bit symbols $\frac{H_\infty(X)}{n} = 1$.

For both positive and negative SCC, we can correctly predict the subsequent bits with $P = \frac{SCC}{2} + 0.5$. So, for an $n$-bit symbol, the probability of each of the most probable values is

$$P_{max} = \max\left(\left(\frac{SCC}{2} + 0.5\right), 1 - \left(\frac{SCC}{2} + 0.5\right)\right)^n.$$

Therefore, for an 8-bit byte, the min-entropy in each byte would be computed from $P_{max}$, computed with $n = 8$. The min-entropy is then computed as

$$H_\infty(X) = -\log_2(P_{max}).$$

For example, we have measured some binary data to have SCC of −0.234, we can compute the min-entropy as follows:

$$P_{max} = \max\left(\left(\frac{-0.234}{2} + 0.5\right), 1 - \left(\frac{-0.234}{2} + 0.5\right)\right)$$
$$= 0.617,$$

$$H_\infty(X) = -\log_2(0.617^8)$$
$$= -\log_2(0.617^8) \approx 5.573.$$

We can plot the min-entropy against serial correlation coefficient. See Figure 19.3.

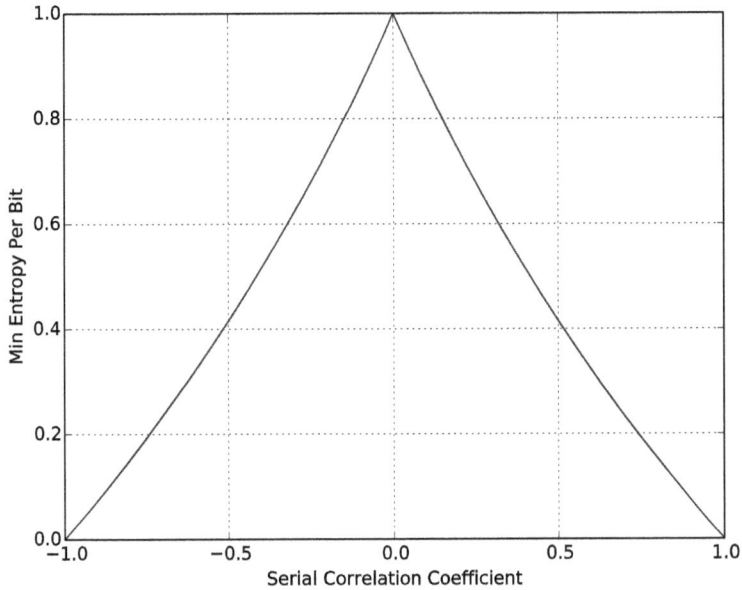

**Figure 19.3:** Min-Entropy as a Function of SCC.

This was generated with the following code:

**Listing 19.1:** Min-Entropy Computed from SCC

```python
#!/usr/bin/env python

import math
import matplotlib
import matplotlib.pyplot as plt

def scc2me(scc):
    p = (scc/2.0)+0.5
    p = max(p,1-p)
    h = -math.log(p,2)
    return h

sccs = [(x-100)*0.01 for x in range(0,201)]
ys = [scc2me(scc) for scc in sccs]

plt.plot(sccs, ys)
plt.xlim([-1,1])
plt.ylim([0,1])
plt.grid(True)
plt.xlabel("Serial_Correlation_Coefficient")
plt.ylabel("Min_Entropy_Per_Bit")

plt.savefig("../img/scc_vs_minentropy.pdf", format='pdf')
```

## 19.4 Distance From Uniform

Another commonly used way of describing the quality of random numbers is to say that the distance of the distribution from the uniform distribution is below some threshold.

Statistical distance is a measure of how different two probability distributions are. "Distance from Uniform" means taking one of those distributions to be uniform, and the other is the distribution we are measuring.

The distance $\epsilon$ from uniform of a distribution $X$ would typically be expressed $|U - X| < \epsilon$. For example, a distance of less than $2^{-64}$ might be expressed as $|U - X| < \epsilon$, $0 \leq \epsilon \leq 2^{-64}$.

Often we are dealing with random bit strings of a known size. In that case the term $U_n$ would refers to a uniform distribution of $n$-bit bit strings, and $X_n$ would refer to the distribution $X$ of $n$-bit bit strings. So,

$$|U_{128} - X_{128}| < \epsilon, \quad 0 \leq \epsilon \leq 2^{-64}.$$

There are many measures of statistical distance. In the case of enumerable sets of numbers, such as bit strings in the context of random number generators, the standard equation for statistical distance is also known as the total variation distance of probabilities. The (mostly useless for our purposes) definition over sigma-algebras is

$$\delta(P, Q) = \sup_{a \in F} |P(A) - Q(A)|,$$

but for enumerable sets of probabilities that make up a discrete distribution $P = (x_1, x_2, \ldots, x_n)$, we have the definition which is entirely usable:

$$\delta(P, Q) = \frac{1}{2} \sum_{x=1}^{n} |P(x) - Q(x)|.$$

This can be easily visualized as the area between the two probability curves, where $P(x) > Q(x)$, but the area where $P(x) \leq Q(x)$ is not counted. Since all distributions add up to 1, those two areas are both equal, and so that is where the $\frac{1}{2}$ term comes from the statistical distance formula.

In Figure 19.4, two nonuniform distributions have been plotted. They both have a slanted sinusoidal distribution. Being probability distributions, the area under both curves must add to 1.

In Figure 19.5, the area between the two distributions where distribution A is greater than distribution B has been shaded in. The area of the shaded parts is equal to the distance between the distributions. This area will always be identical to the unshaded parts, where distribution B is greater than distribution A.

In the case that we are measuring the distance from the uniform distribution of $n$-bit strings, $U_n$ the probability of each point $x$ is $U(x) = \frac{1}{2^n}$. So, for example, if we have

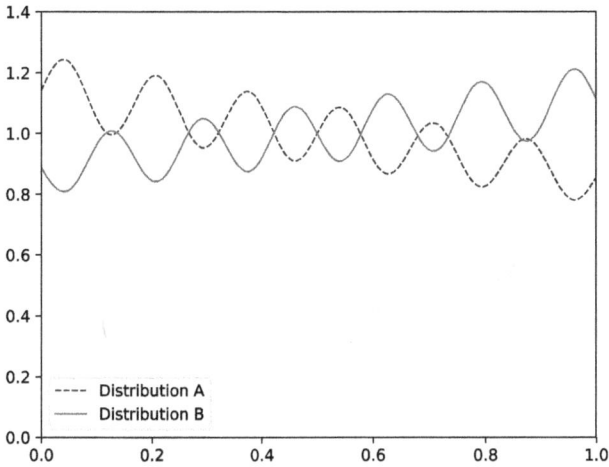

**Figure 19.4:** Distance Between two Distributions.

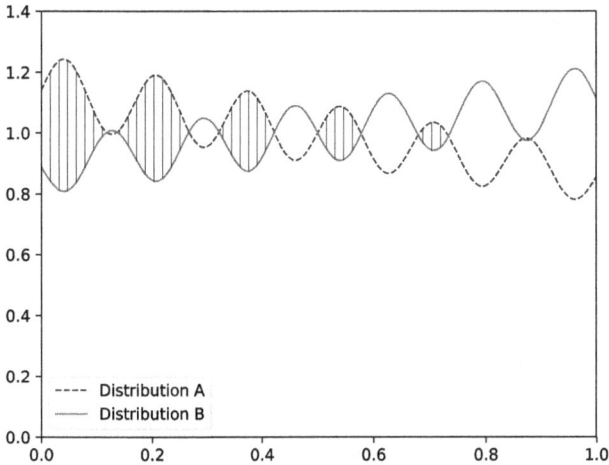

**Figure 19.5:** Highlighted Distance Between two Distributions.

a distribution $X_3$ (see Figure 19.6 (a)) of 3-bit bit strings, such that

$$X_3 = (x_1, \ldots, x_8) = (0.125, 0.1, 0.12, 0.14, 0.125, 0.14, 0.125, 0.125),$$

then the uniform (see Figure 19.6 (b)) distribution

$$U_3 = (0.125, 0.125, 0.125, 0.125, 0.125, 0.125, 0.125, 0.125).$$

Applying the total-variation distance equation, we can write it out in a spreadsheet (see Table 19.1) for easy computation.

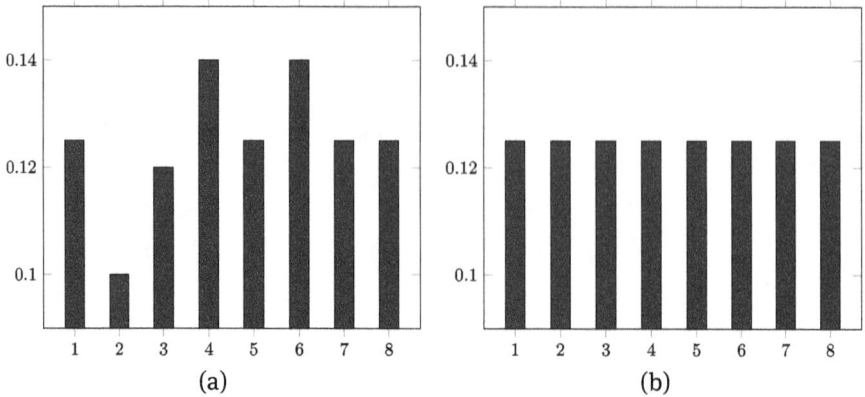

Figure 19.6: (a) $X_3$; (b) $U_3$.

Table 19.1: Distance from Uniform Spreadsheet.

| $i$ | $U$ | $X$ | $U_i - P_i$ | $|U_i - P_i|$ |
|---|---|---|---|---|
| 1 | 0.125 | 0.125 | 0 | 0 |
| 2 | 0.125 | 0.1 | 0.025 | 0.025 |
| 3 | 0.125 | 0.12 | 0.005 | 0.005 |
| 4 | 0.125 | 0.14 | −0.015 | 0.015 |
| 5 | 0.125 | 0.125 | 0 | 0 |
| 6 | 0.125 | 0.14 | −0.015 | 0.015 |
| 7 | 0.125 | 0.125 | 0 | 0 |
| 8 | 0.125 | 0.125 | 0 | 0 |
| Total | 1 | 1 | | 0.06 |
| | $\frac{\sum_i |U_i - P_i|}{2}$ | | = | 0.04 |

So, the distance from uniform distribution is computed by taking the difference between each point on the distributions, turning the negative ones positive, summing them, and dividing by 2 as per the equation, the answer being 0.03.

# 20 Random Methods to Generate $\pi$

## 20.1 Random Method for Computing $\pi$

Given a uniform set of random numbers, it is possible to use them to compute an approximate value for $\pi$. The larger the set of numbers, the more accurate the approximation.

Consider a square sides length $d$ with a circle within it of radius $r = \frac{d}{2}$. The area of the square is $(2r)^2$. The area of the circle is $\pi r^2$. See Figure 20.1.

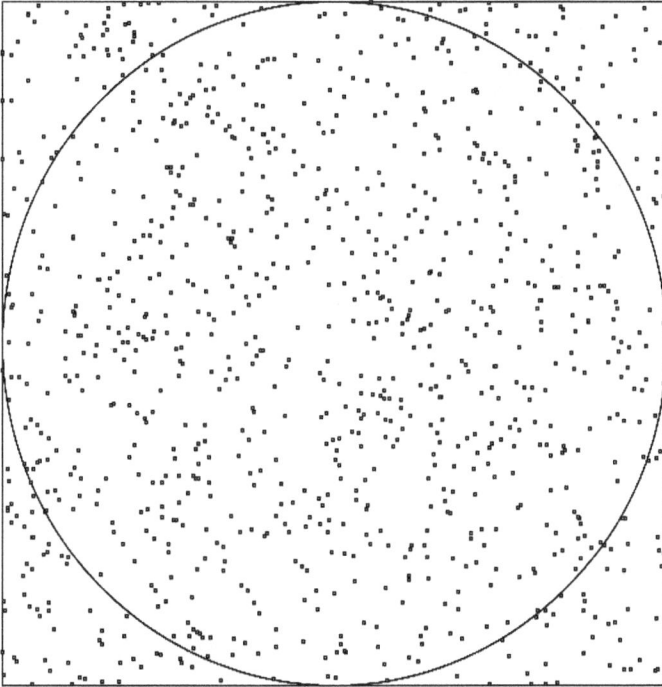

**Figure 20.1:** Random Prediction of Pi.

If you use the random numbers to form uniformly random points within the square, the probability of a point landing inside the circle is

$$\frac{\pi r^2}{(2r)^2},$$

and the probability of landing elsewhere in the square, but outside the circle, is

$$1 - \frac{\pi r^2}{(2r)^2}.$$

https://doi.org/10.1515/9781501506062-020

Given $n$ points, we can therefore expect the number of points $n_{\text{inside}}$ landing in the circle to tend to the ratio time $n$ for large $n$:

$$n_{\text{inside}} \to n\frac{\pi r^2}{(2r)^2}, \quad n \to \infty.$$

Rearranging for large $n$:

$$n_{\text{inside}} \approx n\frac{\pi r^2}{(2r)^2},$$

$$\frac{((2r)^2)n_{\text{inside}}}{n} \approx \pi r^2,$$

$$\frac{(4r^2)n_{\text{inside}}}{n} \approx \pi r^2,$$

$$\pi \approx \frac{4n_{\text{inside}}}{n}.$$

In the following program, we perform this computation, but only over the top right quadrant of the square, so that we are working with positive floating-point numbers. The ratio of inside to total remains the same. We provide the number of points on the command line.

**Listing 20.1:** random_pi.py

```
#!/usr/bin/env python

import sys
import random
import math
rs = random.SystemRandom()

inside = 0
n = int(sys.argv[1])
# Assume r = 1.0 to simplify equation
for i in xrange(n):
    x = rs.random()
    y = rs.random()
    if ((x*x + y*y) <= 1.0):
        inside += 1

pi_approx = 4.0 * inside/n
err = (abs(math.pi - pi_approx)/math.pi)*100.0
print "Pi approximately = %8.6f  Error = %8.6f%%" % (pi_approx, err)
```

Running this with increasing values of $n$, we find the percentage error of the estimate of $\pi$ reduces.

```
$ python random_pi.py 10
```

```
Pi approximately = 3.200000   Error = 1.859164%
$ python random_pi.py 100
Pi approximately = 3.200000   Error = 1.859164%
$ python random_pi.py 1000
Pi approximately = 3.196000   Error = 1.731840%
$ python random_pi.py 10000
Pi approximately = 3.162000   Error = 0.649586%
$ python random_pi.py 100000
Pi approximately = 3.134640   Error = 0.221310%
$ python random_pi.py 1000000
Pi approximately = 3.140320   Error = 0.040510%
$ python random_pi.py 10000000
Pi approximately = 3.141044   Error = 0.017451%
```

Though this is a very inefficient means to estimate $\pi$, it is a means to test the uniformity of random numbers. The SP800-90Rev1a Monte-Carlo-Pi test uses this method, and the resulting percentage error as the figure of merit.

## 20.2 Another Random Method for Computing $\pi$

A standard result in number theory is that the probability that two random integers are coprime is $\frac{6}{\pi^2}$.

So, if we take a large number $n$ of random integer pairs $a, b$ and count the number $n_{coprime}$, where $m$ and $n$ are coprime; if $GCD(a, b) = 1$, then we can expect that, for large $n$, the ratio

$$\frac{n_{coprime}}{n} \approx \frac{6}{\pi^2},$$

$$\pi^2 \approx \frac{6n}{n_{coprime}},$$

$$\pi \approx \sqrt{\frac{6n}{n_{coprime}}}.$$

In the following program, we perform this computation, fetching pairs of 64-bit random integers and counting the pairs that are coprime. We provide the number of pairs on the command line.

**Listing 20.2:** random_pi2.py

```
#!/usr/bin/env python

import sys
import random
import math
from fractions import gcd
rs = random.SystemRandom()
```

```
coprime = 0
n = int(sys.argv[1])

for i in xrange(n):
    a = rs.getrandbits(64)
    b = rs.getrandbits(64)
    if (gcd(a,b)==1):
        coprime += 1;

pi_approx = math.sqrt((6.0*n)/coprime)
err = (abs(math.pi - pi_approx)/math.pi)*100.0
print "Pi_approximately_=_%8.6f__Error_=_%8.6f%%" % (pi_approx, err)
```

Running this with increasing values of *n*, we find that the percentage error of the estimate of π reduces.

```
$ python random_pi2.py 10
Pi approximately = 3.162278   Error = 0.658424%
$ python random_pi2.py 100
Pi approximately = 3.136250   Error = 0.170054%
$ python random_pi2.py 1000
Pi approximately = 3.115885   Error = 0.818308%
$ python random_pi2.py 10000
Pi approximately = 3.128056   Error = 0.430878%
$ python random_pi2.py 100000
Pi approximately = 3.144431   Error = 0.090355%
$ python random_pi2.py 1000000
Pi approximately = 3.140937   Error = 0.020876%
$ python random_pi2.py 10000000
Pi approximately = 3.141278   Error = 0.010008%
```

Comparing these two methods, we find that the first method, using points landing within a circle, is more than twice as efficient as the coprime method:

```
$ time python random_pi.py 1000000
Pi approximately = 3.139340   Error = 0.071704%


real    0m5.772s
user    0m2.975s
sys     0m2.783s


$ time python random_pi2.py 1000000
Pi approximately = 3.138855   Error = 0.087141%


real    0m11.502s
user    0m8.413s
sys     0m3.015s
```

# A Adaptive Proportion Test Cutoff Tables

The following tables are correctly computed tables for the cutoff value $C$ used in the SP800-90B Adaptive Proportion Test.

The columns are computed for blocks of 64, 256, 512, 1024, 2048, 4096, and 65536 symbols. The rows are computed for the entropy per symbol $H$ given in the first column.

$W = 2^{-32}$, 300 Bit Precision

| H | 64 | 256 | 512 | 1024 | 2048 | 4096 | 65536 |
|---|----|-----|-----|------|------|------|-------|
| 0.1 | 64 | 256 | 507 | 999 | 1975 | 3916 | 61540 |
| 0.2 | 64 | 251 | 488 | 953 | 1873 | 3695 | 57583 |
| 0.3 | 64 | 242 | 466 | 905 | 1769 | 3479 | 53851 |
| 0.4 | 64 | 233 | 445 | 858 | 1669 | 3272 | 50347 |
| 0.5 | 63 | 223 | 423 | 812 | 1574 | 3075 | 47064 |
| 0.6 | 62 | 213 | 402 | 768 | 1483 | 2889 | 43991 |
| 0.7 | 61 | 204 | 382 | 726 | 1396 | 2714 | 41117 |
| 0.8 | 59 | 195 | 362 | 685 | 1315 | 2549 | 38428 |
| 0.9 | 57 | 186 | 344 | 647 | 1237 | 2393 | 35915 |
| 1.0 | 56 | 177 | 326 | 611 | 1165 | 2247 | 33565 |
| 2.0 | 40 | 110 | 192 | 345 | 637 | 1200 | 17078 |
| 3.0 | 28 | 69 | 115 | 198 | 354 | 648 | 8724 |
| 4.0 | 20 | 45 | 71 | 117 | 201 | 358 | 4488 |
| 5.0 | 15 | 30 | 46 | 72 | 119 | 203 | 2331 |
| 6.0 | 12 | 21 | 31 | 46 | 73 | 119 | 1228 |
| 7.0 | 9 | 16 | 22 | 31 | 46 | 73 | 658 |
| 8.0 | 7 | 12 | 16 | 22 | 31 | 46 | 362 |
| 9.0 | 6 | 9 | 12 | 16 | 22 | 31 | 204 |
| 10.0 | 5 | 8 | 9 | 12 | 16 | 22 | 120 |
| 11.0 | 4 | 6 | 8 | 9 | 12 | 16 | 73 |
| 12.0 | 4 | 5 | 6 | 8 | 9 | 12 | 47 |
| 13.0 | 3 | 4 | 5 | 6 | 8 | 9 | 31 |
| 14.0 | 3 | 4 | 5 | 5 | 6 | 8 | 22 |
| 15.0 | 3 | 3 | 4 | 5 | 5 | 6 | 16 |
| 16.0 | 2 | 3 | 3 | 4 | 5 | 5 | 12 |
| 17.0 | 2 | 3 | 3 | 3 | 4 | 5 | 9 |
| 18.0 | 2 | 2 | 3 | 3 | 3 | 4 | 8 |
| 19.0 | 2 | 2 | 2 | 3 | 3 | 3 | 6 |
| 20.0 | 2 | 2 | 2 | 2 | 3 | 3 | 5 |

$W = 2^{-48}$, 300 Bit Precision

| H | 64 | 256 | 512 | 1024 | 2048 | 4096 | 65536 |
|---|----|-----|-----|------|------|------|-------|
| 0.1 | 64 | 256 | 511 | 1008 | 1989 | 3937 | 61637 |
| 0.2 | 64 | 255 | 496 | 967 | 1893 | 3725 | 57714 |

https://doi.org/10.1515/9781501506062-021

| | | | | | | | |
|------|-----|-----|-----|------|------|------|-------|
| 0.3 | 64 | 249 | 477 | 922 | 1794 | 3515 | 54004 |
| 0.4 | 64 | 241 | 457 | 877 | 1697 | 3312 | 50515 |
| 0.5 | 64 | 232 | 437 | 833 | 1604 | 3119 | 47243 |
| 0.6 | 64 | 223 | 417 | 790 | 1514 | 2935 | 44178 |
| 0.7 | 64 | 215 | 398 | 749 | 1429 | 2761 | 41309 |
| 0.8 | 63 | 206 | 379 | 709 | 1348 | 2597 | 38624 |
| 0.9 | 62 | 197 | 361 | 672 | 1272 | 2442 | 36113 |
| 1.0 | 60 | 189 | 343 | 636 | 1200 | 2297 | 33764 |
| 2.0 | 46 | 122 | 208 | 368 | 669 | 1244 | 17252 |
| 3.0 | 34 | 79 | 129 | 217 | 379 | 684 | 8858 |
| 4.0 | 25 | 53 | 82 | 132 | 221 | 385 | 4587 |
| 5.0 | 20 | 37 | 55 | 84 | 134 | 223 | 2404 |
| 6.0 | 15 | 27 | 38 | 55 | 84 | 135 | 1281 |
| 7.0 | 13 | 20 | 27 | 38 | 56 | 85 | 697 |
| 8.0 | 10 | 16 | 21 | 28 | 38 | 56 | 390 |
| 9.0 | 9 | 13 | 16 | 21 | 28 | 38 | 225 |
| 10.0 | 7 | 11 | 13 | 16 | 21 | 28 | 135 |
| 11.0 | 7 | 9 | 11 | 13 | 16 | 21 | 85 |
| 12.0 | 6 | 8 | 9 | 11 | 13 | 16 | 56 |
| 13.0 | 5 | 7 | 8 | 9 | 11 | 13 | 38 |
| 14.0 | 5 | 6 | 7 | 8 | 9 | 11 | 28 |
| 15.0 | 4 | 5 | 6 | 7 | 8 | 9 | 21 |
| 16.0 | 4 | 5 | 5 | 6 | 7 | 8 | 16 |
| 17.0 | 3 | 4 | 5 | 5 | 6 | 7 | 13 |
| 18.0 | 3 | 4 | 4 | 5 | 5 | 6 | 11 |
| 19.0 | 3 | 3 | 4 | 4 | 5 | 5 | 9 |
| 20.0 | 3 | 3 | 3 | 4 | 4 | 5 | 8 |

## $W = 2^{-53}$, 300 Bit Precision

| H | 64 | 256 | 512 | 1024 | 2048 | 4096 | 65536 |
|------|-----|-----|-----|------|------|------|-------|
| 0.1 | 64 | 256 | 512 | 1010 | 1993 | 3943 | 61663 |
| 0.2 | 64 | 256 | 498 | 970 | 1899 | 3733 | 57750 |
| 0.3 | 64 | 250 | 480 | 927 | 1801 | 3525 | 54045 |
| 0.4 | 64 | 243 | 461 | 882 | 1705 | 3323 | 50561 |
| 0.5 | 64 | 234 | 441 | 838 | 1612 | 3130 | 47293 |
| 0.6 | 64 | 226 | 421 | 796 | 1523 | 2947 | 44230 |
| 0.7 | 64 | 217 | 402 | 755 | 1438 | 2774 | 41362 |
| 0.8 | 64 | 209 | 383 | 716 | 1358 | 2610 | 38678 |
| 0.9 | 63 | 200 | 365 | 678 | 1281 | 2456 | 36167 |
| 1.0 | 62 | 192 | 348 | 643 | 1209 | 2310 | 33819 |
| 2.0 | 47 | 125 | 213 | 375 | 678 | 1257 | 17299 |
| 3.0 | 35 | 82 | 133 | 222 | 387 | 694 | 8895 |
| 4.0 | 27 | 56 | 85 | 136 | 227 | 392 | 4614 |
| 5.0 | 21 | 39 | 57 | 87 | 138 | 229 | 2424 |
| 6.0 | 17 | 29 | 40 | 58 | 88 | 139 | 1295 |
| 7.0 | 13 | 22 | 29 | 40 | 58 | 88 | 708 |

| 8.0 | 11 | 17 | 22 | 29 | 40 | 58 | 398 |
|---|---|---|---|---|---|---|---|
| 9.0 | 10 | 14 | 17 | 22 | 29 | 41 | 231 |
| 10.0 | 8 | 11 | 14 | 17 | 22 | 29 | 140 |
| 11.0 | 7 | 10 | 11 | 14 | 17 | 22 | 88 |
| 12.0 | 6 | 8 | 10 | 11 | 14 | 17 | 59 |
| 13.0 | 6 | 7 | 8 | 10 | 11 | 14 | 41 |
| 14.0 | 5 | 6 | 7 | 8 | 10 | 11 | 29 |
| 15.0 | 5 | 6 | 6 | 7 | 8 | 10 | 22 |
| 16.0 | 4 | 5 | 6 | 6 | 7 | 8 | 17 |
| 17.0 | 4 | 5 | 5 | 6 | 6 | 7 | 14 |
| 18.0 | 4 | 4 | 5 | 5 | 6 | 6 | 11 |
| 19.0 | 3 | 4 | 4 | 5 | 5 | 6 | 10 |
| 20.0 | 3 | 4 | 4 | 4 | 5 | 5 | 8 |

## $W = 2^{-64}$, 300 Bit Precision

| H | 64 | 256 | 512 | 1024 | 2048 | 4096 | 65536 |
|---|---|---|---|---|---|---|---|
| 0.1 | 64 | 256 | 512 | 1014 | 2001 | 3954 | 61716 |
| 0.2 | 64 | 256 | 502 | 977 | 1910 | 3750 | 57823 |
| 0.3 | 64 | 253 | 486 | 936 | 1815 | 3545 | 54131 |
| 0.4 | 64 | 247 | 467 | 892 | 1720 | 3346 | 50656 |
| 0.5 | 64 | 239 | 448 | 850 | 1629 | 3155 | 47393 |
| 0.6 | 64 | 231 | 429 | 808 | 1541 | 2973 | 44335 |
| 0.7 | 64 | 223 | 411 | 768 | 1457 | 2800 | 41470 |
| 0.8 | 64 | 215 | 392 | 729 | 1377 | 2637 | 38788 |
| 0.9 | 64 | 207 | 374 | 692 | 1301 | 2483 | 36278 |
| 1.0 | 63 | 199 | 357 | 656 | 1229 | 2338 | 33930 |
| 2.0 | 51 | 132 | 222 | 388 | 696 | 1282 | 17397 |
| 3.0 | 39 | 88 | 141 | 233 | 401 | 714 | 8971 |
| 4.0 | 30 | 61 | 92 | 145 | 238 | 408 | 4670 |
| 5.0 | 24 | 44 | 63 | 94 | 147 | 241 | 2465 |
| 6.0 | 19 | 32 | 44 | 63 | 95 | 148 | 1325 |
| 7.0 | 16 | 25 | 33 | 45 | 64 | 95 | 730 |
| 8.0 | 13 | 20 | 25 | 33 | 45 | 64 | 414 |
| 9.0 | 11 | 16 | 20 | 25 | 33 | 45 | 243 |
| 10.0 | 10 | 13 | 16 | 20 | 25 | 33 | 149 |
| 11.0 | 8 | 11 | 13 | 16 | 20 | 25 | 96 |
| 12.0 | 8 | 10 | 11 | 13 | 16 | 20 | 64 |
| 13.0 | 7 | 9 | 10 | 11 | 13 | 16 | 45 |
| 14.0 | 6 | 8 | 9 | 10 | 11 | 13 | 33 |
| 15.0 | 6 | 7 | 8 | 9 | 10 | 11 | 25 |
| 16.0 | 5 | 6 | 7 | 8 | 9 | 10 | 20 |
| 17.0 | 5 | 6 | 6 | 7 | 8 | 9 | 16 |
| 18.0 | 4 | 5 | 6 | 6 | 7 | 8 | 13 |
| 19.0 | 4 | 5 | 5 | 6 | 6 | 7 | 11 |
| 20.0 | 4 | 4 | 5 | 5 | 6 | 6 | 10 |

## $W = 2^{-96}$, 300 Bit Precision

| H | 64 | 256 | 512 | 1024 | 2048 | 4096 | 65536 |
|---|----|-----|-----|------|------|------|-------|
| 0.1 | 64 | 256 | 512 | 1022 | 2017 | 3982 | 61848 |
| 0.2 | 64 | 256 | 510 | 994 | 1936 | 3791 | 58003 |
| 0.3 | 64 | 256 | 498 | 957 | 1847 | 3594 | 54342 |
| 0.4 | 64 | 254 | 483 | 917 | 1758 | 3401 | 50889 |
| 0.5 | 64 | 249 | 466 | 877 | 1670 | 3214 | 47642 |
| 0.6 | 64 | 243 | 449 | 837 | 1584 | 3036 | 44594 |
| 0.7 | 64 | 236 | 431 | 799 | 1502 | 2866 | 41737 |
| 0.8 | 64 | 229 | 414 | 761 | 1423 | 2704 | 39060 |
| 0.9 | 64 | 221 | 397 | 725 | 1348 | 2551 | 36553 |
| 1.0 | 64 | 214 | 381 | 690 | 1277 | 2407 | 34207 |
| 2.0 | 58 | 149 | 246 | 420 | 741 | 1345 | 17640 |
| 3.0 | 47 | 104 | 161 | 261 | 438 | 765 | 9159 |
| 4.0 | 38 | 74 | 109 | 167 | 268 | 447 | 4811 |
| 5.0 | 31 | 55 | 76 | 111 | 170 | 271 | 2568 |
| 6.0 | 25 | 42 | 56 | 78 | 113 | 172 | 1401 |
| 7.0 | 21 | 33 | 42 | 56 | 78 | 113 | 785 |
| 8.0 | 18 | 26 | 33 | 42 | 57 | 79 | 455 |
| 9.0 | 16 | 22 | 27 | 33 | 43 | 57 | 274 |
| 10.0 | 14 | 18 | 22 | 27 | 33 | 43 | 173 |
| 11.0 | 12 | 16 | 19 | 22 | 27 | 33 | 114 |
| 12.0 | 11 | 14 | 16 | 19 | 22 | 27 | 79 |
| 13.0 | 10 | 12 | 14 | 16 | 19 | 22 | 57 |
| 14.0 | 9 | 11 | 12 | 14 | 16 | 19 | 43 |
| 15.0 | 8 | 10 | 11 | 12 | 14 | 16 | 33 |
| 16.0 | 8 | 9 | 10 | 11 | 12 | 14 | 27 |
| 17.0 | 7 | 8 | 9 | 10 | 11 | 12 | 22 |
| 18.0 | 6 | 8 | 8 | 9 | 10 | 11 | 19 |
| 19.0 | 6 | 7 | 8 | 8 | 9 | 10 | 16 |
| 20.0 | 6 | 6 | 7 | 8 | 8 | 9 | 14 |

## $W = 2^{-128}$, 300 Bit Precision

| H | 64 | 256 | 512 | 1024 | 2048 | 4096 | 65536 |
|---|----|-----|-----|------|------|------|-------|
| 0.1 | 64 | 256 | 512 | 1024 | 2030 | 4003 | 61958 |
| 0.2 | 64 | 256 | 512 | 1006 | 1957 | 3823 | 58153 |
| 0.3 | 64 | 256 | 507 | 973 | 1874 | 3634 | 54519 |
| 0.4 | 64 | 256 | 494 | 937 | 1788 | 3446 | 51084 |
| 0.5 | 64 | 255 | 480 | 899 | 1703 | 3263 | 47850 |
| 0.6 | 64 | 251 | 464 | 861 | 1620 | 3088 | 44812 |
| 0.7 | 64 | 246 | 448 | 824 | 1539 | 2920 | 41961 |
| 0.8 | 64 | 239 | 431 | 787 | 1462 | 2760 | 39289 |
| 0.9 | 64 | 233 | 415 | 752 | 1388 | 2608 | 36784 |
| 1.0 | 64 | 226 | 399 | 718 | 1317 | 2464 | 34439 |

| | | | | | | |
|---|---|---|---|---|---|---|
| 2.0 63 | 163 | 266 | 448 | 780 | 1398 | 17845 |
| 3.0 54 | 117 | 179 | 284 | 470 | 808 | 9318 |
| 4.0 44 | 85 | 124 | 186 | 293 | 481 | 4929 |
| 5.0 37 | 64 | 89 | 127 | 190 | 297 | 2655 |
| 6.0 31 | 50 | 66 | 90 | 129 | 192 | 1465 |
| 7.0 26 | 40 | 51 | 67 | 91 | 130 | 833 |
| 8.0 23 | 33 | 40 | 51 | 67 | 92 | 491 |
| 9.0 20 | 27 | 33 | 41 | 51 | 67 | 302 |
| 10.0 17 | 23 | 28 | 33 | 41 | 52 | 194 |
| 11.0 16 | 20 | 23 | 28 | 33 | 41 | 130 |
| 12.0 14 | 18 | 20 | 24 | 28 | 33 | 92 |
| 13.0 13 | 16 | 18 | 20 | 24 | 28 | 68 |
| 14.0 12 | 14 | 16 | 18 | 20 | 24 | 52 |
| 15.0 11 | 13 | 14 | 16 | 18 | 20 | 41 |
| 16.0 10 | 12 | 13 | 14 | 16 | 18 | 33 |
| 17.0 9 | 11 | 12 | 13 | 14 | 16 | 28 |
| 18.0 9 | 10 | 11 | 12 | 13 | 14 | 24 |
| 19.0 8 | 9 | 10 | 11 | 12 | 13 | 20 |
| 20.0 8 | 9 | 9 | 10 | 11 | 12 | 18 |

# B High-Precision Incomplete Beta Function Implementation

The binomial CDF curve is computed as a function of the incomplete beta function. We first encountered this in the SP800-90B adaptive proportion test. In order to avoid running into numerical precision problems, we need to use higher precision floating point representation than is used by the usual libraries.

The implementation used to compute the incomplete beta function used by the adaptive proportion test code is described below. The related Binomial CDF and Binomial Quantile functions are also given.

The regularized incomplete beta function is defined as:

$$I_x(a, b) = \frac{1}{\text{Beta}(a, b)} \int_0^x t^{a-1}(1 - t)^{b-1} dt.$$

Computing this in a computer requires an approximate numerical algorithm. In order to do this with high precision floating point, we need to implement the algorithm directly, instead of calling a library that uses lower precision floats.

Two sets of continued fraction equations for computing the Regularized Incomplete Beta function are given in 26.5.8 and 26.5.9 of *The Handbook of Mathematical Functions*, http://people.math.sfu.ca/~cbm/aands/abramowitz_and_stegun.pdf. Here we use the equations in 26.5.8,

$$I_x(a, b) = \frac{x^a(1 - x)^b}{a \times \text{Beta}(a, b)} \left\{ \frac{1}{1+} \frac{d_1}{1+} \frac{d_2}{1+} \cdots \right\}.$$

The $\frac{1}{1+} \cdots$ notation is shorthand for

$$I_x(a, b) = \frac{x^a(1 - x)^b}{a \times \text{Beta}(a, b)} \cfrac{1}{1 + \cfrac{d_1}{1 + \cfrac{d_2}{1 + \ddots}}}.$$

The odd subscripts of $d_x$ are

$$d_{2m+1} = -\frac{(a + m)(a + b + m)}{(a + 2m)(a + 2m + 1)} x,$$

and the even subscripts of $d_x$ are

$$d_{2m} = \frac{m(b - m)}{(a + 2m - 1)(a + 2m)} x.$$

https://doi.org/10.1515/9781501506062-022

The *Handbook of Mathematical Functions* states, without explanation, that best results are obtained when

$$x < \frac{1+a}{a+b-2}.$$

When experimenting with large $x > \frac{1+a}{a+b-2}$, we find cases where the algorithm does not converge.

To maintain $x$ below that limit, the following symmetry relationship is used to transform $x$ to be below that limit:

$$I_x(a, b) = 1 - I_{1-x}(b, a).$$

Beta$(a, b)$ is the standard beta function, which can be computed from the $\Gamma$ function:

$$\text{Beta}(a, b) = \frac{\Gamma(a)\Gamma(b)}{\Gamma(a) + \Gamma(b)}.$$

The binomial CDF can be computed as a function of the incomplete beta function:

$$\text{BCDF}(n, k, p) = 1 - I_p(k+1, n-k, p).$$

The Binomial Quantile function is the inverse of the Binomial CDF. This is implemented with a binary chop search.

To compute with high precision, the python mpmath library is used with precision set to 300 significant bits.

The above equations for the incomplete beta function are implemented using a recursive algorithm to implement the continued fraction.

**Listing B.1:** Incomplete beta function, recursive implementation

```
#!/usr/bin/env python

import math
from mpmath import *

PRECISION = 300

# Continued Fraction Computation
# 6.5.31 Handbook of Mathematical Functions, page 263
#     Recursive implementation
def ibeta_cf(d,a,b,x):
    if d == 100:
        return mpf('0.0') # end at 100 iterations
    if d == 0: # First term 1/1+|
        mult = ((x**a)*((mpf('1.0')-x)**b))/a
```

```
        mult = mult * gamma(a+b)   # Divide by Beta(a,b)
        mult = mult / (gamma(a) * gamma(b))
        m=0
        return mult*mpf('1.0')/(mpf('1.0')+ibeta_cf(d+1,a,b,x))
    elif ((d % 2) == 1):
        m = (d-1)/2
        result = (a+m)*(a+b+m)*x
        result = -result/((a+(2*m))*(a+(2*m)+mpf('1.0')))
        return result/(mpf('1.0')+ibeta_cf(d+1,a,b,x))
    else:
        m = d/2
        result = (m*(b-m)*x)/((a+(2*m)-mpf('1.0'))*(a+(2*m)))
        return result/(mpf('1.0')+ibeta_cf(d+1,a,b,x))

def ibeta(a,b,x):
    if (x == 0.0 or x==1.0):
        return x
    if x < ((a-1.0)/(a+b-2.0)):
        return ibeta_cf(0,a,b,x)
    else:
        return mpf(1.0)-ibeta_cf(0,b,a,mpf('1.0')-x)

# Binomial CDF
def BCDF(n, k, p):
    return mpf('1.0') - ibeta(mpf(k+1),mpf(n-k),p)

# Find smallest k where BCDF(n,k,p) > alpha
# using binary chop search
# Equivalent to Excel CRITBINOM function
def binomial_quantile(n, p, alpha):
    min = 0;
    max = n;
    mid = min + ((max-min) >> 1)
    keepgoing = True
    while (keepgoing):
        b = B(n,mid,p)
        if (b > alpha):
            max = mid
        elif (b < alpha):
            min = mid
        elif (b == alpha):
            keepgoing = False

        newmid = min + ((max-min) >> 1)
        if (newmid == mid):
            keepgoing=False
        mid = newmid

    if (b < alpha): # Make sure we have smallest b > alpha
```

```
            mid += 1
    return mid
```

An iterative version of the incomplete beta function can be written by computing the $d_x$ coefficients backward from 100 down to 1.

**Listing B.2:** Incomplete beta function, backward iterative implementation

```
def ibeta_cf_backwards(a,b,x):
    f = mpf('0.0')   # running fraction value
    for d in range(100,-1,-1):
        if d == 0: # First Term (last of iteration) 1/1+|
            mult = ((x**a)*((mpf('1.0')-x)**b))/a
            mult = mult * gamma(a+b)
            mult = mult / (gamma(a) * gamma(b))
            m=0
            return mult*mpf('1.0')/(mpf('1.0')+f)
        elif ((d % 2) == 1):
            m = (d-1)/2
            numerator = (a+m)*(a+b+m)*x
            numerator = -numerator/((a+(2*m))*(a+(2*m)+mpf('1.0')))
            f = numerator/(mpf('1.0')+f)
        else:
            m = d/2
            numerator = m*(b-m)*x
            numerator = numerator/((a+(2*m)-mpf('1.0'))*(a+(2*m)))
            f = numerator/(mpf('1.0')+f)

def ibeta_backwards(a,b,x):
    if (x == 0.0 or x==1.0):
        return x
    if x < ((a-1.0)/(a+b-2.0)): # Bring x below required threshold
        return ibeta_cf_backwards(a,b,x)
    else:
        return mpf(1.0)-ibeta_cf_backwards(b,a,mpf('1.0')-x)
```

This uses less memory than the recursive version, but we will see below that it runs slightly slower.

The second set of equations in 26.5.9 of *The Handbook of Mathematical Functions* can also be tried.

**Listing B.3:** Incomplete beta function, backward iterative implementation, alternate equations

```
# An iterative version working backwards, using equations from 26.5.9.
def ibeta_cf_backwards2(a,b,x):
    f = mpf('0.0')   # running fraction value
    for e in range(100,0,-1):
        if e == 1: # First Term (last of iteration) 1/1+|
            mult = ((x**a)*((mpf('1.0')-x)**(b-mpf('1.0'))))/a
            mult = mult * gamma(a+b)
```

```
        mult = mult / (gamma(a) * gamma(b))
        m=0
        return mult*mpf('1.0')/(mpf('1.0')+f)
    elif ((e % 2) == 1):
        m = (e-1)/2
        numerator = m*(a+b+m-mpf('1.0'))*x
        numerator = numerator/((a+(2*m)-mpf('1.0'))* (a+(2*m))
                * (mpf('1.0')-x))
        f = numerator/(mpf('1.0')+f)
    else:
        m = e/2
        numerator = (a+m-mpf('1.0'))*(b-m)*x
        numerator = -numerator/((a+(2*m)-mpf('2.0'))*(a+(2*m))
                -mpf('1.0'))*(mpf('1.0')-x))
        f = numerator/(mpf('1.0')+f)

def ibeta_backwards2(a,b,x):
    if (x == 0.0 or x==1.0):
        return x
    if x < ((a-1.0)/(a+b-2.0)): # Bring x below required threshold
        return ibeta_cf_backwards2(a,b,x)
    else:
        return mpf(1.0)-ibeta_cf_backwards2(b,a,mpf('1.0')-x)
```

These three different implementations were tried in the code to compute the adaptive proportion test cutoff tables (see Table B.1). It was verified that the output matched for the three algorithms and the execution time for each was measured.

**Table B.1:** Execution Time for High-Precision Incomplete Beta Function.

| Algorithm | Time (seconds) |
|---|---|
| Recursive 26.5.8 | 49.23 |
| Iterative 26.5.8 | 50.21 |
| Iterative 26.5.9 | 78.15 |

So the recursive algorithm is the fastest, but it is only slightly faster than the iterative version, and it will need to store 100 intermediate floating point values on the stack while running.

# C Incomplete Gamma Function Implementation

The gamma function and relatives such as the incomplete gamma function are used in various places in the RNG tests described in this book. The gamma function has many uses and interesting properties. However, it is not the goal of this book to teach the mathematics of the gamma function, just the use of it in random number testing and how to implement the variants of the gamma function.

The basic gamma function is available in python in the math library, but functions such as the incomplete gamma function need an additional library, the most common being the scipy library.

In order to undo the dependency on the scipy library for the various RNG tests, a native python implementation of the gamma function and incomplete gamma functions was developed for the code in this book.

The gamma function $\Gamma(x)$ is defined as

$$\Gamma(x) = \int_0^\infty e^t t^{a-1} dt.$$

There are two additional functions, the lower incomplete gamma function $\gamma(a, x)$ and the upper complete gamma function $\Gamma(a, x)$, which divide the gamma function into two parts, split at the point $x$.

The lower complete gamma function is

$$\gamma(a, x) = \int_0^x e^t t^{a-1} dt.$$

The upper complete gamma function is

$$\Gamma(a, x) = \int_x^\infty e^t t^{a-1} dt.$$

Section 6.5.31 of the *Handbook of Mathematical Functions* describes a continued fraction for the lower incomplete gamma function:

$$\Gamma(a, x) = x^a e^{-x} \left( \frac{1}{x+} \frac{1-a}{1+} \frac{1}{x+} \frac{2-a}{1+} \frac{2}{x+} \frac{3-a}{1+} \cdots \right)$$

for $X > 0$ and $|a| < \infty$.

https://doi.org/10.1515/9781501506062-023

This notation is shorthand for the following continued fraction:

$$\Gamma(a, x) = \cfrac{x^a e^{-x}}{x + \cfrac{1 - a}{1 + \cfrac{1}{x + \cfrac{2 - a}{1 + \cfrac{2}{x + \ddots}}}}}.$$

The continued fraction for the lower incomplete function is as follows:

$$\gamma(a, x) = x^a e^{-x} \left( \frac{1}{a-} \frac{ax}{a + 1+} \frac{x}{a + 2-} \frac{(a + 1)x}{a + 3+} \frac{2x}{a + 4-} \frac{(a + 2)x}{s + 5+} \frac{3x}{a + 5-} \cdots \right)$$

or, in longhand notation,

$$\gamma(a, x) = \cfrac{x^a e^{-x}}{a - \cfrac{(a + 0)x}{a + 1 + \cfrac{x}{a + 2 - \cfrac{(a + 1)x}{a + 3 + \cfrac{2x}{a + 4 - \cfrac{(a + 2)x}{a + 5 + \cfrac{3x}{a + 6 - \ddots}}}}}}}.$$

Since $\Gamma(a) = \Gamma(a, x) + \gamma(a, x)$, they can also be computed as

$$\gamma(a, x) = \Gamma(a) - \Gamma(a, x)$$

and

$$\Gamma(a, x) = \Gamma(a) - \gamma(a, x).$$

In a computational setting, this requires two computations, one for $\Gamma(a)$ and one for the incomplete gamma function, both of which require an iterative or recursive algorithm. There is a direct continued fraction for both the upper and lower incomplete gamma functions that are more efficient.

The regularized incomplete gamma functions are the incomplete gamma functions divided by the gamma function. The symbol for the lower regularized gamma functions is $P(a, x)$, and the symbol for the upper regularized gamma functions is $Q(a, x)$:

$$P(a, x) = \frac{\gamma(a, x)}{\Gamma(a)},$$

$$Q(a, x) = \frac{\Gamma(a, x)}{\Gamma(a)}.$$

Software implementations are sometimes unclear about whether they are returning the incomplete gamma function or the regularized incomplete gamma function. For example, the gammainc and gammaincc functions in the python scipy.special library return the regularized incomplete gamma functions $P(a, x)$ and $Q(a, x)$, respectively.

To get $y(a, x)$ and $\Gamma(a, x)$ from scipy.special.gammainc(a,x) and scipy.special.gammaincc(a,x), multiply by $\Gamma(a)$. For example:

```
#!/usr/bin/env python

from scipy.special import gamma, gammainc, gammaincc

def incomplete_lower_gamma(a,x):
    return gammainc(a,x) * gamma(a)

def incomplete_upper_gamma(a,x):
    return gammaincc(a,x) * gamma(a)
```

The python library file gamma_functions.py implements the incomplete gamma functions, using recursive algorithms to implement the continued fractions.

The $\Gamma(x)$ function is universally available in libraries for most languages. In Python, it is available in the math and scipy.special libraries for normal precision arithmetic and in the mpmath and mpfr libraries for arbitrary precision arithmetic.

**Listing C.1:** gamma_functions.py

```
# Continued Fraction Computation
# 6.5.31 Handbook of Mathematical Functions, page 263
#    Recursive implementation
def upper_incomplete_gamma(a,x,d=0,iterations=100):
    if d == iterations:
        if ((d % 2) == 1):
            return 1.0 # end iterations
        else:
            m = d/2
            return x + (m-a)
    if d == 0:
        result = ((x**a) * (e**(-x)))/upper_incomplete_gamma(a,x,d=d+1)
        return result
    elif ((d % 2) == 1):
        m = 1.0+((d-1.0)/2.0)
        return x+ ((m-a)/(upper_incomplete_gamma(a,x,d=d+1)))
    else:
        m = d/2
        return 1+(m/(upper_incomplete_gamma(a,x,d=d+1)))


# 6.5.31 Handbook of Mathematical Functions, page 263
#    Recursive implementation
def upper_incomplete_gamma2(a,x,d=0,iterations=100):
```

```python
    if d == iterations:
        return 1.0
    if d == 0:
        result = ((x**a) * (e**(-x)))/upper_incomplete_gamma2(a,x,d=d+1)
        return result
    else:
        m = (d*2)-1
        return (m-a)+x+ ((d*(a-d))/(upper_incomplete_gamma2(a,x,d=d+1)))

def lower_incomplete_gamma(a,x,d=0,iterations=100):
    if d == iterations:
        if ((d % 2) == 1):
            return 1.0 # end iterations
        else:
            m = d/2
            return x + (m-a)
    if d == 0:
        result = ((x**a) * (e**(-x)))/lower_incomplete_gamma(a,x,d=d+1)
        return result
    elif ((d % 2) == 1):
        m = d - 1
        n = (d-1.0)/2.0
        return a + m - (((a+n)*x)/lower_incomplete_gamma(a,x,d=d+1))
    else:
        m = d-1
        n = d/2.0
        return a+m+((n*x)/(lower_incomplete_gamma(a,x,d=d+1)))

def lower_incomplete_gamma2(a,x):
    return gamma(a)-upper_incomplete_gamma2(a,x)

def complimentary_incomplete_gamma(a,x):
    return 1.0-upper_incomplete_gamma(a,x)
```

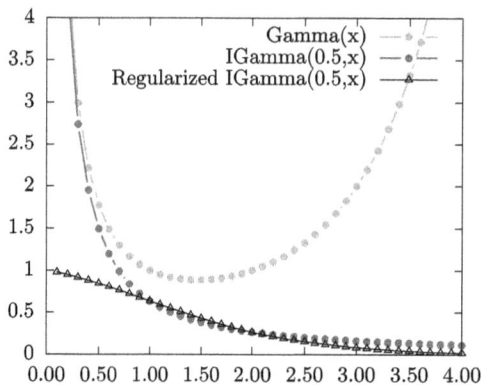

**Figure C.1:** Plots of the Three Gamma Functions.

Figure C.1 shows the results of plotting the output of these functions against some real-valued inputs. These algorithms can also take complex-valued inputs. However, all randomness tests in this book use only real inputs.

We can see how the regularized gamma function transitions between 1 and 0, since at one extreme, the incomplete gamma function approaches the gamma function value, so dividing by the gamma function yields 1 at one extreme. The other extreme asymptotically reaches 0.

# D Software Tool Sources

In this book a number of tools are used to generate and analyze random numbers. All tools are freely available. See the tools appendix for sources for these tools. The code and examples have all been written and tested on Linux and MacOS, but these tools exist for all the usual platforms.

1. python. A dynamically typed programming language that is particularly effective for the small code examples scattered through the book.
   https://www.python.org/
2. R. A programming language oriented to statistics and data analysis. Used in the book for some of the graph plotting and for computing some statistical tables.
   https://www.r-project.org/
3. djenrandom. A command line program to generate random numbers with defined properties. Written to accompany this book.
   https://github.com/dj-on-github/djenrandom
4. ent. A command line program to perform basic statistical tests on random data.
   http://www.fourmilab.ch/random/
5. djent. A reimplementation of ent, with several improvements in file handling, entropy measurement, and symbol size options. Written to accompany this book
   https://github.com/dj-on-github/djent
6. sp800_22_tests. An implementation of the tests in the SP800-22 Rev1a PRNG test specification. Written to accompany this book
   https://github.com/dj-on-github/sp800_22_tests
7. SP800-90B_EntropyAssessment. An implementation of the draft NIST SP800-90b entropy test algorithms.
   https://github.com/usnistgov/SP800-90B_EntropyAssessment
8. rdrand. An update to the standard Python rdrand library to support both RdRand and RdSeed on both Intel and AMD CPUs from within python. Written to accompany this book https://github.com/dj-on-github/rdrand
9. awk, grep, etc ... completely standard UNIX/Linux command line utilities.

https://doi.org/10.1515/9781501506062-024

# E Listing Reference

The files for this book may be downloaded from the Supplementary Information section on the book's page at https://www.degruyter.com/view/product/486349.

A version controlled repository of the files is hosted at https://github.com/dj-on-github/RNGBook_Code.

The filenames associated with the listings throughout the book are as follows:

- `weak_prng.py` : Listing 1.4 on page 13
- `inm_algorithm.py` : Listing 2.1 on page 37
- `xor_iterate.py` : Listing 3.1 on page 49
- `xor_iterate64.py` : Listing 3.2 on page 51
- `rand16.py` : Listing 3.3 on page 53
- `xor_iterate_fips.py` : Listing 3.4 on page 54
- `vnd.py` : Listing 3.5 on page 58
- `vn_table.py` : Listing 3.6 on page 59
- `vn_debiaser.py` : Listing 3.7 on page 60
- `yp_debiaser.py` : Listing 3.8 on page 64
- `blum_whitener_1.py` : Listing 3.9 on page 67
- `blum_whitener_2.py` : Listing 3.10 on page 69
- `cbc_mac.c` : Listing 3.11 on page 75
- `cmac.c` : Listing 3.12 on page 77
- `hmac_extactor.py` : Listing 3.13 on page 80
- `biw.py` : Listing 3.14 on page 87
- `ble.py` : Listing 3.15 on page 90
- `make_ext2_matrices.py` : Listing 3.16 on page 93
- `salsa20.c` : Listing 4.1 on page 111
- `salsa20.c` : Listing 4.2 on page 112
- `salsa20.c` : Listing 4.3 on page 113
- `salsa20.c` : Listing 4.4 on page 114
- `chacha.c` : Listing 4.5 on page 115
- `chacha.c` : Listing 4.6 on page 116
- `blumblumshub.py` : Listing 4.7 on page 117
- `lcg.py` : Listing 6.1 on page 124
- `lcg2.py` : Listing 6.2 on page 124
- `mwc.c` : Listing 6.3 on page 127
- `cmwc.c` : Listing 6.4 on page 128
- `xorshift32.c` : Listing 6.5 on page 130
- `xorshift128.c` : Listing 6.6 on page 131
- `box_muller.py` : Listing 7.1 on page 137
- `ziggurat.py` : Listing 7.2 on page 140
- `zignor.py` : Listing 7.3 on page 143

https://doi.org/10.1515/9781501506062-025

# Bibliography

[1]  Boaz Barak, Russell Impagliazzo, and Avi Wigderson. Extracting randomness using few independent sources. *SIAM Journal on Computing*, 36(4):1095–1118, January 2006.

[2]  Lenore Blum, Manuel Blum, and Mike Shub. Comparison of two pseudo-random number generators. In *Advances in Cryptology: Proceedings of CRYPTO'82*, pages 61–78. Plenum, 1982.

[3]  Manuel Blum. Independent unbiased coin flips from a correlated biased source—a finite state Markov chain. *Combinatorica*, 6(2):97–108, June 1986.

[4]  Jean Bourgain, Nets Katz, and Terence Tao. A sum-product estimate in finite fields, and applications. *Geometric And Functional Analysis*, 14(1):27–57, February 2004.

[5]  G. E. P. Box and Mervin E. Muller. A note on the generation of random normal deviates. *The Annals of Mathematical Statistics*, 29:610–611, 1958.

[6]  Yevgeniy Dodis, Ariel Elbaz, Roberto Oliveira, and Ran Raz. Improved randomness extraction from two independent sources. In *Approximation, Randomization, and Combinatorial Optimization. Algorithms and Techniques*, pages 334–344. Springer, Berlin, Heidelberg, 2004.

[7]  Yevgeniy Dodis, Rosario Gennaro, Johan Håstad, Hugo Krawczyk, and Tal Rabin. Randomness extraction and key derivation using the CBC, Cascade and HMAC modes. In *Annual International Cryptology Conference*, pages 494–510. Springer, 2004.

[8]  Jurgen A. Doornik. An improved ziggurat method to generate normal random samples, January 2005.

[9]  P. Erdős and E. Szemerédi. On sums and products of integers. In *Studies in Pure Mathematics*, pages 213–218. Birkhäuser Basel, 1983.

[10]  Donald E. Knuth. *The Art of Computer Programming, Volume 2 (3rd edn): Seminumerical Algorithms*. Addison–Wesley Longman Publishing Co., Inc., Boston, MA, USA, 1997.

[11]  H. W. Lenstra. Factoring integers with elliptic curves. *Annals of Mathematics*, 126(3):649–673, 1987.

[12]  A. Theodore Markettos and Simon W. Moore. *The Frequency Injection Attack on Ring-Oscillator-Based True Random Number Generators*, pages 317–331. Springer, Berlin, Heidelberg, 2009.

[13]  George Marsaglia and Wai Wan Tsang. The ziggurat method for generating random variables. *Journal of Statistical Software*, 5(8), 2000.

[14]  James L. McInnes and Benny Pinkas. On the impossibility of private key cryptography with weakly random keys.

[15]  Melissa E. O'Neill. Pcg: A family of simple fast space-efficient statistically good algorithms for random number generation. Technical Report HMC-CS-2014-0905, Harvey Mudd College, Claremont, CA, September 2014.

[16]  R. J. Parker. Entropy justification for metastability based nondeterministic random bit generator. In *2017 IEEE 2nd International Verification and Security Workshop (IVSW)*, pages 25–30, July 2017.

[17]  Yuval Peres. Iterating von Neumann's procedure for extracting random bits. *The Annals of Statistics*, 20(1):590–597, March 1992.

[18]  Alfréd Rényi. On measures of entropy and information. In *Fourth Berkeley Symposium on Mathematical Statistics and Probability*, Volume 1, pages 547–561, 1961.

[19]  Andrew Rukhin, Juan Sota, James Nechvatal, Miles Smid, Elaine Barker, Stefan Leigh, Mark Levenson, Mark V. Angel, David Banks, Alan Heckert, James Dray, and San Vo. A statistical test suite for random and pseudorandom number generators for cryptographic applications. Technical Report, National Institute of Standards and Technology, 2000.

https://doi.org/10.1515/9781501506062-026

[20] Claude E. Shannon. A mathematical theory of communication. *The Bell System Technical Journal*, XXVII, 07 1948.

[21] Thomas Shrimpton and R. Seth Terashima. A provable-security analysis of Intel's secure key RNG. In *Annual International Conference on the Theory and Applications of Cryptographic Techniques*, pages 77–100. Springer, 2015.

[22] Standard 754-1985 [Authors not provided by the IEEE]. *IEEE Standard for Binary Floating-Point Arithmetic*. Institute of Electrical and Electronics Engineers, New York, 1985.

[23] Ron Rivest and Robert Silverman. Are 'strong' primes needed for RSA. Cryptology ePrint Archive. Report 2001/007, 2001. https://eprint.iacr.org/2001/007.

[24] Ihor Vasyltsov, Eduard Hambardzumyan, Young-Sik Kim, and Bohdan Karpinskyy. Fast digital TRNG based on metastable ring oscillator. In *International Workshop on Cryptographic Hardware and Embedded Systems*, pages 164–180. Springer, 2008.

# Index

www.ingramcontent.com/pod-product-compliance
Lightning Source LLC
Chambersburg PA
CBHW081037220326

41598CB00038B/6902